Global Perspectives in Policing and Law Enforcement

Policing Perspectives and Challenges in the Twenty-First Century

Series Editor
Jonathon A. Cooper, Indiana University of Pennsylvania

In many respects, policing has evolved over the last two centuries; yet issues that concerned policing in the nineteenth and twentieth centuries continue to be salient to contemporary law enforcement. But how these challenges are manifest to the police today are distinct, as society and politics, too, have evolved. And so understanding the role of police in society, the behavior and organization of law enforcement, the relationship between officers and civilians, and the intersection of theory and praxis remain important to the study of police. To this end, volumes in this series will consider policing perspectives and challenges in the twenty-first century, around the world, and through a variety of disciplinary lenses. Ultimately, this series "takes stock" of policing today, considers how it got here, and projects where it might be going. Policing Perspectives and Challenges in the Twenty-First Century will be of interest and use to a variety of policing scholars, including academics, police executives, and others who study law enforcement.

Titles in the series

Global Perspectives in Policing and Law Enforcement

Edited by
Jospeter M. Mbuba

LEXINGTON BOOKS
Lanham • Boulder • New York • London

Published by Lexington Books
An imprint of The Rowman & Littlefield Publishing Group, Inc.
4501 Forbes Boulevard, Suite 200, Lanham, Maryland 20706
www.rowman.com

6 Tinworth Street, London SE11 5AL, United Kingdom

British Library Cataloguing in Publication Information Available

Library of Congress Cataloging-in-Publication Data

Library of Congress Control Number: 2021933469

ISBN 978-1-7936-3724-6 (cloth)
ISBN 978-1-7936-3725-3 (electronic)

This book is dedicated to all the contributors and their loved ones in recognition of the commitment it took to work from home in the wake of the COVID-19 pandemic that threatened humanity across the globe.

Contents

Acknowledgments

I express sincere gratitude to all the eminent scholars who contributed time and expertise toward this project. I recognize you especially for staying the course during the height of the COVID-19 pandemic. I am additionally grateful to Purdue University Fort Wayne for providing the material support including hiring a graduate assistant for me. Carol Gakii John, your assistance is well appreciated. To my family, my pillar of inspiration, I thank you for the unwavering moral support. Finally, I am grateful to the staff of Lexington Books for editorial and copyediting work in the lead up to the publication of this book.

Introduction

Global Perspectives in Policing and Law Enforcement: Approaches, Challenges, and Opportunities

Jospeter M. Mbuba

Every society has its norms of behavior. Some norms are written down or codified, while others are simply common knowledge to the members. Before the onset of policing as we know it today, the enforcement of both codified and uncodified norms was a collective responsibility of every member of the society. Inefficiencies associated with such collective responsibilities, along with increases in violation of existing norms of behavior, partly due to growth in human population, led to the gradual establishment of bodies tasked with enforcing norms, especially the codified variety. One of the earliest known efforts to establish an official agency to enforce norms of behavior was the passage of the Metropolitan Police Act of London in 1829 by Sir Robert Peel (Kusha, 2013) and the subsequent establishment of the London Metropolitan Police force. This force became the prototype of policing almost throughout the modern world. However, the use of formal "urban" agencies to enforce society's norms, especially in places where rural life is the norm, has been found to paradoxically promote other more severe vices such as "tyranny, privilege, and corruption" (Dinnen & Braithwaite, 2009).

One of the ubiquitous complaints against major police systems in modern era is the mis(use) of the police by wielders of political power as an instrument to advance their political cause and secure the interests of the government of the day. Another equally critical area of complaint against the police is the use of excessive force that often manifests in police brutality (Mbuba, 2017; Yakam, 2019), which, in many parts of the world, has attracted public responses in the form of protests, demonstrations, and even riots. The Black Lives Matter movement, which originated in the United States, is one way in which modern society has rebuked police brutality and demonstrated dissatisfaction with differential treatment of different groups of people by governments through the police power. This book provides an important baseline for assessing the extent to which governments have treated the policing sector as an independent agency tasked with objective law enforcement. Although the represented countries have varied historical roots, the general policing ideology and practice remain the same.

A keen review of historical roots and early beginnings of policing is critical to appreciating the current status of policing and understanding its future trajectories, based on existing and emerging knowledge. However, while research on policing and law enforcement has received significant attention in the last few decades as criminal justice continues to assert its place as a distinct discipline of study in academia, the rate of growth in research on international policing practices and the efforts of political regimes to structure their police organizations to advance their course has been minimal. This book provides an exposition of policing and law enforcement practices, challenges, and opportunities in twenty different countries that were carefully selected to represent diverse geographic regions of the world. Those regions include Africa, Europe, Asia and Oceania, the Americas, and the Caribbean.

The chapters in this book present policing from countries with wide-ranging cultural backgrounds, diverse historical law enforcement experiences, varied social and demographic characteristics, and different approaches to political leadership. However, it is not the aim of the book to compare policing in the selected countries on the basis of organizational structure, practice, or any other basis. Rather, the book aims to provide a framework of policing in each country in relation to their efforts at transitioning to a modern outfit and consequent reforms toward compliance with modern law enforcement dispensations. Ultimately, the book provides critical data for future research into policing and law enforcement as the various chapters highlight major cracks that call for further inquiry. Nearly all modern police agencies are structured along similar chains of commands that utilize common sets of ranks. Most police forces are also organized into units or divisions with specific duty assignments such as crime investigation, anti-narcotics enforcement, internal affairs, grievances and arbitration, public relations, performance monitoring, police training, community outreach, and international affairs, among others. Thus, modern policing is a stark contrast from the rudimentary forebears of law enforcement, whose tenets were simply to act upon crime after it occurs. Today, policing represents a complex multifaceted undertaking that is reactive, proactive, and predictive of social patterns with the aim of preventing crime, ensuring public safety and social order, and safeguard political stability. This book does not aim at interrogating the aforementioned when they fall within the exclusive purview or military responsibilities except on instances when the military and police duties come close to being intertwined (McDavid, Clayton, & Cowell, 2011).

SYNOPSIS OF THE BOOK

This book is organized into four parts. Part one addresses policing in the African continent. Historically, most parts of Africa experienced slavery and colonialism from European countries and the Americas, who were attracted into the continent by the rich natural resources (Rødland, & Wynne-Jones, 2020; Stahl, 2020). In the effort to fight colonialism, resist forced labor, contain theft of natural resources, and stop slavery through involuntary migration, the indigenous peoples fought back, often violently. The early policing attempts in the African continent were therefore the offshoot of the colonizers' efforts to control the uprisings by the native peoples. As various regions of the continent gradually gained independence, they inherited from the colonial administrations some form of a police force that was already viewed by the local people as an agent of repression and therefore held in distrust and disdain. It would take several subsequent decades to transform policing in the continent into modern and transparent agencies that served the interests of the public with fairness and objectivity.

For this book, three countries were considered from the continent of Africa. They are Ghana from western Africa, Kenya from the eastern region, and Zimbabwe from the southern. Each represents a distinct chapter. Chapter 1 focuses on Ghana, formerly the Gold Coast, where the changes in socioeconomic and political environments cascaded by the onset of multiparty democracy in 1993 presented vast transformations to the centralized police system, referred to as the Ghana Police Force. Chapter 2 presents policing in Kenya, where the centralized National Police Service features two parallel police agencies referred to as the Kenya Police Service and the Administration Police Service, respectively, and an ancillary branch referred to as the Directorate of Criminal Investigations, with all three answering to one central command. The third chapter looks at policing in Zimbabwe and how the centrally controlled police service, referred to as Zimbabwe Republic Police, which originated from the British South Africa Police, has evolved through three decades of the presidency of Robert Mugabe.

Part two explores policing in the Europe, a continent considered for long to have the golden standard in policing. Home to Britain that is credited with pioneering contemporary policing, Europe enjoys a relatively stable system of policing. Many European countries are also considered economically more stable than the rest of the world, which largely owes to the historical transfer of resources from their colonies. The import of this stability is that they have been able to develop and sustain policing agencies more rapidly. However, in the recent past, political conflicts have characterized several parts of the continent in ways that hampered economic development and, in other ways, eroded some of the previous advancements in political as well as economic stability (Schäfer et al., 2021).

This part features five countries including Denmark from the northern region, England and Wales from the western, Italy from the southern, and Poland and Serbia from the central part. It encompasses five chapters. In chapter 4, the "battles to define the Danish police" in Denmark are examined, whereby a historical investigation of the structural and organizational reforms occurring between 1863 and 2007 are interrogated. In chapter 5, an account of policing is offered for England and Wales, the two countries in the United Kingdom that share a unified police force while the rest of the United Kingdom—Scotland and Northern Ireland – have independent and separate police forces. The chapter outlines early policing in the country that is believed to be the cradleland of modern day policing as practiced in many parts of the world including several countries covered in this book. The sixth chapter outlines the history and organization of Italy's police forces as well as their practices in various settings. The criminal policy and police response to contemporary issues germane to law enforcement in Italy is presented. Chapter 7 explores the establishment of "Policja" or Polish police and its subsequent legitimation as a centralized, hierarchical, and independent public organization in Poland, along with the several reforms to situate the service within a democratic country. Chapter 8 examines police organization in the Republic of Serbia, where the police is an integral part of the Ministry of the Interior, a cabinet level ministry that protects the security of the republic and prevents activities that threaten constitutional order.

Part three presents accounts of policing and law enforcement practices in two continental regions, namely, Asia and Oceania. Countries included from Asia include China, India, Indonesia, and Malaysia, while Australia and New Zealand represent the Oceania region. This part comprises six chapters. Chapter 9 addresses the nature of policing in China, where public security organs or police departments serving the single-party regime are controlled and used by the Chinese Communist Party to maintain social stability, and where police misconduct has historically been a cause for concern. Chapter 10 focuses on policing in India, a federal system of twenty-eight states and nine union territories, where the police organization is governed by state governments with each state and union territory having its own police force. In chapter 11, the focus is on national police force of Indonesia—Polri—which gained status as a police force after separating from the military in 1999 following the introduction of democratic rule. While police reforms are an ongoing undertaking in the modern world, policing in Indonesia is notable for the continued use of sexism and sexist ideologies in the recruitment of women into the police force.

Chapter 12 focuses on the Royal Malaysia Police, tracing it to the fifteenth century when the sultan exercised absolute power to punish wrong doers, and where the Portuguese and the Dutch established the early forms of law enforcement before the arrival of the British East India Company, whose security system became the forerunner of modern policing. In chapter 13, the origins of Australian policing system are explored in relation to the six states and two territories that comprise Australia. The chapter broadly examines the conflicted role of the police system with indigenous Australians. Chapter 14 examines the New Zealand Police, which was established in 1886 upon the final disbandment of an armed constabulary to become one of the five routinely unarmed police forces in the Organization for Economic Co-operation and Development (OECD), but whose influence by the British police in the 19th century cannot be denied.

Part four explores policing and law enforcement in the Americas and the Caribbean. It comprises six chapters representing the United States from North America, Honduras and Nicaragua from Central America, Jamaica from the Caribbean Islands, and Brazil and Uruguay from South America. Though different in terms of political and economic characteristics, one notable concern in several parts of the region is the prevalence of organized crime, particularly in South America. While much has been achieved in modernizing policing across the region, many challenges still exist. In the United States, issues of prejudice and racism by law enforcement especially against black people continue to whittle down the gains in reforms. The death of George Floyd in May 2020, at the hands of the police during a violent arrest demonstrates that there is much more room for reform against racist practices. Much of the rest of the region continues to struggle with other issues of crime, including gang violence, transnational crimes, and drug trafficking. In chapter 15, an overview is made of policing in the United States, a country that is credited to have co-pioneered modern policing with Britain. The chapter traces policing to the colonial America and illuminates the significance of the English model in modern day law enforcement ideals before delving into the contemporary issues of policing in the country.

Chapter 16 examines policing in Honduras, where violent crime is reported to be one of the highest globally, thanks, in part, to the pervasive power of organized gangs whose physical control rivals that of the government, and whose criminal operations rival those of transnational cartels. Chapter 17 outlines policing in Nicaragua. The Nicaraguan National Police traces its origin to the Sandinista Revolution of 1979. It is organized largely into a community-based policing style that has earned a reputation of great success in relation to other policing jurisdictions in the region. Chapter 18 reflects on the Jamaica Constabulary Force—the police force of Jamaica. Policing is traced to the British colonial systems dating back to 1716 when night watchmen guarded the cities of Port Royal, Kingston, and the parishes of Saint Andrew and Saint Catherine. Chapter 19 covers policing in Brazil, a federal republic and union of twenty-six federal states and the Federal District with fifty-four state police forces that are responsible for policing and law enforcement as anchored in the 1988 constitution, which ended the military regime. Chapter 20 examines the Uruguayan National Police in the Oriental Republic of Uruguay. It explores the history of the force from its origins in 1829 to its current modernization efforts and how those efforts fit into the crime control paradigm in light of the increased rate of crime and violence in the country.

REFERENCES

Dinnen, S., & Braithwaite, J. (2009). Reinventing policing through the prism of the colonial kiap. *Policing & Society*, 19(2): 161–173. https://doi.org/10.1080/10439460802187571.

Kusha, H. (2013). Impediments to police modernisation in Iran, 1878–1979. *Policing & Society*, 23(2): 164–182. https://doi.org/10.1080/10439463.2012.661430.

Mbuba, J. M. (2017). Police ethics. In Robertiello, Gina (Ed.), *The use and abuse of police power in america*. ABC-CLIO, pp. 314–319.

McDavid, H., Clayton, A., & Cowell, N. (2011). The difference between the constabulary force and the military: An analysis of the differing roles and functions in the context of the current security environment in the Caribbean (The Case of Jamaica). *Journal of Eastern Caribbean Studies*, 36(3): 40–71.

Rødland, H., & Wynne-Jones, S. (2020). Archaeological approaches to slavery and unfree labour in Africa. *Azania: Archaeological research in Africa*, 55(4): 417–420. https://doi.org/10.1080/0067270X.2020.1819696.

Schäfer, C., Popa, S. A., Braun, D., & Schmitt, H. (2021). The reshaping of political conflict over Europe: From pre-Maastricht to post-'Euro crisis.' *West European Politics*, 44(3): 531–557. https://doi.org/10.1080/01402382.2019.1709754.

Stahl, A. B. (2020). Slavery in Africa: The spoken subject. *Azania: Archaeological Research in Africa*, 55(4): 528–539. https://doi.org/10.1080/0067270X.2020.1826701.

Yakam, L. T. (2019). Police officers' perceptions of the people's complaints regarding police use of excessive force in Port Moresby, Papua New Guinea. *Contemporary PNG Studies*, 30: 21–41.

Part I

AFRICA

Chapter 1

Policing in Ghana

Joseph Appiahene-Gyamfi

This chapter on policing in Ghana, formerly the Gold Coast, comprises of a brief history of the organization, the mode of operations, and the core mandates of the Ghana Police Service (GPS), which is the sole law enforcement agency in Ghana. The police–population ratio, personnel recruitment and training, service conditions, the GPS in government, challenges facing the police, police–community relations, community policing, police deviance, and the GPS's role in international policing and assignments are covered. Furthermore, Ghana's changing socioeconomic and political environments since 1993, when Ghana embarked on multiparty democracy after more than a decade of military rule, have been examined, along with the sociocultural and political pressures and influences that affect service quality and shape the future of the GPS.

Formerly referred to as the Gold Coast Police Force (GCPF), the GPS is a centralized law enforcement agency with national headquarters in Accra, Ghana's capital city. The GPS is headed by the Inspector-General of Police (IGP), appointed by Ghana's President in consultation with Ghana's highest Presidential Advisory Body, the Council of State (1992, Ghana Constitution [GC], Chap. 15, Art. 202: 1 & 2). The GPS is a public service institution under Ghana's Ministry of Interior. The highest decision-making body of the GPS is a ten-member Police Council (PC), which also advises Ghana's President on matters related to internal security and general policy, among other issues (GC, Chap. 15, Arts. 201 & 203). Per Ghana's Constitution, (Chapter 15, Art 201, [a]) Ghana's Vice President chairs the ten-member PC, although the GPS website claims that the President of Ghana appoints the PC chair (GPS, 2020a).

The IGP, the chief administrator of the GPS is assisted by several Director Generals with Commissioners and Deputy Commissioners presiding over seventeen Directorates. The Directorates, some of which have several Departments, include the Police Management Board, Criminal Investigations Department (CID), Public Affairs, Motor Traffic, and Transport Department, Information Technology (ICT), Operations, Welfare, Medical, Police College, Railways and Ports, and Other Training Institutions and Projects. The two largest Directorates include the CID, which is comprised of twelve departments, and the Operations Directorate, which is comprised of eight departments and units. The departments and units under the CID Directorate are the Interpol, Cyber Crime, Crime Data Services Bureau, Domestic Violence and Victims Support, Homicide, Commercial Crime, Drug Law Enforcement— Narcotic, Anti-Human Trafficking, Central Firearms Registry, Financial Forensic, Anti Armed Robbery Squad, and Forensic Science Laboratory (GPS, 2007, 2020b).

Ghana, a unitary sovereign West African country of approximately thirty-one million people, is currently divided into sixteen administrative regions. (Ghana Statistical Service [GSS], 2020; Ghana Population, 2020). The GPS structure, operations, and administration mimic Ghana's unitary political system. All administrative and policy decisions emanate from the headquarters. For law enforcement purposes, the GPS splits the Greater Accra region into the Accra and Tema regions. Regional Commanders with ranks not below Assistant Commissioner of Police (ACP) administer each region. Within each region are several divisions, districts, stations, and posts. Each division is headed by officers with ranks, not below a Chief Superintendent of Police. The Ashanti and Greater Accra regions have the largest police divisions. There are over 300 police districts in Ghana, and each is headed by at least an Assistant Superintendent of Police. Within the districts are over 1,000 police stations and posts, each headed by at least a Police Inspector—the highest noncommissioned officer rank within the GPS. Each region has a six-member Police Committee (akin to the Police Council), chaired by the Regional Minister, that advises the Police Council on law enforcement and security matters relating to the region (1992 Const., Art. 204). Each district has a Police Committee, headed by the district police commander, to advise the regional police command regarding law enforcement and security issues affecting the district.

A BRIEF HISTORY OF POLICING IN GHANA

The English policing system was introduced in the Gold Coast/Ghana after 1844, when England gained control over some coastal towns through an agreement with the chiefs. Shortly after the agreement, known in Ghana's history as the "Bond of 1844," a 120-member Gold Coast Militia and Police

(GCMP) was created. In 1860, a ninety-member Her Majesty the Queen of England's Messengers Corps replaced the GCMP. In 1873 a new Police Ordinance created the Gold Coast Police Force (GCPF) and abolished the native police systems that coexisted with the GCMP (Arthur, 1989; Ankama, 1983). Because of mistrust of the natives, England recruited all-Hausa constables from Nigeria, which was later absorbed into the Gold Coast Armed Police Force (GCAPF) with new responsibilities (Gillespie, 1955, pp. 9–11, 22, 25, 38). In 1876, the GCAPF was renamed the Gold Coast Constabulary (GCC), and in 1901, the GCC was divided into two parts: a paramilitary unit assigned to the Gold Coast Military and a civil policing unit, titled the Gold Coast Police Force (GCPF) (Osei Mensah, 2018; Tankebe, 2013).

By 1902, two groups, the General and Escort Constables had been created. The General Constable was a "literate" with a minimum educational qualification of Standard VII/Middle School Leaving Certificate. General Constables were deemed to "understand" the law better than the Escort Constables. They were the station orderlies: received and recorded complaints, performed clerical duties, and escorted prisoners; they could rise to become senior officers including the IGP. The Escort Constable was rather an "illiterate" or without any formal educational credential. The main qualification for the Escort Constable, who formed the bulk of the mobile units, performed guard and patrol duties, escorted suspects to and from court, and escorted bullions was physique. According to Coles, Escort Constables, whose highest rank was the Regional Sergeant-Major, often had better memories and made good witnesses, but they nonetheless needed very clear orders, particularly if under stress (Coles, cf. Clayton, & Killingray, 1989, p. 14). The Escort Constable was phased out in the 1970s.

The objective of colonial policing was to keep the native population in perpetual order. The historical sequence that colonial policing progressed through included adjustment and incipient insurrection, reform, reorganization and recruitment, and open revolt. For instance, when faced with renewed challenges and agitation for Ghana's independence, England increased the police size, fashioned it along paramilitary lines, ensured a rigid centralized command structure, and created the SB, CID, and the Mobile Units to deal with rabble-rousers. As Gillespie (1995, p. 8) concluded, "The government of a barbarous country and the exercise of a vague jurisdiction necessitated constant semi-military expeditions," so that "a few dominant civilized men" could "control the great multitude of the semi-barbarous . . . "; and in the King versus The Earl of Crewe, Ex parte Sekgome (1910), " . . . where . . . , the trustee . . . govern a large unsettled territory, peopled by lawless and warlike savages, who outnumber the European inhabitants by more than one hundred to one" (in Shaidi, cf. Mushanga, 1992, p. 11).

Several units were created after the 1894 Police Ordinance formalized policing in the Gold Coast Colony. These included the Marine Unit (MU, 1916), later renamed as the Customs Excise and Prevention Service (CEPS, 1942); the Criminal Investigations Department (CID, 1921); the Special Branch (SB), Signals and Traffic, Mobile/Swat, Fraud Squad, and Immigration Units (1948); Armored and Wireless and Communications Units (1950), and a 12-member all-Ghanaian female unit (1952) (Abbey, 2018; GPS, 2020d). In 1964, the Border Guard Unit (later integrated into the Ghana Armed Forces in 1972) was created to patrol Ghana's borders.

In 1957, the Gold Coast attained independence from England and the GCPF was renamed the Ghana Police Force (GPF). In 1974, the GPF was renamed the Ghana Police Service (Police Force Amendment Decree, Act 350, 1974). The GPS strives to achieve its motto of "Service with Integrity," and its functions of crime prevention, apprehension, and prosecution of suspects, while maintaining law and order (Police Act 350, 1970; GPS, 2020b). Even so, vestiges of colonial legacy continue to hamper effective policing in Ghana (Boateng & Darko, 2016; Tankebe, 2008a, 2010; Aning, 2006). A Commonwealth Human Rights Initiative Report (CHRI, 2009, p. 7) concluded that "colonial style policing . . . left a legacy of regime policing in Ghana; violent, heavy handed and politicised policing . . . to protect the ruling regime's interests, rather than to serve the Ghanaian community" continues.

The GPS is a highly reactive and perhaps, a highly politicized law enforcement agency. Surveys by the Integrity Initiative, the local branch of Transparency International (2000, 2005) found the GPS as the "least trusted, least effective, and most corrupt" institution in Ghana. A low level of cooperation between the police and the citizenry exists. Indeed, most Ghanaians show a significant degree of aversion and disdain toward the police because of their being perceived as corrupt and the brutalities they perpetrate on innocent citizens (Appiahene-Gyamfi, 2003, 1998; Osei Mensah, 2018). Ghana's Commission for Human Rights and Administrative Justice (CHRAJ) has expressed concern about the "deterioration in relations between the Police and the public" and urged both sides to respect each other (CHRAJ, 2013). Challenges facing the GPS include poor service conditions, political manipulation, corruption, cronyism, police brutalities, and illegal application of the law.

RECRUITMENT AND TRAINING

Two colleges train officers above and including the rank of Assistant Superintendent, while over seven depots dotted across Ghana train enlisted constables up to inspectors. Only Ghanaian citizens, eighteen years and older can be recruited. The basic minimum educational qualification for enlistment evolved from no formal education at its inception to a Standard Seven/Middle School Leaving Certificate until the 1990s when it was raised to a Secondary/High School diploma. Recruits with the minimum high school diploma start from constable "class two" after six months of training. Commission into the officer corps requires a college degree/diploma or qualification as an inspector. Thus, the officer corps is made up of those joining without prior experience in policing and qualified serving inspectors. Candidates go through a selection process, including passing an entrance examination and being "physically and medically fit by police standards." The University of Ghana, Legon runs a two-year diploma in Police Administration for personnel aspiring for upward mobility. All training programs are residential. Recruitments are done nationally through media advertisements. Both senior and junior police officers may be sponsored for further training overseas after the initial/basic training in Ghana. The enlistees could be stationed anywhere in Ghana after training. The government gazettes all enlistees after the training and probation period has been served.

Today, the GPS attracts highly qualified/educated Ghanaians, the "better class natives" who once saw policing as "repugnant," and "viewed the natives who enlisted . . . as traitors" because of the job security, improved conditions, and unemployment (Gillespie, 1955, p. 38). Ideally, recruitment is based on merit, but malpractices like corruption, nepotism, in-breeding, patronage, and cronyism have been legend. Rumors abound of politicians enlisting their own relatives and tribes-folks (Arthur, 2012). Faibille (2001) blamed the National Democratic Party and the Provisional National Defence Council governments for recruitment malpractices, which sometimes involved senior officers. In 2015, Commissioner of Police, Patrick Timbilla, then Director General for Human Resources and Administration was arrested and later dismissed for recruitment fraud (Ghanaweb, 2017a). Akin to recruitment abuse is promotion abuse. Malpractices related to enlistment, if not checked, could be detrimental to the efficient operation of the GPS. Improving upon policing calls for a new approach to training, sophisticated methods of selection, diverse training to include proactive nonconfrontational strategies, and emphasis on values and differences that reflect Ghana's ethnic diversity.

POLICE–CITIZEN RATIO

From 120 men in 1844, the police increased to 8,000 men in 1948 (Cole, cf. Clayton, & Killingray, 1989, p. 13). The increase does not match the United Nations' recommended police–population ratio of 1:500. In 2005, the Commonwealth Human Rights Initiative (CHRI) estimated the number of members of the GPS to be 17,806 officers and put the police–population ratio at 1:1,161. In 2014, the National Democratic Congress government claimed the ratio, based on 30,635 personnel, to be 1:784 to the population. In 2017, the New National Patriotic Party government revealed that the GPS had 23,000 personnel, 1:848 of population, and promised to add an additional 23,000 to offset the UN-recommended imbalance (Kwakofi, 2017). The ratio deficit has led to a pitiful police coverage and visibility in most parts of Ghana, including the remote areas and some parts of the major cities and towns. Insufficient personnel and resources have often led to delayed or timely deployment to emergencies or instances of a no-show (Justice Amonoo-Monney Commission, 2006). Enlistment into the GPS slowed between 2012 and 2016 during the National Democratic Congress administration due to conditions imposed by the World Bank (WB) and International Monetary Fund (IMF) that embargoed public service employment in Ghana. Since 2016, the National Patriotic Party government has resumed enlisting more personnel after weaning Ghana off the conditions.

One major problem that compounds the citizen-police ratio, and which will perhaps linger awhile even if massive recruitment occurs, is the lack of office accommodation or what Ghanaians call police stations and living accommodations for personnel. Related to office accommodation is cell/jail accommodation for suspects, which constitutes a study of its own. For now, it can only be asserted that jails/cells, which are normally attached to the stations are overcrowded and inhumane. Several areas of the country are without police presence because of the government's inability to provide stations and personnel. In some areas without police visibility, suspects may be processed by the local chiefs and elders. In areas without police coverage, suspects may be lynched as happened on May 29, 2017, in Denkyira-Obuasi, Central region when some residents gruesomely lynched Captain (posthumously promoted Major) Maxwell Adam Mahama, commander of a military detachment at Diaso, Upper Denkyira, West District of the region on suspicion of being an armed robber (Ghanaweb, 2017b). Several incidents of the citizenry lynching suspected criminals in Ghana, either because of lack of police presence or mistrust of the police or both, have occurred in the past (Appiahene-Gyamfi, 2003; Tankebe, 2010). The police–citizen ratio situation has led to calls for community policing.

COMMUNITY POLICING

Although there is no set-in stone direction on how community policing should work or any preferred strategy to implement one, Ghana's need for a viable and productive community policing system is essential to build a new kind of relationship and partnership with the public before the public mistrust gets out of hand. Given recent calls to defund or abolish policing completely elsewhere, Ghana can seize the opportunity before the agitation gains "global" sympathy. The GPS's Community Policing Unit is headed by a director and operates under the Public Affairs Directorate at the Police Headquarters, Accra. Interestingly, this unit's website has been under construction for several years. The lack of any clear focus or aims and objectives and support suggests that, perhaps, the community policing idea is for public relations rather than to establish a viable partner in crime prevention. Governments fail to understand that community policing is a shared responsibility in neighborhood safety and previous police administrations have been reticent to embrace it.

In 2012, the then Director of the GPS Community Policing Unit (CPU), Chief Superintendent Mohammed Fuseini Suraji, revealed that establishing the CPU was an attempt to deflate the coercive military orientation tag associated with the police. According to Suraji, the CPU was part of a strategic plan to meet community expectations and international standards of policing with regard for basic human rights. Unfortunately, the establishment of community policing continued to be lip-service. Since 2016, the NPP government has recruited remunerated community police officers. On July 3, 2017, the GPS and Ghana's Youth Employment Agency (YEA) announced plans to enlist over 36,000 Ghanaians under a Community Protection Officer (CPO) module of community policing to assist in law enforcement throughout Ghana (Ghanaweb, 2017b). This type of community policing appears to be informed by politics (jobs for NPP sympathizers), but the GPS insists that this cost-effective and community friendly policing seeks to activate the consciousness of Ghanaians in crime prevention, social justice, and community welfare.

Moreover, the quality of training for the community police officers may not be adequate to bring law and order to the doorsteps of Ghanaians. A few weeks of training may not prepare them enough to observe due process and basic human rights. Community police officers perform several auxiliary duties and activities in their communities. They are often deployed alongside the regular police and other security agencies (military, customs, prisons, and fire services) to supervise elections and participate in national celebrations (Ghanaweb, 2020a). A properly implemented community policing could alleviate the shortage of policing in most parts of Ghana and assure rapport and trust between the citizenry and the GPS. As described by Mattessich and Monsey (1997, cf. Maguire & Duffee, 2015, p. 117), community capacity is "the extent to which members of a community can work together effectively, including their abilities to develop and sustain strong relationships, solve problems and make group decisions, and collaborate effectively to identify goals and get work done."

POLICE PROSECUTIONS

One major role of the GPS in Ghana's administration of justice is the prosecution of criminal suspects. This means that in Ghana, the police investigate, arrest, and prosecute criminal suspects. The GPS prosecutes more criminal cases than the Attorney General's Department, which, by law, is the institution mandated to prosecute criminal suspects. Interestingly, to proceed in most of the criminal cases prosecuted by the police, advice is sought from the Attorney General's Department. Police prosecution, a hangover from colonial England, is now a powerful Directorate, the Legal and Prosecution Directorate, headed by a Director General, who is part of the 20-member Police Management Board (POMAB) that helps the IGP run the GPS. Colonial police prosecution was preceded by the appointment of Puisne Magistrates, whom natives referred to as Police Magistrates (PM) in the Gold Coast. Allowing the police to prosecute criminal suspects and serve as judges by England was in clear violation of natural justice, separation of powers, rule of law, common law practice, and the judicial principle that restrained interested parties from sitting, adjudicating, or participating in decisions that affected suspects. As Morris (1972, p. 150 in Shaidi cf. Mushanga, 1992) stated, "The executive gave the law and administered it. Political officers adjudicated upon their own orders and, if need be, upon their own conduct. No court could control them, no lawyer was even allowed to watch them. A native could appeal from Caesar to Caesar but was otherwise without redress. The result was complete subordination of law to policy. The system worked satisfactorily because a soundproof wall round the administration of justice was built so that no echo could reach the outside world" (p. 7).

Bushe (1934, in Shaidi cf. Mushanga, 1992, p. 7), an Assistant Legal Adviser in the Colonial Office, described such practice as a "retrograde step in the colonial administration." Unfortunately, this practice has now been entrenched and no government has had the willpower to stop it.

The PM has been phased out, but police prosecution continues. Police prosecutions raise questions of fundamental fairness and make the GPS too powerful, high-handed, and autocratic. It is worrying that prosecuting suspects is left in the hands of an institution whose personnel may be poorly trained, ill-equipped, high-handed, unchecked, and unaccountable to anyone. Police prosecution could become a gold mine or create avenues and opportunities for corruption, abuse of power, disregard for rule of law, and natural justice. Perhaps, it is time for the GPS to divest itself from prosecuting criminals in Ghana. It is odd for a trained attorney to be seen in court contending on matters of law with a prosecutor who only has six months of police training and no formal legal education. It is still unacceptable, even if the police prosecutor is an attorney, which is hardly the case when sampling more than

90 percent of the police prosecutions. While Civil Rights advocates could campaign to discontinue police prosecution of criminals, ultimately, the onus to discontinue police prosecutions lies with the government.

POLICE DEVIANCE

Police corruption, bribery, brutalities, nepotism, negligence and dereliction of duty, and abuse of power have been documented. Osei Mensah (2018, p. 266) poignantly stated that the police face several challenges including unprofessionalism, bribery, corruption, favoritism, wrongful application of the law, and witness and evidence tampering. The police's use of brute force and shooting of innocent people is well known and documented (Anamzoya & Senah, 2011; Ghanaweb, 2006a; National Commission for Civic Education, 2017). Arbitrary arrests, unlawful detention, sloppy investigations, extorting money and valuables before bail is granted and failure to inform suspects of their right to counsel, contrary to the law, is commonplace (Akosah-Sarpong, 2010; Takyi-Boadu, 2012; Ghana Governance and Corruption Survey, 2001). In September 1998, then Inspector General of Police, Peter Tenganabang Nanfuri called for the overhaul of the GPS to rid it of civilian harassers, unauthorized traffic/motor-checks, unlawful detention of suspects, extorting money from suspects before granting bail, shoddy investigations, and indiscipline; negative components which have become part of its image. Rumors and reports of evidence tampering are profound. Pieces of crime exhibits have either turned into something else or disappeared altogether from police custody. One 2003 report found that exhibits recovered in police-military swoops were neither recorded nor produced for testing as exhibits (Ghanaweb, 2005a). In *Re Republic v Nana Amma Martin*, 1,020 grams of a cocaine exhibit mysteriously turned into sodium carbonate, aka washing soda in custody at the Police Headquarters (Justice Dordzie Committee, 2011). Several commissions of inquiry reports found bribery and corruption, delays in response to crime, and lack of professionalism to be endemic in the GPS (Justice Short Commission, 2019).

In 2000, the government established a National Reconciliation Commission (NRC, 2000) to investigate human rights violations by the police and other security agencies since 1957. The NRC report contained several cases of police corruption and abuse. Moreover, reports by Ghana's Commission on Human Rights and Administrative Justice (CHRAJ) are replete with numerous cases of police deviance (CHRAJ, 2013). There is extensive evidence of police either colluding with criminals or engaging in crime. Moreover, the police have often tipped off suspects to escape, collected private debts, and openly extorted monies (sometimes as little as one Cedi, less than fifty US cents) from motorists (Ghanaweb, 2005b). No IGP or government has been courageous enough to stamp out cronyism, nepotism, bribery, and corruption, especially extortion of money from motorists. Although the police are perceived as being corrupt, over 57 percent of Ghanaians indicated in a survey that they would still report corruption cases to them. (National Commission on Civic Education, 2017). Promotion and transfer malpractices in the GPs are legend (Ghanaweb, 2005b).

Many Ghanaians harbor negative perceptions and antipathy toward the police. For most Ghanaians, the GPS is a corrupt and untrustworthy public institution. Some Ghanaians not only perceive police deviance as normal but suspect government cover-ups. And, some police officers agree. Ghanaians have bemoaned the massive and unbridled police deviance: bribery, corruption, assaulting suspects and defenseless demonstrators, mysterious and unexplained deaths in custody, shooting deaths, evidence tampering, selective justice, and standing aloof while suspects are lynched or set on fire by citizens who claim to have lost confidence in the police (Boateng, 2016; Tankebe, 2008b, 2009, 2011; Appiahene-Gyamfi, 2003; Freiku, 2006; Gomda, 2010). Police deviance has eroded public trust and confidence in the GPS.

To live up to its motto of "Service with integrity," the CHRI suggested the need "to effectively monitor police activities and accountability" and shake off the "colonial legacy that has persisted for too long" (CHRI, 2007, p. 7). According to the CHRI report, "A fundamental part of a modern, democratic and transparent police is . . . accountability to the state . . . community and . . . the law" (p. 8). Accountability calls for an Independent Police Complaints Board, protection from illegitimate political interference, and establishment of community-focused policing that is held to the agreed standards of conduct (Justice Short Commission, 2019).

THE GHANA POLICE SERVICE: FUTURE DIRECTIONS AND CHALLENGES

Although created by colonial England, the GPS has evolved into a viable national law enforcement institution of "repute." As the sole law enforcement organization in Ghana, the GPS attracts highly qualified citizens and has expanded coverage to most parts of the country. The GPS regulates auxiliary security/crime prevention agencies, including private security companies, and licenses weapon sales in Ghana. The GPS has broken several criminal cells, including local and foreign gangs operating in Ghana, and cooperated with regional and international law enforcement agencies to detect crime and bring suspects to justice. The GPS has attempted to "decentralize" its operations and administration, but the IGP continues to wield enormous power as the head. As mentioned earlier, the IGP is assisted in the day-to-day administration by a 20-member Police Management Board (POMAB) comprising Schedule Officers, not below the rank of Deputy Commissioner, stationed at the Headquarters. Through the various Directorates and departments, the GPS assures law and order by detecting crime and apprehending and prosecuting crime suspects. The traditional policing role of order maintenance aside, the GPS provides ancillary services like traffic safety, highway patrol, prosecuting suspects, and security at national, international, sporting, political, leisure, and entertainment events and activities.

Moreover, the GPS provides security detail for Ghana's President, Vice-President, ministers and deputy ministers of state, the Speaker and members of Ghana's Parliament, as well as top/prominent government and public officials, including justices of peace, top civil servants and select prominent Ghanaians (1992 Chap. 15, Art 200 [3]; 1970, Act 350). Furthermore, the GPS provides city, town, village, and residential patrol and utility installations security, as well as security for fees to individuals and institutions. The GPS has been an Interpol member since 1958. Thus, apart from its local law enforcement responsibilities, the GPS through its local Interpol division liaises with counterparts worldwide to "fight" global/international and trans-national crime, including drug, sex, child, human and artifact trafficking, cyber and organized crime, piracy, money laundering, and terrorism. Moreover, the GPS participates in regional and global crime prevention activities and conducts peace-keeping operations in several countries, including Liberia, South Sudan, Somalia, and Sierra Leone under the auspices of the United Nations, the African Union, and the Economic Community of West African States. The GPS is at the forefront in dealing with national disasters and other epidemics, including the coronavirus (COVID-19) and flood and fire response. The GPs continue to team up with the Ghana Armed Forces and the Custom and Immigration Services to patrol Ghana's borders and undertake critical security operations to ensure peace and tranquility in Ghana.

The GPS faces several difficulties, including insufficient and irregular supply of uniforms, constant and irregular transfer of personnel, unfettered political interference and control, and a lack of critical infrastructure, including offices and personnel accommodation. Other difficulties are poor service conditions, including "poor" remuneration, promotion, transfer and enlistment scandals and malpractices, poor educational backgrounds, and lack of proper criminal background screening for enlistees, along with inadequate and outmoded logistics. The government provides free accoutrements, boots, uniforms, and accommodation (barracks or rented) to all personnel. However, irregular supply of uniforms (new uniforms, caps, socks, whistles, and boots used to be supplied biannually) and accoutrements is a recurring problem. It is an open secret that policemen and women could be transferred twice in a year or even within a month from one city, town, village, and/or region to another at a moments' notice. The constant transfer of personnel drains the already scanty police resources since transferees are moved to their new stations at the government's expense. Sometimes transferees must find their own accommodation, which may take months and result in a loss of productivity. Constant transfers affect the personnel and their families (children's education, spouses' work), both financially and in terms of retirement plans. Most police transfers, no matter how well-intentioned, are perceived by the policemen and women as punishment or to get rid of "troublesome" personnel. The transfer of personnel is not just a potential source for nepotism, cronyism, and corruption but also a resource drain since it places undue pressure on personnel accommodation.

As mentioned earlier, the GPS provides free living accommodation to all its personnel. This accommodation policy, another colonial legacy, is difficult to sustain because of the police expansion and Ghana's economic situation. The government's promises of constructing new barracks or providing accommodation are hardly fulfilled. The government provides 20 percent of salary as an allowance for those who do not secure free barracks or rented accommodation.

Ghana's compulsory retiring age for all civil/public service personnel, including the police, is sixty years of age. However, the government often exercises its prerogative power to extend the tenure of some officers, including the IGP's on contract. Exercising this prerogative raises consternation and resentment within the GPS because of its politicization and skewed nature. To discontinue contracts, the compulsory retiring age could be raised to at least sixty-five years, and a law could be passed to enjoin the IGP to serve for one four-year term only. This way, no matter which political party is in power, the current IGP could discharge his or her duties without fear of being retired prematurely. It will instill confidence in, and insulate the IGP, from undue political pressures.

Poor service conditions may contribute to police deviance. As the Justice Archer Commission (1997) report observed, "The present conditions . . . are deplorable . . . woefully undermined, ill-trained and ill-equipped . . . motivation is almost nil and its morale low" (p. 32). The GPS has always faced shortage of patrol vehicles. It is not uncommon to see police officers transporting suspects to and from the courts and custody in public transportation, including through taxicabs. It is also not uncommon for a complainant to provide his or her means of transportation before the police can respond to a call for assistance. In 2001, there were only 145 police vehicles in Ghana (Ghanaweb, 2001). Since 2016, the GPS has received over 740 patrol vehicles, as well as other equipment and machinery, including armored cars to assist in crime prevention efforts, disaster management, and other national emergencies.

For the first time in Ghana's history, the government has procured three helicopters for the GPS to boost its operations. Ironically, some patrol vehicles are pick-up trucks and saloon cars that are hardly designed to carry apprehended suspects. Steps to retrain personnel both at home and abroad to improve professionalism and efficiency have been implemented. However, any innovations may not yield any positive results unless the needless, chronic, unfettered, and pervasive political meddling stops. Since Ghana returned to multiparty democracy in 1993, two political parties, the National Democratic Party (NDC) and the National Patriotic Party (NPP) have governed the country after they won the general elections. That is, the NDC (1993–1999 and 2009–2016) and the NPP (2000–2008 and 2017+)—the two political parties that have ruled Ghana since 1993—always accused each other of using the police to intimidate the citizenry.

The NDC in opposition would accuse the police, including those they either enlisted and/or promoted to their current ranks and positions when they were in power, to be in bed with the NPP government and vice versa. When the police invite an opposition party member for any suspected malfeasance, party supporters besiege the Police Headquarters or the station that invited that person to demand for his or her immediate release. Politicians complain of police "harassment" when they are in opposition. One condemnation of alleged police brutality and harassment was made on March 1, 2006, by then opposition leader and later, President of Ghana, the late John Evans Atta-Mills (Ghanaweb, 2006b). Sadly, police brutalities, including the shooting death of two demonstrators, occurred when Atta-Mills' NDC government was in power in 1995 and continued when he became Ghana's Vice-President, and by virtue of his position, Chairman of the Police Council from 1996 to 1999. Furthermore, under his Presidency (2009–2012), police brutalities continued (Dwamena, 2012; Gadugah, 2010; Ghanaian Chronicle, 2010).

Since the NPP assumed government in 2017, the opposition NDC has constantly criticized them of either manipulating for political gains or politicizing the GPS. Two blunt warnings to the GPS recently came from the NDC member of Parliament for the Ningo-Pampram constituency in the Greater Accra region, Sam George, and the NDC National Communications Director, Sammy Gyamfi; that if the NDC wins political power, any policeman and woman who colluded or was in bed with the NPP government, mistreated NDC supporters, and/or failed to arrest NPP supporters who broke the law will be sacked. Although the NPP government quickly reacted by assuring and encouraging the police to discharge their duties equitably without fear of intimidation, such threats are real and sometimes followed through (Ghanaweb, 2020b). Sadly, no member of Ghana's civil society has yet condemned the threats or even commented on it.

Political manipulation and the problems mentioned have placed the police in an ambivalent position. Suspects are sometimes released because of "an order from above." It is impossible for the police to be at the forefront in Ghana's corruption fight not only because they themselves are complicit but also because politicians vehemently defend their supporters, even in the case of assault, corruption, and even murder. Several crimes including murder are unsolved because suspects are protected, and investigators are threatened with transfer or retirement. The GPS could achieve its mandate and improve its image and credibility if politicians would stop interfering with its work. The situation is so appalling that even when there is an inter/intra NDC and NPP party supporter's fight, it is the police that are blamed for not doing their work.

The GPS has been a male-dominated state institution since its inception. The gender ratio of about six males to one (6:1) female is hardly encouraging. Efforts have been made over the years to recruit more females, but the imbalance will persist for a while. Every command structure and position had previously been headed by males except on the few occasions when female officers were in-charge of Headquarters Administration, the CID and Welfare Directorates, as well as the Domestic Violence and Victim Support Unit (DVVSU) and the Mounted Constabulary. Females also head a few Divisions, Districts, and Stations across Ghana, but not regional commands. It appears that any senior female officer who heads any Unit or Directorate is always on notice—she could be removed at any time. Throughout its history, only once did a female senior police officer come close to becoming the substantive IGP. On January 28, 2009, the most senior female officer, and perhaps, the most senior police officer overall then, Elizabeth Mills-Robertson, was appointed the Acting IGP by then President Evans Attah-Mills. However, any hope of confirming her as the first substantive female IGP in Ghana was short-lived because her male junior colleague, Paul Tawiah Quaye, was appointed the substantive IGP only a few months later, on May 16, 2009. Elizabeth Mills-Robertson was retired from the Service after Quaye's appointment. Recently, the first female Commandant of the Winneba Police College, who is also the first female Director General of CID and currently the Director General of the Welfare Directorate, Maame Yaa Tiwaah Addo-Danquah has bemoaned the pervasive sexism and misogyny within the GPS. According to Tiwaah, female officers are harassed and discriminated against daily (Ghanaweb, 2020a). According to Maame Tiwaah, any initiative by a female or any woman who aspires to be in a higher position is met with stiff opposition and name-calling from her male counterparts. Maame Tiwaah's assertion reinforces what many gender advocates have complained about as institutionalized sexism. Hence, despite the achievement and tremendous contributions they have made and continue to make, policewomen still suffer from gender stereotypes. There is little wonder that even though there are more women in Ghana than men when it comes to policing, the ratio is different (Abbey, 2015).

CONCLUSION

Although the GPS has since its inception evolved into the sole law enforcement institution in Ghana, numerous challenges confront it. These include the difficulty in shaking off its colonial loots and legacy, human rights violations, cronyism, bribery, and corruption. As the CHRI (2007, p. 8) report observed,

> Despite a series of . . . commissions and committees that began in 1951, the police have not been pulled into line with the modern democracy that Ghana is today; at different times reform has been undermined by political turmoil or discarded because of a lack of political will for change.

The same 2007 CHRI report concluded that,

> Ghana's police are ready for reform, and Ghana's community is ready for a police service that reflects its role as a model of successful and stable democratic change. . . . It is time that the decades of discussion and debate around police reform translates to tangible change, and the final shaking off of a colonial legacy that has persisted for too long (p. 7).

The GPS must be attuned to Ghana's contemporary sociopolitical contexts by deflating its coercive colonial paramilitary orientation and should move toward a proactive community-oriented policing that is responsible to the people and respects human rights. Creating independent or bipartisan civilian review boards, introduction of early warning systems, improved response time to distress calls, installing video cameras in patrol vehicles, and/or officers wearing body cameras, and swiftly sanctioning those who break the law could help the police win public trust and confidence (Justice Short Commission, 2019). Furthermore, the GPS must be insulated from undue political interference. Police prosecution of criminal suspects must end, period!

To address the century-old accommodation deficit, personnel could be stationed in their hometowns or home districts. This could be achieved by aggressively decentralizing or "localizing" policing in Ghana (as obtained in some countries), where every town employs its own qualified residents to police. This policy shift, while resolving the perennial accommodation deficit, may also greatly reduce brutalities, nepotism, and corruption. Given Ghana's social system, it is unlikely that locals will extort money from and/or brutalize their own folks.

A new "paradigm" may be needed to shift contemporary policing and police administration in Ghana to a new level that is responsive to the safety and welfare of the citizenry. One extreme shift, albeit radical, could be a complete breakup of the GPS into two, three, or four autonomous law enforcement entities, each with a well-defined mandate. For instance, the Motor Traffic Unit could be separated from the GPS and renamed the Ghana Motor Traffic and Highway Patrol Police. After all, the Special Branch, (now BNI) the Border Guard Unit, and the Customs and Preventive Services, which used to be part of the GPS were detached successfully (Fordjour, 2009). Another consideration could be the creation of a separate autonomous agency (akin to the USA Secret Service) to protect very important personalities (VIPs) or dignitaries, including Presidents and Parliamentarians. The break-up and creation of separate specialized law enforcement organizations could be done in a bi-partisan way, but skeptics may be apprehensive because of Ghana's experience under President Nkrumah who formed his own Presidential Guard, which according to critics, was better resourced and equipped than the regular military and police. Conscientization or public education and political will could be important in any "paradigm" shift. If approached properly and if public support could be garnered, a break-up could go a long way to release some of the burdens of the GPS and ensure better management, monitoring, and efficiency. To live up to its motto of "Service with Integrity" the GPS must address the challenges confronting it while policymakers improve upon service conditions, which every police commission of inquiry has bemoaned as being poor, although no one knows what better service conditions are or how much is enough in Ghana.

Improved police–community relations could reduce crime significantly. Policymakers and civil society could address the systemic problems and declining public confidence in the police. Edelsten (cf. Clayton & Killingray, 1989), an Assistant Superintendent of the Gold Coast police stationed in Accra in a 1944 address titled, "The Cooperation between the Police and the Public," solemnly stressed mutual cooperation between the police and the citizenry as the core police mandate to preserve peace and prevent crime. Edelsten admonished all and sundry to "remember that the immense unseen 'preventative' power of the police, which enables the community organizations to function smoothly and effectively, is the creation not of their material power and strength, but of the respect, regard, and affection in which they are held by the majority of their fellow citizens" (pp. 4–5).

Without respect, regard, and affection from the very public it seeks to protect, the GPS may not be successful in achieving its mandate. As the CHRI report suggested, "A fundamental part of a modern, democratic and transparent police service is accountability—accountability to the state, accountability to the community and accountability to the law . . . ensures that police officers are community focused and held to the agreed standards of conduct" (2007, p. 8). The police must strive to protect the citizenry rather than being agents of the government, avoid the display of machismo, keep the "Sovereign's Peace" and represent the community when carrying "out duties that by law belong to all the citizenry" (Clayton & Killingray, 1989, pp. 4–5). This way, Ghanaians may establish unalloyed confidence in the GPS, which is hardly "repugnant" to "the better class natives" (Gillespie, 1955, p. 38). Ghanaians should always remember that "A stitch in time saves nine."

REFERENCES

Abbey, E. E. (2018). Women in police uniform: Genesis of the story. Category: Feature Article (25 August 2018). https://www.graphic.com.gh/features/features/women-in-police-uniform-genesis-of-the-story.html. Retrieved 7 July 2020.

Akosah-Sarpong, K. (2010). Ghana, African police corruption, indiscipline, national security and freedom: Understanding Ghana's overburdened police. http://www.thegambiaecho.com/Homepage/tabid/36/articleType/ArticleView/articleId/1890/Default.aspx. Retrieved 13 May 2020.

Anamzoya, A., & Senah, K. (2011). Internal control and disciplinary mechanisms in Ghana Police. http://www.cleen.org/Police%20Internal%20Control%20in%20West%20Africa.pdf. Retrieved 02 February 2020.

Aning, E. K. (2006). An overview of the Ghana Police Service. *Journal of Security Sector Management,* 4(2): 1–37.

Ankama, S. K. (1983). *Police history: Some aspects in England and Ghana.* Silken Books.

Appiahene-Gyamfi, J. (1998). Violent crime in Ghana: The case of robbery. *Journal of Criminal Justice,* 26(5): 409–424.

Appiahene-Gyamfi, J. (2003). Urban crime trends and patterns in Ghana: The case of Accra. *Journal of Criminal Justice,* 31(1): 13–23.

Arthur, C. (2012). Juicy salary led to police recruitment fraud. Source: citifmonline.com. http://www.ghanaweb.com/GhanaHomePage/NewsArchive/artikel.php?ID=242346&comment=0#com. Retrieved 12 June 2020.

Arthur, J. (1989). Ghana: colonial influence and political development in an African Country. *Criminal Justice International,* 5(4): 9–16.

Boateng, F. D., & Darko, I. N. (2016). Our past: The effect of colonialism on policing in Ghana. https://journals-sagepub-com.ezhost.utrgv.edu/doi/full/10.1177/1461355716638114 https://doi-org.ezhost.utrgv.edu/10.1177/1461355716638114. Retrieved 14 March 2020.

Boateng, F. D. (2016). Students and the police in Ghana: Mixed feelings. *Police Practice and Research,* 17(6): 555–569. http://dx.doi.org/10.1080/15614263.2015.1086877. Retrieved 13 May 2020.

Clayton, A., & Killingray, D. (1989). *Khaki and blue: Military and police in British Colonial Africa.* Center for International Studies, Ohio University.

Commission on Human Rights and Administrative Justice Report (2013). http://www
.chrajghana.org. / Retrieved 25 March 2020.

Commonwealth Human Rights Initiative Annual Report. (2007). The police, the people,
the politics: Police accountability in Ghana. http://www.humanrightsinitiative.org/
publications/police/police_accountability_in_ghana.pdf. Retrieved 16 April 2020.

Commonwealth Human Rights Initiative Annual Report. (2004). Sarvodaya Enclave,
New Delhi. https://www.humanrightsinitiative.org/content/our-documents Retrieved
20 March 2020.

Constitution of the Republic of Ghana. (1992). Tema: Ghana Publishing Corporation.

Dwamena, N. Y. (2012). President Mills under fire over growing insecurity. http://
www.africanstandardnews.org/index.php?option=com_content&view=article&id
=520:nana-yaw-dwamena-ghana&catid=3:newsflash&Itemid=89. Retrieved 21
March 2020.

Faibille, E., Jnr. (2001). How NDC ruined police service: Recruits practice "Stand
and load." *Independent Newspaper,* 1 November 2001, pp. 1, and 8.

Fordjour, A. (2009). A review of the conflicting roles of the BNI and Ghana
Police Service. https://www.ghanaweb.com/GhanaHomePage/NewsArchive/A
-Review-of-the-Conflicting-Roles-of-the-BNI-and-Ghana-Police-Service-173175.
Retrieved 15 March 2020.

Freiku, S. R. (2006) Rotten eggs on police faces . . . damage control on Kuasi murder
backfires http://ghanaian-chronicle.com/rotten-eggs-on-police-facesdamage-con-
trol-on-kumasi-murder-backfires/. Retrieved 22 April 2020.

Gadugah, N. (2010). AFAG alarmed over insecurity in Ghana. http://www.moderng-
hana.com/ news/302760/1/afag-alarmed-over-insecurity-in-ghana.html. Retrieved
16 April 2020.

Ghana Governance and Corruption Survey: Evidence from households, enterprises
and public officials (English). (2001). Washington, DC: World Bank Group. http://
documents.worldbank.org/curated/en/749401468253174124/The-Ghana-gover-
nance-and-corruption-survey-evidence-from-households-enterprises-and-public
-officials. Retrieved 31 July 2020.

Ghana Integrity Initiative (GII) of Transparency International (TI). (2005). "Voice of
the People" survey (Southern Ghana). Project Completion Report. Sponsors: PTF,
UK. https://www.tighana.org/programs/overview/. Retrieved 5 April 2020.

Ghana Integrity Initiative (GII) of Transparency International (TI). (2000). https://
www.tighana.org/programs/overview/. Retrieved 5 April 2020.

Ghana Police Service Act. (1970, Act 350). Ghana Pub. Corp. Printing Division,
Accra-Tema.

Ghana Police Service. (2007). Police administration: A brief history. www.ghanapo-
lice.org/police_admin/index.htm. Retrieved 08 February 2012.

Ghana Police Service. (2020a). Police Council. https://police.gov.gh/en/index.php/
the-police-council/. Retrieved 6 March 2020.

Ghana Police Service. (2020b). Ghana Police Service. https://police.gov.gh/en/.
Retrieved 6 March 2020.

Ghana Police Service. (2020c). Ghana Police Service. http://www.ghanapolice.com/.
Retrieved 6 March 2020.

Ghana Police Service. (2020d). Brief histroy of Ghana Police Service. https://police .gov.gh/en/index.php/our-history. Retrieved 26 June 2020.

Ghana Population. (2020). Country meters. https://countrymeters.info/en/Ghana. Retrieved 12 April 2020.

Ghana Statistical Service. (GSS, 2020). Quick overview. https://statsghana.gov.gh/. Retrieved 12 April 2020.

Ghanaian Chronicle. (2010). Alliance for Accountable Governance on the State of Increasing Insecurity in Ghana. http://ghanaian-chronicle.com/features/alliance-for-accountable-governance-on-the-state-of-increasing-insecurity-in-ghana/. Retrieved 14 May 2020.

Ghanaweb. (2001). Police have only 145 vehicles: General news of Monday, 20 August 2001. www.ghanaweb.com. Retrieved 24 February 2020.

Ghanaweb. (2005a). Rot in Police Service exposed: General news of Monday, 18 July 2005. http://www.ghanaweb.com/GhanaHomePage/NewsArchive/artikel.php?ID =244370. Retrieved 25 March 2020.

Ghanaweb. (2005b). Police urged to improve upon crime fighting strategies. https:// ghanaweb.com/GhanaHomePage/crime/Police-urged-to-improve-upon-crime -fighting-strategies-96881. Retrieved 16 March 2020.

Ghanaweb. (2006a). Cops torture man into coma: General news of Thursday, 19 January 2006. *Ghanaian Chronicle*. https://www.ghanaweb.com/GhanaHomePage/ NewsArchive/Cops-torture-man-into-coma-97828. Retrieved 12 April 2020.

Ghanaweb. (2006b). Atta Mills condemns Police brutalities. *GNA General News*. March 2006. http://www.modernghana.com/news/95934/1/atta-mills-condemns -police-brutalities.html. Retrieved 12 April 2020.

Ghanaweb. (2017a). Timbilla sacked: General news 25 January 2017. *Ghana Star*. https://www.ghanastar.com/stories/cop-patrick-timbilla-sacked/. Retrieved 14 March 2020.

Ghanaweb. (2017b). Police to recruit 36,000 for community policing. *General news*, dailyguideafrica.com. http://dailyguideafrica.com/police-recruit-36000-community-policing/. Retrieved 14 March 2020.

Ghanaweb. (2017c). How Captain Mahama was killed: The inside story. *Daily Guide*. https://dailyguidenetwork.com/captain-mahama-killed-inside-story/. Retrieved 12 April 2020.

Ghanaweb. (2020a). Female police bemoans sexism at workplaces: General news of Thursday, 23 July 2020. *Daily Guide Network*. https://www.ghanaweb.com /GhanaHomePage/NewsArchive/Female-police-bemoans-sexism-at-workplaces -1014613. Retrieved 23 July 2020.

Ghanaweb. (2020b). Ignore Sammy Gyamfi's threats: Interior minister to police, soldiers. *Starr FM*. https://www.ghanaweb.com/GhanaHomePage/politics/Ignore -Sammy-Gyamfi-s-threats-Interior-Minister-to-police-soldiers-1018120. Retrieved 12 March 2020.

Gillespie, W. H. (1955). The Gold Coast Police, 1844–1938. With illustrations by C.R. Edelsten and from other sources. Unknown Binding.

Gomda, A. R. (2010). Six cops arrested for murder: *General news* Friday, 12 March 2010. *Daily Guide.* https://www.ghanaweb.com/GhanaHomePage/NewsArchive/browse.archive.php?date=20100312. Retrieved 12 July 2020.

In Republic v Nana Ama Martin: Cocaine turns into washing soda after certification by police forensic lab. (2011). *Daily Graphic General News* http://www.ghanaweb.com/GhanaHomePage/NewsArchive/artikel.php?ID=225563. Retrieved 12 April 2020.

Justice Agnes Dordzie Committee. (2011). Report of committee of inquiry into the police CID and NACOB petition to the chief justice over "washing soda cocaine." Ghana Pub.

Justice Archer Commission. (1997). Inquiry into the Ghana Police Service. Ghana Pub.

Justice Emile Short Commission of Inquiry into Ayawaso West Wuogon Bye-Election Violence (2019). Ghanaweb (2019). https://starrfm.com.gh/2019/09/download-govt-white-paper-on-aww-commissions-report/. Retrieved 20 January 2020.

Kwakofi, E. (2017). Gov't working to address 23, 000 police deficit. *Citifmonline.com/Ghana.* http://citifmonline.com/2017/12/govt-working-to-address-23-000-police-deficit-ambrose-dery/.

Maguire, E. R., & Duffee, D. E. (Ed.) (2015). *Criminal justice theory: Explaining the nature and behavior of criminal justice.* Routledge.

National Commission for Civic Education, Ghana. (2017). Survey on public perception on the state of corruption, public accountability, and environmental governance in Ghana. http://sia.arapghana.eu/web/uploads/documents/PUBLIC_ACCOUNTABILITY__ENVIRONMENTAL_GOVERNANCE_.pdf. Retrieved 1 August 2020.

National Reconciliation Commission. (2005). Final report. Ghana Pub.

Osei Mensah, R. (2018). Assessment of training practices in the Ghana Police Service. *Journal of Law, Policy, and Globalization,* 79: 265–273.

Police Service Act. (1970, Act 350). Ghana Pub.

Shaidi, L. P. (1992). Traditional, colonial and present-day administration of criminal justice. In Mushanga, T. Mwene (Ed.), *Criminology in Africa.* UNICRI, Pub. No. 47.

Takyi-Boadu, C. (2012). Avuyi exposes rot in police. *Daily Guide Ghana.* http://www.dailyguideghana.com/?p=50713. Retrieved 25 May 2020.

Tankebe, J. (2008a). Colonialism, legitimation, and policing in Ghana. *International Journal of Law, Crime and Justice,* 36(1): 67–84.

Tankebe, J. (2008b). Police effectiveness and police trustworthiness in Ghana: An empirical appraisal. *Criminology and Criminal Justice,* 8(2): 185–202.

Tankebe, J. (2009). Public cooperation with the police in Ghana: Does procedural fairness matter? *Criminology* 47: 1,265–1,293.

Tankebe, J. (2010). Public confidence in the police: Testing the effects of public experiences of police corruption in Ghana. *British Journal of Criminology* 50: 296–319.

Tankebe, J. (2011). Explaining police support for the use of force and vigilante violence in Ghana. *Policing & Society*, 21(2): 129–149. doi:10.1080/10439463.2010.540663.

Tankebe, J. (2013). In search of moral recognition? Policing and eudaemonic legitimacy in Ghana. *Law & Social Inquiry*, 38(3): 576–597.

Chapter 2

Policing in the Republic of Kenya

Structure and Practice

Jospeter M. Mbuba

This chapter presents the organizational structure and operational practices of the police in the Republic of Kenya. It highlights the history of policing in the country, presents police administration and law enforcement processes, and discusses pertinent issues facing the police service in the country. Kenya utilizes a centralized law enforcement system embodied in a national agency called the National Police Service (NPS). The NPS was established by the Constitution in 2010 as a successor of the former Kenya Police Force, which had eroded public trust due to lack of professionalism and the frequent use of unnecessary force even under favorable circumstances. The police system was thus recreated not as a *force*, but as a *service* to the public. The objectives and functions of the NPS, as listed on its official website, are to strive for the highest standards of professionalism and discipline among its members; prevent corruption and promote and practice transparency and accountability; comply with constitutional standards of human rights and fundamental freedoms; train staff to the highest possible standards of competence and integrity, and to respect human rights and fundamental freedoms and dignity; and foster and promote relationships with the broader society (see also Constitution of the Republic of Kenya, 2010). The NPS is headed by an Inspector-General, who is appointed by the President with the approval of Parliament. The NPS consists of two parallel state agencies, namely, the Kenya Police Service and the Administration Police Service, each of which is headed by a Deputy Inspector-General. The two agencies are augmented by an investigative arm, referred to as the Directorate of Criminal Investigations, which is headed by a Director that also answers to the Inspector-General.

BACKGROUND

The system of policing used in Kenya was inherited from the British colonial rule that ended in 1963 when the country gained independence. In the early years of colonial era, the British used armed guards, who later became the first organized law enforcement system in the country. By the end of the nineteenth century, the colonial administration had organized a police structure with police stations in a few parts of the country. This effort was consolidated in 1902 to form the British East Africa Police, which in 1920, had the name officially changed to the Kenya Police (Mbuba & Mugambi, 2011).

Along with the Kenya Police was the Administration Police, a parallel state law enforcement agency established in 1929 to help the colonial administration enforce village-level policies. By that time, the Administration Police was aptly referred to as Tribal Police. Both the Kenya Police Service and the Administration have the joint mission to "maintain law and order, preserve peace, protect life and property, prevent and detect crime, apprehend offenders, and enforce the law" (ibid., p. 5). The only discernible additional functions of the Administration Police officers were to secure government buildings and provide border patrols. The enactment of a new constitution in 2010 reformatted the inherited colonial system of policing to reflect the sociodemographic dynamics and to recreate the long-lost public trust in the police. The novel system still features the regular police, now called the Kenya Police Service, and the Administrative Police. The two, along with the Directorate of Criminal Investigations, comprise the National Police Service.

The functions of the National Police Service include "the provision of assistance to the public when in need; maintenance of law and order; preservation of peace; protection of life and property; investigation of crimes; collection of criminal intelligence; prevention and detection of crime; apprehension of offenders; enforcement of all laws and regulations; and performance of any other duties as prescribed by the Inspector-General" (National Police Service Act, Laws of Kenya, Act 11A of 2011). Although Kenya's government is devolved to counties with each of the forty-seven counties having a police commander, yet the policing itself is not devolved. The chain of command emanates from the Inspector-General. County Governors have no control or supervisory role over the police within the counties. Instead, the Inspector-General of Police designates from among the county commanders in each county, the most senior officer from either the Kenya Police Service or the Administration Police Service, to coordinate the operational command and control of the county (see Mbuba, 2018). The national government may therefore exercise direct control over an errant county governor by, for example, dispensing "the full force of the law," which, in Kenya's political and administrative lingua franca, is an expression for unleashing police brutality.

They may also recall the police bodyguards of the perceived delinquent Governor (Mbuba, 2018).

POLICE ADMINISTRATION IN KENYA

As previously stated, Kenya's National Police Service (NPS) comprises two parallel agencies, the Kenya Police Service and the Administration Police Service. While for the most part, the two augment each other in law enforcement, there are still some instances of effort duplication (Okia, 2011). Administratively, the two agencies have an identical chain of command from the entry-level police position up to the Inspector-General, as explained further on in this chapter. Apart from the main policing functions, the management and operations of Kenya's National Police Service are overseen by a civilian body called the National Police Service Commission (NPSC). The NPSC's specific duties are to recruit, promote, and transfer police personnel; discipline errant officers; manage training curriculums; determine the terms of service for the police service; manage the organization of the service; manage the National Police Reserve; submit annual reports; and make recommendations to the national government on conditions of service. A second civilian body, called the Independent Policing Oversight Authority (IPOA), exists to prevent the police from misconduct, such as the violation of citizens' privacy or suspects' constitutional rights. The functions of IPOA include holding the police accountable to the public, ensuring professionalism and discipline in the police service, and hearing complaints by and against the police.

Besides the three branches of the NPS, viz, the Kenya Police Service, Administration Police Service, and the Directorate of Criminal Investigations, the NPS is organized into administrative directorates. The directorates are created by the Inspector-General and can be disbanded if the Inspector-General finds them no longer viable. The administrative directorates are headed by Directors, who report to the Inspector-General. Each directorate is further operationalized into sections, which detail the overall functions of the directorate. A condensed overview of the directorates as found on the official website of the NPS is presented below (see www.nationalpolice.go.ke).

- *Directorate of Police Reforms*: This directorate evaluates the police performance against set goals and implements the strategic and annual workplans. It also lobbies for and mobilizes resources on police reforms from external stakeholders.
- *Directorate of Administration, Planning, and Finance*: This directorate oversees general police administration, supply chain management services, and planning and fiscal matters within the police service.

- *Directorate of Operations Audit*: This directorate develops annual budget and prioritizes allocation of resources. It establishes standards for investigation and prosecution of crimes and maintains the national police records and archives. Overall, it oversees quality assurance.
- *Directorate of Counter-Violent Extremist and Organized Crime*: This directorate was created to counter and combat transnational crimes including terrorism, cyber-crimes, money laundering, human trafficking, as well as the trafficking of narcotics, arms, and other contraband. .
- *Directorate of Corporate Communication*: This directorate is to enhance the image of the police service by conveying accurate information especially in the wake of the media, which for the most part covers only scandalous events. This is the mouthpiece of the NPS.
- *Directorate of Legal and Crime Affairs*: This directorate provides legal opinion, coordinates legal matters within the police service, and represents the police service in court and other places where legal matters may arise.
- *Directorate of Command, Control and Communication*: This directorate oversees the emergency call and dispatch centers as well as the critical incidence management, which includes the management of closed-circuit televisions and automatic recognition of vehicle registration plates, among others.
- In addition to the administrative directorates, there is an office of the *Chief of Staff*, who answers directly to the Inspector-General, and whose duties include the management of the corporate affairs of the NPS, coordination of police associations, police welfare, and other support services.

Police Units

To address the varied policing needs across the country, the Inspector-General of the National Police Service creates policing units and departments that deal with specialized issues of law enforcement. The units and departments are created as needs arise and can be abolished with changing circumstances. Both the Kenya Police Service and the Administration Police Service have their own sets of units or departments, whose names directly describe the nature and purpose of the unit. Some of the key units of the Kenya Police Service include the Anti-Stock Theft Unit, General Service Unit, Railways Police Unit, Tourism Police Unit, Marine Police Unit, Kenya Airports Police Unit, Kenya Police Airwing, Kenya Police Dog Unit, Diplomatic Police Unit, Traffic Law Enforcement Unit, Presidential Escort Unit, and the Kenya Police College (Mbuba, 2017).

The Administration Police Service, on the other hand, has such units as the Rapid Deployment Unit, Rural Border Patrol Unit, Peace Corps Unit, Vital Installations and Strategic Points Unit, Security of Government Buildings

Unit, Finance Service Protection Unit, Administration Police Training College, Administration Police Service Air Support Unit, Administration Police Senior Staff College, and Administration Police Band (ibid.). Some units have survived several police regimes due to the nature of the problems that they are meant to address. A few examples of Kenya Police units are described below.

Anti-Stock Theft Unit

The Anti-Stock Theft Unit is a mobile service unit trained specifically to protect against cattle rustling and general stock theft. Livestock keeping is a fundamental economic activity in rural Kenya where nearly every household keeps a few farm animals to supplement family income. There are also pastoral communities whose only economic activity is keeping large herds of cattle, sheep, and goats as their main source of family livelihood. Loss of livestock to raiders would give them a devastating blow. With such importance being attached to livestock keeping, there was a need to create a concrete police unit that is equipped to combat livestock theft. The Anti-Stock Theft Unit is one of the oldest and remains largely intact.

General Service Unit (GSU)

The General Service Unit is the police unit that is specially trained to combat riots. Because this unit is the most conspicuous during riots, the GSU officers represent the police image in the perception of many people. The unit provides support and backup to other police units and departments during emergency situations, which are mostly in the form of civil disorder. The unit also provides security to the State Houses and State lodges as well as vital installations and strategic points (Mbuba, 2017).

Traffic Law Enforcement Unit

One of the main functions of policing in Kenya is to enforce traffic law by patrolling highways and country roads. A special police unit, the Traffic Law Enforcement Unit, is responsible for this function. The unit inspects vehicles on the roads for roadworthiness, controls load and passenger capacity, and regulates speed limits. Traffic police officers use roadblocks to control traffic and pull to the side any vehicles suspected of any violations. Police roadblocks are made of spiked metal frames laid across the road to compel oncoming vehicles to stop for inspection. At night, lantern lamps are placed next to the spiked frames to warn motorists of the presence of the police roadblock. At police roadblocks, vehicles are inspected for contraband and drivers are searched if probable cause exists. The most common target of police inspection on highways is public passenger vehicles, locally referred to as *matatus*, against overloading of passengers. Heavy-duty transportation vehicles are also commonly stopped. To signal to an approaching vehicle to stop for police inspection, officers stand by the roadside around the road-block with a raised hand while gesturing with the other hand to pull to the side. The use of roadblocks has been criticized for offering the police ample opportunities to obtain bribes from motorists who are eligible for police scru-tiny. Other functions of the traffic police include ensuring that vehicles have proper registration and are appropriately insured. The unit also directs traffic at roundabouts or traffic circles and major intersections and helps in clearing the way for senior government officials. Moreover, the unit conducts driver-license tests and issues the necessary documentation to prospective drivers in addition to conducting annual inspections of vehicles for roadworthiness.

Kenya Airports Police Unit

This unit, which is based at the main airport in the country—Jomo Kenyatta International Airport—provides security at all airports. It prevents air-travel related crimes such as hijackings, bomb-related terrorism, and drug traf-ficking, among others. Other functions of this unit include investigation of traveler complaints such as lost and delayed luggage, provision of security to aircraft, escort of items of high value and persons wanted by foreign law enforcement, guarding of vital installations within airports, and provision of security to VIPs while on airport grounds (Mbuba, 2017).

Kenya Police College

Unlike other police units, which have responsibilities tied to law enforce-ment, the Kenya Police College is the academy that trains newly hired per-sonnel to serve as police officers. Although the college is now augmented by several other basic police training schools in the country, it is the oldest and arguably the most comprehensive police academy in Kenya. The college traces its roots to the merger of police training efforts by the British colonial government, and the establishment of a unified college at Kiganjo, a camp that was initially occupied by Italian prisoners of war (Mbuba, 2017). The top administrator of the college, who bears the title Commandant, answers to the Deputy Inspector of the Kenya Police Service. All police training schools in the country, whether serving the Kenya Police Service or the Administration Police Service, use a common harmonized training curriculum.

Rural Border Patrol and Maritime Units

Like the Kenya Police Service, the Administration Police Service also fea-tures various units, whose names reflect the purpose for which the units were created. The Rural Border Patrol Unit is one such unit, affiliated with the Administration Police Service. The unit reinforces the functions of the immigration personnel in ensuring the safety of Kenya's borders by patrolling against crimes such as trafficking in contraband and other transnational crimes. Kenya's neighboring countries include Ethiopia to the north, Tanzania to the south, Somalia to the east, Uganda to the west, and South Susan to the north-west. The country also borders the Indian Ocean to the south-east, hence a separate unit—the Maritime Police Unit, was formed to provide security along the coastal line as well as around the many lakes in the hinterland. The Unit conducts surveillance against introduction of contraband by sea, piracy, illegal immigration via arriving ships, as well as other coastal criminal activities, such as illegal fishing on Kenyan waters. Moreover, the Marine Police Unit provides rescue operations during emergencies along the coastal waters.

Security of Government Buildings Unit

This is a unit of the Administration Police Service. The unit exists to guard government buildings and key infrastructure, such as power generating and distribution installations, the railway system, and main water treatment points. The unit also provides security at the residences of senior government personnel and escort of money on transit between commercial entities. While this unit offers "free" services to government entities, private citizens can also hire the service, for example, in the transportation of goods of value when armed escort is deemed necessary.

Police Ranks

Police ranks in the Kenya's policing system include the following from entry position to the top command: Constable, Corporal, Sergeant, Senior Sergeant, Inspector, Chief Inspector, Assistant Superintendent, Superintendent, Senior Superintendent, Commissioner, Assistant Inspector-General, Senior Assistant Inspector-General, Deputy Inspector-General, and Inspector-General. Unlike all the other ranks, Deputy Inspector-General and Inspector-General are not meritorious but constitutional offices competitively filled by Presidential appointments through an interview process vetted by the National Police Service Commission.

In the chain of command, the entry-level rank is the Constable, who conducts patrols, followed by the Corporal, the first noncommissioned officer (NCO). Corporals oversee outposts and supervise Constables (Mbuba, 2017). Police Sergeants, who are also NCOs, oversee armory at police stations and, where circumstances permit, may be assigned the command of patrol bases. The senior-most NCO is the Senior Sergeant. Police Inspectors and Chief Inspectors are leadership positions. They comprise the "inspectorate" category and provide operational leadership at the subcounty level (ibid.). Police Superintendents manage policing affairs at the county level, while Police Commissioners head the county command and supervise law enforcement at the county level. The various categories of police Generals manage policies and procedures at the national level.

National Police Reserve

To supplement the police strength, especially in rural areas where the service is not readily available, the police in Kenya use the services of volunteers. Anyone above the age of eighteen and below the age of fifty-five may apply to become a volunteer. The volunteers are provided some basic training as authorized by the Inspector-General and upon successful recruitment, they join a special police category called the National Police Reserve. Police reserve officers serve for a nonrenewable term of five years, except in cases of emergencies, during which they may be recalled to duty. Reserve officers are designated by their ranks, such as Sergeant or Inspector, followed by the suffix "R" designating "Reserve." Like regular police officers, the police reserve officers are armed and uniformed and are deployed in specific areas, with defined commands and supervision structures (National Police Service Act 11A, 2011, Section 110). Although they are a volunteer service, officers of the National Police Reserve are remunerated or compensated with allowances as appropriate.

RECRUITMENT AND DEPLOYMENT

While the National Police Service in Kenya oversees law enforcement and crime prevention, recruitment of police candidates, deployment, and discipline of officers are conducted by two separate civilian bodies, namely, the National Police Service Commission (NPSC) and the Independent Policing Oversight Authority (IPOA), covered further on in this chapter. The National Police Service Commission was created by the Constitution. According to Article 246 of the Constitution, the mandate of the NPSC includes the recruitment and appointment of persons to the police service and determining promotions and transfers within the National Police Service. The Commission also observes due process and exercises disciplinary control including the removal of indicted persons from the police service (Republic of Kenya, 2010). Although it is a civilian body headed by a chairperson who is not a police officer, it is notable that among the members of the NPSC are the Inspector-General of the National Police Service and the two deputies who head the Kenya Police Service and the Administrative Police Service, respectively.

In recruiting personnel into the police service, the NPSC considers educational as well as physical eligibility of candidates. Educational eligibility is usually below the eligibility for university education, although university graduates may also apply to join police service. To attract more women into the historically male-dominated profession, affirmative action is exercised occasionally. Even then, the African culture does not encourage women to take up position of authority as this robs them of the culturally idolized femininity. Thus, even with affirmative action, it is still difficult to attract enough women into the police service. Once recruited and successfully trained, female officers are still offered differential treatment at deployment as many are posted to less-dynamic stations, such as airports, instead of the more demanding stations such as the Anti-Stock Theft or General Service units.

POLICE CORRUPTION AND LAW ENFORCEMENT PROCESS

One of the most common complaints against the police in Kenya is lack of accountability and undemocratic practices. According to Hope (2015), "(T)he basic tenets of democratic policing require the police to, among other things: uphold the law; be accountable to democratic oversight institutions outside their organization that are specifically designated and empowered to regulate police activity; be accountable to the communities they serve; be ethical and transparent in their activities; give the highest operational priority to protecting the safety and rights of individuals; be representative of the community they serve; and seek to build professional skills and conditions of service that support efficient and respectful service delivery to the public" (p. 91). This lack of professionalism and accountability, along with undemocratic practices, is believed to have exacerbated the wide-ranging post-election violence of 2008, which was triggered by disputes arising from the presidential election of 2007 (Noyes, 2013; Hope, 2015). This called for increased police reforms (Osse, 2016) and explains why police reforms were subsequently added as a recommendation on how to prevent or mitigate future civil disorder (Noyes, 2013).

Even under the current law, much of policing and police conduct against citizens require only "reasonable cause to believe" that there is need for police intervention. According to the National Police Service Act 11A of 2011, the "general powers of police officers" provide that a police officer, exercising reasonable cause, may regulate and control traffic; stop and detain any person whom the officer "finds in possession of anything contrary to any written law"; break into a suspect's home; and arrest any person accused of committing an aggravated assault. By implication, police officers use discretion to stop motorists, forcefully enter private premises, and detain whomever they have "reasonable cause" to suspect of violation of law. This broad use of discretion in lieu of a warrant creates the necessary conditions for abuse of police power and corrupt practices. The police have abused their powers this way to settle political (see Opalo, 2018) and personal vendettas, and it forms the most widespread basis of citizens' complaints against the police.

Over the recent years, the police service has been used by the executive to suppress political detractors. But perhaps the most referenced abuse of police authority was the unleashing of police brutality against unarmed and helpless citizens in a disguised attempt to quell the post-election violence of 2007 (Hope, 2015). This heightened the already existing clamor for police reforms and respect for human rights and the rule of law (Hope, 2015, p. 91). Police officers have the discretion to make arrests, but the factors that justify an arrest without a warrant are general and are left to individual officer's interpretation. Although an arrested person has the right to be informed of the reason for their arrest, a motivated officer can always find reason to arrest anyone due in part to the fluidity of the definition of "suspicion of crime involvement" or "being about to commit a crime." Thus, the police have been accused of extorting money from citizens who fear arbitrary arrests.

An arrested person is afforded the opportunity to deposit a bond and secure release until the trial date. In the Kenyan case, the opportunity to deposit bond is offered at either of two stages: with the police if the alleged offense is bailable and the arrest was not under warrant, or in court, again if the alleged crime is bailable. Once the person is aligned in court, the role of police depends on the level of the court. In lower-level courts that are presided over by magistrates, called Magistrates' Courts, the police serve as prosecutors (Mbuba, 2017). In the superior courts, that is, the High Court, the Appeals Court, and the Supreme Court, the police serve in such other capacities as documenting the charges on charge sheets, maintaining custody of crime suspects, and supervising witnesses in the courtrooms.

DEVOLVED GOVERNMENT AND CENTRALIZED POLICING

The current Kenyan constitution, which came into effect in 2010, created a two-tier government that comprises the national government and forty-seven semi-autonomous county governments. While most services such as education, health, and agriculture are regulated at the county level, policing remains centralized, answering to a central command that is headquartered at the capital city, Nairobi. While each county must have a County Policing Authority that law enforcement needs and prioritizes police resources, counties must rely on the national government for execution and implementation of the identified policing needs. However, the challenge is that some counties need more police resources, depending on some endemic needs such as cattle rustling and intertribal border disputes.

LEVELS OF POLICING

Kenya is rich in cultural diversity with norms of behavior that vary widely. Standard norms in one culture may not be acceptable in another. In response to this normative variation, government leaders at the village level, called chiefs and assistant chiefs, depending on the area of jurisdiction, enforce community-specific norms. Violation of village-level norms constitutes infractions that are punishable by small fines, communal work, or other agreed-upon sanctions that are not necessarily legislated. Formal law enforcement essentially begins at the smallest police service unit, the police station. Police stations are created by the Inspector-General and are equitably distributed throughout the country. A police station is headed by an officer with the title of Officer Commanding Police Station, locally referred to as OCS. Police stations do not only serve the public, but they also receive and record complaints against police misconduct. Large police stations, particularly in sparsely populated counties, tend to have outposts for enhancement of service delivery. The outposts are called police posts. High population density urban areas also tend to have police outposts, but in this case, they are referred to as patrol bases. Police posts and patrol bases are managed by noncommissioned officers, including Corporals and Sergeants, that is, lower-ranking supervisors who have not yet earned formal rank documentation.

CRIME INVESTIGATION

The authority of crime investigation in Keya is vested in the Directorate of Criminal Investigation (DCI). This includes investigation of all organized crimes, white-collar crimes, and other acts of violations of law. However, police officers generally have the power to investigate common street crimes, albeit with the help of the DCI as crime complexity warrants. There are DCI officers at each level of government, including national, county, and sub-county levels, with a centralized chain of command that emanates from the national Director of Criminal Investigation. While DCI officers are police officers with all the responsibilities in respect of crime control, DCI personnel are trained to investigate crimes of a serious nature, such as, homicide, human trafficking, money laundering, drug trafficking, terrorism, and other organized types of crime.

Specialized Crime Investigation

In Kenya, crimes that occur on an ongoing basis with gradual but significant effect on the larger society are investigated by stable commissions that are created by the constitution. Such crimes as corruption, discrimination, abuse of human rights, and the misuse of state office are left to commissions, whose members are drawn from ethnically diverse backgrounds. Membership to such commissions is limited to specific number of renewable or nonrenewable terms. Some of the major commissions include the following:

Ethics and Anti-Corruption Commission

This commission investigates violations of ethics by state and public officers. It receives complaints from the public and, depending on the outcome of the commission's investigations, the commission recommends to the Director of Public Prosecutions the prosecution of acts of corruption, bribery or economic crimes or violation of codes of ethics. The commission also recommend appropriate action against perpetrators if found guilty of the violations (Ethics and anti-corruption commission Act, Laws of Kenya, Act 22 of 2011).

Kenya National Commission on Human Rights

This commission investigates complaints about the violation of human rights. It receives complaints from the public but may also institute investigations on its own without overt complaints. Human rights, as constitutionally defined, include the rights to life, privacy, free expression, free association, assembly, movement, and family, among others. The commission may recommend judicial action to the Director of Public Prosecutions against human rights violations if conciliation, mediation, and other out-of-court settlements are not successful (Kenya National Commission on Human Rights Act, Laws of Kenya, Act 14 of 2011).

National Gender and Equality Commission

The constitution of Kenya decrees that everyone is equal before the law and bars discrimination, directly or indirectly, against any person on the grounds of "race, sex, pregnancy, marital status, health status, ethnic or social origin, color, age, disability, religion, conscience, belief, culture, dress, language or birth" (Kenya Constitution, Article 27). To support the enforcement of this decree, the National Gender and Equality Commission investigates allegations of discrimination based on the above grounds. The commission may either initiate its own investigations or may base investigations on complaints received from the public, in relation to violations of the principle of equality and affront to the freedom from discrimination. In particular, the commission conduct audits on the status of special interest groups including minorities, marginalized groups, persons with disability, women, youth, and children, and makes appropriate recommendations (National Gender and Equality Commission Act, Laws of Kenya, Act 15 of 2011).

Commission on Administrative Justice

This commission investigates allegations of misconduct and abuse of power in public administration by state agencies as well as state and public officer, both at the national and county governments. Misconduct of state officers represents a unique category of crime that is hard to control by use of regular police surveillance. Thus, this commission "investigates complaints of abuse of power, unfair treatment, manifest injustice or unlawful, oppressive, unfair or unresponsive official conduct within the public sector" (Commission on Administrative Justice Act, Laws of Kenya, Act 23 of 2011). Any reported administrative injustice, discourtesy, incompetence, misbehavior, inefficiency or ineptitude within the public service are all investigated by this commission. When violations are discovered, they are reported to the National Assembly or to the Director of Public Prosecutions for prosecution. To be able to discharge this mandate, the commission has the power to summon and to require that statements be given under oath or affirmation.

National Cohesion and Integration Commission

As a multiethnic country, the Kenyan government recognizes the need for each ethnic community to feel a sense of inclusion into mainstream governance and decision making. The law bars the treatment of people differentially along the lines of ethnicity, including harassment, victimization, and discrimination, especially in access to jobs. Thus, this commission investigates, either on its own accord or on request from any institution, office, or person, any issue affecting ethnic and racial relations. Depending on the outcome, the commission recommends to the government, the criteria for deciding whether any public office or officer has committed acts of discrimination on the ground of ethnicity or race (National Cohesion and Integration Act, Laws of Kenya, Act 12 of 2008).

POLICE MISCONDUCT

Police corruption is a phenomenon reported in almost every policing jurisdiction across the world, albeit with varying degrees of manifestation. One of the most

reported forms of police corruption in Kenya takes place in the transport industry. Police enforce traffic rules and elect roadblocks along highways and country
roads in order to stop and inspect vehicles and motorists suspected of crime
involvement. Notably, the police target motorists whose vehicles are not road-
worthy for reasons such as broken taillights, dysfunctional turn signals, improper
or lack of insurance coverage, or overloading of cargo or passengers. They also
target vehicles driving at higher speeds than the posted limits. All these cases
provide ample opportunities for the police to receive bribes that are either readily
offered by motorists or demanded by the police. The amounts of bribes vary with
the extent of overloading, level of speeding, type of vehicle, and other factors.
Road patrols are usually conducted on foot, with a police vehicle parked within
reach. Since it takes time for the officer to walk to the stopped vehicle and to go
around conducting a roadworthiness inspection, some impatient motorists will
readily offer bribes and save their time (Mbuba, 2017, pp. 134–135).

Another area through which police misconduct is manifested in Kenya is
discrimination. In racially diverse societies, discrimination often involves
differential treatment based on race. Kenya, which is home to more than
forty tribes and subtribes, many of which are distinct communities with distinct cultures and languages, experiences police discrimination mostly along
tribal lines. Police discrimination also takes a socioeconomic dimension. For
example, officers often ask for rides from citizens who go to the police station
to report crimes. They may, alternatively, ask the citizens to provide money to
fuel police cars. A citizen who owns a car or has the wherewithal to fuel the
police car, is advantaged with respect to obtaining police response. The ability to provide a ride to a police officer also inherently influences the officer's
discretion in favor of the person responsible for the officer's transportation
(Mbuba, 2017, pp. 135–136). Other bases of police discrimination, though
not as widespread, include age, gender, and religion (ibid., p. 136).

To tame drunkenness among police officers, the Kenyan law makes it illegal
for police officers to drink alcohol while in uniforms, referring to "while on
duty." It is important to note here that the focus is not on the officer, but on the
person, who sells alcohol to the officer. The Alcoholic Drinks Control Act states
that "any person who knowingly sells, supplies or offers an alcoholic drink to an
authorized officer or to a police officer in uniform . . . commits an offense and is
liable to a fine not exceeding fifty thousand Kenya shillings or to imprisonment
for a term not exceeding three months, or to both" (Laws of Kenya, Chapter
121A). Since most people, especially businesspeople, would like to be in good
terms with the police in anticipation of future incidents when they might need
police help, it is difficult enforce this law and it is also unlikely that violators
will be apprehended as the violation favors the police—the custodian of law.

In Kenya, police misconduct is handled by a civilian agency called the
Independent Policing Oversight Authority (IPOA), which was established

by an Act of Parliament following the enactment of the 2010 Constitution. IPOA was created to hold the police accountable to the public, to instill professionalism and discipline in the police service, and to ensure independent oversight in handling of complaints by and against the police. According to the Independent Policing Oversight Authority Act, 2011, the overarching function of the Authority is "to investigate complaints related to disciplinary or criminal offenses committed by any member of the Service, whether on its own motion or on receipt of a complaint, and make recommendations to the relevant authorities, including recommendations for prosecution, compensation, internal disciplinary action or any other appropriate relief, and to make public the response received to these recommendations" (Laws of Kenya, number 35 of 2011). Other functions of IPOA include monitoring, reviewing, and auditing of investigations and actions taken by the Internal Affairs Unit of the police service in response to complaints against the police, and inspecting police premises, including detention facilities, to ensure compliance with all provisions of the law.

Police Role in Public Prosecution

In addition to the wide array of law enforcement and public safety responsibilities, police officers in Kenya serve an additional role—as prosecutors in lower courts, which are courts that are presided over by magistrates. They are called lower courts as opposed to superior courts such as the Appeals Courts and the Supreme Court, where prosecution is conducted by the Attorney General through the state counsel. Lower courts also hear and process most types of crimes. One of the most common criticism of the use of police officers as prosecutors is that while the police have only a working understanding of the law, they cannot effectively confront defense attorneys who are highly trained in specific aspects of law. The consequence of this inadequacy is two-fold: loss of convictions even in obvious cases of guilt, and unwarranted continuances or postponement of trial proceeding as police prosecutors ask for more time to repackage their evidence. However, only officers who have attained the rank of inspector can serve as prosecutors and even then, they conduct prosecutions in lower courts in which only misdemeanor and low-degree felonies are processed.

SUMMARY AND CONCLUSION

Kenya utilizes a policing system that mirrors Britain's and most other countries that were subjects to British colonialism. The country has a centralized police service, the National Police Service (NPS), headed by an Inspector-General (IG) The NPS features two parallel agencies, that is, the Kenya Police Service and the Administration Police Service, each headed by a Deputy Inspector-General, who answers to the IG. In addition, the NPS has an investigative branch called the Directorate of Criminal Investigations, headed by a Director, who also answers to the IG. The more pervasive types of crimes, such as corruption, hate crimes, and discrimination in access to public resources are investigated by full-time commissions created by the government. While the functions of both the Kenya Police Service and the Administration Police are law enforcement and crime control, the Administration Police Service is more involved in providing security to government buildings and facilities as well as patrolling the country's borders, although instances in which the duties of the two police services overlap are not uncommon.

In some rural communities where police services are not readily available, the NPS employs trained volunteers in the name of the National Police Reserve. Although they are volunteers, police reserve officers have police authority and are renumerated but work as needs arise. Police management in the country is run by civilian government agencies. Training, deployment, and discipline are overseen by the National Police Service Commission, while a second civilian agency, the Independent Policing Oversight Authority, conducts investigations into reported police misconduct. The police service in Kenya is anchored in the constitution that was enacted in 2010, following decades of widespread clamor for a new constitutional order and police reforms.

REFERENCES

Constitution of the Republic of Kenya. (2010). Republic of Kenya.

Commission on Administrative Justice Act, Laws of Kenya, Act. 23 (2011). http://www.kenyalaw.org.

Encyclopedia of the Nations. (2010). http://www.nationsencyclopedia.com/economies/Africa/Kenya.html.

Ethics and Anti-corruption Commission, Laws of Kenya, Act 22. (2011). http://www.kenyalaw.org.

Hope, K. R. (2015). In pursuit of democratic policing: An analytical review and assessment of police reforms in Kenya. *International Journal of Police Science & Management*, 17(2): 91–97. https://doi.org/10.1177/1461355715580915.

Kenya National Commission on Human Rights, Laws of Kenya, Act 14. (2011). http://www.kenyalaw.org.

Mbuba, J. M. (2017). *Policing in Eastern Africa: A Focus on the National Police Service in Kenya*. Law Africa Publishers.

Mbuba, J. M. (2018). Devolution without devolution: Centralized police service implications in a decentralized government in Kenya. *Journal of Pan African Studies*, 11(8): 165–181.

Mbuba, J. M., & Mugambi, F. N. (2011). Approaches to crime control and order maintenance in transitional societies: The role of village headmen, chiefs, subchiefs, and administration police in rural Kenya. *African Journal of Criminology and Justice Studies*, 4(2): 1–12.

National Cohesion and Integration Act, Laws of Kenya, Act 12. (2008). http://www.kenyalaw.org.

National Gender and Equality Commission, Laws of Kenya, Act 15. (2011). http://www.kenyalaw.org.

National Police Service Act 11A. (2011), Section 24. http://kenyalaw.org.

National Police Service, Kenya. (2020). http://www.nationalpolice.go.ke/.

Noyes A. (2013) Cleaning house in Kenya's Police Force. *Foreign Policy*, 30 December. http://www.foreignpolicy.com/articles/2013/12/30/cleaning_house_in_kenyas_police_force.

Okia, O. (2011). The role of the police in the postelection violence in Kenya 2007/08. *Journal of Third World Studies*, 28(2): 259–275.

Opalo, K. O. (2018). Another disputed election batters Kenya's institutions. *Current History*, 117(799): 187–193. https://doi.org/10.1525/curh.2018.117.799.187.

Osse, A. (2016). Police reform in Kenya: A process of "meddling through." *Policing & Society*, 26(8): 907–924. https://doi.org/10.1080/10439463.2014.993631.

Chapter 3

Policing and Law Enforcement in Zimbabwe

Jephias Matunhu and Viola Matunhu

The Zimbabwe Republic Police (ZRP) is a centrally controlled system that originated from the British South Africa Police (BSAP) in 1980 when the country attained its independence from Britain. Section 219 (1) of the Constitution of Zimbabwe (Amendment # 20) Act 2013 creates the ZRP, whose mandate is to maintain law and order. Some of the initiatives used by the ZRP to stimulate community participation in policing include the neighborhood Watch Committee, Junior Call, Crime Consultative Committees, and Village Anti-Stock Theft Committee. Systemic corruption in the police is one of the pervasive challenges that the new political dispensation in Zimbabwe is battling. This chapter is written by civilians with life experiences of policing in Zimbabwe. The authors examine some of the policing dynamics in Zimbabwe, partly under Robert Mugabe (First Republic) and under Emerson Dambudzo Mnangagwa (Second Republic).

INTRODUCTION

The Zimbabwe Constitution (Amendment #20) Act 2013 Section 219 (1) provides that there be a Zimbabwe Republic Police (ZRP) to detect, investigate, and prevent crime (Zimbabwe Constitution, 2013). Human rights promotion should be the major thrust of the ZRP. Dowding et al. (2004) describes human rights as independent standards of fairness or legitimacy that are formally established by law. The values of this centrally controlled police service are integrity, commitment, professionalism, accountability, and transparency. Police performance is open to scrutiny by Human Rights Watchdogs and the general public.

The ZRP is an organized and complex system that is divided into specialized units that include, for instance, the Support Unit, which is responsible for public order management, major disaster and hostage situation management, protection of vital installations and VIPs; border patrols; and anti-stock theft and sub aqua duties. There is also the Zimbabwe Formed Police Unit, which is a Southern African Development Committee (SADC) standby force responsible for the safety and security of the SADC, United Nations, and the African Union personnel and missions. Another unit is the Minerals and Border Control Unit, which is responsible for the security of minerals and other natural resources as well as the enforcement of laws that protect public infrastructure and utilities in the country. Moreover, there is the Criminal Investigation Department (CID), which investigates all serious crimes under the following units: Interpol; Records and Technical Services; Crime; Police anti-Corruption; Commercial Crimes; Criminal Intelligence; and Minerals, Flora, and Fauna. This chapter focuses mainly on policing in the last decade of the First Republic (under former president Robert Mugabe) and the two years in the Second Republic (under President Emerson Mnangagwa). The chapter pays close attention to community policing by the ZRP. The terms Police and ZRP are used interchangeably, and so are Second Republic and New Dispensation. The authors of the chapter are civilians living in Zimbabwe.

HISTORY

The ZRP evolved from Cecil John Rhodes's initially all-white British South Africa Company Police (BSACP). The Police came into being after Rhodes had secured the Rudd Concession and the Royal Charter from the British Government in 1889. William Bodle, the first to suggest a company police, later became the Commissioner of the Police. By 1895, the Police had recruited black watchers (*mabhurakwacha*) to police black Africans in Rhodesia, which is now referred to as Zimbabwe.

The colonial police force mistreated the Africans, resulting in resentment by the black people. This necessitated the police to live in police camps, away from the public. In 1980, Prime Minister Robert Mugabe remodeled the repressive and tyrannical police force in line with the needs and aspirations of a newly found nonracial society. The British South Africa Police (BSAP), Auxiliaries, Zimbabwe People's Revolutionary Army, and Zimbabwe African National Liberation Army were integrated to form the Zimbabwe Republic Police. In 1982, Wiridzayi Nguruve was appointed the first black Commissioner-General of the new police force. The Robert Mugabe Administration removed Nguruve from the post in 1985 due to the police's involvement in illicit drug trafficking (Mandaza, 2016).

Some former white BSAP members who were irked by the massive structural and ideological changes in the police force resigned and left for then apartheid South Africa. In 1985, Henry Mukurazhizha became the second black Commissioner-General of the Police, replacing Nguruve. In 1994, Augustine Chihuri succeeded Mukurazhizha, and, in 2018, President ED Mnangagwa replaced Chihuri with Godwin Matanga in accordance with Section 221 (1) of the Zimbabwe Constitution.

The ED Mnangagwa Administration removed Chihuru on account of corruption and abuse of office during the late Robert Mugabe rule. The Second Republic Prosecutor-General, Mr. Kumbirai Hodzi, filed an application in the High Court of Zimbabwe seeking the freeze of over twelve immovable properties and a range of vehicles and farm equipment owned by Chihuri. The former Police boss, who is currently in self-imposed exile, is also being charged for diverting over U.S.$32 million of public funds into family companies (Nehanda Radio, 2020).

In 1984, Robert Mugabe made a legitimate and befitting plea to transform the public image of the police. He envisioned a police force that incorporated with the civil society in policing. Mugabe's directive marked a watershed for the transformation of the police to a people-oriented one. It was about seeking the needs of the community and being responsive in the delivery of services. In May 1986, a community relations scheme was rolled out. The scheme successfully repaired the fractured relations between the police and the public as evidenced by cordial social interaction between the police and the public. The community was now involved in community policing.

Vigilantes were established for the purposes of accommodating the aspirations of the community in areas of service delivery, human rights, and new policing philosophies. For instance, the Neighborhood Watch Committee scheme is one of the major community-oriented programs meant to contain crime in residential areas. The scheme is voluntary and open to medically fit and eligible adults. Their roles include marking property, reporting suspicious activity, patrolling neighborhoods, and improving home security, which reduce opportunities for crime and increase the chances of detection. Notably, Mugabe had formally transformed the police force into a police service.

The rebranding of the police force into a police service led to the creation of the Information Systems and Information Technology department and resulted in the development of strategic, tactical and service plans in the Service. In addition to that, the Police Service Charter, strategic links with Interpol and other organizations improved the image of the police service (Mandaza, 2016). However, the public image of the Police deteriorated to the lowest ebb during the 2007–2009 hyperinflationary period as police brutality and other forms of blatant disrespect of the Law increased. By 2016, Mugabe had successfully turned the country into a police state amid political, social, and economic recession. Mugabe's ruling party, the Zimbabwe African National Union-Patriotic Front (ZANU (PF)) was facing serious infighting, leading to the dismal of Vice President ED Mnangagwa from office in 2017. The Second Republic, under President Mnangagwa, who replaced Mugabe in November 2017, had a daunting task of reestablishing a cordial relationship between the public and the Police.

THE ZRP ORGANIZATION

The Constitution of Zimbabwe regards national safety and security as a priority. In compliance with this constitutional requirement, the ZRP is expected to be in service daily, all year round. For purposes of executing this mandate, the police service is divided into well-synchronized units, each with unique duties and responsibilities. The Duty Uniform Unit is responsible for general policing. Members of this branch perform their duties in uniform. Crime prevention, detection, and arrests of law breakers form the bulk of their duties. The ZRP has a military wing called the Support Unit which is armed and performs its duties in uniform. The Unit is trained in military tactics for the purposes of restoring peace and order where necessary. In the past, the Unit assisted the duty uniformed police to quell unlawful violent and destructive demonstrations.

The ZRP has a Technical Unit staffed with members with specialized technical skills and specific professions such as medical doctors, teachers, laboratory technicians, electricians, and ICT specialists. Civilian artisans and technicians who join this Unit undergo basic police training before they are attested to serve the Organization. The Criminal Investigations Department of the ZRP comprises members operating in civilian attire who are trained in the special skills of crime investigations. The Unit investigates economic and noneconomic crimes. Members of this unit work closely with the Zimbabwe Anti-Corruption Commission. The Commission, which is administered under the Office of the President and Cabinet, is one of the chapter 13 institutions constitutionally mandated to combat crime and corruption. The duties of the Police Protection Unit of the ZRP are to manage the Presidential Motorcade, as well as provide security services to very important persons including diplomats. All members of the Police are free to join any unit on the strength of their qualifications, skill, or attributes (http://www.zrp.gov.zw).

ZRP RECRUITMENT AND ELIGIBILITY

Recruitment into the lowest rank on attestation for regular general police duties (Constable) commences at a local ZRP Station. The advertisement of intention to recruit is publicized in local media, at community meetings, and at local career guidance activities (http://www.zrp.gov.zw) by the local ZRP Officer in Charge. To be considered for the rank of Constable, applicants must have attained their eighteenth birthday and must not be more than twenty-two years of age at the time of appointment. In terms of educational qualifications, the applicants must have passed a minimum of five Ordinary Level subjects with Grade C or better in not more than three sittings, of which English language and mathematics are compulsory (http://www.zrp.gov.zw). The other requirement is that such persons should be of good character, in addition to having a good background, with no criminal record or pending criminal proceedings against them (http://www.zrp.gov.zw).

The applicants must also fulfill health requirements as recommended by a Police Medical Officer. For equity reasons, each of the ten political provinces of Zimbabwe is allocated a number of places in each squad of twenty-one recruits per intake (http://www.zrp.gov.zw). The quantum of recruits per province per intake is determined by the provincial population size against the national population size. Technically, the higher the provincial population, the more the number of recruits per intake. The computations are based on population statistics as reflected by the Zimbabwe Statistical Office (ZimStat).

The application procedure for the post of Constable is different from that of persons wishing to enter the Police Service as technicians or for other specialized services. For Constables, applicants are to approach the Officer in Charge of the Police Station nearest to them. The Officer in Charge will interview the applicants and ensure that the fingerprints of successful applicants are recorded and vetted to prevent unsuitable elements from joining the Service. The next step is the administration of preentry tests (Aptitude Tests) at approved centers to further test the suitability of the applicants for the job (http://www.zrp.gov.zw). The assessment protocol at this stage includes physical tests and oral interviews by a ZRP panel. Successful applicants are placed on a waiting list that is maintained at the Police General Headquarters in Harare. When vacancies do occur in the Service, names of the applicants to be considered for appointment are drawn from the Waiting List on a first-come, first-serve criterion (http://www.zrp.gov.zw).

Applications for the posts of technicians follow a different route from the one stated earlier. To qualify to enter the Service at that level, applicants must have served a recognized apprenticeship and qualified as a journeyman in the Class 1 and 2 Category. The applicants must be holders of at least five Ordinary Level (http://www.zrp.gov.zw) passes, including the English language. Applications for this category are lodged with the Police General Headquarters and only in response to advertisements for vacant posts. The advertisements are publicized in the national print and electronic media. The applicants are advised to submit or post their written applications to the Staff Officer [Recruiting] at the Police General Headquarters.

ZRP TRAINING

The three major national training depots are the Morris and Chikurubi depots in Harare and the Ntabazinduna depot in Bulawayo. The carrying capacity of the three training institutions is about 3,600 per year (http://www.zrp.gov .zw). The training programs conducted at these Depots are the following: two-year graduate training; six months recruit training; three months training for technicians, and induction training for medical doctors.

The ZRP Staff College at Morris Depot in Harare is the highest training center in the Service. The College was (http://www.zrp.gov.zw) founded in 1981 in terms of the Police Act, Chapter 11:10. The College seeks to enhance the efficiency and effectiveness of officers in the Police Service. This is to be attained through sharpening the administrative and operational capabilities of Officers at various levels (http://www.zrp.gov.zw). Notably, the College is an associate college of the University of Zimbabwe and is also an affiliated college of the Bindura University of Science Education. The College offers diplomas in Business Management, Adult Education, and Law, in collaboration with the University of Zimbabwe and a diploma in Public Relations with the Bindura University of Science Education.

LEGAL FRAMEWORK OF POLICING IN ZIMBABWE

Zimbabwe is a constitutional democracy with a centralized police service. The constitutional provisions guiding public policing in the country are largely impressive although operationally, there exist uncouth police officers who are violating human rights for selfish reasons. Focusing on human rights, section 49 of the Zimbabwe Constitution (Amendment #20) Act, 2013, provides the right to personal liberty (Zimbabwe Constitution, 2013). More explicitly, Section 49(1) states thus: Every person has the right to personal liberty, which includes the following rights: (a) not to be detained without trial and (b) not to be deprived of their liberty arbitrarily or without just cause.

Section 50 (4) of the national constitution provides that accused persons should be charged or be informed of the reasons for their detention. The police sometimes detain accused persons in holding cells prior to arraying them before the courts of law. The public opinion is divided, with some, especially those in the opposition politics, believing that the police is captured by the ruling party. The political tiff in the country stemmed from the

2018 disputed elections where the Movement for Democratic Change (MDC) President Nelson Chamisa narrowly lost to the ZANU (PF) president, ED Mnangagwa, resulting in the opposition leader escalating the dispute to a televised Constitutional Court where he lost the case.

Section 50(1b) of the Constitution spells out the rights of arrested and detained persons by stating that any person who is arrested must be permitted, without delay, to enjoy two rights. These include: (i) the right to counsel at the expense of the State, to contact their spouse or partner, or a relative or legal practitioner, or anyone else of their choice and (ii) at their own expense, to consult in private with a legal practitioner and a medical practitioner of their choice and to be informed of their right to dignity promptly. There are no serious public contestations of how the Police are discharging their mandate in this regard.

The supreme law provides that accused persons must be treated humanely and with respect for their inherent dignity and must be released unconditionally or on reasonable conditions, pending a charge or trial, unless there are compelling reasons justifying their continued detention by the ZRP. There is no consensus among the people of Zimbabwe on whether or not the police are observing this constitutional requirement. Judging from the public sentiments, many people feel that the Police are operating below their expectations, although there has been a tremendous improvement from how the ZRP operated during the end days of the First republic.

The Constitution provides that accused persons have the right to challenge the lawfulness of their arrest in person. The people of Zimbabwe are increasingly becoming aware of their rights and are increasingly making use of the law courts for justice. In the past, the police were losing many of the cases they brought to court due to their weak understanding of the law. The situation is improving as more and more police officers are gaining access to appropriate training in criminal procedures.

Section 53 of the Constitution provides that the police should protect the accused person's freedom from torture or cruel, inhuman, or degrading treatment or punishment. In other words, no person, including the ZRP officers, has the right to subject any other person to physical or psychological torture. In 2020, opposition politicians Hon Majome, Ms. Mamombe, and many others claimed to have been abducted, tortured, and secretly released by the Second Republic police. The arrest, torture, and release script were also played by journalists, medical doctors, and other professionals. The general feeling of some political analysts is that the scripts are being stage-managed in pursuit of the opposition politicians' relentless clamor for a regime change agenda.

In order to offer protection against self-incrimination, section 50 (4) of the Constitution decrees that any person who is arrested or detained for an alleged offense has the right to remain silent and to be informed promptly of their right to remain silent and of the consequences of either remaining silent or not. The public opinion is that there are times when the police forces the accused persons to make statements and thereby violates their right to remain silent.

The Constitution is also clear on the rights of detained persons. It provides, under section 50(5), that a detained person has the right to be informed promptly of the reason for their detention and, that, at their own expense, they can consult in private with a legal counsel of their choice. The law provides that the police should protect the accused person's right to counsel and the right to be visited while in custody by their spouses, partners, relatives, religious counselors, and or their legal counsel.

The police sometimes detain the accused persons in their police cells pending court hearings. The law provides that the conditions of detention should be consistent with human dignity, including the opportunity for physical exercise and the provision, at the State's expense, of adequate accommodation, ablution facilities, personal hygiene, nutrition, appropriate reading material and medical treatment (Constitute, n.d.). While the public opinion may suggest that the living conditions in police holding cells are poor, the conditions are consistent with the overall Zimbabwe economic conditions that exist everywhere across the country.

The Constitution also protects the right to privacy, through section 57, which includes the right not to have anyone's home or premises entered or searched, or property seized, without their permission. The section also offers similar protections against infringement into private communications and the health status of individuals. Although this law applies to the police and their treatment of civilians, it is common for the police to violate it, especially in regards to suspects who are unaware of this particular constitutional right.

THE POLICE AND CRIME PREVENTION

The Zimbabwe police service utilizes various strategies in preventing crime. In particular, given the growing trend in cybercrime, public awareness and civic education have gained importance as the public has to be informed about the operations of the police service and how the internet is being used to undermine police work and promote lawlessness. For instance, on August 24, 2020, Interpol released a statement alerting the public on the possible use of social media to spread propaganda and advertise weapons that could be used in large-scale criminal activities.

The ZRP also runs television, radio, and other media programs to educate the public on crime and crime prevention. The programs include information regarding human trafficking, sexual offenses, drug trafficking, gender-based violence, child abuse, theft, robbery, commercial crimes, and cyberbullying. Persons on the police-wanted list or fugitives are also mentioned in an appeal to the community that urges them to assist in apprehending criminals. Thus, the police involves the community in crime prevention and the maintenance of order; the community, in turn, acknowledges police initiatives and gets involved accordingly. One of the strategies used by the Zimbabwe police to stimulate interest in community policing among secondary school students is the Junior Call. This involves introducing the students to basic law, human rights, foot drill, and general policing (Zimbabwe Republic Police, n.d.). The intentions of the program are highlighted by the same source as, promotion of law-abiding conduct among youths; presenting a nucleus of youths with sound basic knowledge of police work; producing a disciplined child through molding them to become responsible and sympathetic citizens; offering useful information and training to potential police candidates; and providing assistance to identify and correct risky behavior in young people.

The Junior Call program is expected to produce law-abiding youths who can contribute positively to the development of the society. This is to be achieved through the promotion of the physical, mental, moral, and social growth of the pupils (Zimbabwe Republic Police, n.d.). Through the creation of awareness and the provision of the law about such behaviors as child abuse, the ZRP can confront and minimize the prevalence of such vices as children are exposed to the law at an early stage.

Community policing is more rigorous during festive seasons (*Herald*, 2019). The police undertake patrols, especially in the urban areas, where the crime rate is high.

During the festive seasons, the police maintain increased vigilance in urban areas by ensuring that there is a contingent of "plain clothes" officers mingling with the public on a daily basis. Apart from that, the police developed the Crime Consultative Committees, whose purpose is to coalesce the police and the community to share ideas of mutual concern (Zimbabwe Republic Police, n.d.) through formal meetings, suggestion boxes, hotlines, WhatsApp, and text messaging. The Crime Consultative Committees are composed of opinion leaders, community leaders and the business community, government departments, and nongovernmental organizations. Crime reduction and positive police–public confidence have been recorded in communities that have adopted the Committee model (Zimbabwe Republic Police, n.d.). While crime cannot be eliminated, the Committees initiative goes a long way in monitoring adherence to the rule of law.

At every police station, the ZRP keep records of monthly arrests and convictions. A visit to several police stations by the authors of this chapter revealed that the police are systematic in terms of keeping records of habitual criminals, displaying criminals on the *WANTED* list, and recording road traffic accidents in the respective policing jurisdictions as well as document-ing the contact information of VIPs in those areas. Other means through which the ZRP has been able to improve its policing performance include crime mapping and joint command. Such joint commands enable the police to synchronize their activities as each district becomes aware of the policing issues and itineraries of their neighboring police stations.

The general view of the public is that the ZRP is one of the best in the region in terms of training and competence, as confirmed by Professor Jonathan Moyo, one of the post–Robert Mugabe political fugitives who also served as a cabinet minister during the First Republic that ended in November 2017.

The police are aware of common criminal perpetrators. Commissioner Dumbura has identified them as illegal beer outlet operators, pick pock-eters, *mushikashika* (illegal transporters in urban areas), and thugs. The Commissioner claims that his organization executes its duty without fear or favor. While the Commissioner's public statement is important, corruption in the police has made it difficult for it to live up to this promise. Lack of such resources as vehicles has made it difficult for the highly skilled Police ser-vice to be at the right place at the right time. Despite these challenges, many people believe the ZRP is doing a splendid job.

The same Commissioner of the Police identified the most troublesome types of crimes during festive periods as unlawful entry and theft cases because some people leave their houses unattended when traveling. The Commissioner urged people to put up security measures to curb such criminal activities during the festive seasons. Concerning robbery during the festive seasons, the Commissioner alerted the public thus,

> be wary of robbery cases. Robbers pounce on unsuspecting public. Do not move around with large sums of money. Hiking transport at undesignated pick up points puts you in danger. Be alert and vigilant. Memorize police telephone numbers and contact police as soon as you come across any suspicious criminal activities. (*Herald*, 2019)

A brief survey by the authors of this chapter concerning memorizing Police telephone numbers revealed that over 69 percent of the public including the authors of this chapter had not memorized the ZRP telephone numbers.

The public has, on several occasions, praised the ZRP for being proactive and for bursting notorious crime syndicates such as the "amashurugwi," a network of criminals who have been terrorizing all the gold-rich parts of the country, killing innocent people using machetes, robbing mines of their minerals, and sometimes seizing mining claims from innocent miners. The enthusing development from the public's perspective is the high-profile arrest, by the police, of one of the country's most wanted armed robbers,

Musa Traj Abbul on the night of August 25, 2020, in Beitbridge. The criminal had been on the run for over twenty years, masterminding armed robberies in Zimbabwe. Other high-profile cases by the police being applauded by the public include but are not limited to the arrest of former cabinet ministers Mupfumira, Undenge, and Obadia Moyo.

Road policing is another cause of concern in the country, especially during festive seasons. During the seasons, carnage statistics spike. The Police usually put strong warnings to the motoring public such as, "There will be police roadblocks and increased traffic enforcements to arrest violators of regulations and impound unroadworthy vehicles. There are no kind of words for those who choose to be on the wrong side of the law" (*Herald*, 2019). The Police set up 24-hour road blocks and conduct routine day and night patrols in the suburbs and such vigilance is increased during the festive seasons. The following is one of such messages from the Police to the public, "The joyful but somewhat relaxed and carefree mood of the moment is the breeding ground for crime. Let your celebratory mood be compounded with a measure of alertness, self-control and security-consciousness" (*Herald*, 2019).

The police are linked to Neighborhood Watch Schemes for tightening security in communities in compliance with the notion that (Chigudu, 2015) community projects and programs are better achieved through community participation and involvement. The scheme involves residents becoming more responsive to the risk of crime and acting to protect their own and neighbor's property (Zimbabwe Republic Police, n.d.). Such activities include reporting suspicious activity, patrolling neighborhoods, and improving home security, which minimizes the opportunity for crime and increases the chances of detection at the same time, increasing community participation in policing (The Herald, 2019).

CORRUPTION IN THE POLICE SERVICE

This section is built on the notion that evidence of good policing is the absence or minimization of crime. Corruption is intentional unlawful acts by police officers aimed at personal gains in exchange for selectively enforcing or manipulating rules, procedures and arrests (Chene & Jennet, 2007). The corruption ranges from petty and bureaucratic corruption to the criminal infiltration of the state, state capture and other forms of political corruption (Chene, 2009). This section deals with petty corruption.

In 2011, Transparency International ranked Zimbabwe 154 out of 182 countries in terms of its level of corruption and the police has not been spared in this ordeal. In 2019, the Transparency International Corruption Perceptions Index ranked the nation 158 out of 180 countries (Trading Economics, 2020) with the police being labeled the most corrupt institution. Public experiences seem to suggest that the police under former President Mugabe was more corrupt than the Police under his successor, President Mnangagwa.

In terms of the cost to the nation, Transparency International (2016) stated that Zimbabwe was losing U.S.$1 billion every year due to corruption. Thus, the act has the potential to divert resources away from growth initiatives (Kim & Conceição, 2010). This has compelled President Mnangagwa's Administration to declare a zero tolerance policy on corruption. This declaration has resulted in an increase in the number of reported cases of graffiti, not only in the police service but across professions.

The public is excited about how the police are arresting the culprits of corruption; however, it is the rich and well-connected persons who are unhappy with the zero tolerance policy. Fighting corruption has increased the rift between President Mnangagwa and corrupt powerful syndicates. The authors of this chapter opine that such bitter persons wish to have the President ousted from power before he gets them nabbed for their misdeeds. The Police and the Zimbabwe Anticorruption Commission (ZACC) are unearthing high levels of corruption in urban councils. The public is enthused by this stance of the current national leader as acts of corruption in and by the ZRP has disadvantaged many people.

The Afrobarometer (2015) revealed that 25 percent of survey respondents had paid a bribe to the police to obtain a service or to defeat the cause of justice. During Mugabe's rule, corruption in the police had attained the highest levels despite the fact that the police had a contractual duty to plug corruption and maintain law and order in the country. The then-Police Commissioner, General Augustine Chihuri, was accused of lining his pockets with money collected by his officers at road blocks. The ruthless roadblocks tarnished the public image of the police. Corrupt road traffic police officers had turned road blocks into "mobile banks" from which they could openly withdraw funds. The quantum of police roadblocks had increased by a huge margin; for instance, the route from Zvishavane to Harare through Gweru City (420km) had about sixteen of them.

In July 2020, a number of police officers including a deputy director for the Criminal Investigation Department's Commercial Crimes Unit Assistant Commissioner were nabbed by the ZACC for crimes relating to unlawful selling of land belonging to the Harare City Council. It is alleged that the six officers connived with a magistrate and a City Council employee to sell residential stands in Kuwadzana suburb (Ndlovu, 2020) to illegitimate beneficiaries, thereby swindling the Council of U.S.$1 million.

In August 2020, President Mnangagwa intensified his blitz on corruption by targeting high profile officers. Senior CID officers were arrested by the ZACC, which was working in collaboration with the Special Anti-Corruption

Unit housed in the President's office. They were charged with the miraculous disappearance of dockets, procurement of vehicles, service uniforms, and equipment. The blitz dragged to court Thomas Mabgwe, who is facing bribery charges for allegedly receiving two residential stands from Felix Munyaradzi's company, Delatfin Civil Engineering (Bulawayo24, 2020). Previously, Mabgwe had arrested many high-profile people including other police officers on fraud charges.

The Shona idiom *mbudzi inofura payakasungirirwa* (a hungry goat will feed from where it is captured) is commonly used by the police to justify the unlawful act. Writing about corruption and its effect on justice and human poverty, Transparency International Corruption Perceptions Index (2019) concluded that out of most government officials, the police are the most corrupt. Such a practice by the Police as duty bearers defeats the course of justice and it is against the founding spirit of the police. Acts of corruption in the police deal a heavy blow to free justice as poor people are left to rot in jail while rich people bribe their way to freedom. Public experience is that where a poor person is caught by the police engaging in a corrupt deal with a rich person, the poor person is always the loser, even though the law criminalizes both the giver and the receiver of a bribe.

COMMUNITY POLICING OF POLITICS AND STOCK THEFT

The police have a role to play in enforcing laws that govern the politics of the day. The Bill of Rights in chapter 2 of the Constitution plays an important role in deciding whether conduct is in conflict with public policy or the community's perception of justice. Section 59 of the Constitution provides that every person has the right to freedom of assembly and association, and the right not to assemble or associate with others and that no person may be compelled to belong to an association or to attend a meeting or gathering.

Some quarters of the public hold the view that the police are politicized (Chan & Dixon, 2007) and suffer from a culture of impunity. Human Rights watchdogs and opposition politics in Zimbabwe express a low degree of trust in the reliability of the police. In their view, the Police is an instrument of oppression. The ZRP denies this allegation, claiming that they exercise their duties without fear or favor.

The July 31, 2020, planned demonstrations by the opposition parties amid a spike in COVID-19 cases was one of the litmus tests for the police. The position of the Police was that they were in support of the right to demonstrate peacefully as enshrined in the Zimbabwe Constitution but were against violence or any act that infringed upon other people's rights. Therefore, the planned demonstration was not cleared by the police, citing claims by the organizers that they meant to force Mnangagwa out of Office by August 1, 2020. Two days before the demonstrations, the ZRP Commissioner-General, Godwin Matanga stated that the planned demonstrations were illegal and warned that the police was ready to enforce the law. Some sections of the society believed that the Police is right to protect them from a click of power-hungry and devious individuals bent on assuming power by any means necessary.

Recently, Job Sikhala, an opposition politician, was arrested by the police and charged with incitement to commit public violence as defined in section 187(1)(a) as read with section 36(1)(a) of the Code, alternatively, incitement to commit public violence as defined in section 187(1)(b) of the Code as read with section 36(1)(b) of Code. The alternative charge for him was incitement to partake in a gathering with intent to promote public violence, breaches of peace or bigotry as defined in section 187(1)(a) of the Code as read with section 37(1)(a) of the Code. The accused denies the charges citing that he was only exercising his constitutional right to freedom of expression.

Turning to livestock, the Anti-Stock Theft Unit of the police is responsible for supporting the Government's resolve to build the national livestock herd. The Unit co-ordinates anti-stock theft activities in their respective areas. Speaking during an anti-stock theft campaign meeting held by the (Zimbabwe Republic Police, n.d.) National Anti-Stock Theft Unit in Mbembesi, Matabeleland North Province, Chief Ndondo said, "I am impressed by the introduction of Village Anti-Stock Theft Committee initiative; it will help us a lot and must be therefore taken seriously by all traditional leaders across the country."

The significance of involving traditional leaders in rural policing is expressed by Mathonsi and Sithole's (2017) claim that rural communities have a strong trust in the traditional leadership system and that dispute resolution by traditional leaders is effective. Policing in an environment where oaths are a deterrent to impunity and recurrence is made easier because of fear of death or misfortune when one tells lies under oath.

In an unsolicited casual dialogue between a cattle rustler with the authors of this chapter, a Masvingo Province villager confessed about how he stole cattle and got nabbed by the police after being sold out by villagers to the local chief, who in turn alerted the local anti-stock theft police unit.

Traditional leaders are also at the heart of improved policing and in dispute resolution. One of the hanging fruits in traditional leadership involvement in policing is that disputes are disposed of more quickly (Mathonsi and Sithole, 2017) in traditional tribunals than in conventional law courts, where statutory oaths have no significant effect on false testimonies.

CONCLUSION

The chapter highlighted the legal framework controlling community policing in Zimbabwe. The ZRP evolved from Cecil John Rhodes' BSACP, which was racist. The ZRP was established in 1980 by the Mugabe Administration who later changed the ZRP from being a police force to a police service. The Police has about seven specialized units whose functions are controlled by the law. Despite there being a perfect legal provision controlling the operations of the police, the chapter noted that corruption in the police service and resource constraints are some of the factors affecting the performance of the Police. Neighborhood Watch Committees, Junior Call, Crime Consultative Committees, and Village Anti-Stock Theft Committee are some of the strategies used to involve communities in policing. The public opinion of the performance of the police is mixed with some praising it and others critiquing it. The chapter concludes that despite the challenges being faced in the country, the police service is playing a very important role in enforcing the law and that their strength is linked to community participation and involvement in policing.

REFERENCES

Afrobarometer. (2015). AD56: Police corruption in Africa undermines trust, but support for law enforcement remains strong. https://afrobarometer.org/publications/ad56-police-corruption-africa-undermines-trust-support-law-enforcement-remains-strong. Retrieved 10 August 2020.

Bloomberg. (2016). "Diamond Smuggling Cost Zimbabwe Economy $13 Billion", Mugabe Says. https://www.bloomberg.com/news/articles/2016-03-04/correct-zimbabwe-may-have-lost-over-13b-in-diamond-revenue. Retrieved 10 August 2020.

Bulawayo24. (2020). Zacc descends on police top brass. https://bulawayo24.com/index-id-news-sc-national-byo-191450.html. Retrieved 10 August 2020.

Bulawayo24. (n.d.) https://bulawayo24.com/. Retrieved 10 August 2020.

Chan, Janet, & David Dixon. (2007). The politics of police reform: Ten years after the Royal Commission into the New South Wales Police Service. *Criminology & Criminal Justice* 7, no. 4: 443–468.

Chene, Marie. (2009). Low salaries and the culture of per diems and corruption, Transparency International/U4 Helpdesk.Chr Michelsen Institute, Bergen, Norway. https://www.u4.no/publications/low-salaries-the-culture-of-per-diems-and-corruption. Retrieved 10 August 2020.

Chene, Marie. (2015). Zimbabwe: Overview of corruption and anti-corruption. Transparency International & U4 Helpdesk. https://www.u4.no/publications/zimbabwe-overview-of-corruption-and-anti-corruption/. Retrieved 10 August 2020.

Chigudu, Daniel. (2015). Assessing policy initiatives on traditional leadership to promote electoral democracy in Southern Africa. *Mediterranean Journal of Social Sciences* 6, no. 1 S1: 120.

Constitute. (n.d). https://www.constituteproject.org/. Retrieved 17 August 2020.

Dowding, Keith, Robert E. Goodin, and Carole Pateman. 2004. Justice and democracy: essays for Brian Barry.

Jennet, Victoria & Chene, Marie. (2007). Anticorruption complaints mechanisms. Transparency International/U4 Helpdesk.Chr Michelsen Institute, Bergen, Norway. https://www.u4.no/publications/anti-corruption-complaints-mechanisms .pdfKim. Retrieved 17 August 2020.

Mandaza, I. (2016). The asking of a securocrat state in Zimbabwe. https://www .theindependent.co.zw/. Retrieved 20 June 2020.

Miller, D. (2004). "Democracy and Public Goods". In Dowding K., Robert, E.G., and Pateman, C. , eds. *"Justice and Democracy"*. P. 59-78. Cambridge, CUP, Schuyler, Robert Livingston.

Mathonsi, N., & Sello Sithole. (2017). The incompatibility of traditional leadership and democratic experimentation in South Africa. *African Journal of Public Affairs* 9, no. 5: 35–46.

Ndlovu, Mandla. (2020). ZACC arrests four police officers, magistrate over massive Harare land scam. https://bulawayo24.com/index-id-news-sc-national-byo. Retrieved 18 June 2020.

Nehanda Radio. (2020). Chiluri case-more properties unearthed. https://nehandaradio .com/2020/06/04/chihuri-case-more-properties-unearthed/. Retrieved 7 September 2020.

Namsuk, & Pedro Conceicao. (2010). The economic crisis, violent conflict, and human development. *International Journal of Peace Studies*: 29–43.

Reliefweb. 2007. Hungry Zimbabwean police officers turn to corruption for survival. https://reliefweb.int/report/zimbabwe/hungry-zimbabwean-police-officers-turn-cor ruption-survival. Retrieved 13 August 2020.

Herald. 2019. JUST IN: ZRP warns corrupt cops. Accessed August 14, 2020. https:/ /www.herald.co.zw/just-in-zrp-warns-corrupt-cops/.

Zimbabwe Independent. (2016). World Economic Forum: Global Competitiveness Report 2015–2016.

Transparency International. (2014). An analysis of transparency and accountability in land sector governance in Zimbabwe 2013. https://landportal.org/library/resources /mokoro6033/analysis-transparency-and-accountability-land-sector-governance. Retrieved 13 August 2020.

Trading Economics. (2020). Zimbabwe corruption rank. https://tradingeconomics. com/zimbabwe/corruption-rank. Retrieved 20 August 2020.

Zimbabwe Constitution. (2013). Amendment (No. 20), Act, 2013. Government Printers.

Zimbabwe Republic Police. (n.d). http://www.zrp.gov.zw/. Retrieved 12 August 2020.

Zimbabwe Statistical Agency. (2020). Fidelity Printers.

Part II

EUROPE

Chapter 4

Battles to Define the Danish Police

*Police Reform and the Transformation
of Organizational Ideals and Practices*

Mikkel Jarle Christensen

This chapter contributes to a historical investigation of the battle to define the Danish police. The focal point of the analysis is the contest to (re)define the police in relation to large structural and organizational reforms between 1863 and 2007. Involved in the contest to define good policing were different stakeholders that included the political level, different social groups within the police itself, and other stakeholders trying to affect the direction of the police. The battles between these stakeholders shaped the development of the Danish police, including which ideas and practices it valued most. The analysis provides an overview of the police's most important historical developments seen through the battle to define it.

BACKGROUND AND APPROACH OF THE CHAPTER

Before proceeding with the analysis of the battles to define the Danish police, this short section will briefly introduce the state of Danish police research. Danish (and to some extent other Nordic) scholarship on the police can be grouped into three categories. It includes research conducted in close cooperation with the police, criminological/anthropological perspectives, and historical research. Researchers sometimes publish in more than one category.

The first category covers consultancy or practice-oriented research conducted in close cooperation with and often solicited by the police or carried out by the Ministry of Justice's research unit (Kyvsgaard, 2001, 2018; Pedersen, M. L., 2014). This scholarship analyzes problems and challenges co-identified by the police, such as the trust in Danish police before and after large reforms (Balvig, Holmberg, & Højlund 2011). In a broader perspective, the police have been crucial in funding and supporting (especially early) Danish research (Holmberg, 2003; Balvig & Holmberg, 2005; Koch, 1985).

Criminological studies are probably the most prominent in the Nordic context. The work of Danish criminologists has contributed important knowledge on the criminal justice system (Klement, 2016, 2020; Johansen, 2015; Minke, 2010), using, for instance, qualitative methods to analyze the stereotypes that guide police meetings with citizens (Holmberg, 2003). Other researchers have investigated police involvement in particular forms of internationalized criminal justice cooperation (Vendius, 2015) and how police officers use surveillance technologies (Sausdal, 2018a, 2018b). A small number of anthropological studies inspired by the sociology of knowledge production have focused on investigative work and the patterns of perception and organization that structure how police develop knowledge (Hestehave, 2013; Hald, 2011).

Historical research has also been supported by police funding and cooperation. Early research was focused, in particular, on the role of the police during the Second World War (Koch, 1994; Stevnsborg, 1992). Besides these studies, scholars have contributed crucial insights on the development of the Danish police nationally (Stevnsborg, 2010), locally (Mührmann-Lund, 2015), and with regard to different units and organizational branches (Pedersen, K. P., 2014). Of particular relevance for this chapter, researchers have investigated the development of a uniformed detective branch (Strand, 2011) and the reform history of the Danish police (Christensen, 2012). Furthermore, the police's organizational development has been analyzed using original police archives (Stevnsborg, 2016).

This chapter builds mainly on scholarship on the Danish police's history, but takes on a more sociological approach to studying this institution's development. The idea is to portray the police through the social, political, and professional forces that competed to define it. As famously remarked by Max Weber, the state is characterized by monopolizing the legitimate deployment of physical force within its boundaries (Gerth & Mills, 1946). Since the police have been given much of the responsibility to exercise physical force on behalf of the state (Bittner, 1973), what constitutes good police work has often been the bone of contention. This has also been the case in Denmark. The question of what constitutes good policing, both in the form of what the police ought to do and how it is best organized, has been debated particularly when the police were reformed. The chapter's objective, based especially on Christensen (2012, 2016), is on police reforms and the stakeholders that debated the police during these reform periods. In particular, reforms in 1863/1871, 1911, 1938, 1973, and 2007 will be discussed. The chapter will also briefly highlight important events that followed the last reform in 2008 (for English language accounts of this reform and its aftermath see, Schaap,

2020; Holmberg & Balvig, 2013; Kruize & Jochoms, 2013; Degnegaard, 2010). Reforms of police forces have become more common and frequent, and a broad scholarship on reform processes, effects, and evaluation of these effects exist, including literature specifically on the Nordic countries (Holmberg, 2019; Cameron, 2017; Johannessen, 2015; Granér, 2017; Holmberg, 2014). However, these studies focus mainly on recent reforms that coexisted with the expansion of the private security sector (Volquartzen, 2019) and not on how police reforms were linked to broader historical developments.

This chapter takes a historical and sociological perspective to introduce the Danish police's longer lines of development and contextualizes recent changes. The battle to define these processes was defined by the political level and by different stakeholders within the police and, particularly in later reforms, stakeholders from the private sector. In the quest to reform the police, international linkages were also present, often through particular stakeholders' arguments to make or remake the Danish police from the mold of international role models. National stakeholders responded to wider international circulations of police ideals, but local power dynamics often defined how such ideals were imported. Analyzing the reforms and the debates about them allows for a critical understanding regarding how the Danish police have developed and the social, political, and professional forces that defined this development. The chapter also outlines important elements of transformation in the Danish state and administrative apparatus over the centuries and how they were linked to police reforms. In particular, the chapter shows how the norms of good policing changed over time—from an idea of good police being linked to maintaining a fixed social balance within absolutist society, over civic policing that served both the new liberal democracy and old power elites in the nineteenth century, to industrialized effective and efficient policing in the twentieth century that was challenged in the twenty-first century by new ideas of flexible and projective policing. In identifying and analyzing the core norms of what was perceived as good policing in different periods, the chapter is inspired by the work on different regimes of worth in the work of French sociologist Luc Boltanski and collaborators (Boltanski, Claverie, & Offenstadt, 2007; Boltanski & Chiapello, 2005; Boltanski & Thévenot, 2006).

FROM GOOD POLICE TO POLICE FORCE

To contextualize the first major police reform in 1863, the police before this reform will be briefly introduced. Like many police forces in continental Europe, the creation of the first Danish police was linked to an absolutist form of governance. In Denmark, the 1665 constitution was one of the most clear-cut legislative examples of absolutism in the period (Ekman, 1957). Shortly after the formal establishment of absolutism, in 1682, the first Chief of Police (*Politimester*) was appointed by the Danish king (Koch, 1981). Initially, the Chief of Police had jurisdiction only over Copenhagen, the country's capital and seat of the king, but this jurisdiction was soon expanded to the entire kingdom. The police force originally operated as a private endeavor under the mandate of the king. This meant that whereas the Chief of Police was under royal authority, the police were not salaried. The Chief of Police had to generate income and was not particularly popular among Copenhagen's citizenship due to his methods of doing so (Stevnsborg, 2010, pp. 13–19). The Chief of Police was also active in ensuring the king's financial income. Formal police powers were expanded to include the ability to perform searches of private properties, something that was related to the desire to control the trade guilds (Koch, 1981). The impetus behind the expansion of police power in a Danish context was linked to the royal house trying to become an economic factor. The police were tasked with maintaining good order and controlling some of the organizations that competed with (and often outcompeted) royal efforts to secure revenue.

In this period, the term police itself had a double meaning (Christensen, 2011). It described the normative goal of maintaining and keeping "good police" in the sense of ensuring good mores and reproducing balances of social life (especially in Copenhagen and larger cities), a connotation related to the German tradition of police science (Neocleous, 2006; Tamm, 2008; Härter, 2010). As the police organization gained institutional footing, the concept also began to refer to the group of individuals tasked by the king with establishing good police. This shift was driven by the emergence of a state bureaucracy increasingly able to enforce specific rules.

The idea of creating a police organization seems to have come from abroad. The first national piece of police legislation, from 1701, was inspired by France. One of the authors of this order, Danish inventor Ole Rømer, who had designed some of the fountains at the castle at the French royal palace of Versailles, became chief of police in 1705 (Christensen, 2006). A later order of 1791 created the legal framework for other local forces by establishing regional royal appointees (*amtmænd*) outside of the capital (Pedersen, 1998). The development of the police as an organization was subject to local interpretation. In other words, whereas the absolutist state was an active factor in creating new police forces at the legislative level, local governance structures also experimented with and pushed for the creation of actual police units (Mührmann-Lund, 2015). In addition to forming the legal skeleton around which the police as a force was created and proliferated, the two orders also, to a certain extent, regulated relations between the police and citizens, mediating some of the controversies surrounding the first Chief of Police.

By the first half of the nineteenth century, the concept of police referred mainly to a uniformed force of officers with authority to use force. This was related to the expansion of a bureaucracy around the police. In 1814, the first Danish Director of Police for Copenhagen was appointed. Until 2007, this title was only used for the capital. In 1815, the position of Minister of Justice was created. In 1821, all Chiefs of Police and the Director of Police in Copenhagen had to have a university law degree. This legal monopoly on senior management positions was linked to the fact that the Danish police and prosecution service are formally part of the same organization (Langsted, Garde, & Greve, 2014, pp. 19–20).

In this period, the police in Copenhagen had around sixty officers (Blüdnikov & Christensen, 1982, p. 9). In the same period, and inspired by the creation of liberal democracies in the United States, France, and Belgium, liberal movements gained influence in the Danish context. Before the fall of the absolutist monarchy, the police was used to control these nascent liberal movements. In response, these movements increasingly criticized the police for suppression that took the form of both surveillance and physical violence (Svane-Mikkelsen, 1969). As the liberal movements gained traction, Danish absolutism and its police were reformed.

THE BATTLE TO DEFINE THE CIVIC POLICE

The Danish system was reformed into a constitutional monarchy with the royal system's support. However, this support was conditioned by revolutions in other parts of Europe, especially in 1830 and 1848; the latter directly influencing the king's decision to support a constitutional monarchy. On June 5, 1849, a new constitution was signed. It established a parliament with two houses, maintaining royal influence over the appointment of government. Although this system had democratic traits, the right to vote and to stand for election was limited to a select group of wealthy male citizens (Bjørn, 2019). Suffrage was extended to women in 1915. The new parliament consisted of the emerging liberal movements as well as stakeholders tied to the monarchy. These constitutional arrangements gave rise to considerable controversies in the latter half of the nineteenth century, a period in which Denmark was still a heterogeneous state with a Danish and German-speaking population. However, Denmark lost its southern (and main German-speaking) duchies to Prussia in 1864 (Neergaard, 1892). The police was reformed in 1863.

The police were heavily criticized in the decades after the fall of absolutism. In particular, liberals claimed that it had not kept up with the times and still did not respect the civic virtues written into the constitution. Civic in this context refers to respect for citizens closely linked to ideals developed around the concept of civil rights. The criticism particularly criticized what was perceived as an indiscriminate use of force, something that was supposed to be a thing of the past (Svane-Mikkelsen, 1969). This criticism could also be found on the parliament floor, where debates about police reform intensified in the early 1860s. As liberals argued, the police needed to be reformed so it mirrored the constitutional monarchy's new spirit and moral force (Christensen, 2012, p. 57). These police reform's stakeholders were mainly the liberal and conservative forces of parliament and the highest echelons of police management. To reform the police in 1863, the liberal and conservative parliament members looked to London, where what was considered a modern police force had been implemented in 1829. A key reformer in Denmark, Bille, published a travel book from the country that featured two chapters on the police of the English capital (Bille, 1857) and the Danish police sent an officer to London to investigate its advantages. As such, Danish reformers were part of a bigger circulation of police ideas. Despite some parliament members raising doubts if the London police system was as rosy as its Danish promoters made it out to be (Christensen, 2012, p. 61), this system was finally chosen as the model on which to reform the Copenhagen police.

The police organization for Copenhagen adopted, in particular, the detective branch of the Metropolitan Police. Whereas Danish police had previously been involved in detective and investigative work (Pedersen, 2014; Søller, 1866), the organizational differentiation into distinct police branches was an innovation in the 1863 reform. The Police of Copenhagen now consisted of three branches (or directorates). The uniformed police, the detective branch, and the health police. Each directorate had one commanding officer who reported directly to the Director of Police. The health police did not exist in London. In Copenhagen it reproduced some broad tasks related to the maintenance of good order inherited from the absolutist police. After the reform, the uniformed police consisted of 210 patrolling officers assigned specific beats in the capital. The officers were barracked in six districts of the city. Seventeen officers were selected for duty as detectives, but the number was doubled as early as 1864 (Strand, 2011, p. 49). Detectives received a higher salary and were perceived to be the elite of the police. The uniformed police patrolled Copenhagen's streets at regular intervals and were supposed to treat all citizens with hospitality and fairness. They were also given new, discreet blue uniforms. The detective branch investigated all crimes indiscriminately using the latest technologies. This was the case in theory, at least. In practice, the police's civic virtues still applied to very few citizens and were not extended, for instance, to the nascent socialist movement.

A similar reform of the police outside of Copenhagen was attempted in 1871. In this case, reformers argued for creating a detective branch (sometimes referred to as judicial police) in the districts outside of the capital, but local political levels resisted this initiative. The idea of having a minimum number of detectives in all Danish districts was considered too costly. It was also seen as contrary to the principle of municipal self-governance. The 1871 reform did give the Ministry of Justice a certain amount of control as local police rules had to be approved by the ministry in Copenhagen. Like the police of Copenhagen's reform, the 1871 reform contained rules of police powers, including their ability to use physical force to make arrests. This was seen as important, especially with regard to controlling what was seen as a problem of vagabonds that moved across jurisdictional lines across the country.

The police reforms established new principles for policing in Denmark. However, the organizational ideas linked to these principles mainly affected policing in the capital city of Copenhagen. The state of policing across the country was still highly heterogeneous. Outside of the capital, especially larger districts slowly moved in the direction of more differentiated police forces organized in branches similar to the one formed in Copenhagen. On the basis of such initiatives, local governments drove the slow homogenization of police forces. This new police evolved at different speeds. The new police also mirrored the power dynamics of early constitutional monarchy. As such, it defended this system against new political developments, particularly against the socialist movements that emerged as a political force in the late nineteenth and early twentieth century. Despite significant repression from the police, this movement would help define the direction of later police reforms. As would the new police associations formed as part of wider unionization of labor in Denmark.

THE INDUSTRIAL POLICE

The Danish police was reformed several times in the twentieth century as it moved toward an increasingly national form of organization, maintaining elements of municipal control. These reforms coexisted with and were related to Danish society's wider industrialization and the creation of a welfare state after the Second World War, driven especially by the social democratic party. This development also expanded the stakeholders involved in police reforms as newly created unions became party to negotiations. In other words, the political level was expanded to include the social democrats and other parties and, at the level of the police, negotiations extended beyond top management to include police unions and associations. A similar pattern of union influence was visible in the rest of Scandinavia (Christensen, 2014).

As industrialization and urbanization recalibrated Danish capitalism and society, unions of wage laborers became influential (Pedersen, 1982). Closely linked to the social democratic party, these unions worked to improve workers' working conditions and rights. In the 1880s and 1890s, the Danish labor market was characterized by considerable conflict between employers and employees, leading to one of the largest per capita losses of working hours (due to strikes and lockouts) in Europe during the nineteenth century (Kristiansen, 2014 p. 29). The September compromise of 1899 between employers and employees (sometimes referred to as the constitution of the Danish labor market) formalized a truce between the two sides (Due, Madsen, Jensen, & Martin, 2000). Employers accepted employees' right to negotiate as a collective, and employees accepted employers' right to lead and direct labor. The compromise was generally seen as a victory for the employers. However, the unions became stronger in the decades following the agreement. The principles of the September compromise of 1899 still govern the Danish labor market, resulting in a system that is subject to negotiations between employers and employees. State legislation only becomes relevant in cases of deadlock. The strong position of police unions in negotiating twentieth-century reforms was linked to this particular structuration of the Danish labor market and the power it helped unions achieve. However, this power has been waning over past decades, as evidenced in the 2007 reform where the private industry was influential, and police unions had less impact.

Danish police employees slowly and carefully began to organize and unionize in the late decades of the nineteenth century. The first discreet attempt at organizing police labor came from a choir organized by staff in Copenhagen's Police in 1884. Whereas the choir soon turned its attention to questions related to the rights, wages, and influence of staff, the social purpose was maintained to avoid management suspicion. The rest of the country, especially larger cities, had created a differentiated police organization, divided into branches as in Copenhagen (Christensen, 2012, pp. 81–84). This incremental homogenization was a direct driver for police unionization. Police staff in the second-largest city in the country, Aarhus, created a Police Association in 1901, slightly masked as was case in Copenhagen. This association also hosted the founding meeting of the National Police Union on June 3, 1902, against local police management's will. The Police of Copenhagen, however, would not join the National Union until 1910. The unionization of police staff was directly inspired by similar developments in other labor fields, including in the public sector that also saw unions' creation, for instance, for railway workers. Police recruits often came from working-class families where unionization was well developed. For the National Police Union, central points of debate during the first years were the uneven opportunities of promotion in the different districts and the relatively low wages of police officers across the country. The training of police officers was also on the agenda. The police unions themselves had initiated the first education of officers and pushed for the state to take over. In 1914, the Ministry of Justice allocated funds to create the first national police academy (Christensen, 2012, pp. 97–98).

An internal point of contention between police staff was the distinction between patrolling officers and detectives, the latter receiving a higher salary. Despite the differences between these two groups, they coexisted somewhat uneasily in the same union. This contention was also fueled by a 1911 reform that established a state-controlled detective branch (Strand, 2011, pp. 133–184). This branch was partly financed by Danish fire assurance companies advocating a stronger investigation of fires (Christensen, 2012, pp. 86–93) and consisted of thirty-six officers that operated nationally, and had jurisdiction over fire cases, murder, and specific theft cases. This jurisdictional arrangement meant that the national detective branch often came into conflict with local police forces. The work of the national detective police was closely associated with nascent scientific approaches to police work, such as biometrics and fingerprints. Whereas the national detective branch was not the only domestic player in the push for new scientific methods, their role as an elite group was intimately connected to the emergence of new technologies and police officers' training to deploy these technologies in solving crimes. The first Danish verdict based on fingerprints was given in 1916 (Strand, 2011, p. 96). In 1938, this particular detective branch was folded into the national police force.

A 1919 reform created a new interest group in the police: The association of the Chiefs of Police of municipal police forces (*Politimesterforeningen*). This association, not formally a union, organized all sixty-five heads of local police forces that shared formal responsibility for districts' police. In addition, they all had the legal, university education mandatory for this position. Despite these commonalities, there were significant differences between these heads of police linked to their police force's size. The smallest police force in 1919 was in Hurup in the Northern part of Jutland. It consisted of the Chief of Police, *politimester* d'Auchamp, two administrative assistants, and two police officers. Collectively and despite the differences between their districts, the Chiefs of Police group was closely related to the Ministry of Justice, who had appointed them to their respective positions in the municipal landscape. The association of Chiefs of Police attained the formal right to negotiate on behalf of police management in 1921 (Christensen, 2012, pp. 110–112). The association fought for better wages and pensions and to maintain its position as the main professional negotiator of police affairs. For the association, strong local management was crucial for the maintenance of police autonomy.

The interwar period and the police reforms in this period were affected by larger international developments. The crack on Wall Street chocked financial systems across the world and decimated economies. Across Europe, extremist political parties emerged and solidified. Adolf Hitler gained dictatorial powers in Germany in 1933. These developments were also felt in Denmark, where shots were fired in parliament in 1930. The Danish Nazi party was formed in 1930 and had three members elected to parliament. The Danish communist party had two members elected in 1932, despite a massive anti-communist campaign driven by the social democrats who had had been in government since 1924 (except for between 1926 and 1929) and governed the country through the 1930s on close cooperation with a liberal party (*Radikale Venstre*). In negotiation with other parties, the government developed a reform agenda designed to curb the effects of the financial crisis and, at the same time, limit the political influence of extremist parties that included the communists and the national-socialists. In the mid-1930s, the government initiated a wide range of social reforms that systematized and codified terms of employment of state employees, including working-class and middle-class citizens. The reforms increased the state's influence and developed a state-wide system where richer municipalities diverted resources to poorer ones and created a system of insurance-based social security (Steincke, 1935).

The police reform of 1938 was both related to previous debates about nationalizing the police and a product of the political forces behind the reforms that created the contours of the welfare state. The reform created a National Police but only gave it administrative competencies. Proponents of the reform saw policing as essentially a state task and referred to the need for effective management structure to command police activity to parts of the country where it was most needed. Reformers also highlighted the complexity of crime as a reason to pool resources and ensure that sufficient investigative capabilities were available across the country (Strand, 2011, pp. 179–185). The Ministry of Justice maintained control of the reform process, negotiating with the police unions and associations individually thus avoiding a reform commission. Especially the uniformed and detective branches were at odds. The former claimed the latter was given credit (both symbolically and in terms of wages) for its work, and the latter legitimized its position with reference to the need for an elite force. Whereas both of these groups supported the nationalization of the police (if it would bring more transparent rights and rules beneficial to their group), the Chiefs of Police were skeptical that this change would undermine their autonomy as leaders of the now seventy-two Danish police districts.

The focus of the 1938 reform was to create effective police that could function as a smooth bureaucracy that allowed for police intervention all over the country, even if the system created dual management (Christensen, 2012, pp. 124–153). The reform created a national police organization and a national Director of Police (*Rigspolitichef*) but only gave this director administrative resources and powers. The national Director of Police was in charge of transfers of personnel, promotions, police equipment, the Police Academy, the traffic police, the immigration police, the police intelligence system, and the police's central registry. The competence to make executive decisions was still under the purview of the seventy-two chiefs of police, whereas § 114 of the new police code allowed the National Police Director to make arrangements through negotiation with relevant police districts in case a specific police task demanded cooperation between such districts. This paragraph was hotly disputed, potentially giving the National Police Director power to coordinate across police districts. The power balance of the national police vis-à-vis municipal districts would continue to be debated throughout the twentieth century.

The 1938 police consisted of 2,571 uniformed officers and 640 detectives. This force barely hit the streets before the country's German occupation in 1940. The Danish government cooperated with the occupying force, which meant that the enlarged police cooperated with the Germans. This cooperation became increasingly tense from the end of 1942 and ended formally on August 29, 1943 (Stevnsborg, 1992). On September 19, 1944, German forces arrested and deported about 2,000 Danish police officers. This meant that the Danish police were in a peculiar double position after the war. The police had worked closely with the German forces until 1943 and was hated by much of the resistance movement. However, the police had also been the subject of deportations, and escaped officers had often joined the resistance. After the war, 1,673 new positions were created in the Danish police. Most new employees had been hired during the war where the numbers of police officers increased dramatically.

The 1938 police that focused on effectiveness lasted until 1973, where a new reform targeted making the police more efficient (Christensen, 2008). The focus on efficiency was related to the creation of a police that could deliver good service in what was now a highly industrialized society with a large welfare state. Partly related to these developments, the Danish administrative landscape was reformed in 1970 when more than 1,000 municipal units were disbanded and merged with larger municipalities. The country now had 277 municipalities, often centered on urbanized centers. The 1973 police reform was linked to these transformations. The reformed police was also supposed to respond to new threats of an international world. Denmark had become a member of the North Atlantic Treaty Organization (1949) and the European Economic Community or EEC (1972). Members of the reform commission featured representatives from the unions and the association of police chiefs.

To create efficient and sustainable police districts, the commission developed calculations of what it took to keep a police station operative round the clock. It assessed that at least 40 uniformed officers were needed.

Accordingly, each new police district was to be built around one main station with at least this capacity, typically located in the district's largest city. Besides centralizing police units into sustainable districts, the reform discussed the level of service police gave citizens, mirroring wider debates about welfare state services that were expanded in the 1960s and 1970s. The result of the police reform of 1973 was a police force organized in 54 different districts seen to be able to deliver the required police service. The police districts were also folded into the strategy of Denmark's military defense in case of a Soviet invasion (Stevnsborg, 2016, pp. 191–331).

As part of the effort to rationalize police service, the commission worked to define what police service meant, It identified no less than 228 different police responsibilities, some of which had roots in the nineteenth century. In trying to define which tasks were most important, the three groups within the police did not always agree, often preferring services controlled by their own group. In general, the three groups (lawyers, detectives, and uniformed personnel) competed to define what good service meant in the context of a reformed police organization. These differences aside, the 1973 reform continued the focus on effectiveness, but crucially supplemented this with efficiency and a language of police services. The decades after the reform were particularly characterized by community policing experiments that were also in vogue internationally (there is a large literature on community policing, see, for instance, Fielding, 1995; Brogden & Nijhar, 2013). In the Danish (and Nordic) context, community police seemed just as entrenched in the 1990s as it seemed old-fashioned in debates about the reforms of the twentieth-first century (Balvig & Holmberg, 2004; Holmberg, 2005). Community policing, legitimized by what Boltanski calls the domestic regime of worth (Boltanski & Thévenot 2006, pp. 90–98), has generally played a relatively small role in debates about the transformation of the Danish police.

During the twentieth century, Danish police were reformed several times. Early reforms were especially characterized by developing new stakeholders in the police and focused on creating effective police. The different groups within the police competed to define what this effectiveness meant, arguing for either a solid foundation of uniformed police, the further development of an elite force of detectives, or increased autonomy of police management. The 1938 reform was a compromise between these positions and between social democratic ideas of centralization and a more conservative or liberalist preference for local governance. The 1973 reform took up some of the same problems but added a focus on efficiency, service, and rationalization that would become hallmarks of later reforms. In the late twentieth century, the Danish police were national at the administrative level and municipal at the executive level. However, the national police would slowly take on more operative powers linked to the administration of important technologies and databases and as the contact point for international cooperation (Strand, 2011, pp. 371–410; Stevnsborg, 2016, pp. 427–472).

THE PROJECT POLICE

The latest reform in 2007 was characterized by new norms for police work related to projective competencies and ideas of adaptability, flexibility, and problem-oriented policing. These ideals were linked to a wider transformation of capitalism (Sennett, 2007; Boltanski & Chiapello, 1999) that was reoriented toward some of the same norms. The new focus on projective norms did not push out legitimation patterns that called for effective and efficient policing. However, it challenged the bureaucracy built around the police as an organization, claiming its structure hindered flexible, problem-oriented work, and collaboration across professional divides. As such, the idea of police that could adapt to different projects and problems challenged the professional balances established in the twentieth century and the equilibrium between uniformed officers, detectives, and legal professionals. In addition to challenging these established professional divides, some of the legwork of the reform was tasked to a private consultancy firm, and the commission set up to handle the reform process included agents from private industry. This development was linked to wider norms of New Public Management in the Danish public sector and a new culture of capitalism that gave privilege to adaptive and even what was seen as creative ways of working.

New Public Management (Hood, 1995) or the use of private business ideals in the public sector, made its way into debates about the Danish public sector in the 1990s (Greve, 2006). The core idea, influenced by especially liberal and neo-liberal policymakers, was that the welfare state had to be controlled and constantly evaluated to be cost-effective and efficient. In order to achieve this, assessment and measurement of the public sector's effectiveness and efficiency had to be created and put under government or parliamentary control. With regard to the police, early implementations of measurement of effectiveness and efficiency were implemented in 1991 when the so-called multiannual agreements were first negotiated. These agreements were negotiated between police management and the government. They specified the minimum number of police officers (the Danish police currently employs around 11,000 officers), the allocation of resources to the police, and established targets for the output generated from resources. The police were increasingly measured according to criteria co-defined outside the police, often politically defined and supported by consultancies from the private sector. The police unions and organizations were no longer considered the main experts on their own effectiveness and efficiency.

The first, among the police highly controversial, report written by external stakeholders was published in 1995 in cooperation between the Ministry of Finance and PA Consulting Group (Finansministeriet & Group, 1995). This cooperation also signified a broader shift in the Danish ministerial landscape. Whereas the Ministry of Justice had previously been at the center of national administration and had been crucial, especially for the criminal justice sector, the Ministry of Finance was now quintessential for determining what was considered a good use of public finances (Jensen, 2003). The Ministry of Finance's dominance and its reliance on ideals from and collaboration with external consultancy firms was central for the latest reform of the Danish police. This has also entrenched the multiannual agreements as a permanent governance mechanism in the Danish police. The ability to fulfill identified goals is central for the finances of the National Police and individual districts. The bonuses of management are also reliant on living up to indicated performance measures.

In addition to this culture of measurement, the 2007 police reform was affected by the emergence of what has been called a new spirit of capitalism (Boltanski & Chiapello, 1999; Boltanski & Chiapello, 2005). This new pattern of norms criticized earlier ideals of capitalism for being too rigid and inflexible. Simply put, the classic norms of the industrial society privileged ideas of bureaucracy, craftsmanship, productivity, and clearly defined hierarchies of professional roles. The new projective spirit of capitalism was legitimized through reference to plasticity, adaptability, the ability to connect and disconnect from particular professional relations, and the expertise to work across disciplinary, organizational, and institutional boundaries (Sennett, 2007). Whereas these forms of legitimation of capitalism did not push out ideas of productivity, effectiveness, and efficiency, it created new normative patterns for what professionals and organizations were supposed to do and how institutions ought to be organized. The latest multiannual agreements between the Danish police and the political level exemplify this. Whereas the agreements still specified particular output goals such as reducing case processing time, it also focused on particular projects seen to be important in specific periods. For instance, organized crime and cybercrime have been defined as an area of interest in past agreements (Justitsministeriet, 2018).

In the 2007 reform, the 54 police districts were reduced to 12 (mirroring a larger municipal reform where 271 municipalities were reduced to 98). The consultancy firm KPMG (Klynveld Peat Marwick Goerdeler) was tasked with the preparatory work, and the commission was populated with the usual stakeholders from the police and Ministry of Justice as well as external members, some of which came from the private sector (Christensen, 2012, p. 98). The report detailed the lack of clear and transparent management in the police that was largely a product of the 1938 and 1973 reforms. This was partly due to the muddy division of power between the districts' management and the National Police. It was seen as an impediment to a systematic and targeted use of resources to secure output. Instead of this management structure, KPMG suggested management in which the National Police had executive power. Based on this recommendation, the National Police now has operational as well as administrative competencies.

The reform was also critical of the previous bureaucratic structure of police work, including the professional divisions between legal professionals, uniformed and detective police. This structure was seen as an impediment to creating larger, analytically trained, flexible police units. As argued in the preparatory commission, the complexity of crime was central for importing police ideals linked to intelligence or problem-oriented policing forms (Ratcliffe, 2016). In the committee's eyes, this form of policing should not depend only on police trained staff. It would benefit from the inclusion of other experts and analysts. In order to produce solid intelligence needed to solve crimes, police officers had to be able to work in teams organized across professional divides, to be able to adapt and even innovate.

This meant that the previous balance between police professionals was seen as old-fashioned. The removal of professional boundaries was legitimized with reference to police work's constantly changing characteristics and the need to create police districts that could handle all forms of crime. Whereas the police union and the Chiefs of Police resisted this change, the focus on creating flexible forms of organization won. This argument was supported in particular by the commission's external members, including its head, Erik Bonnerup, a trained mathematician who had worked in several Danish ministries and large banks and was used to spearhead other reforms after his retirement in 2000. Bonnerup also played an important part in the Danish municipal landscape's structural reform that preceded the police reform.

In the eyes of Bonnerup, KPMG, and the majority of the commission, the division into specialized units was an obstacle to effective, efficient, and, especially, flexible police work. It meant that police work was fenced off into different staff categories and did not focus on solving crimes or delivering the requested outcomes. As a result, the detective police were disbanded. It merged with the uniformed police through what is now called investigation units. Whereas these units are formally not a distinct branch, they are still, to a certain extent, seen as detective units by police officers that thus reproduce, against the will of reformers, a specific professional culture. Concerning the legally trained police management, the reform did away with the Chief of Police's old privileged position. The heads of the twelve new districts would be called Directors of Police. These positions could now also be filled by professionals without a legal education, ending the legal monopoly on top management positions in the police established in 1821. As of 2021, most Directors of Police still have legal training, but the first Director of Police with a police background was appointed in 2015. As a result of the disappearance of forty-two police districts and most Chiefs of Police (the title is still used for the Police of Greenland and the Faroe Islands both of which are part of the Kingdom), the Chiefs of Police association was disbanded.

The period since 2007 has been characterized by what can be seen as an extended reform period, as has also been the case in other countries (Savage, 2007). Whereas the 2007 reform focused on the police districts, soon after the reform, attention turned to the National Police. Not included in the original reform, but given new powers as part of it, the National Police underwent a reform that placed this part of the police even more centrally in the Danish hierarchy. The National Police reform was driven as a more internal process that has not been the subject of research. In the new organization of the police, the large national police units that work with intelligence gathering and intelligence-led policing have accumulated increased power (Strand, 2011, pp. 303–328). These units are also frequently at the frontline of international cooperation, even if the value of international police work remains disputed in the wider police organization (Christensen, 2018).

The reform of 2007 challenged the police and its forms of organization. In many ways, the reform remains ongoing and still affects policing in Denmark. The quest to define the police before and after the reform relied on the different regimes of worth. Police were still supposed to be civic, but also effective and efficient. In addition, building on norms and ideals developed as part of the new spirit of capitalism, during recent decades, the police were also supposed to be adaptive, flexible, and able to respond to different threats without being caught in what was perceived as old-fashioned bureaucratic structures. These norms were often in conflict with each other and shaped debates about policing. Linked to the advent of projective norms of policing, the historical role of police staff (whether specialized in detective work, uniformed or legally trained) as experts on their own work was challenged by external perspectives.

CONCLUSION

The Danish police have undergone considerable changes since it was established to ensure the power of the absolutist king and his revenue. The creation of a constitutional monarchy, inspired by revolutions in other parts of the world, led to the creation of a new police tasked with being civic and upholding the constitution. Inspired by the Metropolitan Police in London, this civic police maintained the balance between liberal and conservative elites and suppressed new socialist movements. In the twentieth century, civic norms were challenged by a focus on effectiveness. The small civic police units supported by local governance structures were criticized for being ineffective in dealing with larger forms of more complex crime. In 1938 a National Police was established to enable the deployment of police officers nationally, but local police management maintained operative control. This police focused on effectiveness were linked to a larger expansion of the welfare state that aimed to mediate the tension between extreme leftwing and rightwing political mobilization. It was also built around the influence of the police unions and organizations that had become crucial stakeholders in police reforms. These stakeholders were also influential in the 1973 reform that focused on making sure the police was an efficient provider of specific services and used its resources in the best way possible. Ideas of efficient police service were related to the wider expansion and reform of the welfare state. The 2007 reform challenged police staff and its influence on policing based on new projective police norms. Good policing was now perceived also as being adaptable, flexible, and unhindered by the bureaucracy that the police unions and the chiefs of police represented.

These different norms are still used to legitimize and give direction to police practices. The police is supposed to respect civil and human rights, be effective in its practices while remaining efficient in its use of resources. In addition, the police is often expected to be able to remain flexible and adaptable to new forms of crimes and threats. The normative patterns formed around these at times conflicting ideals have consequences for the deployment of police resources and the organization of police work, including the prioritization of specific police units and practices. Ultimately, these norms have consequences also for police interactions with citizens. Because of their consequential effects on police organizations and practices, the conflicts between different norms are important for understanding the state of police. Battles to promote specific constellations of police norms still structure debates about the Danish police. These norms and the balance between them are bound to affect the state of policing also outside of Denmark.

REFERENCES

Balvig, F., & Holmberg, L. (2004). *Politi og tryghed: Forsøg med nærpoliti i Danmark*. Djøf Forlag.

Balvig, F., Holmberg, L., & Nielsen, M. P. (2011). *Verdens bedste politi*. Jurist- og Økonomforbundet.

Balvig, F., Holmberg, L., & Nielsen, M. P. H. (2009). Politireformen år to: Befolkningens og samarbejdspartnernes syn på politiet i november/december 2008.

Bille, C. (1857). *Skizzer fra England*, København..

Bittner, E. (1973). *The Functions of the Police in Modern Society*. National Institute of Mental Health.

Bjørn, C. (2019). *Kampen Om grundloven*. Lindhardt og Ringhof.

Blüdnikov, B., & Bent C. (1982). Politiet og Jødefejden i København 1819. *Politihistorisk Selskabs Årsskrift*: 5–38.

Boltanski, L., Claverie, E., Offenstadt, N., & Van Damme, S. (2007). Affaires, scandales et grandes causes (de Socrate à Pinochet). *Les Essais (Paris. 2003)*.

Boltanski, L., & Chiapello, E. (2005). The new spirit of capitalism. *International Journal of Politics, Culture, and Society*, 18(3–4): 161–188.

Boltanski, L., & Ève, C. (1999). *Le nouvel esprit du capitalisme*. Gallimard.

Boltanski, L., & Thévenot, L. (2006). *On Justification: Economies of Worth* (Vol. 27). Princeton University Press.

Brogden, M., & Nijhar, P. (2013). *Community Policing*. Routledge.

Cameron, I. (2017). The Swedish police after the 2015 reform: Emerging findings and new challenges. *Policing: A Journal of Policy and Practice*.

Christensen, D.C. (2006). Rømer som strømer. *Politihistorisk Selskab Årsskrift*: 27–49.

Christensen, M. J. (2008). At urbanisere og at policere er det samme. *Politihistorisk Selskabs Årsskrift*: 61–95.

Christensen, M. J. (2011). Da politien blev til politiet: Om kritik og begrebslige forskydninger. In *Liber Amicorum Ditlev Tam* (pp. 259–271). Djøf Forlag.

Christensen, M. J. (2012). *Fra det evige politi til projektpolitiet*. Jurist-og Økonomforbundets Forlag.

Christensen, M. J. (2014). Skabelsen af det moderne skandinaviske politi: Udkast til en komparativ historisk sociologi. In *Motmæle* (pp. 49–61).

Christensen, M. J. (2017). The import/export of police models: Danish 19th-century police reform between elites of revolution and reaction. *Journal of Historical Sociology*, 30(4): 845–867.

Christensen, M. J. (2018). International prosecution and national bureaucracy: The contest to define international practices within the Danish Prosecution Service. *Law & Social Inquiry*, 43(1): 152–181.

Degnegaard, R. (2010). *Strategic Change Management: Change Management Challenges in the Danish Police Reform*. Copenhagen Business School.

Due, J., Madsen, J., Jensen, C., & Martin, S. (2000). The September Compromise: A strategic choice by Danish employers in 1899. *Historical Studies in Industrial Relations*, (10): 43–70.

Ekman, E. (1957). The Danish royal law of 1665. *Journal of Modern History*, 29(2): 102–107.

Fielding, N. G. (1995). *Community Policing*. Oxford University Press.

Finansministeriet, & P. A. Consulting Group. (1995). Turnusundersøgelse af politiet, politiets administrative arbejdstilrettelæggelse og teknologianvendelse. Kbh.

Gerth, H. H., & Mills, C. W. (1946). Politics as a vocation. *Essays in sociology* (pp. 77–128).

Granér, R. (2017). Literature on police reforms in the Nordic countries. *Nordisk politiforskning*, 4(2): 138–148.

Greve, C. (2006). Public management reform in Denmark. *Public Management Review*, 8(1): 161–169.

Hald, C. (2011). *Web without a Weaver-on the Becoming of Knowledge: A Study of Criminal Investigation in the Danish Police*. Universal-Publishers.

Hestehave, N. K. (2013). *Proaktiv kriminalitetsbekæmpelse*. Samfundslitteratur.

Holmberg, L. (2003). *Policing Stereotypes: A Qualitative Study of Police Work in Denmark*. Galda & Wilch.

Holmberg, L. (2005). Policing and the feeling of safety: The rise (and fall?) of community policing in the Nordic countries. *Journal of Scandinavian Studies in Criminology and Crime Prevention*, 5(2): 205–219.

Holmberg, L. (2014). Scandinavian police reforms: Can you have your cake and eat it, too? *Police Practice and Research*, 15(6): 447–460.

Holmberg, L. (2019). Continuity and change in Scandinavian police reforms. *International Journal of Police Science & Management*, 21(4): 206–217.

Holmberg, L., & Balvig, F. (2013). Centralization in disguise: The Danish police reform, 2007–2010. In *Centralizing Forces?* (pp. 41–57). Eleven International Publishing.

Holmberg, L., & Kyvsgaard, B. (2003). Are immigrants and their descendants discriminated against in the Danish criminal justice system? *Journal of Scandinavian Studies in Criminology and Crime Prevention*, 4(2): 125–142.

Hood, C. (1995). The "new public management" in the 1980s: Variations on a theme. *Accounting, Organizations and Society*, 20(2–3): 93–109.

Härter, K. (2010). Security and "Gute Policey" in Early Modern Europe: Concepts, laws, and instruments/Sicherheit und "Gute Policey" im frühneuzeitlichen Europa: Konzepte, Gesetze und Instrumente. *Historical Social Research/Historische Sozialforschung*: 41–65.

Jensen, L. (2003). Den store koordinator. *Finansministeriet som moderne styringsaktør*. Jurist-og Økonomforbundets Forlag.

Johannessen, S. O. (2015). Reforming the Norwegian police–cultural change as a restoration of organizational ideologies, myths, and practices. *Nordisk politiforskning*, 2(2): 167–182.

Johansen, L. V. (2015). *Personen bag straffen: Forhandlingen af viden om sigtede*. Djøf Forlag.

Justitsministeriet. (2018). *Mål- og resultatkontrakt for politiet*. Copenhagen.

Klement, C. (2016). Crime prevalence and frequency among Danish outlaw bikers. *Journal of Scandinavian Studies in Criminology and Crime Prevention*, 17(2): 131–149.

Klement, C. (2020). Studies of immigrant crime in Denmark. *Nordic Journal of Criminology*, 21(1): 11–31.

Koch, H. (1981). Politimyndighedens oprindelse (1681–1684) ORGANISATION OG BEFØJELSER. Historisk Tidsskrift.

Koch, H. (1985). *Politiets effektivitet efter strukturændringen af 1. april 1973*. Kbh.

Koch, H. (1994). *"Demokrati-Slå til!": Statslig Nødret, Ordenspoliti og Frihedsrettigheder 1932–1945*. Gyldendal.

Kristiansen, J. (2014). *Den kollektive arbejdsret*. Djøf Forlag.

Kruize, P., & Jochoms, T. (2013). The police system in Denmark: Towards a completion of the national police. In *Contested Police Systems: Changes in the Police Systems in Belgium, Denmark, England and Wales, Germany, and the Netherlands.* (pp. 59–88).

Kyvsgaard, B. (2001). Kriminalitet, retshåndhævelse og etniske minoriteter. *Crime, Justice, and Ethnic Minorities*, 32–41.

Langsted, L. B., Garde, P., Greve, V., & Elholm, T. (2019). *Criminal Law in Denmark*. Kluwer Law International BV.

Minke, L. A. K. (2010). Fængslets indre liv:-med særlig fokus på fængselskultur og prisonisering blandt indsatte.

Mührmann-Lund, J. (2015). Good order and the police. *Scandinavian Journal of History*, 1–20.

Neergaard, N. T. (1892). *Under Junigrundloven: en Fremstilling af det danske Folks politiske Historie fra 1848 til 1866* (Vol. 1). Philipsen [Bd. 2:] Gyldendal.

Neocleous, M. (2006). Theoretical foundations of the "new police science." In *The New Police Science: The Police Power in Domestic and International Governance* (pp. 17–41).

Pedersen, K. P. (1998). *Enevældens amtmænd: danske amtmænds rolle og funktion i enevældens forvaltning 1660–1848*. Djøf/Jurist-og Økonomforbundet.

Pedersen, K. P. (2014). *Kontrol over København: Studier i den sene enevældes sikkerhedspoliti 1800–48*. Syddansk Universitetsforlag.

Pedersen, M. L. (2014). Gang joining in Denmark: Prevalence and correlates of street gang membership. *Journal of Scandinavian Studies in Criminology and Crime Prevention*, 15(1): 55–72.

Pedersen, P. J. (1982). Union growth in Denmark, 1911–39. *Scandinavian Journal of Economics*: 583–592.

Ratcliffe, J. H. (2016). *Intelligence-Led Policing*. Routledge.

Sausdal, D. (2018). Everyday deficiencies of police surveillance: A quotidian approach to surveillance studies. *Policing and Society*: 1–17.

Sausdal, D. (2018). Pleasures of policing: An additional analysis of xenophobia. *Theoretical Criminology*, 22(2): 226–242.

Savage, S. (2007). *Police Reform: Forces for Change*. Oxford University Press.

Schaap, D. (2020). Police trust-building strategies. A socioinstitutional, comparative approach. *Policing and Society*: 1–17.

Sennett, R. (2007). *The Culture of the New Capitalism*. Yale University Press.

Steincke, K. K. (1935). The Danish social reform measures. *Int'l Lab. Rev.*: 31, 620.

Stevnsborg, H. (2020). *Politiet 1938–47. Bekæmpelsen af spionage, sabotage og nedbrydende virksomhed*. Lindhardt og Ringhof.

Stevnsborg, H. (2010). *Politi 1682–2007*. Samfundslitteratur.

Stevnsborg, H. (2016). *Magt, krig og centralisering. Dansk politi 1945–2007*. Djøf Forlag.

Storch, R. D., & Engels, F. (1975). The plague of the blue locusts: Police reform and popular resistance in northern England, 1840–57. *International Review of Social History*, 20(1): 61–90.

Strand, F. (2011). *Efterforskningens anatomi: Kriminalpolitet 1863–2007*. Jurist-og Økonomforbundets Forlag.

Svane-Mikkelsen, J. (1969). Københavns politi og forholdet til offentligheden omkring enevældens ophør. *Historiske meddelelser om København*: 55–164.

Søller, I. C. (1866). *En opdagelsesbetjents erindringer fra en tiaars virksomhed under Kjøbenhavns Politi*. København.

Tamm, D. (2008). *Repertorium der Policeyordnungen der Frühen Neuzeit: Band 9: Danmark og Slegsvig-Holsten-Dänemark und Schleswig-Holstein*. Vittorio Klostermann.

Vendius, T. T. (2015). Proactive undercover policing and sexual crimes against children on the internet. *European Review of Organised Crime*, 2(2): 6–24.

Volquartzen, M. (2019). *Politi og Privat Vagtvirksomhed: Retlige perspektiver på opgavefordelingen mellem politiet og den private sikkerhedsbranche*. Doctoral dissertation, Det Juridiske Fakultet.

Chapter 5

Police in England and Wales

Timi Osidipe and Jonathan South

Understanding policing in the United Kingdom can be a complex process. Practical considerations inform the complexities of different legal structures and devolution of policing at both policy and operational levels. First, the United Kingdom comprises four countries, namely England, Wales, Scotland, and Northern Ireland. While England and Wales share the same legal infrastructure, Scotland and Northern Ireland have their independent systems and laws. Second, England and Wales have a unified police force, while Scotland and Northern Ireland each have a single police force. This chapter focuses on public police in England and Wales. As a social institution funded by the taxpayer, the police perform law enforcement duties, including but not restricted to law and order maintenance, state security, and crime reduction. Legitimacy, structure, and functions are three core aspects of the police that inform policing practices and the basis for its evaluation (Mawby, 2011, pp. 17–46). Policing in England and Wales has undergone a series of reforms since its establishment in the nineteenth century. Indeed, it is a vast area of study. Therefore, areas covered in this chapter were selected based on their importance to police and policing narratives in England and Wales and in line with this book's scope.

This chapter is structured into three main sections. The first section gives a brief overview of public police in England and Wales, reflecting on several important historical facts and some key reforms in the twentieth and twenty-first centuries in order to provide background information. As the historian Edward Hallett Carr noted, history consists of a corpus of ascertained facts. Their interpretation is important in evaluating a current event, situation, or practice (Carr, 1985). By extension, a historical survey will help readers appreciate how public police have evolved in England and Wales since the nineteenth century. The second section analyses the approach to policing in England and Wales. We acknowledge that there are diverse approaches to policing. However, this section will focus on neighborhood policing and problem-oriented policing (POP). The third section discusses police powers; in this case, stop and search and its impact on crime and minority ethnic groups.

HISTORY AND CURRENT STRUCTURE OF THE POLICE IN ENGLAND AND WALES

Historical documents suggest that the police and policing existed in various forms in England before the nineteenth century. Examples were communal/customary policing, parish constables, Bow Street Runners, Docks and Ports Police, Justice of the Peace, constables of the castle, and watchmen (Emsley, 1996, 2011; Rawlings, 2011, pp. 47–71). Nonetheless, the genesis of what is usually referred to as the modern public police in England and Wales came through the Metropolitan Police Act 1829, after which Metropolitan Police Service (MPS) was established in London. Sir Robert Peel, the then Home Secretary, has been credited for the Metropolitan Act 1829 and the nine policing principles, which became famously known as "*Peelian Principles*" (Rawlings, 2011). Since 1829, the police have had radical changes and reforms. The various reforms reflected events, situations, and broader socioeconomic and political developments of those centuries. While the nineteenth-century reforms were more of a response to industrialization, the twentieth and twenty-first century reforms were triggered by micro and macro-level factors. These involve social conflicts in the society, growing inequality, social spatial distancing, technological advancements, and new criminal opportunities, new crime types and patterns, globalization, immigration, and a marked shift to the political right and adoption of neoliberal principles in managing the public sector (e.g., agencification, performance management, market-oriented principles and rise of network type governance framework) (Karn, 2013, p. 5).

These reforms evidencing the police's transformation were introduced through a plethora of Acts of Parliament and several policy interventions (Newburn, 2011, pp. 90–114). Of importance is the politicization of law and order by successive political parties through campaign slogans and governance approaches, particularly from the 1980s (Newburn, 2011, pp. 90–114). Failure, scandals, miscarriages of justice, and erosion of public confidence led to the police's uncharitable characterization. The urban riots in Brixton, London in 1981 and the Lord Scarman Report (1982) on the disorder, the involvement of the police in the 1984 miners' strike, not to mention Sir William Macpherson Report (1999) on the death of Stephen Lawrence, were decisive events in the history of Policing in England and Wales in the twentieth century. In addition, the use and abuse of police powers—in the case of stop and search, and disproportional representation of black, and minority ethnic communities (BME) in the CJS continue to draw attention to the police and policing practices in England and Wales.

The White Paper—"Policing in the 21st Century: Reconnecting Police and the People"—is the defining document on which the current structure of the police in England and Wales is based (Home Office, 2010). The paper was published during the coalition government: Conservatives and Liberal Democrats (2010–2015). At the core of the twenty-first-century reform is the concept of "democratic accountability" premised on the notion that the citizens, people, and communities must have a central role in how they are policed. It represents a move away from the government's total control of the police (previously based on the tripartite arrangement: Home Office, Police Authority, and Local Chief Constables) to more of public ownership (House of Commons, 2008; Home Office, 2010). A notable aspect of these reforms is the introduction of Police and Crime Commissioners (PCCs) elected by the communities[1] every four years. According to the Home Office (2010, p. 3), the introduction of a PCC is to "make the police more accountable, accessible and transparent to the public and make our communities safer." The PCC is to hold the Chief Constable to account on crime and anti-social behavior in communities, and they also have the power to sack a Chief Constable (Brown, 2020a; Home Office, 2010).

Other responsibilities include working with the Chief Constable and community safety partners (in the spirit of multiagency working and partnership, for example, health, local authorities, and fire and rescue services). The purpose is identifying local issues on community safety, crime and disorder and other policing matters and devising strategies to address them—this is called the police and crime plan (Brown, 2020a; Bryant & Bryant, 2019, p. 29). Under the provisions of the Police and Crime Act 2017, PCCs are allowed to assume responsibility for their local fire and rescue services in addition to the police (Brown, 2020a). Some PCCs have already taken over fire and rescue, thus becoming Police, Fire, and Crime Commissioner.[2] PCCs set the annual budget and decide at what level to set the annual council tax precept (which accounts for around 34 percent of the funding PCCs receive and is paid directly by the local taxpayers) (Home Office, 2019). The Local Police and Crime Panel (PCP), which is usually made up of locally elected councils and lay members of the public, oversee PCCs (LGA, 2011). The following Acts of Parliament consolidated the reforms proposed in the White Paper: Police and Social Responsibility Act, 2011; Crime and Courts Act, 2013; and Anti-social Behavior, Crime and Policing Act, 2014 (Brown, 2020a).

There are forty-three Home Office territorial police forces in England and Wales and three specialist police forces—British Transport Police (BTP),

The Civil Nuclear Constabulary (CNC), and the Ministry of Defense Police. BTP is under the Department for Transport, while the CNC is overseen by the Department for Business, Energy and Industrial Strategy (Brown, 2020a, p. 16). The MoD Police guards and protects MoD establishment across the UK (Bryant & Bryant, 2019). Although democratic accountability has shifted power to the PCCs at the local level, the Home Office still oversees the forty-three police forces in England and Wales. The Home Office provides national policy agendas, performs oversight functions such as the publication of Strategic Policing Requirement (SPR), convening the National Police Board (NPB), and providing funding (Brown, 2020a; Home Office, 2015, 2020a). The majority of government funding for the police forces in England and Wales is provided by the Home Office and is agreed by the UK Parliament annually (Home Office, 2020a, p. 4).

The Chief Constable is in charge of the day-to-day operations of the police. The four types of personnel that work in the police forces are police officers, police specials (volunteer police officers), Police Community Support Officers (PCSO), and civilian support staff (Brown, 2020a). Futhermore, some private companies and charities do policing work, e.g., G4S, Securitas AB, Serco Group Plc (see Lister & Jones, 2016; Rogers, 2018, for more detail on plural policing). The PCSOs who are unsworn officers were introduced under section 8 of the Police and Reform Act, 2002. Although they wear uniforms, they do not have the power to arrest (Bryant & Bryant, 2019). PCSOs work with police constables in the policing of local neighborhoods. They have other powers such as controlling the traffic, entering and searching premises, and removing abandoned vehicles. Their wider remit is to reduce crime, disorder, and anti-social behavior in local communities (College of Policing, 2015). Police Specials (also known as Special Constables) are volunteer police officers, and they work on a part-time basis. Civilian support staff does a wide range of tasks within the police force.

The police have core operational duties that involve protecting life and property, preserving order, preventing the commission of offenses, detecting and reducing crime, and bringing offenders to justice (see Home Office, 2004). It is important to stress that the police deal with more "noncrime" incidents than crime-related ones. Its duties are enshrined in the various police legislations and the common law. The two operational characteristics of the police involve independence and policing by consent. According to Roger and Lewis (2007, p. 17), the public's support is the foundation on which the second characteristic—"policing by consent" is built. Independence of the police means that they operate without political interference (Brown, 2020a).

The Metropolitan Police Service (MPS), popularly known as the Met, is the largest police force in England and Wales. It is responsible for policing the thirty-two boroughs of London. Recent statistics show that MPS has

44,000 police officers and staff.[3] MPS plays a central role in counter-terrorism in Britain (Brown, 2020a). Other bodies linked to the police in England and Wales are the National Crime Agency (NCA), which deals with serious and organized crime such as illegal firearms, cybercrime, fraud, drug trafficking, modern slavery, human trafficking, and organized immigration. The College of Policing, established in 2012, is a professional body responsible for providing skills, education, and standards to the police force in England and Wales (Brown, 2020a). National Police Chiefs Council (NPCC) coordinates police forces in the UK. Among other things, NPCC supports the implementation of standards and policies set by the College of Policing and Counterterrorism. NPCC replaced the Association of Chief Police Officers. The Association of Police and Crime Commissioners (APCC) is an organization that represents PCC's at a national level. Her Majesty's Inspectorate of Constabulary, Fire and Rescue Services (HMICFRS) is an independent body responsible for assessing the police forces' efficiency and effectiveness and fire and rescue services.

When put in contrast internationally, attention is often drawn to a distinct feature of Policing in England and Wales: Officers do not routinely carry lethal weapons, although many carry other protective equipment such as a baton, CS gas, and tasers. The historical context regarding this decision can be located at the birth of the "new police" because before this time, those undertaking policing duties had carried lethal weapons (Waddington & Wright, 2011, pp. 72–89). However, historical and social events such as the French revolution, rapid urbanization, and social unrest, as seen in the Gordon Riots and the massacre at Peterloo following a public rally, should be considered (Emsley, 1996; Reiner, 2012). It shows that the act attempted to mitigate both the symbolic nature of state power and cases of state violence. Theoretically speaking, policing by consent seeks to tread a fine line between co-operation and the exercise of power by the police, as Ignatieff explains, "Support for the police, then as now, was inherently unstable" (Ignatieff, 2005, pp. 25–29). When looking back at the *Peelian* principles, some of the police's issues surrounding the public are equally relevant and challenging to what is happening today. The debates around risk, public safety, and officers carrying firearms in England and Wales will continue. However, in the eyes of some people that legitimate lethal power puts the police above the public, and this can have consequences for how "policing is done" "the traditional unarmed image of the British bobby has faded" (Reiner, 2005, p. 680).

Following the global financial crisis of 2007/2008, the Coalition government embarked on austerity measures set out in the Comprehensive Spending Review (CSR). These austerity measures significantly impacted public spending. Similarly, the Winsor Review (2011) looked at the police officer and staff remuneration conditions. The review made 183 recommendations, including but not limited to reduced hours, redundancies, abolishing special priority payments, and two years pay freeze, except for officers youngest in the police. Therefore, from 2010 to 2011, there was a reduction of 5.68 percent (a loss of 6,800) in frontline officer numbers across England and Wales (Neyroud et al., 2016, p. 25). The overall estimate of the impact from 2010 to 2015 was 34,000 reduction in police numbers (police officers, staffs, and PCSOs) (HMIC, 2014). However, part of the current government's agenda is to recruit additional 20,000 police officers in England and Wales by March 31, 2023 (Home Office, 2020b, p. 6). There is also a diversity agenda in the recruitment process to increase the number of ethnic minority officers in the police workforce.

The statistics on the police strength and workforce are published biannually by the Home Office. There are two strands to these statistics. First, one is produced in July, showing the workforce situation on March 31, and second, another one is produced in January, showing the workforce on September 30 in the previous year (Allen et al., 2020, p. 4). As of March 31, 2020, there were 210,620 workers employed by the forty-three territorial police forces in England and Wales.

The proportion of police officers from Black, Asian, and Minorities has increased. In 2010, the percentage was 4.7, and in 2020, it was 7.3 percent (Home Office, 2020b, p. 28). As of March 31, 2020, 30 percent were mixed ethnicity, 17.3 percent were from black or black British ethnicity, 42.3 percent were from Asian or Asian British backgrounds, and 11 percent were from Chinese or other ethnicities. The ethnic minority group accounts for 4 percent in the senior ranks—the chief inspector or above. This representation of ethnic minorities in the police, if compared to the proportion of the general population, is low. The Metropolitan Police Service has the highest minority ethnic officers at 15 percent (Allen et al., 2020; Home Office, 2020b, p. 29).

What this section has been able to provide is an overview of police in England and Wales. History and current structure of the police covered in this section give insight into the police force's tapestry.

APPROACHES TO POLICING IN ENGLAND AND WALES

There is a diverse range of policing styles used across the forty-three Home Office police forces such as neighborhood policing, intensive enforcement ("zero tolerance" or "broken windows"), hotspots policing, predictive policing, problem-oriented policing, collective efficacy, and evidence-based policing (Home Office, 2006, p. 4). This section will focus on neighborhood policing and problem-oriented policing.

Neighborhood Policing

The genealogy of neighborhood policing in England and Wales is an interesting one, for example, community policing, reassurance policing, to neighborhood policing (Innes, 2005). In the United Kingdom, its adoption is associated with John Alderson's work, the chief constable of Devon and Cornwall, who saw it as a base level function supported by the response and investigative policing (Higgins, 2018). According to Bryant and Bryant (2019, p. 53), in community policing, the police seek to involve various communities in their locality to achieve local policing objectives. Community policing involves prioritizing the needs of the community and relationship building between the police and community. It also focuses on improving communication, reorienting the police, involving the community in decision making, and identifying crime and disorder problems in communities. Lastly, it provides solutions to them (Innes, 2005; Longstaff et al., 2015).

The precursor of neighborhood policing was the National Reassurance Policing Programme (NRPP), piloted in the sixteen areas between October 2003 and March 2005 (Higgins, 2018; Quinton & Morris, 2008). It was modeled on the signal crimes perspective (SCP), which asserts that crime and disorder impact how individuals perceive their communities and their safety. NRPP pilots were introduced to bridge the "reassurance gap," particularly the discrepancy between crime levels and public confidence and perceptions causing a crisis of legitimacy (Higgins, 2017, 2018; Quinton & Morris, 2008). Following the evaluation of the sixteen sites and the perceived improvements of public perceptions of crime, disorder, and decrease in levels of victimization, anti-social behavior, and improved image of the police, the Neighborhood Policing Programme (NPP) was rolled out nationally (in England and Wales) in April 2005.

As Quinton and Morris (2008) observed, NRPP and NPP have three main delivery mechanisms, which are increasing police visibility, involving the community in identifying local priority, and collaborative problem-solving approach. Neighborhood policing' is a policing tactic in which police forces build relationships with their community so that they can work together to combat crime (Brown, 2020a, p. 27). Quinton and Morris (2008, p. 1) note that the main purpose of NPP is to increase the contact between the police and the public in defined local geographic areas in order to make the work of the police more responsive to the needs of local people. It is more about partnership working between the public, police, and other partner agencies within the defined geographic areas (see also Brown, 2020a; Innes, 2005). NPP is citizen-focused policing (see also Home Office, 2006, p. 14; Innes, 2005; Johnston, 2005).

The introduction of NPP coincided with the New Labour Governments' (1997–2010) focus on "new localism," community cohesion (Home Office, 2006) and the vision for neighborhood policing was contained in the White Paper "Building Communities, Beating Crime" (Home Office, 2004). As noted in the White Paper:

> By 2008 we want every community to benefit from the level and style of neighborhood policing that they need. This will involve dedicated teams of police officers, community support officers and wardens providing a visible, reassuring presence, preventing and detecting crime and developing a constructive and lasting engagement with members of their community. (Home Office, 2004, p. 7)

The White Paper also mentioned that "the main thrust of our reforms is to pass power from the political centre to local citizens and communities, to create new democratic accountabilities and scrutiny, and to reinforce the role of elected councillors in local policing" (Home Office, 2004, p. 16).

The principles of neighborhood policing are: first, *visible and accessible policing*—this entails regular contact with the community and local people; second, *influence*—that is, communities influencing crime and disorder decisions; third, *interventions*—working with communities and partners to solve problems; four, *answers*—sustainable solutions to problems and feedback on results (Home Office, 2006, p. 4). The Police Reform Act 2002 introduced the Police Community Support Officer role, to work in and with local communities as part of neighborhood policing teams (NPTs) (Brown, 2020a; College of Policing, 2015, p. 60). It is also important to add some political context from the formation of Community Safety Partnerships (CSP's), under sections 5–7 of the Crime and Disorder Act 1998. This was a recognition that crime and disorder were often complex in origin and solutions and that it would take a partnership approach to tackle these issues. It also sought to devolve decision-making to a more local level. There are about 300 CSPs in England and Wales (MOJ, 2013).

The Home Affairs Committee's recent session identified neighborhood policing's value concerning visibility and reduction in crime and disorder, improved community relations, alongside supporting counter-terrorism measures (House of Commons, 2018). However, recent research by Higgins (2018) identifies challenges facing neighborhood policing—this involves a shortage in frontline staff, erosion of traditional outputs, heavy workloads, a combination of neighborhood policing techniques with reactive local policing, and variation in the remits of PCSOs.

Problem-Oriented Policing (POP)

Herman Goldstein developed POP in 1979 (Bryant & Bryant, 2019; Borrion et al., 2020). POP aims to understand and identify the genesis of crime and disorder problems in communities. Goldstein (1979) defines it as identifying specific problems through systematic analysis of data and engagement with the community to hear their concerns. POP highlights the importance of involving various actors and agencies using a problem-solving framework (Home Office, 2006). It is different from the traditional reactive, incident-driven standard policing model (Home Office, 2006; Karn, 2013, p. 4). SARA—Scanning, Analysis, Response, and Assessment is part of POP framework. "Scanning" involves the police identifying and prioritizing potential problems on crime and disorder. The "analysis" involves the police analyzing the identified problem(s) to develop an appropriate response. The "response" is developing and implementing interventions designed to solve the problem(s). "Assessment" entails assessing the impact of the response on the targeted problem(s) (Weisburd et al., 2008, p. 7).

In the UK, it is also referred to as "problem-oriented partnerships" or "problem-solving policing" (Sidebottom et al., 2019, p. 6). POP use in England and Wales is part of a broader government strategy to crime and disorder in communities. It was built on the National Intelligence Model,[4] and intelligence-led policing (see also Higgins, 2018; Sidebottom et al., 2020). The College of Policing (no date) observes that POP is effective, efficient, reduce demands, fosters innovation, promotes innovation, and promotes satisfaction and morale. Recent research by Sidebottom et al. (2020) on POP in twenty of the forty-three territorial police forces in England and Wales reveals a wider acceptance of POP's impact in reducing crime and disorder. It also found that the police forces endorsed the SARA model and its extension OSARA (O stands for objectives). Sidebottom et al. (2020) argue that there are challenges in multiagency working and overstretched neighborhood policing teams despite its acceptance.

POLICE POWERS: A CASE OF STOP AND SEARCH

Stop and search is one of the powers available to Police Officers in England and Wales (Brown, 2020b) and remains a constant topic of debate despite attempts by the government to regulate and curtail the use of the police's powers. This regulation predominantly comes from Code A of the Police and Criminal Evidence Act, 1984, which states officers must use the power "fairly, responsibly, with respect for people being searched, and without unlawful discrimination" (Home Office, 2014). These codes of practice sought to curtail abuses of power and the nature of the state and citizen relationship that came under its predecessor, namely the old "sus laws" from The Vagrancy Act, 1824 where officers could search "idle and disorderly persons, and rogues and vagabonds" (Reiner, 2015, p. xi). The language is value-laden and open to interpretation when officers use their discretion and decision-making.

According to Bryant and Bryant (2019, p. 166), stop and search is an umbrella term given to the nineteen or more powers to detain people for searches. The powers to stop and search someone are contained in several different legislations, often based upon what illegal item is being sought in the search. Therefore, what offense may have been or about to be committed. Following legislation changes since the Police and Criminal Evidence Act (PACE) 1984, two fundamentally different stop and search types exist. The first type requires the officer to have some form of reasonable suspicion that the person about to be searched has an item (Section 1 of the PACE, Section 47 of the Firearms Act 1968, and Section 23 of the Misuse of Drugs Act, 1971).

The second type requires no suspicion (see Section 60 of The Criminal Justice and Public Order Act 1994 and Section 47 A of The Terrorism Act, 2000). This power allows the police to stop and search without any grounds of suspicion. However, it requires a senior officer to reasonably believe that an incident of serious violence is likely to or has occurred. Section 60 searches are often used in incidents involving football or gang-related violence and have been criticized because it is ineffective, open to abuse, and damages police–community relations (Brown, 2020b, p. 7). It is worth noting at this point that significant changes were made to stop searches under The Terrorism Act 2000 following what is referred to as the Gillan judgment. This followed previous powers to search under section 44 of the Act, where officers could search without reasonable grounds to be formulated of anything being possessed. The authority had to be applied for a senior officer who gave authority for officers to stop and search where they felt it was expedient to prevent acts of terror. Despite over 600,000 searches being undertaken between 2000 and 2009, there was no conviction for a terrorist offense (Anderson, 2015, p. 20). There have been significant falls over the last ten years in the authorizations and subsequent searches, with a high of 150,174 individual Section 60 searches in 2008/2009 to 18,081 in the year 2019/2020 (Home Office, 2020c). As mentioned earlier, powers under the Terrorism Act 2000 were reformed following concerns over using the powers and effectiveness rates.

Due to criticism and reforms, the use of stop and search has declined considerably. According to Brown (2020b, p. 15), recent evidence shows that around 577,000 searches were conducted in 2019/2020: 58 percent. It is fewer than in 2009/2010 but still 52 percent higher than in 2018/2019.

In 2019/2020, the highest rate of stop and search was conducted by the Metropolitan Police Service at 48 percent, while only five forces conducted 64 percent of all searches—the MPS, Merseyside, West Midlands, Essex, and South Yorkshire Brown (2020b, p. 15). One way of looking at an individual search's effectiveness is to consider the number of searches that resulted in an arrest (presumably something was found that may have resulted in an offense being committed). This percentage has changed annually since 2001/2002 and has a high of 17 percent searches resulting in an arrest in 2016/2017 and 2017/2018. Secondly, a low of 9 percent between 2009 and 2012 was also observed. Debates continue over whether this is an effective deterrent or prevention strategy.

Stop and search remain controversial (Bradford & Tiratelli, 2019) and, in some cases, found to have been conducted illegally. In addition, research has shown that stop and search targets minorities (Bryant & Bryant, 2019). Evidence shows that black, minority, and ethnic (BME) people are more likely to be searched than white people. BME people were four times more likely to be searched than white people in 2019/20 (Brown 2020b, p. 15). The black people are the most affected as they were nine times more likely to be searched than white people (Brown, 2020b, p. 16). Brown (2020b) note that the disparity between the search rates for black and white people has increased since 2009/2010. It is the result of a larger reduction in the number of white people searched than black people. Between 2009/2010 and 2019/2020, white people's rate fell by 65 percent, while black people's rate fell by 53 percent (Brown, 2020b, p. 21). In order to promote accountability and transparency and identify good and bad practices by police officers, forces have adopted a national "Best Use of Stop and Search Scheme" (also known as BUSSS). It also invites community members to sit on Stop and Search Scrutiny Panels to assess the manner and legality of stop and searches within their locality. More broadly speaking, stop and search have been found not to reduce crime effectively (Bradford & Tiratelli, 2019).

CONCLUSION

While policing remains a heavily contested area of public life, it is a vital social function that protects people from harm and preserves life and limb. However, it is undoubted that past failings and high-profile incidents have damaged the reputation of policing and the trust and legitimacy it seeks to develop. A reform agenda of policing in England and Wales is continuing as recruitment strategies aim for graduate-level qualifications, and applicants from more diverse communities are being sought. It is an interesting time for policing in England and Wales and discussions about what the police function is and what it should be over the coming years are of paramount importance as our society's nature and types of harm evolve. One example of this can be seen in terminology. For example, are the organizations a police service or a police force?

While in some ways, it could be viewed as a simple choice of words. To others, it is the exercise of oppressive state power over its citizens. This point brings us back to where this chapter started—the Metropolitan Police Act of 1829, and how decisions made almost 200 years ago are reemerging to signpost how the philosophy of policing, its role and function in a changing society. Also, coming to the limelight is how it recruits, educates, trains its officers, and applies the law firmly and fairly to prevent crime and promote public tranquility. Policing in England and Wales is dealing with a significant and diverse demand on its resources. These resources have been significantly reduced since 2009/10, and officer numbers have started to rise again.

NOTES

1. The following are not overseen by PCCs Metropolitan Police Service, the City of London Police, and Greater Manchester Police.

2. Examples are West Mercia, Staffordshire, and Cambridgeshire.

3. https://www.met.police.uk/police-forces/metropolitan-police/areas/about-us/about-the-met/structure/.

4. The National Intelligence Model is a business process. The intention behind it is to provide focus to operational policing and to achieve a disproportionately greater impact from the resources applied to any problem. It is dependent on a clear framework of analysis of information and intelligence allowing a problem solving approach to law enforcement and crime prevention techniques. The expected outcomes are improved community safety, reduced crime, and the control of criminality and disorder leading to greater public reassurance and confidence (Home Office, n.d., p. 6).

REFERENCES

Anderson, D. (2012). The Terrorism Acts in 2011: Report of the Independent Reviewer on the Operation of the Terrorism Act 2000 and part 1 of the Terrorism Act 2006. https://assets.publishing.service.gov.uk/government/uploads/system/uploads/attachment_data/file/243552/9780108510885.pdf.

Allen, G., Kirk-Wade, E., & Arthur, R. (2020). *Police Service Strength*. [Briefing Paper Number SN-00634]. House of Commons Library. https://researchbriefings.files.parliament.uk/documents/SN00634/SN00634.pdf.

Borrion, H., Ekblow, P., Alrajeh, D., Borrion, A. L., Keane, D. K., Mitchener-Nissen, T., & Toubaline, S. (2020). The problem with crime problem-solving: towards a second generation POP? *British Journal of Criminology,* 60: 219–240. https://doi:10.1093/bjc/azz029.

Bradford, B., & Tiratelli, M. (2019). Does stop and search reduce crime? *UK Justice Policy Review* Issue 4. Centre for Crime and Justice Studies. https://www.crimeandjustice.org.uk/sites/crimeandjustice.org.uk/files/Does%20stop%20and%20search%20reduce%20crime.pdf.

Brown, J. (2020a). Policing in the UK. [Briefing Paper Number 8582]. House of Commons Library. https://researchbriefings.files.parliament.uk/documents/CBP-8582/CBP-8582.pdf.

Brown, J. (2020b) Police powers: Stop and search. [Briefing Paper Number 3878]. House of Commons Library. https://researchbriefings.files.parliament.uk/documents/SN03878/SN03878.pdf.

Bryant, R., & Bryant, S. (Eds). (2019). *Blackstone's Handbook for Policing Students*. Oxford University Press.

Carr, E. H. (1992). *What is history?* (40th Anniversary ed.). Palgrave Macmillan.

College of Policing. (2015). *National Policing: Police Community Support Officer: Operational Handbook*. College of Policing. https://recruit.college.police.uk/pcso/Documents/National_Policing_PCSO_Operational_Handbook.pdf.

College of Policing. (n.d.). Implementing and sustaining problem-oriented policing: A guide. College of Policing. https://whatworks.college.police.uk/Research/Documents/Problem-solving_implementation_guide.pdf.

Emsley, C. (1996). *The English Police: A Political and Social History* (2nd ed.). Routledge/Taylor & Francis.

Emsley, C. (2011). The birth and development of police. In T. Newburn (Ed.), *Handbook of policing* (2nd ed.) (pp. 72–89). Taylor and Francis.

Goldstein, H. (1979). Improving policing: A problem-oriented approach, *Crime & Delinquency*, 25: 236–258. https://doi.org/10.1177/001112877902500207.

Higgins, A. (2017). *Neighbourhood Policing: A Police Force Typology*. Police Foundation. http://www.police-foundation.org.uk/2017/wp-content/uploads/2017/06/neighbourhood_policing_a_police__force_typology.pdf.

Higgins, A. (2018). *The Future of Neighbourhood Policing*. Police Foundation. http://www.police-foundation.org.uk/2017/wp-content/uploads/2010/10/TPFJ6112-Neighbourhood-Policing-Report-WEB_2.pdf.

HMIC. (2014). *Policing in Austerity: Meeting the Challenges*. HMIC. https://www.justiceinspectorates.gov.uk/hmicfrs/wp-content/uploads/policing-in-austerity-meeting-the-challenge.pdf.

Home Office. (2004). *Building Communities, Beating Crime: A Better Police Service for the 21st Century*. Home Office. https://assets.publishing.service.gov.uk/government/uploads/system/uploads/attachment_data/file/251058/6360.pdf.

Home Office. (2006). *Neighbourhood Policing: Progress Report*. Home Office. https://delta.bipsolutions.com/docstore/pdf/13509.pdf.

Home Office. (2010). *Policing in the 21st Century: Reconnecting Police and the people*. [Cm7925]. https://assets.publishing.service.gov.uk/government/uploads/system/uploads/attachment_data/file/118241/policing-21st-full-pdf.pdf.

Home Office. (2014). *Police and Criminal Evidence Act CODE: A revised code of practice for the exercise by police officers of statutory powers of stop and search police officers and police Staff of requirements to record public encounters.*

Home Office. https://assets.publishing.service.gov.uk/government/uploads/system/uploads/attachment_data/file/903810/pace-code-a-2015.pdf.

Home Office. (2015). *The strategic policing requirement*. Home Office. https://assets.publishing.service.gov.uk/government/uploads/system/uploads/attachment_data/file/417116/The_Strategic_Policing_Requirement.pdf.

Home Office. (2019). *Police Funding for England and Wales: Statistical Bulletin 10/19*. Home Office. https://assets.publishing.service.gov.uk/government/uploads/system/uploads/attachment_data/file/815102/police-funding-england-and-wales-2015-to-2020-hosb1019.pdf.

Home Office. (2020a). *Police Funding for England and Wales 2015–2021*. [Statistical Bulletin 16/20]. Home Office. https://assets.publishing.service.gov.uk/government/uploads/system/uploads/attachment_data/file/900017/police-funding-england-and-wales-2015-to-2021-hosb1620.pdf.

Home Office. (2020b). *Police workforce, England and Wales, as at 31 March 2020*. Home Office. https://assets.publishing.service.gov.uk/government/uploads/system/uploads/attachment_data/file/905169/police-workforce-mar20-hosb2020.pdf.

Home Office (2020c) *Stop and search data tables* (2nded). Home Office. https://assets.publishing.service.gov.uk/government/uploads/system/uploads/attachment_data/file/935121/stop-search-police-powers-procedures-mar20-tables.ods accessed 26/11/2020.

Home Office, (n.d.). *National Intelligence Model: Code of practice*. http://library.college.police.uk/docs/npia/NIM-Code-of-Practice.pdf.

House of Commons. (2008). *Home Affairs: Seventh report. Session 2007–08*. House of Commons Library. https://publications.parliament.uk/pa/cm200708/cmselect/cmhaff/364/36402.htm.

Home of Commons. (2018). *Policing for the Future. Tenth Report of Session 2017–2019*. House of Commons Library. https://publications.parliament.uk/pa/cm201719/cmselect/cmhaff/515/515.pdf.

Ignatieff, M. (2005). Police and people: The birth of Mr Peel's blue locusts.' In T. Newburn (Ed.), *Policing key readings* (pp. 25–29). Routledge.

Innes, M. (2005). Why "soft" policing is hard: On the curious development of reassurance policing, how it became neighbourhood police, and what this signifies about the politics of police reform. *Journal of Community and Applied Social Psychology*, 15: 156–169. https://doi:10.1002/casp.818.

Johnston, L. (2005). From community to "neighbourhood" policing: Police community support officers and the "police extended family" in London. *Journal of Community and Applied Social Psychology*, 15: 241–254. http://doi:10.1002/casp.820.

Karn, J. (2013). *Policing and Crime Reduction: The evidence and the implications for practice*. Police Foundation. http://www.police-foundation.org.uk/2017/wp-content/uploads/2017/06/police-foundation-police-effectiveness-report.pdf.

Lister, S. C., & Jones, T. (2016). Plural policing and the challenge of democratic accountability. In S., Lister & M. Rowe. (Eds), *Accountability of Policing* (pp. 192–213). Routledge.

LGA. (2011). *Police and Crime Panels: Guidance and Role and Composition*. Local Government Authorities. https://cfgs.org.uk/wp-content/uploads/Police-and-Crime-Panels-general-guidance.pdf.

Longstaff, A., Willer, J., Chapman, J., Czarnomski, S. & Graham, J. (2015). *Neighbourhood Policing: Past, Present and Future: A Review of Literature*. Police Foundation. http://www.police-foundation.org.uk/2017/wp-content/uploads/2017/06/neighbourhood_policing_past_present_future.pdf.

Macpherson, Sir William. (1999). *The Stephen Lawrence Inquiry: Report* [Cm 4262-I]. https://assets.publishing.service.gov.uk/government/uploads/system/uploads/attachment_data/file/277111/4262.pdf.

Mawby, R. I. (2011). *Models of policing*. In T. Newburn (Ed.), *Handbook of policing* (2nd ed.) (pp. 17–46). Taylor and Francis.

Ministry of Justice. (2013). *Statutory partnerships and responsibilities*. Minister of Justice. https://assets.publishing.service.gov.uk/government/uploads/system/uploads/attachment_data/file/389746/statutory-partnerships.pdf.

Neyroud, P., Loader, I., Brown, J., & Muir, R. (2016). *Policing for a better Britain: Report of the Independent Police Commission*. http://library.college.police.uk/docs/Policing-for-a-better-Britain-summary-2013.pdf.

NICS. (2000). *The National Intelligence Model*. National Criminal Intelligence Service. http://library.college.police.uk/docs/npia/NIM-Code-of-Practice.pdf.

Newburn, T. (2011). Policing since 1945, in T. Newburn (Ed.), *Handbook of Policing* (2nd ed.) (pp. 90–114). Taylor and Francis.

Quinton, P., & Morris, J. (2008). Neighbourhood policing: The impact of piloting and early national implementation. Online Report 01/08. Home Office. https://openeyecommunications.typepad.com/Uploads/NHPImpactReport.pdf.

Rawlings, P. (2011). Policing before the police. In T. Newburn (Ed.), *Handbook of Policing* (2nd ed.) (pp. 47–71). Taylor and Francis.

Reiner, R. (2005). Policing a postmodern society, in T. Newburn (Ed.), *Policing Key Readings* (pp. 675–697). Routledge.

Reiner, R. (2012). *The politics of the police* (4th ed.). Oxford University Press.

Reiner, R. (2015). *Stop and search: The anatomy of a police power*. Palgrave Macmillan.

Roger, C., & Lewis, R. (2007). *Introduction to Police Work*. Willan Publishing.

Rogers, C. (2018). Plural policing in England and Wales: Thoughts and discussion. *Forensic Research & Criminology International Journal*, 6(5): 397–340. https://doi.org/10.15406/frcij.2018.06.00235.

Scarman, Lord. (1982). *The Scarman Report*. Penguin Books.

Sidebottom, A., Bullock, K., Armitage, R., Ashby, M., Clemmow, C., Kirby, S., Laycook G., & Tilley, N. (2020). *Problem-Oriented Policing in England and Wales 2019*. College of Policing. https://whatworks.college.police.uk/Research/Documents/Problem-oriented_policing.pdf.

Shearing, C. D. (1992). The relation between public and private policing. *Crime and Justice: Review of Research*, 15: 399–508. http://www.jstor.org/stable/1147622.

Theodoulous, S. Z., & Roy, R. K. (2016). *Public Administration: A Very Short Introduction*. Oxford University Press.

Waddington, P. A. J., & Wright, M. (2011). Police use of force, firearms, and riot-control. In T. Newburn (Ed.), *Handbook of Policing* (2nd ed.) (pp. 72–89). Taylor and Francis.

Weisburd, D., Telep, C., Hinkle, J., & Eck, J. (2008). *Effects of Problem-Oriented Policing on Crime and Disorder*. U.S. Department of Justice. https://www.ncjrs .gov/pdffiles1/nij/grants/224990.pdf.

Winsor Review. (2011). *Independent Review of Police Officer and Staff Remuneration and Conditions: Part 1 Report*. National Archives. http://library.college.police.uk/ docs/Winsor-Part2-vol1.pdf.

Chapter 6

Criminal Policies in Action

Italian Police Forces, Discretionary Powers, and Selective Law Enforcement

Giulia Fabini and Alvise Sbraccia

The authors of this contribution have undertaken research in the sociocriminological sphere from a critical and deconstructive perspective, focusing on the relationship between criminal phenomena and institutional reactions[1]. It is only in the setting of this relationship that criminalization processes take place and can be analyzed. A part of these research efforts, therefore, involves meeting the people who work in the field of institutional control and the individuals who may engage in illegal practices. Among all the institutional actors involved (penitentiary staff, social workers, lawyers, judges, public health personnel, consultants, criminologists, etc.), the focus of the present chapter is on the members of Italy's various police forces, which include several separate organizations.

Given the difficult relationship between sociological research and police practices, the behavior of police officers can be observed as part of ethnographic studies, as long as the researcher can access areas where the police operate. Their practices can then be interpreted also in the light of the sense attributed to them by the other actors involved; be they groups of drug dealers or residents of the streets where they play their trade or judges in the law courts (Sbraccia, 2015; Fabini, 2017a). Police officers should then explain their strategic options and decision-making processes in their own words (Wilson, 2000). However, Italy's police forces take a mistrustful attitude toward sociological research, and opportunities to conduct interviews with their members are very rare (Della Porta, 1998). The Italian literature in *police studies* that has been able to count on their cooperation is very limited. This historical problem has affected efforts to analyze police's discretionary powers and *selectivity*. The nature of the latter can be hypothesized and deduced from the police forces' statistical output regarding the individuals affected by identity checks on the street, stop-and-search actions, arrests, and so on. Unfortunately, the qualitative dimension of their operating practices still remains largely uninvestigated in Italy.

In the following pages, we briefly outline the history and organization of Italy's police forces and then consider their practices in various operational settings: in combating organized crime and street crime, in immigration control, in penitentiaries, and in keeping public order. Our approach focuses on *criminal policies in action*, which are shaped by discretionary use of power and selectivity in control measures. This matters where police practices exhibit too little clarity, which is tantamount to displaying a genuine lack of *accountability*.

HISTORY AND ORGANIZATION OF ITALY'S POLICE FORCES

The Italian police forces are intricately organized in various bodies. There are four forces operating nationwide (Carabinieri, Polizia di Stato, Guardia di Finanza, and Polizia Penitenziaria), and local police forces serving municipalities or provinces. All police forces serve in the role of judicial police. The Polizia di Stato (PS) and Polizia Penitenziaria (PP) are civil police divisions. The PS employ approximately 98,500 people and answer to the Ministry of the Interior. They have general responsibilities, but focus particularly on security and public order, especially in the larger towns and cities. The PP answers to the Ministry of Justice and operates inside prisons. The Carabinieri (CC) and the Guardia di Finanza (GdF) are military police divisions. The CC (110,000 units) answers to the Ministry of Defense. As the PS, it has general responsibilities, also in security and public order, but the CC has a more capillary diffusion than the PS, often representing the only police presence in small towns. The GdF (62,800 units) answers to the Ministry of the Economy and Finance and deals specifically with economic or fiscal crimes and customs illegalities. The local police forces are at the service of local (municipal, provincial, or metropolitan) authorities and only operate within their territories. Originally used for traffic control, their activities have expanded over time (Selmini, 2010), together with the growing importance in the public debate of security and decorum in urban settings since the 1990s (Crocitti & Selmini, 2017). A clear sign of such change comes from the local police forces being equipped with firearms. More recently, the decision to trial the use of tasers by local police has originated some debate (Bertaccini, 2019). The different forces have largely similar responsibilities in terms of the territories to control and the scope of their action. This gives rise to overlaps and can make coordination difficult (particularly between the PS and the CC).

Such a proliferation of police forces is the outcome of historical processes that we can only very briefly outline here. The Corpo dei Carabinieri Reali, the ancestor of today's CC, was established in 1814, and since 1861 held the responsibility of defending the nation's borders. The Corpo delle Guardie di Pubblica Sicurezza, from which today's PS derived, was established in 1852, was responsible for security and public order, and operated in the larger towns and cities all over the country. Under fascism, Mussolini first unified the two forces and then separated them again: the Corpo dei Carabinieri remained faithful to the King, while the Corpo delle Guardie answered to the government, bearing witness to a dualism of power at the time that may seem incomprehensible in today's Republic (Bertaccini, 2009).

Numerous efforts have been made to reorganize Italy's various police forces. The elimination of compulsory military service in Italy during 2005 coincided with preferential routes being adopted for the PS to employ personnel coming from the army's ranks. This may well have led to a remilitarization of the PS—which was converted from a military to a civil police force in 1981 (Di Giorgio, 2016)—with possible repercussions on its operations in Italy's towns and cities, and in the way it handles public order.

Policing and Criminal Policy in Italy Today

As we write this chapter, Italy's police forces are returning to their ordinary activities after an intensive period of responding to the institutional problems posed by COVID-19 pandemic, that led to a temporary, but radical, operational, and symbolic redefinition of policing in Italy (Canestrini, 2020). This took shape in the police turning their attention to the behavior of the population as a whole, which came under exceptional restrictions on freedom of movement. These restrictions were reinforced by the police conducting spot checks and imposing penalties (fines) on tens of thousands of people. Simply put, the political decision to entrust the police with monitoring of compliance with social distancing prompted an intense, though short-lived, effort that disrupted the police's usual practices of patrolling. They had to largely disregard people who were routinely the object of police checks (the homeless, migrants, young people, sex workers, etc.), with the partial exception of vehicle checks. Of course, the lockdown measures affected the most visible illegal activities too, as confirmed by a statistical reduction in crime rates, especially in regards to street crime. Leaving aside the specific contingency, various authors have noted how the pandemic had the potential to trigger an authoritarian shift in the way in which Italian society is monitored and disciplined, even alluding to an experiment in the limitation of democracy (Algostino, 2020). Bearing in mind that Italy has lived through a fascist dictatorship and that its police forces are constantly called in to deal with "emergencies," scenarios warranting a state of emergency (Agamben, 2005) did not materialize with the diffusion of COVID-19. Special powers and reinforced organizational structures have been employed in the last thirty years for the police to combat two different forms of criminality: the Mafia (organized crime) and street crime (microcriminality). Nonetheless, the logic of the emergency seems to pervade the whole horizon of a policing activity that is often (presented as) an action to combat-specific enemies.

To give an example, we can take the field of underage criminality. In the last decade, the threat to society posed by underage immigrants appears to have weakened, and the time is now ripe for the police and criminologists to turn their attention to the offspring of immigrants, the second generations and beyond (cf. Waters, 1990; Marietti & Scandurra, 2017). The risks of jihadist radicalization seem to stem from an ambiguous association between *foreign fighters* and *homegrown terrorists*, leading to the profiling of an aggressor, who is always characterized ethnically, as well as ideologically, with an emphasis on their religious leanings (Khosrokhavar, 2014; Roy, 2016). Although Italy (unlike other European countries) has not experienced major jihadist attacks, the country's police forces have been allocating relevant investigative resources in this area. This is because the country is seen as a logistic base for organizations in the galaxy of Islamic terrorism. The Italian police have a heavy burden of memories from the country's own season of political terrorism. The subversive actions of extreme left- and right-wing revolutionary groups destabilized Italy and shed a great deal of blood, especially in the years 1968–1985. The police's part in the story is controversial, however. They took action to protect democratic legality with a huge investment of resources, and the sacrifice of human lives, but some were also involved in attempted reactionary coups and terrorist attacks alongside people in high office in the government, the secret services, and NATO (Ganser, 2005). Nowadays, intelligence work involves keeping track of important communication media (telephones, social networks, the web), but also demands an operational network capable of monitoring a territory that is increasingly complex, partly because of the fragmented distribution of foreigners.

Given the picture of a criminal policy focused on managing phenomena that are presented as emergencies, and therefore, removed from the normative and operational logic of the ordinary, the issues of selectivity and discretionality take on a crucial sociological relevance. This applies particularly to those forms of criminality that have given rise in recent decades to peaks of social alarm.

ORGANIZED CRIME AND STREET CRIME

The terrorist strategy adopted by the Mafia in the early 1990s, culminating in a series of assassinations of high-profile figures, such as the magistrates Falcone and Borsellino (Stille, 1995), triggered a harsh institutional response. The metaphor of the "war" on Cosa Nostra was not used only in the political discourse or the media's representations of the State's action. Specific forms of punishment were implemented in high-security prisons (see section 4). Special police corps were established under district managements (DDA), coordinated by an interforces National Antimafia Directorate (DNA). Starting with the "Vespri Siciliani" operation (which involved strategic objectives in Sicily), the Italian army was involved in vast surveillance operations. The logic of emergency took over in a historical context in which organized crime raised the level of the conflict with the use of explosives. The Mafia's usual strategy, that aimed to coexist with the legitimate powers, was temporarily abandoned in favor of a more militaristic approach.

By the second half of the 1990s, another emergency was emerging. While crime rates remained stable, a prolonged wave of moral panic (Maneri, 2018) developed over micro-criminality, with heavy emphasis on the part played by immigrants in street crime (stealing, robberies, illicit drug dealing). This second emergency betrayed its semantic connotation, establishing a long-term horizon of criminal policy (still dominant today) that led some authors (Firouzi Tabar, 2014) to identify the particular boundaries of an Italian security paradigm that reflected the international debate on penal populism (Rivera Beiras, 2005). The fallout of the economic and financial crisis that characterized the last twenty years in Italy has certainly counterbalanced the rhetorical core issue of people's concerns about criminality. The dynamics behind the acquisition and retention of political consent, nonetheless, seem to be stably anchored to the issue of combating widespread forms of micro-criminality, especially in the towns and cities. Seen from this point of view, the countrywide involvement of the army in patrolling activities is significant. The symbolic value of using army personnel in daily patrolling activities seems to reinforce the sociocultural picture of a permanent emergency. Such a process has ambivalent effects on the police. On one hand, it adds value to their role, given a criminal policy that tends to propose repressive and preventive solutions with a focus on police operations. On the other, it places a considerable political pressure on police forces, which are increasingly called on to deal with complex social problems that go beyond their operational and institutional capabilities. Clearly reflecting Stanley Cohen's analytical findings (1972), waves of successive emergencies have focused time and again on stereotypic figures of an internal enemy, sometimes attributing them ethnically or racially to delineated criminal specializations. A succession of alarms has defined the cultural horizon of Italy's criminal policy in the last twenty-five years, with talk of "Romanian robbers," "North African or sub-Saharan drug dealers," "Albanian or Nigerian pimps," "Gypsy thieves," and so on.

It may be useful to add that it is only in these last twenty-five years that Italy has really come to be one of the Western countries of immigration, in terms of the demographic relevance of the phenomenon. The criminalization of foreigners has therefore come about remarkably quickly, with their over-representation in the judicial and penitentiary statistics. The latest alarms have been closely related to the reconfiguration of the internal enemy. The specific concept of *crimmigration* (Stumpf, 2006) appears to have played a crucial part in charting the course of criminal policy today, and—taking our approach—this cannot be separated from the reiteration of representations rooted in culturalist racism (Howe, 1988; Cunneen, 2001). Despite ample pockets of the autochthonous *underclass* persisting in the suburbs of the towns, especially in the largest cities of southern Italy, a partial shadow seems to have been cast over the processes of its criminalization in the public debate.

We lack the space in the present paper for an account of the very complicated geographical patterns of criminality in Italy, but it is worth noting that distinguishing between organized crime and micro-criminality is not always very useful. It is clear, for instance, that concentrating the fight against drug dealing on foreign pushers in the street can hardly solve the core issue of their relationship with the distribution network behind them; often monopolized by autochthonous criminal organizations and sometimes part of international networks. Using flexible forms of cooperation and conflict, these organizations have recently abandoned the idea of engaging the State in armed conflict. With the economic dynamism of organized crime in Campania (*Camorra*) and Calabria (*'Ndrangheta*), the Mafia has regained the capacity to penetrate the country's legal production sectors (Arlacchi, 1987; Saviano, 2008; Sergi & Lavrogna, 2016), launching their investments (through recycling practices) well beyond national borders. In times of economic and banking crises, their pervasive presence is a renewed and extremely worrying challenge for the police, who have to combat economic illegalities involving enormous sums of money. This is not just a matter of repressing local rackets or containing acts of intimidatory violence that aim to influence the competition in the context of a capitalist economy. Such activities of control are important, but they refer to a purely parasitic concept of organized crime. Instead, the interaction between economic criminality, political corruption and organized crime now delineates productive and speculative relations that can profoundly disrupt the country's economic system. In such a framework (Gounev & Ruggiero, 2012), the police have to rely on complex investigation methods, using their economic, computing, and personnel resources to combat money-laundering activities within the fabric of the wider economy and in the virtual arena of financial transactions.

The topic of the focused use of limited resources in the setting of strategies for institutional control is fundamental to the sociological analysis of police in any country, and should therefore be approached systematically, and additionally, from a comparative perspective. Needing to consider only the specifics regarding Italy in this chapter, we have identified two macro environments that we consider decisive, where discretionality must be exercised: organized crime and street crime. Our analytical perspective aims to identify the elements of selectivity in terms of working practices (mechanisms for deciding who is a suspect; discretionality in choosing which urban areas to focus on; which crimes to prioritize). Naturally, these choices refer to a limited range of possibilities, conceptually and empirically distinct from the abstract and unachievable goal of full compliance with the principle of legality. Such elements of selectivity do not only involve the working practices of the police, however. They are also shaped by interactions between them, i.e. by decisions relating to criminal policy that selectively orient the police's resources toward politically defined goals. So, it seems obvious that much effort has gone into controlling migrations and immigrants in the last thirty years; diverting resources needed to combat other forms of illegality with a huge economic and social impact. We now turn to focus on how this institutional control is organized.

MIGRATION CONTROL AND THE CRIMINALIZATION OF IMMIGRANTS

In Italy, every aspect of immigration control is under the responsibility of the police (Quassoli, 2013), from tracing, detaining, and deporting irregular migrants, to issuing residency permits. This combination of functions gives rise to overlapping practices aiming to apply the law on immigration while simultaneously trying to prevent and repress crime (Chiodi & Quassoli, 2000).

The handling of asylum seekers is also largely up to the police, including the process of identifying and fingerprinting them—even using force to do (Sciurba, 2017). Most asylum seekers in Italy are accommodated in an extraordinary circuit managed by the *prefetti* (local-level employees of the Ministry of the Interior, coordinating the police forces). This often consists of large centers far away from residential areas, where asylum seekers are kept in poor living conditions (Firouzi Tabar, 2019).

The police track down irregular migrants, report any immigration-related crimes, or recommend their detention (Campesi & Fabini, 2020) and possible deportation. Italy has no organization corresponding to the United States Immigration and Customs Enforcement (ICE), and patrolling the country's internal borders is mainly up to the PS. The police's selective control practices are often directed against migrants or "racialized" ethnic minorities, possibly in response to a demand for reassurance coming from Italy's "residents," and for purposes other than to control territorial borders. They may temporarily move certain individuals perceived as "problematic" or "dangerous" from certain parts of a city. Yet, the police are faced with an "illegal migrant" who is almost impossible to expel, and whose "illegality" they have to manage (Fabini, 2017b). They cannot impose all the rules, and are rather somewhat forced to engage in a negotiation with migrants (Fabini, 2019). They sometimes threaten to use force and sometimes look the other way ("Go somewhere else. Don't show your face around here.") Migrants who experience the most accentuated police surveillance are those suspected of being involved in drug dealing.

It is a different story for the patrolling of the country's external borders. There is a specific section of the PS, the immigration and frontier police, which works alongside: Frontex (Campesi, forthcoming), the European Border and Coastguard Agency coordinating border control operations; and the GdF, responsible for customs control. The limited data available to the public on the external borders control is difficult to interpret. The informal and arbitrary nature of the police's action emerges from episodes of refoulement that are not recorded as such, or the informal transfer of migrants rounded up by the police in Ventimiglia (Italy-France border) and transferred to Taranto's Hotspot (immigration center in southern Italy), for the sole purpose of "making things easier at the border" (Ferri, 2019).

Two troublesome issues have been brought to the fore so far: (1) the fact that the migrant population is managed entirely by the police, whose actions are only open to the control of their legality if someone takes them to court, which creates opportunities for abuse, blackmail, and violence; (2) the police's discretionary powers, in a situation where they have a limited capacity to dedicate time, space and resources to migrants, are implemented in selective mechanisms that lack transparency and are probably influenced by the migrants' nationalities and their perceived social dangerousness. This specific "dangerousness" is amplified by the fact that they are managed by the police in a sort of continuum of detention. It suffices to mention, for example, that Italy's repatriation centers continued to hold migrants during the COVID-19 lockdown even though the closure of the country's borders made it impossible to expel anybody (Roman, 2020), thus revealing their real nature as "prisons for foreigners" (Mazza, 2013). In fact, the system also absorbs a sizable proportion of Italy's foreign population, with effects that we will discuss in the next section.

THE POLICE AND THE ITALIAN PRISON SYSTEM

In the two previous sections, we outlined how the Italian police forces are involved in managing phenomena of great social complexity relating to political and economic domains that certainly cannot be brought down to the disciplinary sphere of criminology. The distinction made by Ruggiero (1999) between crimes of the weak and crimes of the powerful, drawing on Sutherland's seminal contribution (1985), seems useful for framing the selective nature of the criminalization processes, especially with regards to the most severe punishments involving imprisonment. The overrepresentation of socially subordinate layers of society among prison populations is so common in Western countries that it has become a historical constant. Data on the social characteristics of Italy's prisoners confirm this selective element in its criminal justice system. In fact, the levels of corruption, typical of a very damaging link between political criminality and economic criminality, would lead us to expect a more balanced representation of the different social classes among the people serving sentences, but the Italian penitentiary system has all the features of a container for marginality (Associazione Antigone, 2020). The social composition of its prison population has changed enormously in the last twenty-five years, however. The criminalization processes that shape it have been influenced by a gradual increase in the proportion of individuals coming from ethnic groups employed in the lowest ranks of illicit economic activities, who are the most exposed to the selective attention of the police and to the risk of imprisonment (Sbraccia, 2008). Italy's prisons are thus becoming increasingly multiethnic (with an average incidence of 34 percent of foreigners nationwide, up to 50 percent in some regions). Prisons are governed by the PP, which accounts for more than 80 percent of the personnel. Today's prison populations are characterized by variable degrees of marginality and growing levels of internal conflict, which shape an institutional environment that is difficult to manage. Opportunities for resocializing prisoners are limited due to overcrowding and cuts in public spending. The public health system struggles to contain the rising levels of medical conditions inside prisons, particularly with regards to drug dependence and psychiatric disorders. Prison personnel working in the treatment sphere and prison managers are badly short-staffed. The resulting present and future scenarios thus seem to revolve largely around policing the Italian penitentiary system. The public discourse of the penitentiary police unions tends to emphasize the deterioration of these institutions, attributing it to the desperation and violence of the inmates, and proposes increasingly "closed" forms of detention. Exponents of a guarantist culture note how such proposals would lead to a further limitation of inmates' rights, a worsening of their material living conditions, and harsher punishments. Extending and differentiating the prisons' high-security circuits (for sentences related to organized crime, political subversion and terrorism) to be run by special penitentiary police forces adopting very strict methods raises the prospect of a militarized prison management.

The power of the police seems to be growing in the ordinary detention circuits as well. For instance, it is often an informal action by the police that decides the criteria for allocating prisoners to the various sections. This means that the prevailing distribution model gives rise to ethnically character-ized sections, concentrating foreigners by their geographical region of origin, and consequently pooling together the poorer inmates who have the least sup-port of friends and relatives on the outside. Qualitative sociological research in the area of prison studies in Italy (Sbraccia & Vianello, 2016) has shown that this model is often seen by prison staff (and the PP in particular) as use-ful for the purposes of internal security and to combat conflict within prisons. Study findings and direct observations (Santorso, 2016) have demonstrated, however, that establishing ethnically homogeneous groups of inmates tends to exacerbate interethnic conflicts in the communal areas, weakens the bonds of solidarity between inmates, and makes relation-building between prisoners and guards more difficult. In fact, there tend to be more episodes of violence and self-harm in the "African" sections, which make the day-to-day working of the prison staff more difficult too. The stress deriving from such conditions is to be considered in interpreting the violent behavior of some members of the PP. Various incidents have led to a now sizable series of legal proceedings that sometimes even refer to cases of alleged torture.

In short, as part of the specific process of criminalization of foreigners in Italy, the penitentiary system seems to stabilize their socially disadvantaged status, while presenting a picture that confirms the idea that foreigners engage in more aggressive and dangerous forms of criminality. Many foreign inmates participated in the recent wave (March 2020) of prison revolts prompted by the restrictions imposed due to COVID-19, including eleven of the thirteen who died as a result of those events. The specific social threat attributed to prisoners of the Islamic religion (almost exclusively foreigners) has combined with a change of heart regarding the positive value of religious practices in prison to produce a new scenario. A cooperation between the secret services and the PP has given rise to methods of monitoring individuals who "might be suspected" of radicalization, and special separate high-security sections have been created for people accused of crimes related to jihadist terrorism, including any form of ideological and financial support (Ronco, Sbraccia, & Torrente, 2019).

In light of our interpretation of criminal policy structure in Italy, the way radicalization behind bars is managed and represented prompts us to look at how political dissent is managed too, and how any associated illegal activi-ties are repressed. The relationship between criminal policy and political criminality can unquestionably be seen as part of the wider picture of public order. As we wrote in our introduction, this area is constantly being reshaped, especially by the contingent depiction of the "emergencies" to deal with. It is an area with uncertain boundaries, which may contain all the ways for governing disorder (Palidda, 2000) that involve the police, from migration control to managing violence in football stadiums, and from combating the Mafia to patrolling the streets where drug dealers operate. So, now we turn our attention to a policing action, at times and in settings, where dissent is expressed explicitly and is more closely anchored to the political domain.

POLICE AND PUBLIC ORDER

The police's handling of political demonstrations is another dark chapter in Italy's history. The demonstrations against the G8 in Genoa in July 2001 descended into police acts of violence, abuse and torture, even leading to the death of one of the protesters, Carlo Giuliani, during clashes on the streets (Della Porta & Reiter, 2006). What happened in Genoa is by no means the first example of the police' use of force to keep public order. In the 1960s and 1970s, there were social and political conflictuality in Italy that often exploded in confrontations on the streets. Without going into details, the fact remains that maintaining public order is a highly discretionary activity that warrants careful attention because it is crucial to safeguarding democracy.

Della Porta (1998) explains that three general principles seem to guide the police's action in protest settings: seeking a mediation with the demonstrators; avoiding the use of coercive means during protests wherever possible; and collecting information so as to punish certain types of behavior later on, or for the purposes of prevention. She identifies two anomalies in the case of Italy: (i) mediation practices follow no standardized procedure, but are conducted informally; and (ii) there are no clear limits on the collection of information about demonstrators, which is done in Italy by an ad hoc department of the PS, the *Digos* (political police). To this list we would add that the limits imposed on the use of force during demonstrations are not formalized. The proper use of the means available to the police is established not by law, but in the police manuals (Gargiulo, 2015).

Della Porta (1998) identifies four specific models for dealing with public order: cooperation, negotiation, ritualistic standoff, total control. The fourth model is typically used in football stadiums (De Biasi, 1998) and features a conspicuous presence of the police, who may intervene directly, and also with the use of force against a "delinquent mob." It is worth adding that, when it comes to public order, the police training manuals still in use today contain considerations reminiscent of Lombroso and draw on Sighele's views regarding the irrationality of the crowd (Gargiulo, 2015). It is also interesting to note how "exceptional" means designed to respond to exceptional challenges have been normalized and used in other situations as well. This is the case of the DASPO; legislation originally devised in the interest of public order in football stadiums that prohibited fans known to have been disruptive in the past from attending further sporting events. In 2017, the "urban DASPO" was created; a flexible tool for temporarily removing individuals from certain parts of a city for ill-defined reasons of decorum and urban security (Torre, 2019).

In recent years, we have seen an increasingly conspicuous use of preventive policing measures against political militants (expulsion orders, compulsory residence orders, prohibitions from residing in specific municipalities, and so on). These actions have the effect of preventing some people considered "dangerous" from taking part in demonstrations, and thereby weakening protest movements (Algostino, 2019; Senaldi, 2016). We have also seen political militants being accused of very serious crimes (of association for the purposes of terrorism or subversion of the state, for instance) that have led to very lengthy legal proceedings, which can serve as a punishment in themselves, even when the final verdict is "not guilty" (Chiaramonte, 2019).

Returning to the topic of managing public order, this can clearly turn into unlawful institutional violence. During the mentioned days of the G8 in 2001, there were reports of police violence and torture. One of the worst episodes concerned the assault on the Diaz school, when hundreds of police in riot gear forced their way into the school during the night, indiscriminately hitting out at the many demonstrators sleeping there. Another involved the Bolzaneto CC station, where demonstrators who had been arrested were kept standing for hours, and reportedly beaten, threatened, humiliated, and denied sleep. In both cases, the police violence was condemned after years and years of legal proceedings, but it proved impossible to identify the individuals responsible because they were not wearing their police ID. There is no proper system for ensuring accountability, which should be available to fight back a distorted *esprit de corps* and the wall of silence covering up the violence of some members of the Italian police forces.

The problems of containing illegal police behavior are not limited to the sphere of political conflicts. As we write, there is a trial underway against a group of CC accused of deliberately misleading the investigation into the killing of Stefano Cucchi in Rome in 2009, who died while spending four days in a room on the protected ward at a hospital after he had been arrested. A previous lengthy trial to ascertain who was responsible for his death concluded that he had been badly beaten by the CC officers who arrested him. Another case that made national headlines and placed the police's operations under the scrutiny of the magistrates and public opinion was the death of eighteen-year-old Federico

Aldrovandi in Ferrara in 2005, who had been stopped by four members of the PS. It is worth recalling that three of the four policemen condemned for his death were met with a standing ovation lasting five minutes when they arrived at the national conference of the police's independent union (SAP) in 2014.

But something may be changing. There has recently (July 2020) been news of a whole station of the CC being impounded following investigations conducted by the GdF at the request of the Public Prosecutor's office. The extremely grave accusations (torture, kidnapping, unlawful arrest, drug dealing) involve members of the CC and crimes that seem to have gone on for years, pointing to the existence of a full-blown criminal organization. If the accusations are confirmed, it will be clear that such criminal behavior has benefited from many people looking the other way. The Public Prosecutor's "forceful" intervention (a whole police station had never been impounded before) could be a sign that the institutions responsible for monitoring police legality are taking a new attitude, and no longer prepared to condone levels of arbitrary behavior and impunity that are incompatible with the constitutional order. Given the operational and cultural challenges mentioned in this chapter that the police will continue to face in modern-day Italy, we are hopefully seeing a change that has become inescapable.

NOTE

1. The present contribution was conceived and undertaken jointly by the two authors, but for the purposes of editorial acknowledgment, sections 1.1, 1.3, and 1.5 are attributable to Giulia Fabini, and sections 1.2, 1.2, and 1.4 to Alvise Sbraccia.

REFERENCES

Agamben, G. (2005). *State of Exception*, trans. Kevin Attell. University of Chicago Press.

Algostino, A. (2020). COVID-19: Primo tracciato per una riflessione nel nome della Costituzione.

Algostino, A. (2019). Sicurezza urbana, decoro della smart city e poteri del prefetto. Note intorno alla "direttiva Salvini sulle zone rosse" (n. 11001/118/7 del 17 aprile 2019) e ad alcune recenti ordinanze dei Prefetti di Bologna, Firenze e Siracusa.

Arlacchi, P., & Ryle, M. H. (1986). *Mafia Business: The Mafia Ethic and the Spirit of Capitalism* (Vol. 3, p. 4). Verso.

Associazione Antigone. (2020). *Il Carcere ai Tempi del Coronavirus: XVI Rapporto sulle Condizioni di Detenzione*. Antigone. https://www.antigone.it/news/antigone -news/3301-xvirapporto.

Bertaccini, D. (2018). Dotazione di armi comuni ad impulsi elettrici e interpretazione autentica sulle armi in dotazione alla Polizia municipale. In *Il decreto Salvini*

– *Immigrazione e sicurezza – Commento al d.l. 4 ottobre 2018, n. 113, conv. con mod. in legge 1 dicembre 2018, n. 132*, edited by Francesca Curi. Ospedaletto (PI), Pacini, 249–260.

Bertaccini, D. (2009). *La politica di polizia.* Bononia University Press.

Campesi, G. (forthcoming). *Policing Mobility Regimes: Frontex and the Production of the European Borderscape.* Routledge.

Campesi, G., & Fabini, G. (2020). Immigration detention as social defence: Policing dangerous mobility in Italy. *Theoretical Criminology*, 24(1): 50–70.

Canestrini, N. (2020). COVID-19 Italian emergency legislation and infection of the rule of law.

Chiaramonte, X. (2019). *Governare il conflitto: La criminalizzazione del movimento No TAV.* Mimesis.

Crocitti, S., & Selmini, R. (2017). Controlling immigrants: The latent function of Italian administrative orders. *European Journal on Criminal Policy and Research*, 23(1): 99–114.

De Biasi, R. (1997). *The Policing of Hooliganism in Italy.* European University Institute.

Della Porta, D., & Reiter, H. (2006). *The Policing of Global Protest: The G8 at Genoa and Its Aftermath.* Routledge Ashqate.

Della Porta, D. (1998). Police knowledge and protest policing: Some reflections on the Italian case. *Policing Protest: The Control of Mass Demonstrations in Western Democracies,* 6: 228.

Di Giorgio, M. (2019). Per una polizia nuova: il movimento per la riforma della Pubblica Sicurezza (1969–1981). *Per una polizia nuova*: 1–301.

Fabini, G. (2019). Internal bordering in the context of undeportability: Border performances in Italy. *Theoretical Criminology*, 23(2): 175–193.

Fabini, G. (2017a). These are crimes for poor people and sex workers! Reading Europe through immigration crimes and local frames of dangerousness. *Etnografia e ricerca qualitativa*, 10(3): 415–434.

Fabini, G. (2017b). Managing illegality at the internal border: Governing through differential inclusion in Italy. *European Journal of Criminology*, 14(1): 46–62.

Firouzi Tabar, O. (2019). L'accoglienza dei richiedenti asilo tra segregazione e resistenze: un'etnografia a Padova e provincia. In *Lungo i confini dell'accoglienza. Migranti e territori tra resistenze e dispositivi di controllo*, edited by Giulia Fabini, Omid Firouzi Tabar, and Francesca Vianello. ManifestoLibri, 173–210.

Firouzi Tabar, O. (2014). Una rassegna di ricerche sulla percezione dell'insicurezza in Italia: forza e vulnerabilità del paradigma sicuritario. *Studi sulla questione criminale*, 9(3): 73–92.

Ganser, D. (2005). *NATO's Secret Armies: Operation Gladio and Terrorism in Western Europe.* Routledge.

Gargiulo, E. (2015). Ordine pubblico, regole private. Rappresentazioni della folla e prescrizioni comportamentali nei manuali per i Reparti mobili. *Etnografia e ricerca qualitativa*, 8(3): 481–512.

Gounev, P., & Ruggiero, V. (Eds.). (2012). *Corruption and Organized Crime in Europe: Illegal Partnerships.* Routledge.

Maneri, M. (2018). *Media Hypes, Moral Panics, and the Ambiguous Nature of Facts.* Urban Security as Discursive Formation.

Marietti, S., & Alessio S. (2017). *Guardiamo Oltre: Quarto Rapporto di Antigone sugli Istituti Penali per Minorenni,* Antigone. http://www.ragazzidentro.it/rapporto-2017/.

Palidda, S. (2000). *Polizia postmoderna: Etnografia del nuovo controllo sociale.* Feltrinelli Editore.

Palidda, S. (2010). Revolution in police affairs. In *Conflict, Security and the Reshaping of Society (Open Access).* Routledge, 128–138.

Quassoli, F. (2013). "Clandestino": Institutional discourses and practices for the control and exclusion of migrants in contemporary Italy. *Journal of Language and Politics,* 12(2): 203–225.

Rivera Beiras, I., & Almeda, E. (2005). *Política criminal y sistema penal: Viejas y nuevas racionalidades punitivas* (Vol. 41). Anthropos Editorial.

Roman, E. (2020). Rethinking immigration detention during and after COVID-19: Insights from Italy." https://www.law.ox.ac.uk/research-subject-groups/centre-criminology/centreborder-criminologies/blog/2020/06/rethinking.

Ronco, D., Sbraccia, A., & Torrente, G. (2019). *Prison Deradicalization Strategies, Programmes and Risk Assessment Tools in Europe.* Università di Torino.

Roy, O. (2016). The Islamization of radicalism. *Mada Masr,* 11.

Ruggiero, V. (1999). *Delitti dei deboli e dei potenti: Esercizi di anticriminologia.* Bollati Boringhieri.

Santorso, S. (2016). The prison city: Space, community, and ethnicization processes. *Etnografia e Ricerca Qualitativa,* 2.

Saviano, R. (2008). *Gomorrah: A Personal Journey into the Violent International Empire of Naple's Organised Crime System.* Farrar, Straus and Giroux.

Sbraccia, A. (2008). *More or less eligibility? Theoretical perspectives on the imprisonment process of irregular migrants in Italy.* Cisdig.

Sbraccia, A. (2015). Drugs and drug control in Italy. In *Pan-African Issues in Drugs and Drug Control,* edited by Anita Kalunta-Crumpton. Ashgate, 307–328.

Sbraccia, A., & Vianello, F. (2016). Introduzione: Carcere, ricerca sociologica, etnografia. *Etnografia e ricerca qualitativa,* 9(2): 183–210.

Sciurba, A. (2017). Categorizing migrants by undermining the right to asylum: The implementation of the hotspot approach in Sicily. *Etnografia e ricerca qualitativa,* 10(1): 97–120.

Selmini, R. (2010). Cosa fa la polizia municipale e come cambia la sua identità. *Quaderni di Citta sicure,* 36: 85–125.

Senaldi, A. (2016). *Cattivi e Primitivi: Il Movimento No Tav tra discorso pubblico, controllo e pratiche di sottrazione.* Ombre corte.

Sergi, A., & Lavorgna, A. (2016). *'Ndrangheta': The Glocal Dimensions of the Most Powerful Italian Mafia.* Springer.

Stanley, C. (1972). *Folk Devils and Moral Panics: The Creation of the Mods and Rockers.* MacGibbon & Kee.

Stille, A. (1996). *Excellent Cadavers: the Mafia and the Death of the First Italian Republic*. Vintage.

Stumpf, J. (2006). The crimmigration crisis: Immigrants, crime, and sovereign power. *Am. UL Rev.*, 56: 367.

Sutherland, E. H. (1985). *White Collar Crime: The Uncut Version*. Yale University Press.

Torre, V. (2018). Estensione del DASPO (art.20 d.l. 113/2018, conv. con modd. da l. n. 132/2018 – art.6, co.1, l. n.401/1989). In *Il decreto Salvini – Immigrazione e sicurezza – Commento al d.l. 4 ottobre 2018, n. 113, conv. con mod. in legge 1 dicembre 2018, n. 132*, Edited by Francesca Curi, Ospedaletto (PI): Pacini, 261–263.

Waters, R. (1990). *Ethnic Minorities and the Criminal Justice System*. Aldershot: Avebury.

Wilson, C. P. (2000). *Cop Knowledge: Police Power and Cultural Narrative in Twentieth-Century America*. University of Chicago Press.

Chapter 7

The Police and Policing in Poland

Monika Baylis

The history of the Polish police links to its establishment and the legitimation of professional policing in Poland. The organization was established in 1919 and since then, it has been a subject of various reforms to cultivate and endorse its role in the democratic country. In this chapter, the origins of modern police in Poland and how this development was achieved will be analyzed. This also includes the current nature of pragmatic approaches and methods used to address social order and crime trends. Hence, the following concepts will be covered: centralized and decentralized models of policing, police patrol, police training and education, police ethics and discretion applied, police–community relations, and the police's role in the central government. This will demonstrate the importance of legal and extra–legal factors that can affect its democratic accountability as well as the inter–dependence of policing in the transnational state system. The chapter will finish with a brief conclusion to prompt critical thinking concerning the politics of policing and society in modern Poland.

DEVELOPMENT OF "POLICJA" AND POLICING (1919–1990)

The word "Policja" originated from a Greek term "*politeja*" which means "managing a city/town" (Pieprzny, 2003, p. 11). This has been often linked to a process that is commonly labeled as "policing" that can be carried out by a variety of agents: professionals employed by the state in an organization, such as the Police or City Guards formation in Poland (Skiba, 2015). However, the term is broad because it can involve various activities, such as maintaining social order by patrolling the streets, investigating recorded crime and disorder by gathering evidence, and securing the safety of the state (Letkiewicz & Majer, 2011). The "policing" is frequently viewed as the process, which has become the central aspect of social control (Bowling, Reiner, & Sheptycki, 2019).

Social control has been defined differently by many scholars. For instance, Cohen (1985) argued that the concept can be understood as control processes to respond to behavior that people regard as deviant, problematic, and worrying, whereas Marenin (1982) added that the notion can intertwin with particular structures of social dominance, such as the police or the State. This can be seen in the Polish context, where it is mainly the police and the State that are responsible for social control (Skiba, 2015).

In Poland, the State is represented by the government, which consists of the Sejm ("Sejm") and the Senate ("Senat") (opis.sejm.gov.pl, 2016). These two organizations are behind numerous legislations or certain regulations, which shape the police legitimacy, work, and education since the establishment of the Polish Police called "Policja" (Letkiewicz & Majer, 2011). Therefore, a common argument stated by Polish scholars is that the development of the police has been mainly driven by constant changes that take place within Polish society and the country itself (Majer, 2015; Misiuk, 2018). These changes have been frequently viewed as political, economic, and social factors that have had not only an impact on public perception of police legitimacy (Czaspska, Radomska, & Wojcik, 2016) but have also influenced the administrative structure of the organization (Skiba, 2015).

"Policja" was formally created during the interwar period (1918–1939) and was a highly centralized, hierarchical, and independent public organization (Misiuk, 2008). For instance, in 1919, the Chief Commander oversaw six provincial police headquarters, but this number increased to sixteen in 1925 (Skiba, 2015). The main role of the Polish Police was to prevent crime, maintain social order, and ensure the State's security. However, they were replaced by a new uniformed organization called the Citizen's Militia on the July 27, 1944 (Letkiewicz & Majer, 2011). The Citizen's Militia was based on a militaristic model that consisted of various uniformed policing units including the Road Patrol, Criminal Investigation Department, and Crime Prevention Unit, with the main Police Headquarters called "Komenda Glowna Policji" located in Warsaw, the current capital of Poland. The same is true for the previous organization, which was also controlled by the Chief Commander, who was responsible for 80,000 officers by 1945 (Skiba, 2015).

Further administerial and legislative changes that took place due to the political system, such as the Communist regime of 1945–1989, contributed to the creation of a "political police" (Majer in Szymaniak & Ciepiela, 2007) in Poland. For instance, on the July 20, 1954, a new *decree* was issued to give new police powers to the organization and on December 1956, some specialized units, such as "Zmotoryzowane Odwody Milicji Obywatelskiej" (ZOMO), located mainly in urban areas, were established. They aimed to control riots or address any form of political resistance and were often used by the State during December 1970 and the period of 1981–1983 (Skiba, 2015). This changed the original nature of policing in the country into a "Soviet style" that was based on the secret police model and intelligence-led policing (Skiba, 2015). Hence, along with "Sluzba Bezpieczenstwa" (SB) (the Security Service) that was established in 1954, the Citizen's Militia was responsible for maintaining social control and order until May 10, 1990. Their "style of policing" toward some Polish citizens was openly questioned on numerous occasions by many Polish politicians, Polish media, and society itself. Examples include during and after the introduction of Martial Law on December 13, 1981; the Miners' strike at the Wujek coal mine in Katowice on December 16, 1981; and after the fall of Communism in 1989 (Dudek & Zblewski, 2008). The critics argued that both organizations frequently used an oppressive and militaristic approach that could be viewed as a violation of human rights in terms of freedom of expression and the right to protest. A social debate about the real legitimacy or "independent" nature of the formation began in the 1950s (Dudek & Zblewski, 2008; polskieradio.pl, 2017).

It would be useful to comment further on the subject, however, there is limited empirical research carried out on the methods used by the Citizen's Militia during that time. Also, the available literature is very descriptive in nature by discussing mainly the structural changes of the organization, for example, the development of criminal investigation units or the role of profiling in general (Skiba, 2015). Perhaps, this reflects the fact that during the Soviet time Polish Criminology remained marginal in terms of both teaching and research (Krajewski, 2004) and the Evidence-Based Practice (EBP) developed slowly in Poland (Baylis & Matczak, 2019). The "Militia" was formally replaced with the introduction of the Police Act 1990 on April 6, where the Polish government created a new uniformed and armed formation called "Policja" (Police Act, 1990). This mirrored not only the political changes in Poland, such as the fall of the communism era but also economic developments, such as the beginning of Polish capitalism (Misiuk, 2018). Since then, the structure of the "Policja" has changed slightly to reflect the modern trends of policing democratic Poland, and Polish Police have become both "a force" and "a service" by taking over many functions that have been outlined in the Police Act of 1990.

The Police Act 1990 was and still is one of the most important legislations in the history of Polish policing (Misiuk, 2018) and consists of two main components. The first part describes the role and functions of the organization (e.g., maintaining national security and social order), whereas the second part discusses various police powers that dictate how policing shall be carried out by a police officer (Police Act, 1990). The Act also states that the structure of the organization is based on a centralized and hierarchical model, which is made up of regional and local police units/commands that were embodied in the highly centralized policing system on July 10, 1991 (Misiuk, 2008). However, this view was questioned by Majer (2007), who argued that on some levels, the Polish policing system can be viewed as decentralized because of the role and the influence of local authorities, such as the council, over the selection of local Police Commanders and in providing financial support for establishing new police stations (Skiba, 2015).

THE NEW "POLICJA" AND ITS CURRENT STRUCTURE (1991–2020)

Today's Polish Police service is divided into the Main Headquarters of Polish Police and sixteen regional command units that are controlled by their commanders. Each unit has its own subdivisions that are responsible for different activities within the police force/service, for example, dealing with crime prevention, criminal investigation, traffic control, aviation service, and counterterrorism (info.policja.pl, n.d.).

According to info.policja.pl, n.d., the organization's main goal is to serve and protect the people and to maintain public order and security, whereas the basic police duties involve the protection of people's health and life, the protection of property, the protection of public safety and order, creating and organizing "community policing" and crime prevention activities, detecting crimes and misdemeanors, arresting people who committed crimes, controlling regulations regarding public life and public spaces, and cooperating with police forces from other countries and international organizations (info .policja.pl, n.d.).

There are other police services that assist the Polish Police, such as the Central Bureau of Investigation, the Internal Bureau of Police conduct, the Central Subdivision of Counter-Terrorism Unit "BOA," and the Central Forensic Laboratory of the Police. Each of these services specializes in addressing different criminal activities, and therefore, performs different functions. For instance, the Central Bureau of Investigation (CBSP) that was established in 2000 focuses on identifying and combating organized crime and identifying terrorist threats (antyterroryzm.gov.pl, n.d.), whereas the Internal Bureau of Police Conduct (BSWP) investigates police misconduct and corruption (policja.gov.pl, n.d.). To differentiate them, different police uniforms, powers, and training are given to reflect their differing roles. The most common police uniforms that can be often seen by the public are either dark blue or black. They are frequently worn by police prevention units.

The police patrol consists of double crewing, which means that two officers are usually sent to an incident (Ciarka, 2009). If the incident requires the involvement of officers from other countries, the Polish police can use the "mixed police patrol approach" (Ciarka, 2009). This form of multinational collaboration, such as joining Slovakian (Ciarka, 2009) or German patrols (Burchardt, 2020) begun after the 1990s and became more popular since Poland joined the EU and the Polish accession to the Schengen area that occurred in 2007 (Ciarka, 2009). Although international collaboration has always been welcomed by all agencies involved (Krystians, 2012), some important issues were highlighted as well. For instance, according to Styczynska and Beamount, (2017), police patrols that consist of German-Polish officers can face legal and administrative obstacles, which may lead to inconsistencies and delays in the management of administrative procedures. There are also differences with regards to police traditions and overall, cultural differences have a sizable impact on police work (-ibid., 2017). Thus, the process of combining two different policing systems where the law differs can be complex and dynamic.

In Poland, police working hours are eight per day, five days a week, however, in specific circumstances, this can be extended to twelve and the officers can work during weekends, according to the updated October 9, 2014, version of the Order of the Minister of Interior Affairs and Administration, initially tabled on October 18, 2001. During their working hours, the police mostly rely on the knowledge gained from their previous and current training as well as their experience by the length of service (Kiszlo, 2015), which plays an important role in the officers' professional progression process (Baylis & Matczak, 2019).

Police Training, Education, and Rank Structure

In Poland, all police officers or police cadets are trained and educated by four police training centers in Pila, Slupsk, Legionowo, and Katowiceas, as well as one Police Academy in Szczytno. These are part of a two-tiered system of police learning and education in Poland that is delivered in the form of compulsory basic training followed by optional in-service training (Baylis & Matczak, 2019).

The 142-day police basic training consists of 1,142 hours of lectures that focus on public safety, public order, investigating cases of missing persons and items, criminal investigation, and road traffic control. These different subjects/topics are delivered by internal staff or "associate/contracted" teachers (Bogdalski, 2014). Each person who wishes to join the organization must pass the police entrance exams and complete the basic police training (Baylis & Matczak, 2019). This allows the police officer to perform basic police duties but only in four different units, namely crime prevention, criminal investigation, operational/technical support, or logistics (Gawronski, 2015). Officers willing to pursue further training may opt for a 6-month course of advanced training currently delivered only by the Police Academy in Szczytno (Baylis & Matczak, 2019).

The advanced police training is based on various modules, such as the psychology of management, leadership, administrative law, youth offending, criminology, police strategies, cybercrime, and terrorism (Baylis & Matczak, 2019). The eligibility criteria to undertake this training involves being already employed by the Police, holding a higher education degree, and having served for at least 3 years in the same formation (Baylis & Matczak, 2019). This is crucial because this is the only way to reach the highest rank in policing in the Polish context. It is often understood as "hierarchical career progression" or the "promotion process" by other European scholars (Boag-Munroe et al., 2017).

The police ranking structure in Poland begins at Constable, followed by Senior Constable, Sergeant, Senior Sergeant, and Staff Sergeant, in ascending order of seniority. These ranks are noncommissioned and holders are categorized as junior police officers. The next higher category, Senior Police Officers, who are also noncommissioned, include the ranks of Junior Aspirant, Aspirant, Senior Aspirant, and Staff Aspirant. Above them is the category of Junior Supervisors. This includes the ranks of Deputy Commissioner, Commissioner, and Chief Commissioner. Officers holding these ranks are commissioned. Moving up is the category of Senior Supervisory Police, which is also commissioned, and contains the ranks of Deputy Inspector, Junior Inspector, and Inspector. The topmost category is Staff Police Officers, which is commissioned and includes the categories of Chief Inspector and Inspector General of Police at the helm.

To be promoted to a higher rank in Poland, police officers must follow the educational model stated in the Police Act of 1990 or four different Regulations of the Minister of Internal Affairs and Administration (Baylis & Matczak, 2019). The requirements can also be determined by the Chief Commander of Polish Police, who is also in charge of police recruitments, while the Department of Control (the Supreme Audit Office) carries out annual inspections to improve or control the current system of police learning and education in the Polish context (Baylis & Matczak, 2019).

The Police Current Numbers

By the January 1, 2019, the Polish Police had employed approximately 100,000 police officers and 12,000 civilians (info.policja.pl, n.d.). Although these numbers do not specify how many of them were female, the same organization argued in 2019 that every fifth officer is a woman (ibid.). This has often been questioned by Polish scholars.

According to Rudnicka (2017), female officers were underrepresented in 2017; out of the 96,586 serving police officers, only 13,280 were women, which mirrored similar arguments presented by Basinska and Wiciak (2015). Basinska and Wiciak (2015) implied that the female officers who work now for all police units have much higher degrees in comparison to their male colleagues, and they often face gender discrimination that stops them from being promoted. For instance, in 2013 only 57 women out of 1,722 available vacancies were holding higher positions in the uniformed formation (Basinska & Wiciak, 2015). However, both authors agreed that more and more women are joining the Polish Police, suggesting the "macho culture" is decreasing slowly due to social changes within the Polish society, such as the new construct of womanhood or structural changes within the formation, such as the establishment of specialized units that tackle the process of stereotyping women (Basinska & Wiciak, 2015; Rudnicka, 2017). These processes are frequently linked to improving procedural justice and police work in Poland that are usually discussed through the lenses of police legitimacy (Czapska, Radomska & Wojcik, 2016).

Procedural Justice and Police

It would be useful to offer one definition of procedural justice for the Polish policing context. However, Czapska, Radomska, and Wojcik (2016) stated that it is a broad concept, which is frequently viewed through the application and perception of law, crime prevention, or public trust (Sunshine & Tyler, 2003). Thus, it is challenging to draw final conclusions with factors that influence the police procedural justice and work in Poland because the "issue of quality of legitimation remained on the margins of theoretical considerations" (Czapska, Radomska & Wojcik, 2016, p. 455). The only source of information is the Public Opinion Research Centre that conducts a public opinion poll that runs every six months. The study consists of a representative sample of adult residents and asks about their views on trust in various public institutions, for example, the courts and the government (Czapska, Radomska & Wojcik, 2016).

According to Policja.pl (2018), 72 percent of Polish citizens rate Police work as "good" and since 2016, the low-level crime rate, which includes theft or robbery, is decreasing due to their professional approach. For instance, in 2017, there were 490,711 criminal offenses recorded, which was lower in comparison to the 553,767 offenses committed during 2015 (Ibid.). However, the professional approach is a broad and subjective term (Baylis & Matczak, 2019) because the police and the public can perceive it differently. This links to the perception of police legitimacy and the impact of police legitimacy on public cooperation with the police, which can be related to the procedural fairness of the police (Czapska, Radomska, & Wojcik, 2016) or "formal rules of justice" (Baran, 2017). Both concepts are based on the law in the Polish context, thus, in practice, all activities that are undertaken by the police must be conducted within the limits set by the act of law (Baran, 2017).

A similar view was presented by Plywaczewski (1997), Stando-Kawecka (2015), and Krajewski (2012), who also added that the police response is driven by a model of law, which dictates the specific actors involved in addressing different criminal activities. Plywaczewski (1997) noted that when policing organized crimes such as drug trafficking or money laundering, the police work with local and international criminal justice systems like the local judges and the International Criminal Police Organization (INTERPOL) (Plywaczewski, 1997). Stando-Kawecka (2015) highlighted the importance of youth judges in policing youth crime, whereas Krajewski (2012) pointed out the role of Polish procuracy when discussing prosecution in general in Poland. This suggests that the police decision-making process can be influenced by the law and the Polish Criminal Justice System. However, it is challenging to argue differently because there are limited empirical studies that examine the process of law administration by various police units, which is based on the process-based model (Czapska, Radomska, & Wojcik, 2016). The current police work and practice rely mainly on the quality of police training, international cooperation (Styczynska & Beaumont, 2017; Baylis & Matczak, 2019), or the process of understanding the law; highlighting the role of police discretion in general.

Police Discretion and Decision-Making

The police discretion is not defined in Polish law, instead, the police's "good practice" has been addressed in more detail in the police code of ethics that is part of the Order of Police Commander, Number 805 from December 31, 2003. According to the Order (Article 2), "Each police officer shall follow the rules of social cohesion, whereas his/her work shall reflect the ethos of police role obeying the rule of law and improving the public trust towards the organization." The same document lists other attributes that each police officer shall have when performing his/her duties. These are kindness and impartiality in racial, national, religious, political, and worldviews or other forms of prejudice (Order of Police Commander, Number 805 from December 31, 2003, article 6). The police officer also has the power to decide how to carry out their roles but this process needs to respect human dignity and human rights (Order of Police Commander, Number 805 from December 31, 2003, article 4).

If the police officer faces challenging situations, he/she can rely on his/her supervisor, who shall offer his/her support (Order of Police Commander, Number 805 from December 31, 2003). However, what if the police officer does not understand the law and the situation fully or the superior does not offer emotional and professional support? These questions are important, especially as some Polish scholars argue that Polish criminal and civil law can be ambiguous (Novak, 2013), which means that the interpretation can be subjective (Zielinski, 2012; Bogucki, 2019), or some officers can face mobbing in their organization (Sanecki, 2017). Kapusta (2017) added to this by stating that the current operational law is inadequate as it allows the police to use covert surveillance, which is contrary to the basics of human rights. This highlights the need to review current legislation and examine the process of decision-making in general to improve the policing system, as police accountability has become a subject of political (Blaszczak, 2017) and public criticism since 1990 (Kapusta, 2017; Rapacki, 2020).

Political and Public Discourse on the Police Work

The political influence over the work of Polish police has been frequently discussed in social media and has dominated the public debate (Baczynski, 2020; Rapacki, 2020). This means that the "Policja" has faced various allegations including the use of force, ignorance, or favoritism when securing public demonstrations (Rakusa-Suszczewski, 2018) or providing safety to local politicians who take part in public gatherings when performing their duties (e.g., during the elections to the European parliament in 2009) (Jakubowski, 2009).

To protect and defend the organization's independence known as "apolitycznosc" and their image, the role of a press officer was established in 2002 (Krawczyk, 2018). Since then, the press officers work in municipal and district police stations and are the main sources of information about criminal, road, or preventive events that occur locally or regionally (Krawczyk, 2018). An official Facebook account created in 2010 and a Twitter account created in 2016 have been added to promote the police work as well. Grodek (2020) claimed that the Facebook account enables the organization to shape their image, which is mainly based on the argument that the police consists of human beings: "I am human being and nothing human is alien to me" (Grodek, 2020). This shows that interaction with Polish society has undergone a massive transformation since the 1990s and has become one of the most important tools in improving public relations and trust. However, this process can be challenging for any public policing authority. For instance, Krawczyk (2018) argued that press officers frequently questioned the professionalism of the journalists they dealt with. By professionalism, the officers referred to a lack of appropriate knowledge on the specific police work or qualifications that can improve the quality of the message that is transmitted to the public through the television, the press, or the Internet (Krawczyk, 2018). Krawczyk (2018) also stated that press officers preferred to pass or comment on specific subjects over the phone instead of arranging press conferences and that they were more willing to collaborate with reliable journalists. This approach was explained as a way of obeying the media law and other considerable police regulations, as the press officers are aware of the media's influence over the public's perception toward police work (Krawczyk, 2018).

Furthermore, an additional question shall be posed in future studies: What about the co-dependent relationship between the media and the police, which may have an impact on the quality of the material that is presented to the public? By answering this question, we could argue that various factors can be established to improve police legitimacy. This follows a common argument presented by Grimmelikhuijsen and Meijer (2015), according to whom the literature suggests that social media can increase perceived police legitimacy by enabling transparency and participation. However, the notion of transparency can be viewed as an assurance of accountability of the actors who represent specific organizations in any modern democratic state, as it has been often linked to the visibility and performance of various institutions (Brucato, 2015). In the Polish context, the behavior and the "performance" of police officers have to reflect the ethos of the formation itself but what happens when the police officers break the law and their "abusive behavior" is recorded and posted on social media or shown on television? This is what happened in Poland in 2016, where the case of Igor Stachowiak from Wroclaw, who died in police custody during May 2016, was presented and discussed by one of the most popular Polish television channels called TVN (TVN24.pl, 2017). The program featured video footage of a tasering incident obtained by a TVN journalist, which showed brutal scenes of police officers using a taser repeatedly on a 25-year-old suspect who was in handcuffs and lying on the floor of a toilet at the police station. The police behavior triggered massive media and public reactions including public demonstrations outside the police station where the event took place. The then Minister of Interior Affairs and Administration, Mr. Mariusz Blaszczak, expressed his disappointment and requested a further investigation of the case by the public prosecutor (TVN24, 2017).

Although the public prosecutor established that Igor's death was not caused by the police officer's behavior (rmf24.pl, 2017), some police officers involved in the event were sent to prison (Harlukowicz, 2020). Additionally, the Ombudsman (Commissioner of human rights) put an official request in 2017 to the Minister of Justice to investigate similar cases that took place in different parts of Poland (rpo.gov.pl, 2019). However, according to the same source, there has not been a reply questioning the slow response of the Polish officials, the police officers' integrity, and police culture in general (Ibid., 2019). Instead, the government's response was to introduce police training on how to use body-cameras in 2017 (rpo.gov.pl, 2019), which aimed to improve police transparency (policja.pl, 2019). Since then, the police training has been rolled out across Poland, whereas further police reforms have been introduced, for example, the Programme of the Modernisation of Polish public services; Police; Customs and Border Services and Fire Service and Government Protection Bureau (2017–2020) (Baylis, 2017). The government officials and the police believe that these changes will improve already existing community policing that was established after 1989 in the Polish context and address public mistrust (Ernest, 2016).

COMMUNITY POLICING AND POLICE REFORM (2017–2020)

Community policing is not defined directly in Polish law (Ernest, 2016). It often involves other actors, such as the local council, schools, or social services, who can assist the organization with addressing youth crime or minor criminal activities to improve local neighborhoods and the family and community life in general (Ostrzycka, 2015). The reactive approach was changed into proactive, where police officers called "Dzielnicowy" or the Neighborhood officers began to actively communicate and work with Polish communities by arranging public meetings and discussing various issues concerning crime and social disorder, reminiscent of the American community policing strategy (Ernest, 2016). However, the role of the Neighborhood officer was first seen as part of intelligence-led policing and was mostly chosen as the first step in the police career because some officers viewed it as a part of "soft-policing" (Ernest, 2016).

"Soft-policing" consisted of community crime prevention activities and maintenance of community safety. It was believed that this strategy would improve the relations between the police and the Polish public, who would take responsibility for their own safety by actively communicating and collaborating with the police (Urban, 2000). However, the make-up of the community the police work with is established by the Neighborhood Team officer called the "Dzielnicowy" (Ernest, 2016). The work of the "Dzielnicowy" was first questioned by the Supreme Audit Office in 2008 known as the NIK ("Najwyzsza Izba Kontroli"). This independent state audit body is subordinate to the Sejm (lower chamber of the Polish Parliament) (nik.gov.pl, n.d.) and has a mission to safeguard public spending. It conducted an inspection of the prevention strategy that was delivered by the Neighborhood Team officers in 2007 and published in an official report in 2008. The findings revealed that although the officers were performing their duties according to the law, they were also given additional work that stopped them from strengthening community relations, while some of them were not specifically trained for their role (Supreme Audit Office, 2008).

Other issues were identified as well. The geographical area they were responsible for was variable; there was a shortage of technical equipment, such as computers and printers; and the supervisors were not able to offer any bonus pay for the purpose of boosting the officers' morale and performance (Supreme Audit Office, 2008). Therefore, public perception over the importance of the NPT officers' work has decreased (Supreme Audit Office, 2008). Similar findings were revealed in 2016 by the same institution. However, on this occasion, the Supreme Audit Office highlighted a lack of vision shown by the main Police Headquarters with respect to the unutilized potential of the 8,000 NPT officers, questioning the purpose of their existence and the lack of appropriate regulations that could help to specify their duties (Supreme Audit Office, 2016). This was magnified by another finding, which showed that 81 percent of the Polish public (1,002 participants) did not personally know their NPT officer (Supreme Audit Office, 2016). To address these issues, the Polish government introduced the Programme of the Modernisation of Polish public services: Police, Customs and Border Services, Fire Services, and the Government Protection Bureau (2017–2020), and added to the existing model of policing through a newly established rank of NPT officer known as the "starszy dzielnicowy" (Baylis, 2017).

The Programme of the Modernisation of Polish public services: Police, Customs and Border Services, Fire Services and Government Protection Bureau (2017–2020) has been presented by the Polish government as one of the most important police reforms that occurred since the introduction of the Police Act in 1990 (Baylis, 2017) and has been positively welcomed by these different public bodies (policja.pl, 2019). This means that 9 208 940 PLN ("Polish Zloty") (nik .gov.pl, 2018) was given to these organizations, which allowed them to buy much needed equipment and improve their work in general. For instance, the police have spent most of the money on buying new police cars, body-cameras, and computers, and opening new police stations across the country (nik.gov.pl, 2018; infosecurity24.pl, 2019). However, it is difficult to discuss both subjects further because empirical studies on the effectiveness of community policing in Poland are limited (Czapska & Szafranska, 2015). At the same time, police reform has been seen, so far, as a short-term solution to improve the financial situation and tackle the other challenges that the police faces, including staff shortage, lack of strategy for improving the role of the NPT's officers, and a lack of a unified communication system (Supreme Audit Office, 2018). Finally, the academic debate focuses mostly on the need for adjusting current legislation

(Krawczyk, 2018; Misiuk, 2018) as well as empirically studying the highly centralized policing system in Poland (Olszewski, 2014) instead of focusing on the evaluation of the recent police reforms.

CONCLUSION

In this chapter, the history of the Polish police, which was established in 1919, has been presented and discussed. It was demonstrated that the Polish police organization has gone through various reforms to cultivate and endorse its role in a democratic country. These reforms were also linked to the need to establish and legitimate professionalism in policing in Poland, which is based on a highly centralized system, but which is starting to reflect decentralization. Various legal and extralegal factors have affected police accountability and their transparency, and have shaped the police work in general. However, the question of the interdependence of policing in the transnational state system remains, and this can be addressed by carrying out further legislative reforms and making significant changes to the police practice. This includes examining, in more detail, the political influence over the choices made by various actors of democratic policing and the operational practice of police officers, as there is limited empirical research on decision-making and their operational work in general. This would raise the awareness of the policing system within the Polish context and other actors. It would also highlight the different aspects of police work, focusing mainly on the scholarly debate on descriptive analysis of the current law and the system itself.

REFERENCES

Antyterroryzm.gov.pl. (n.d.). The Central Bureau of Investigation of the National Police Headquarters. Retrieved August 26, 2020, https://www.antyterroryzm.gov .pl/eng/anti-terrorism/institutions-and-servi/the-police/the-central-bureau-of/656 ,The-Central-Bureau-of-Investigation-of-the-National-Police-Headquarters.html.

Baran, B. (2017). Procedural justice standards in disciplinary proceedings of the police officers. *Roczniki Administracji i Prawa*, 17: 289–299.

Basińska, B. A., & Wiciak, I. (2015). Kobiety w wydziałach logistyki Policji. *Zeszyty Naukowe Uniwersytetu Szczecińskiego. Problemy Zarządzania, Finansów i Marketingu*, 41: 223–236.

Baylis, M. (2017). "Police reforms and community policing in Poland 2017–2020." In *British Society of Criminology* . Retrieved August 24, 2020, https://bscpostgrads .wordpress.com/2017/10/25/police-reforms-and-community-policing-in-poland -2017-2020-by-monika-baylis/.

Baylis, M., & Matczak, A. (2019). Tracking the evolution of police training and education in Poland: Linear developments and exciting prospects. *Police Practice and Research*, 20(3): 273–287.

Blaszczak, M. (2017) The police shall be apolitical. I am afraid we have not managed to avoid it. Retrieved August 26, 2020, https://tvn24.pl/polska/upolitycznienie -policji-alarm-zwiazkowca-i-policjanta-ra776289-2493584.

Boag-Munroe, F., Donnelly, J., van Mechelen, D., & Elliott-Davies, M. (2017). Police officers' promotion prospects and intention to leave the police. *Policing: A Journal of Policy and Practice*, 11(2): 132–145.

Bogdalski, P. (2014). Practical use of officers of police forces as teachers in the process of education for internal security: Models of a"rotational post"and"associate lecturer". *Nauka, bezbednost, policija*, 1: 97–110.

Bogucki, O. (2019). O konstytutywnej współzależności wyjaśniania i identyfikowania czynności konwencjonalnych. *Ruch Prawniczy, Ekonomiczny i Socjologiczny*, 81(2): 51–65.

Bowling, B., Robert, R., & James, S..(2019). *The Politics of the Police*. (5th ed.) Oxford University Press.

Brucato, B. (2015). The new transparency: Police violence in the context of ubiquitous surveillance. *Media and Communication*, 3(3): 39–55.

Burchardt, T. (2020, January 17). Bedzie bezpieczniej. Wspolne niemiecko-polskie patrole policji [It will be safer. German-Polish patrols].. Retrieved August 26, 2020, https://gorzow.tvp.pl/46243753/bedzie-bezpieczniej-wspolne-niemiecko -polskie-patrole-policji.

Ciarka, M. (2009). Polsko-słowackie patrole policji. Uwarunkowania prawne i praktyka na przykładzie województwa małopolskiego. *Bezpieczeństwo. Teoria i Praktyka*, 1(1–2): 71–76.

Cohen, S. (1985). *Visions of social control: Crime, Punishment, and Classification* Polity.

Czapska, J., & Szafrańska, M. (2015). *Analiza społecznych konsekwencji policyjnego programu w zakresie community policing*.

Czapska, J., Radomska, E., & Wójcik, D. (2014). Police legitimacy, procedural justice, and cooperation with the police: A Polish perspective. *Varstvoslovje*, 4.

Dudek, A., & Zblewski, Z. (2008). *Utopia nad Wisłą: Historia Peerelu*. Wydawn. Szkolne PWN.

Gawroński, P. (n.d.). Trajectories of training system for police and border force: An overview. In *Dydaktyka zawodowa: Dylematy i wyzwania [Professional didactics: Dilemmas and challenges]*, 329–340.

Grimmelikhuijsen, S. G., & Meijer, A. J. (2015). Does Twitter increase perceived police legitimacy? *Public Administration Review*, 75(4): 598–607.

Gródek, A. (2020). *Wykorzystanie Facebooka w zarządzaniu wizerunkiem Polskiej Policji*.

Harlukowicz, J. (2020, April 17). The police officers responsible for Igor Stachowiak's death are behind bars now in Wroclaw.wyborcza.pl. Retrieved August 26, 2020, https://wroclaw.wyborcza.pl/wroclaw/7,35771,25877434,policjanci-skazani-za -znecanie-nad-igorem-stachowiakiem-juz.html.

Info.policja.pl. (n.d.) The police staff numbers for 2019. Retrieved August 26, 2020, https://info.policja.pl/inf/organizacja/stan-zatrudnienia/49216,Stan-zatrudnienia -na-dzien-1-stycznia-2019-roku.html.

Info.policja.pl. (n.d.) The structure of police main headquarters. Retrieved August 26, 2020, https://info.policja.pl/inf/kierownictwo-i-struktu/struktura-kgp/86025 ,Struktura-Komendy-Glownej-Policji.html.

Info.policja.pl. (n.d.) The Polish police. Retrieved August 26, 2020, https://info .policja.pl/ine/about/190685,The-Polish-Police.html.

Infosecurity24.pl. (2019, June 13). 3 mld zloty to reform the policing services in this year). Retrieved August 15, 2020, https://www.infosecurity24.pl/3-mld-zlotych-na -modernizacje-sluzb-w-tym-roku.

Izabela, S. & Beamount, K. (2017). *Easing Legal and Administrative Obstacles in EU Border Regions: Case Study No. 8, Police Cooperation, Complexity of Structures and Rules on the Border (Germany–Poland)*. European Commission. Retrieved August 26, 2020, https://ec.europa.eu/regional_policy/sources/docgener /studies/pdf/obstacle_border/8_policy_cooperation_germany-poland.pdf.

Jakubowski, P. (2009). Strategie triki i błędy partii politycznych w kampanii parlamentarnej 2007.

Kapusta, M. (2017). *Administracyjnoprawne zagadnienia ingerencji Policji w wolności i prawa człowieka* (Doctoral dissertation).

Kiszło, T. Bezpieczeństwo Własne Policjantów Oddziału Prewencji Policji W Białymstoku W Trakcie Interwencji.

Krajewski, K. (2004). Crime and criminal justice in Poland. *European Journal of Criminology*, 1(3): 377–407.

Krajewski, K. (2012). Przestępczość w II Rzeczpospolitej w świetle danych statystycznych. *Archiwum Kryminologii*, XXXIV: 531–568.

Krawczyk, D. (2018). Organizacja i zakres działań media relations oficerów prasowych jednostek policji. *Studia Politicae Universitatis Silesiensis*, 22: 75–94.

Krystians, P. (2012). Polsko-niemiecka współpraca służb policyjnych (Lubuskie-Brandenburgia). *Rocznik Lubuski*, 38(1): 243–258.

Letkiewicz, A. & Majer, P (2011). *Polska Policja [Polish Police]*. Wyzsza Szkola Policji w Szczytnie.

Magda, E. (2016). Idea community policing w pracy polskiej Policji. *SCIENTIFIC PAPERS*, 61.

Majer, P. (2015). The anniversary of establishing the Polish police: The refelctions. *Policja 997*.

Majer, P. (n.d.). The model of Militia between 1944–1990. In *Policja w Polsce.Stan obecny i perspektywy [Police in Poland. Current situation and future perspectives]*.

Marenin, O. (1982). Parking tickets and class repression: The concept of policing in critical theories of criminal justice. *Contemporary crises*, 6(3): 241–266.

Misiuk, A. (2008). *Historia policji w Polsce: Od X wieku do współczesności*. Akademickie i Profesjonalne.

Misiuk, A. (2018) Policja Polska w świetle wypowiedzi komendantów głównych Policji w latach 1990–2018. *Securitologia*, 1: 107–126.

Nik.gov.pl. (2018). The overview of the Programme of modernisation of Polish public services.

Nik.gov.pl. (n.d.) About the Supreme Audit Office. Retrieved August 20, 2020, https://www.nik.gov.pl/o-nik/.

Nowak, A. (2013). Cyberprzestrzeń jako nowa jakość zagrożeń. *Zeszyty Naukowe AON*, 5–46.

Opis.sejm.gov.pl. (2016). Discover Sejm. http://opis.sejm.gov.pl/en/index.php.

Ostrzycka, M. (2015). Idea community policing jako źródło innowacyjnych metod współpracy społeczności lokalnych z policją w Polsce. *Przegląd Prawniczy Uniwersytetu im. Adama Mickiewicza*, 5: 111–130.

Pieprzny, S. (2011). *Policja: Organizacja i funkcjonowanie*. Wolters Kluwer.

Plywaczewski, E. (1997). Organised crime in Poland. *Transnational Organised Crime*, 3.

Police, Customs and Boarder Services, Fire Service, and Government Protection Bureau. (2017–2020). Retrieved August 20, 2020, https://www.nik.gov.pl/plik/id,21396,vp,24037.pdf.

Policja.gov.pl. (n.d.). The Internal Bureau of Police conduct. Retrieved August 26, 2020, https://policja.pl/pol/bswp/67855,Biuro-Spraw-Wewnetrznych-Policji.html.

Policja.pl. (2018). Lower number of crimes, the lowest level of fear of crime and the highest level of public trust towards the police. Retrieved August 26, 2020, https://www.policja.pl/pol/aktualnosci/161497,Mniej-przestepstw-rekordowe-poczucie-bezpieczenstwa-i-wysokie-zaufanie-do-Policj.html.

Policja.pl. (2019, February 19). The body worn cameras have been given to police officers from Rzeszow. Retrieved August 20, 2020, https://www.policja.pl/pol/aktualnosci/169851,Kamery-trafily-na-mundury-rzeszowskich-policjantow.html.

Policja.pl. (2020, February 6). The police reforms are almost finished. Retrieved August 19, 2020, https://www.policja.pl/pol/aktualnosci/169260,Realizacja-Programu-Modernizacji-Sluzb-Mundurowych-na-polmetku.html.

Rakusa-Suszczewski, M. (2018). Polityka krzywdy PiS. *Przegląd Socjologiczny*, 67(2): 119–138.

Rapacki, A. (2020, July). The politics were always there (at the police level), however, it was not so much of it then. Retrieved August 26, 2020, https://obywatele.news/rapacki-polityka-zawsze-wkraczala-do-policji-ale-nie-zawsze-bylo-to-takie-natarczywe/.

Rmf24.pl. (2017). Ziobro: The usage of the taser has not been the reason of the death of Igor Stachowiak. Retrieved August 26, 2020, https://www.rmf24.pl/fakty/polska/news-ziobro-uzycie-paralizatora-nie-bylo-przyczyna-smierci-igora-,nId,2397434.

Rpo.gov.pl. (2019, May 15). Three years after the death of Igor Stachowiak. The official statement of the commissioner of human rights. Retrieved August 20, 2020, https://www.rpo.gov.pl/pl/content/trzy-lata-po-smierci-igora-stachowiaka-oswiadczenie-rpo.

Rudnicka, M. (2017). Specyfika rozwoju zawodowego kobiet w Policji–rola płci w strukturach dyspozycyjnych. *Społeczeństwo. Edukacja. Język*, 5.

Sanecki, G. (2017). Przejawy mobbingu w środowisku pracy policjantów. *Annales Universitatis Mariae Curie-Skłodowska, sectio J–Paedagogia-Psychologia*, 29(4): 115.

Skiba, F. (2015). Policja w Polsce. *Działalność Formacji na obszarze aglomeracji miejskiej, Szczytno: Wyższa Szkoła Policji w Szczytnie.*

Stańdo-Kawecka, B. (2015). Juvenile justice in Poland. *Juvenile Justice in Global Perspective*: 291–326.

Sunshine, J., & Tyler, T. R. (2003). The role of procedural justice and legitimacy in shaping public support for policing. *Law & Society Review*, 37(3): 513–548.

Supreme Audit Office. (2008, March). Informacja o wynikach kontrolii wykonywania funkcji prewencji przez dzielnicowych w Policji [The results of control regarding the role of neighbourhood police officers – prevention units]. Retrieved August 20, 2020, https://www.nik.gov.pl/kontrole/wyniki-kontroli-nik/pobierz,px_remote _kob_p_07_090_2007052908203811180419638_01,typ,kk.pdf.

Supreme Audit Office. (2019, April 28). NIK o pracy dzielnicowych [NIK about the work of neighbourhood police officers]). Retrieved August 21, 2020,https://www .nik.gov.pl/ aktualnosci/nik-o-pracy-dzielnicowych.html.

TVN24.pl. (2017, May 20). Smierc w komisariacie. Reportaz Superwizja. Retrieved August 26, 2020, https://tvn24.pl/polska/smierc-igora-stachowiaka-w-komisaria-cie-zobacz-reportaz-superwizjera-ra741647-2506787.

TVN24 2017. (2017, May 24). Trzy minuty kwadransa poswiecil minister smierci Igora Stachowiaka.. Retrieved August 26, 2020, https://tvn24.pl/polska/sej-mowe-przemowienie-mariusza-blaszczaka-o-smierci-igora-stachowiaka-ra742693 -2454580.

Urban, B. (2000). *Zachowania dewiacyjne młodzieży*. Wydaw. Uniwersytetu Jagiellońskiego.

Zasady Eytki Zawodowej Policjanta [the Order of Police Commander, Number 805 from 31st of December 2003]. Retrieved August 26, 2020 https://isp.policja .pl/isp/prawa-czlowieka-w-poli/akty-prawne-i-dokumenty/9072,Zasady-etyki -zawodowej-policjanta.html.

Zieliński, A. (2012). Postępowanie cywilne. *Kompendium, Warszawa*, 2–3.

Chapter 8

Ministry of Internal Affairs and Police Organization in the Republic of Serbia

Dalibor Kekić, Filip Kukić, and Miloš Milenković

The police organization in the Republic of Serbia is an integral part of the Ministry of the Interior. In addition to the MoI General Police Directorate, there are also departments for emergency management, analytics, telecommunication and information technologies, international cooperation, affairs and planning, human resources, material and financial affairs, and internal control of police.

In terms of organizational structure parameters, namely departmentalization and decentralization of decision-making, the General Police Directorate represents a hybrid organizational structure and is mostly centralized. In addition to the headquarters of the General Police Directorate, within which Functional Directorates are located, it is territorially composed of twenty-seven Regional Police Directorates. Each of these directorates has at least three or more police stations on a territorial basis.

Relations between the police and the community are monitored daily through the media, and the media outlet is the Department of Media and Communication in the Cabinet of the Minister of Internal Affairs. The police perform their duty mainly through tasks and activities such as: demanding, theatrical, on-call duty, and so forth.

INTRODUCTION

Internal affairs are the activities stipulated by law that are performed by competent state authorities in order to provide security to the Republic of Serbia and its citizens and ensure the exercise of citizens' rights as laid down in the constitution and law. The Ministry of Interior (MoI) performs the state administration's internal affairs in a manner that ensures equal protection and exercise of freedoms and rights set out in the constitution for every person and citizen. In the performance of internal affairs, only such measures of coercion may be used that are envisaged by the law, thereby causing as few harmful consequences as possible for citizens and their associations, companies, institutions, and other organizations.

The MoI is a cabinet-level ministry in the Government of Serbia responsible for the protection of the security of the Republic of Serbia and detection and prevention of the activities aimed at undermining or overthrowing the constitutional order. This includes protection of life, safety and property of citizens, prevention and detection of criminal offenses, finding and apprehending perpetrators of criminal offenses and bringing them to competent authorities, maintenance of public peace and order, securing public gatherings and other assemblies of citizens, protection of certain persons and facilities, road traffic safety, border crossing checks, control of movement and stay within the border area, control of movement and stay of foreigners, provision, possession and carrying of weapons and ammunition, production and trade of explosive materials, flammable liquids and gases, fire protection, citizenship matters, personal identification, travel documents, checks on permanent and temporary residences, staff training, and other tasks envisaged by the law (Ministry of Interior).

To ensure that these tasks are performed, the MoI has at its disposal local and national police services with municipal and district branches throughout the country. Their core responsibilities are crime prevention, criminal apprehension, investigations, customs and border control, counterterrorism, anti-corruption, anti-narcotics, and disaster relief. Moreover, through its local branches, the MoI is also responsible for issuing passports and personal identification to citizens.

Organizational structure of the MoI of the Republic of Serbia relies on functional grouping of jobs in an old but also the most widespread form of grouping jobs into organizational sectors. The law stipulates that the MoI, which is established by the Law on Ministries, performs the internal affairs of the state administration. Thereby, in accordance with the nature of the tasks and duties assigned to the MoI, the law regulates the boundaries within which the police may operate to accomplish the tasks. In accordance with the nature of the tasks and duties assigned to this Ministry, the Law on Police in a special way (in relation to other) regulated bases of and structured police organization.

The organization of the police in Serbia is centralized, meaning that decisions on regulations, procedures, authorizations, and so forth are made at the level of the ministry and applied nationally and locally. Therefore, its hierarchical structure is vertically differentiated, whereby the higher the managerial level of the hierarchy, the higher the level of managerial authority (i.e., decision power), but also the responsibility. The Minister of Interior makes all decisions on the functioning of the MoI, whereby the manner of its management is poorly regulated. On the contrary, but for the purpose of lawful and democratic performance of internal affairs, the civilian government, and various NGOs and international organizations influence the Minister of the Interior in making decisions and organizing the work of the MoI. There is a high degree of decentralization of the affairs in the MoI, but the chain of command and responsibility is also clearly defined.

Functional structure of the group positions is the oldest but also the most widespread form of grouping jobs into organizational sectors. Exactly such grouping of positions was done during the classification of the MoI, forming six sectors and one directorate:

• Sector for analytics, telecommunication, and information technologies,
• Sector for international cooperation, European Union (EU) affairs and planning,
• Sector for human resources,
• Sector for material and financial affairs,
• Sector for internal control of police,
• Emergency management sector.

The Sector for analytics, telecommunication and information technologies performs tasks that primarily provide conditions for the functioning of the General Police Directorate and other organizational units of the MoI (i.e., functioning and protection of the information system and network infrastructure). The activities of the sector refer to the organization, development, and operation of the integrated information system of the Ministry.

Furthermore, this sector is involved in planning, construction, supervision and use of telecommunication systems and crypto security systems as well as planning, monitoring, and implementation of measures in the field of information security. For the citizens of the Republic of Serbia, this sector performs a significant part of the work through the preparation, processing, and personalization of travel documents and identification documents. In order to ensure the protection of personal data, standards in line with the highest EU standards are applied and monitored.

The Sector for international cooperation, EU affairs, and planning is responsible for planning and organizing the European integration process, setting directions and goals in the priority areas of work of the MoI and equalizing the procedures to those set by EU. The sector works on planning and managing projects financed by the EU funds and other international sources.

The Sector for Human Resources performs tasks that provide conditions for the smooth functioning of the General Police Directorate and other organizational units of the MoI, in connection with the function of human resources management. The Sector, in coordination with other organizational units of the Ministry, creates and implements human resources development strategies and human resources management policies. It harmonizes processes, systems, and practices of human resources management with strategic goals and the needs of the Ministry and evaluates and improves management quality of human resources throughout the Ministry's sectors.

Sector for Material and Financial Affairs establishes, manages, and coordinates the work of the logistics department at the level of the Ministry, reviews and analyzes the needs of the General Police Directorate and organizational units at the headquarters of the Ministry. It manages and monitors immovable and movable property in the regime of use of the Ministry and performs commercial and property storage activities.

The Sector for Internal Control of Police performs internal control over the work of police officers and other employees in the Ministry, especially with regard to respect and protection of human and minority rights and freedoms in performing official tasks and exercising police powers, that is, in performing tasks within the legal and lawful scope (Ministry of Interior).

The Emergency management sector performs normative, administrative, organizational-technical, preventive, operational, programing, planning, informational, and other activities. The purpose of this sector is organizing and implementing measures for the protection and rescue of people, material and cultural goods, and the environment from natural disasters, technical-technological accidents—accidents and catastrophes, consequences of terrorism, war and other major accidents. The head of the sector may decide to form specialist protection and rescue teams from the members of the sector, depending on the specificity of intervention.

The General Police Directorate of the MoI is organized into what many consider a seventh sector. It is responsible for the performance of police duties, which are, together with the competences and powers, governed by the Law on Police.

THE GENERAL POLICE DIRECTORATE OF THE MINISTRY OF THE INTERIOR

The organization of the headquarters of the General Police Directorate is composed of functionally (diagonally) connected organizational units, with a well-established hierarchical structure of police stations and substations, so that they perform tasks within their scope, covering the entire territory of the Republic of Serbia. Police duties are performed by uniformed and crime investigation officers such as employees who exercise police powers, as well as the personnel having special or specific tasks, which are directly related to police duties. In addition, special purpose police units have been formed at the Headquarters of the General Police Directorate, which differ from its functionally and territorially differentiated organizational units in that they are intended for performing special security tasks.

The General Police Directorate Headquarters comprises the following organizational units:

Bureau of the Police Director,
Department for the Improvement of the Work of the General Police Directorate,
Directorates at the Headquarters (12),
Coordination Directorate for Kosovo and Metohija,
The General Police Directorate also comprises twenty-seven regional police directorates.

Grouping of positions was done during the classification for the organizational unites of the General Police Directorate in the seat. Organizational units of the General Police Directorate in the seat:

1. Department for improvement of work of General Police Directorate,
2. Bureau of the Police Director,
3. Criminal Investigations Directorate,
4. Directorate for International Operational Police Cooperation,
5. Uniformed Police Directorate,
6. Security Unit Protecting Specific Persons and Facilities,
7. Protection Unit,
8. Traffic Police Directorate,
9. Border Police Directorate,
10. Administrative Affairs Directorate,
11. Operations Center,
12. Gendarmerie,
13. Special Anti-Terrorist Unit,
14. Helicopter Unit,
15. Coordination Directorate for Kosovo and Metohija.

Organizational units of the General Police Directorate outside the seat are Regional Police Directorates, and there are twenty-seven territorially differentiated organizational units. These regional police directorates are divided according to geographical categories. Each regional police directorate, in terms of territorial differentiation, consists of police stations in the seat and outside the seat of the regional police directorate. The main task of the organizational units of the general directorate outside its headquarters is to perform all tasks within its competence in the territory for which they were formed. Regional police directorates are the basic territorial organizational units of the Directorate (Ministry of Interior).

This kind of organizational structure of the general police directorate suggests that this is a hybrid organizational structure. Territorial differentiation of a regional police directorate coincides with administrative territorial structure. Namely, the area of one police station is equal to the administrative territory of one municipality (Stevanović, 2019, pp. 134–144).

COMPOSITION OF POLICE STATIONS

The security sector is the basic unit territory of the police, and it is formed in the area of the police station and includes a certain natural and security unit, where the security situation can be efficiently monitored and the execution of tasks and duties within the scope of work of the MoI can be organized. The security sector covers the area of one or more local communities. The traffic sector is formed in the area of the traffic police station or police station and includes a number of streets, squares, and intersections in cities and larger settlements, or roads outside populated areas, and on freeways, highways, and regional roads. Police stations' staff of general and traffic jurisdiction, through stage, patrol, operational activities, traffic control and regulation, and other activities, perform their duties in the security sector.

Police affairs and tasks are mostly related to the field as security issues are mostly manifested on the ground, which further implies that officers from police stations perform the largest volume of police work. Thus, they are the first to be "hit" by various events. The heads of the sector and police officers who know their community, territory, and potential security issues perform assignments in the security sector. Citizens are the first to notice "sectoral police officers"; they are in constant contact with them, and it is unnecessary to discuss the importance of citizens' perception of police activities and police organization in general for any society. Good relations between the police and citizens are a prerequisite for achieving a satisfactory level of security in the community. The head of the sector also participates in the organization of work and assigns the tasks to officers, keeps the necessary records, and performs other tasks assigned to him by superior officers from the units that are ranked higher in hierarchy (Subošić, 2019, pp. 118–126).

In addition to the head of the sector and uniformed police officers, a certain number of criminal investigation police operatives in civilian clothes perform the tasks and duties in the sector as well. All security affairs are performed in the security sector, which is very important to emphasize. Although the security sector enters the domain of the territorial organization of the police service, it is also a stronghold for all other bodies dealing with security affairs. Any activity related to a security event undertaken by any subject of the security system begins with the collection of information in the local community (i.e., police officers who are familiar with local security and local issues).

Sectoral affairs have numerous points of contact with the new concept of community policing. In Serbia, affairs in the security sector are traditionally nurtured. As part of the sectoral affairs, the police organization adapted to local needs, and officers in the sector, by the nature of their work, established certain relations with citizens. However, within the concept of community policing and the application of methods and techniques remains the possibility of improving these relations. There is a wide range of programs and techniques that result from community policing, which can improve sectoral affairs—geographical focus, emphasis on prevention, problem-oriented approach, positive interactions with citizens, the concept of teamwork, and so forth.

Police officers' district area and patrol activities are the basic way of territorial and preventive-repressive performance of police affairs, with the aim of maintaining public order, preventing crimes and misdemeanors, apprehending their perpetrators, bringing them to the competent authorities and assisting people in the security sector. Both activities can be performed on foot, while the officers' activity is usually performed by hiring a uniformed police officer in one officers' district area, with the possibility of hiring at least one more police officer for security reasons. The Chief of the Regional Police Directorate determines the patrol and stage areas within the security sectors by a written decision, depending on the number and importance of the facilities; population density; traffic densities; states of public order and peace; structure and number of committed crimes and misdemeanors; and other circumstances of importance for security reasons (Subošić, 2019, pp. 94–95).

Officers' district areas are formed in cities, larger settlements, industrial centers, and certain tourist settlements. The officers' district area is being formed in a smaller part of the security sector. The patrol area is a part of the security sector that is larger than the officers' district area. The first category security sectors usually contain two patrol regions, while the sectors contain only one patrol region.

Operational activities are aimed at identifying crimes and their perpetrators. This activity accomplishes preventive and repressive tasks. Preventive tasks are solved mainly through criminal checks, gathering information, restricting movement in a certain area, determining the identity of persons, surveillance, and criminal control. The permanent duty service in organizational units of the police is organized continuously in all organizational units of the police.

Police stations within regional police directorates are organizationally formed to perform all police work and cooperate with bodies and organizational units of local government on the territory of one municipality. Police stations typically include a crime prevention department (group), police substations (one or more of the same competencies), and department (group) for administrative affairs, while in border municipalities police stations additionally have a group for border control and administrative affairs. The police substation consists of uniformed police officers. However, whether a police station will have substations depends on the size of the municipality that the police station covers.

A Police substation (sometimes more than one), may be with or without police departments. The area of the police station is a part of the territory where police officers perform specific tasks to ensure greater security in the local area. On the territory of the police station, criminal investigation officers play the most important role in the suppression of crime. The criminal investigation police is responsible for carrying out and organizing work pertaining to the detection and combat of all forms of organized crime. Moreover, the officers of this department plan and organize information and reporting, and coordinate the service and application of operational-technical and tactical measures to clarify and document all criminal offenses in accordance with the law.

Police Affairs

Police of the Republic of Serbia apply the police intelligence model, thereby managing police affairs based on criminal intelligence information, which is the basis for making performative decisions in police affairs.

Crime prevention and community security are developed through problem-oriented policing and the implementation of prevention programs and planning activities. Nonpolice partners that contribute to solving various security problems of the community are also supported, with the aim of developing a security culture and strengthening community awareness about the importance of prevention. The police perform activities of prevention, detection, and clarification of criminal offenses using modern criminal and other scientific disciplines and legally prescribed methods, measures, and actions in order to fight against the various forms of crime and terrorism. Some of these tasks include, but are not limited to, observations of territories, points of interest, objects, persons, or groups and the collection of information from various sources (i.e., written, oral, telephone, anonymous), and so forth. Using a combination of these techniques and methods, the police detects and arrests perpetrators of criminal acts and misdemeanors and brings them to the competent authorities.

Furthermore, police affairs include the maintenance and safeguarding of public order at sporting events and other public gatherings, whereby the proportion of police at these events as well as the type of officers corresponds to the potential threat (i.e., dealing with football fans or securing the fun festival). The police assist the competent authorities, individuals, and legal entities in order to enable the safe implementation of enforcement. The tasks of regulation and control, providing assistance in traffic on the roads, riot control, and other tasks in the field of safety are performed in the manner prescribed by the law and regulations in the field of traffic safety. Safeguarding affairs are graded as regular safeguard, extraordinary safeguard, and special safeguard. Security protection of certain persons and facilities includes the undertaking of preventive and security measures, measures of preventive and technical protection, measures of physical protection, and measures of preventive and medical protection.

State border control, activities related to the movement and residence of foreigners, asylum, cross-border crime, irregular migration, and readmission are performed in the manner prescribed by law and bylaws and international regulations. In order to achieve the optimal level of efficiency in the use of human and technical resources, the tasks are organized based on the situational analysis and risk assessment, following an established risk analysis.

Certain tasks and tasks performed by the police in Serbia are not very typical for some other European police. In addition, individual affairs are not regulated by single acts, but by a series of several acts. So, the tasks determined by the regulations on weapons, private security and detective activity are performed in the manner prescribed by law and bylaws that regulate the conduct of administrative procedures and the procedure of supervising the application of regulations in these areas. The security protection of the MoI is one of the important tasks of the police. The police, in accordance with their scope determined by law, prepare for action during a state of emergency or war and perform other tasks and duties.

With the arrival of the multiparty political system of the former Yugoslavia, the reform processes of the security system, including the police, has started. General goals of the new program orientations of Serbian police activity reflected in increasing efficiency in work, creating stronger relations between citizens and the police, and so forth. The two most important concepts of policing that have emerged are community policing and the police intelligence model.

Community policing involves a partnership between the police and citizens. Both work together to identify and solve problems in the community. There have been some positive results in the application of this concept in the Republic of Serbia, but it should be said that it has not been fully implemented yet. The reasons lie in a number of political, economic, social, historical and other factors. Police culture, still burdened by the achievements of the previous system, has stood in the way as a stumbling block to the new concept.

The term Police-Intelligence Model (Intelligence-led Policing) means the system according to which criminal-intelligence information forms the basis for defining priorities, strategies, and operational goals in the field of prevention and suppression of crime and other security threats. Furthermore, it is used for the adoption of appropriate decisions on operational police affairs and actions, rational engagement of available personnel, and allocation of material and technical resources. It is a new concept of data management in the police (similar to those of intelligence agencies) and management of material and human resources. Successful implementation implies some small changes in the internal organization and systematization of jobs, along with some substantial changes. The introduction of a police intelligence model is an obligation from chapter 24 ("Justice, Freedom, and Security") of negotiations for accession to the EU. The MoI of Serbia is undertaking significant activities in order to fully implement the model according to the issued manual that describes the specific details of the model, specific activities, and measures.

Forms of Police Activity

In the Republic of Serbia, internal affairs are affairs determined by law, by the performance of which the competent government bodies realize the security of the Republic and its citizens and ensure the realization of the other rights of citizens determined by the Constitution and the law. The MoI performs the internal affairs of the state administration. Within the MoI, the general police directorate acts as the operational body in charge of police affairs, by applying police measures, actions, and police powers.

Analyzing the legal enumeration of police affairs (i.e., their scope), affairs are marked as detection and clarification of criminal offenses, misdemeanors, and other offenses as well as their prevention and suppression. It is important to note that criminal offenses and misdemeanors form a dominant part of police activities. Crime prevention and crime suppression activities such as pretort and posttort conduct of the police permeate the entire activity of the police.

In Serbia, there is a strictly centralized system of state administration that cannot be assessed as sufficiently effective in the fight against crime or in ensuring the safety of citizens. Therefore, the possibility of transferring some competencies to local governments should be seriously considered (Subošić, 2019, pp. 58–62). For instance, the criminal investigation police is organized and specializes in crime prevention. Within the criminal investigation police, specializations for certain forms of crime are represented. The Traffic Police specializes in traffic safety, that is, control and regulation of traffic on the roads. The Border Police specializes in the control of crossing the state border, securing the state border and controlling the movement of persons in the border zone.

In addition to police officers of general jurisdiction, criminal investigation police officers also play an active role in combating crime on the territory of the police station. The criminal investigation police is responsible for carrying out and organizing work in detecting and combating all forms of organized crime, as well as preventing and combating other forms of crime (Milidragović & Milić, 2019, pp. 63–81). It further plans and organizes timely information and reporting, coordination of the work of services, and the application of operational-technical and tactical measures in order to clarify and document all criminal acts.

The police of general jurisdiction undertake, independently or in cooperation with the criminal investigation police, various measures and actions with the aim of combating crime. Police officers of general jurisdiction perform a much wider range of tasks than the members of the criminal police specialized in combating crime. A high level of specialization in the police provides the blade for battling specific problems while at the same time being too narrow for many other offenses. Thereby, police officers of general jurisdiction provide greater support and ensure smoother processes in obtaining the organization's goals. For instance, special task units are engaged when the complexity exceeds the capabilities of general jurisdiction officers (Milidragović & Milić, 2019, pp. 63–81). Such units include gendarmerie, special antiterrorist unit, units for protections of special persons and affairs, helicopter unit, police brigade, and intervention units.

Activities and tasks related to the implementation of the concept of community policing are the exclusive competence of police officers of general competence. The fact that this concept is also important for the criminal investigation police has unfortunately been ignored so far, because it is wrongly perceived and performed in repressive activities. The activities of the criminal investigation police are understood exclusively as post-criminal, and they are expected to shed light on criminal acts and catch the perpetrators. Their cooperation with citizens is based on gathering information important for the criminal processing of a certain criminal act.

Specific purpose police units are intended for tasks whose complexity exceeds the capabilities of police units intended to perform regular security tasks. These units are intended for the suppression of serious forms of crime, civil riots, terrorism, armed riots, as well as for the performance of other specific security tasks. Permanent specific purpose police units operate continuously. Therefore, these are the police units that exist regardless of the need for their current engagement. Such units include Gendarmerie, the Special

Antiterrorist Unit, the Unit for Protections of Special Persons and Affairs, the Helicopter Unit, the Police Brigade (within the Police Regional Directorate for the City of Belgrade), but also Intervention Unit 92 (within the Police Regional Directorate for the City of Belgrade).

There are also periodical specific purpose police units. Examples of such units are the police intervention units, the negotiating team, and the operative groups in the criminal investigation police. Since in some extreme cases (emergencies), regular members are not enough, an alternative to solving the problem can be found in the subsidiary police. However, the problem is that the subsidiary police is still not relevant as a subsidiary instrument in the police due to the current political circumstances and machinations (the basic problem is the current situation in Serbian society).

The position of the public prosecutor and the police in the phases of reconnaissance of criminal offenses and perpetrators, which precede the court criminal procedure, is regulated by procedural codes on a strict hierarchical relationship of these bodies. In all situations, the public prosecutor is the superior body to the police. In the preinvestigation, the public prosecutor directs the activity of the police, while in the investigation phase, the prosecutor is the joinder. Because the performance of their functions is based on a solid hierarchical principle (functional hierarchy), from which the leading role of the public (state) prosecutor springs, it is not possible to talk about cooperation between the public prosecutor and the police other than in an order-execution relationship. The relationship between the public prosecutor and the police is influenced by the regulations of the function of criminal prosecution and the function of reconnaissance of criminal acts and perpetrators, contained in the criminal procedural and organizational procedural law (Đurđić et al., 2017, pp. 36–41).

The public prosecutor and the police appear as the bodies of the procedure in the investigation, when he/she entrusts it with the implementation of evidentiary actions. The pretrial judge is not authorized to take evidentiary actions at all, but appears only as a protector of freedoms and rights during the investigation. The public prosecutor in the investigation may take any evidentiary action, and its results have the same evidentiary force as if it had been taken by a court or before a court. In addition, the competent public prosecutor may entrust the police with the performance of certain evidentiary actions. In order to have probative value, the police must take them in the procedural form prescribed for the evidentiary action entrusted to the police, such as when that action is taken before a court. The attitude of the public prosecutor from the preinvestigation is reflected in the investigation and it is obvious that the public prosecutor, as a body of procedure, has a superior position over the police. The public prosecutor may request criminal-technical assistance from the police. The law authorizes the public prosecutor for cases when he/she needs forensic, analytical or any other police assistance in connection with the investigation, to request that assistance, and the police are obliged to provide the requested assistance.

Control of Police

Sector for internal control of police is tasked with the internal control of police. There are two other bodies within the organizational structure that are responsible for internal oversight: the Department for Legality Oversight of Policing and the Section for Legality Monitoring and Oversight in the Gendarmerie.

Internal oversight of policing can take a number of different forms. The most basic of these is hierarchical oversight, which rests on the fact that each officer answers to his or her superior and is similar to a military chain of command. This form of oversight is not insignificant as officers of any rank depend, to an extent, on their immediate superiors, and can also act across the boundaries of the General Police Directorate and extend as far as the MoI, to whom the General Police Director answers.

The Internal Audit Service audits business processes within the competence of the MoI as defined by the Law on Ministries, in the manner provided by the Rulebook on common criteria for organization and standards and methodological instructions for conducting and reporting internal audit in the public sector. The scope of work of internal audit also includes the audit of EU funds, as well as all other resources provided by other international bodies and institutions, intended for the implementation of international programs and projects in accordance with concluded international agreements. The Internal Audit Service cooperates with the sector for internal control of the MoI, the State Audit Institution, other state bodies, and international and domestic professional institutions and associations.

The National Assembly, the Government, the Protector of Citizens, and the courts control the MoI. Independent regulatory bodies also exercise democratic control: the State Audit Institution, the Commissioner for Information of Public Importance and Personal Data Protection, and the Commissioner for the Protection of Equality. The National Mechanism for the Prevention of Torture, established based on the European Convention, has been developed as an important segment of the democratic control of the work of the Ministry of the Interior (Stevanović, 2019, pp. 245–269).

The Anti-Corruption Agency initiates and conducts the procedure for determining conflicts of interest or violations of the law by MoI officials. In the form of a notification, it warns the body about the nonsubmission of reports on the property and income of MoI officials, the right to use apartments for official needs, property and income of spouses, and so forth. The

Commissioner for the Protection of Equality has a control function over the work of the police, and the following mechanisms are available to him: procedure for citizens' complaints, conciliation procedure, opinion and recommendations, issuance of warnings in case of noncompliance with recommendations, and so forth.

Control of the police affairs by citizens is provided in the first place through the possibility of filing complaints if they believe that actions or omission of police officers in the performance of official tasks has violated human rights and civil liberties. Also, the subject of the complaint may be the work of an organizational unit within the MoI. The first-instance procedure for reviewing complaints takes place before the immediate superior of the police officer to whom the complaint relates, while the second-instance procedure is conducted before a commission of three members. In addition to the representatives of the MoI, the members of the commission are also representatives of the public, appointed by the Minister. The Minister appoints the public representatives on the proposal of professional public and nongovernmental organizations (dealing with the protection of human and minority rights). Members of the commissions in police administrations are elected on the proposal of local government bodies.

Citizens can also control the police through other means and institutes such as petitions or local plenums of citizens. In the practice of the Serbian police, the use of these legal possibilities has not been recorded so far, but can be expected with the development of the society and the consciousness of the citizens.

Police–Community Relations

The MoI entrusted the representation of the Ministry in public, information and cooperation with the media; with the daily activities of the Bureau for Cooperation with the Media, an organizational unit in the Cabinet of the Minister of the Interior. By daily monitoring of the published information on MoI's activities in the media, the Bureau enables the Ministry to react in a timely manner to incorrectly presented information. By analyzing the way in which the media present the activities of the MoI, the authorities in the Ministry gain insight into the opinion of the public, as well as the problems of citizens related to the work of the MoI. The Bureau for Cooperation with Media is in constant contact with all spokespersons from the regional police directorates.

In relations with the media, the police act in accordance with the law and according to professional guidelines issued by the Minister. At the level of regional police directorate, they perform the task of communicating with the media spokespersons. There is no formal employee in any police department appointed solely as spokesperson, whose sole task would be to communicate with the media. Acting as media contacts is just one of their duties. Spokespersons consult with investigating judges and competent public prosecutors and seek the consent of judicial authorities to provide information, so as not to jeopardize the efficient conduct of criminal proceedings.

Public opinion has a great influence on the activities of the police and is a significant corrective mechanism. The public can condemn or praise certain police activities, especially those related to the suppression of crime, riots, traffic safety, and the like. To prevent public dissatisfaction, police executives must respond in a timely manner and check the attitudes, opinions and views of the public before undertaking activities that may cause public outcry (i.e., when providing police assistance in enforcement of law).

At the request of the journalist on the requested topics, the spokesperson or the authorized person should respond as soon as possible and no later than forty-eight hours from the receipt of the request. If they are due to the interest of the investigation or some other reason (i.e., data is based an official secret), police cannot respond to a journalist's request. However, an explanation must be provided to the journalist or editor without delay. Trust in the police in the Republic of Serbia grows along with the perception of transparency, while it decreases if the police work is politicized. Although the public perceives that there is high politicization and corruption in the police, it is obvious that it does not significantly affect the trust in the police. Therefore, it appears that the citizens recognize the importance of police for their safety and security despite noticing the ubiquitous of corruption or lack of trust due to the influence of politics on the operational work of the police.

Public research from 2018 indicates that there is a picture of the existence of deep corruption in Serbia. For only three of the twelve institutions offered, the perception of corruption is below 50 percent, while the health, police, judiciary and media are at the top of the list when it comes to the perception of corruption. That is why it should come as no surprise that the citizens of the Republic of Serbia rely primarily on themselves and not on state institutions when it comes to security. In the Republic of Serbia, only one in four citizens trust the police to protect them (Đorđević & Elek, 2018, pp. 4–8).

CONCLUSION

Organization of the police in Serbia is unique and centralized. Centralization of police in Serbia stems from the fact that its structure is vertically differentiated, where the relation is valid. Grouping of positions was done during the classification of the Ministry. There are six sectors and a General Police Directorate. Organizational units at the headquarters of the General Police

Directorate are formed so that they are functionally (diagonally) connected to the appropriate organizational units of Regional Police Directorates, police stations and substations, so that they perform tasks within their scope in the entire territory of the Republic of Serbia.

Police affairs and tasks are mostly related to the field, because security issues are also manifested on the ground. The security sector is the basic unit territory of the police and it has been formed in the area of the police station and includes a certain natural and security unit, where the security situation can be efficiently monitored along with the execution of tasks and duties. The security sector is the basic territorial unit of the police, and it has been formed in the area of the police station and includes a certain natural and security unit, where the security situation can be efficiently monitored along with the execution of tasks and duties.

Serbian police apply the Police Intelligence Model in performing police affairs. It is a new concept of data management in the police, management of material and human resources. Crime prevention and crime suppression activities such as pretort conduct and posttort conduct of the police, permeate the entire activity of the police.

There are bodies within the organizational structure that are responsible for internal oversight—Sector for Internal Control, Department for Legality Oversight of Policing, and the Section for Legality Monitoring and Oversight in the Gendarmerie. The Anti-Corruption Agency and citizens can also control the police.

Public opinion has a great influence on the activities of the police and it has been a significant corrective mechanism in the Republic of Serbia. Information and cooperation with the media is handled through the daily activities of the Bureau for Cooperation with the Media, an organizational unit in the Cabinet of the Minister of the Interior.

REFERENCES

Association of Public Prosecutors and Deputy Public Prosecutors of Serbia, Kingdom of Netherlands. [Original: Đurđić, Vojislav, i drugi. (2017). *Javno tužilaštvo i policija*. Udruženje javnih tužilaca i zamenika javnih tužilaca Srbije, Kraljevina Hollandija].

Đorđević, Saša, and Elek, Bojan. (2018). *The Public in Serbia on Police: Results of the 2018 Public Opinion Survey*. Belgrade Centre for Security Policy.

Đurđić, Vojislav, Ilić Goran, Lazić Radovan, Miletić Livija Panić, Lazović Lazar, Nenadić Svetlana, Dedić Miljan, Zorić Tomo, Jovanović Dragan, Porubović L. Vujanović and Bošković M. Matić. (2017). *Public Prosecutor's Office and Police*.

Milidragović, Dragan, and Milić, Nenad. (2019). Results and problems of police of general jurisdiction in combating crime. *NBP: Journal of Criminalistics and Law,* 24(1): 63–81. [Original: Milidragović, Dragan, and Milić, Nenad. (2019). ''Rezultati i problemi policije opšte nadležnosti u suzbijanju kriminala. *"NBP: Žurnal za kriminalistiku i pravo,* 24(1): 63–81.]

Ministry of Interior. (n. d.) The General Police Directorate of the Ministry of the Interior. Accessed July 7, 2020 Retrieved. http://mup.gov.rs/wps/portal/en/ directorate.

Stevanović, Obrad. (2019). *Security management.* University of Criminal Investigation and Police Studies. [Original: Stevanović; O. (2019). Bezbednosni menadžment. Kriminalističko-policijski univerzitet].

Subošić, Dane. (2019). *Police Organization and Operations.* University of Criminal Investigation and Police Studies. [Original: Subošić, Dane. (2019). *Organizacija i poslovi policije.* Kriminalističko-policijski univerzitet].

Part III

ASIA AND OCEANIA

Chapter 9

The Chinese Police

Structure, Police–Public Relations, and Deviance

Mengliang Dai and Yunyun Yang

As an instrument of social control, the criminal justice system is structured differently in different countries. In China, the public security organs (or the police departments), the procuratorates, and the courts constitute the basic elements of the Chinese criminal justice system. They form an important state machinery analogous to workshops in a factory in which the public security organs perform the first procedure and provide the other two organs the materials for later processing.[1] Due to the critical role of the public security organs, the Chinese Communist Party (CCP) uses them as a weapon of self-preservation and has strengthened its control over the police organs under Chairman Xi's leadership. The public security organs have undergone several reforms in their organizational structures and leadership.

This chapter mainly selects three aspects and presents an overview of Chinese policing. First, it describes the leadership system and organizational components, especially with regard to the recent reform of special public security organs and the Chinese People's Armed Police Force (CPAPF). Then, it discusses the causes of worsening police–public relations. Lastly, the chapter describes police deviance, including the types and causes. In short, in a one-party regime, public security organs are deemed the most important tool for maintaining social stability. It is hard to relax the tensions between citizens and the police. This issue is exacerbated by the surety that police deviance will frequently occur.

BRIEF HISTORY

There was no official police agency when the CCP was formally established in July 1921. To protect the Central Committee of the CCP and its leaders, gather intelligence, rescue the detained, and send intelligence to revolutionary base areas, the Central Intelligence Agency (*zhongyang teke*) was created in 1927. It successively set up the general office, intelligence office, action office, and traffic office. Guo (2012) thought that the agency played an important role in shaping the philosophy, mechanism, and organizational structure of the CCP regimes' public security organs. The State Political Security Bureau (*zhengzhi baoweiju*) was also set up when the CCP established the Chinese Soviet Republic in November 1931. Its mission was mainly concerned with investigating, suppressing, and wiping out counterrevolutionary activities and with the extermination of banditry. On February 17, 1939, due to attempts by traitors and die-hards to infiltrate and destroy the work of the party, the CCP set up the Social Affairs Department, which became the leading agency for the elimination of traitors. As Xu and Yang (2018) mentioned, all of these agencies took on some wartime characteristics, and their works went beyond traditional policing functions. The Social Affairs Department had been structured as an intelligence agency, rather than as a security services agency (Guo, 2012). With the establishment of the People's Republic of China (PRC), the CCP decided to scrap the Social Affairs Department and set up the MPS. On November 5, 1949, the inaugural meeting was held in Beijing. The establishment of the MPS was an important step toward the institutionalization of the CCP's security apparatus (Guo, 2012). In the 1950s, to defend the regime, the police devoted themselves to putting down counterrevolutionaries, launched an anti-drugs campaign, and shut down brothels. In the 1960s and 1970s, due to the Great Proletarian Cultural Revolution, the public security organs implemented military regulations. After the downfall of the Gang of Four in 1976, the policing work was gradually restored.

THE ORGANIZATIONAL STRUCTURE

Leadership System

Before understanding the leadership system of the public security organs, the authoritative feature needs to be noted. In a one-party state, the CCP has an absolute monopoly on power and controls all sectors of the country (Kornai 1992). Although the party and the government are nominally separate, the actual leadership is in the hands of the CCP. Party committees and party groups are established at all levels, through which the CCP can achieve control in all organizations (Wright, 2015). Therefore, the public security organs are also under the absolute leadership of the CCP.

Specifically, the leadership system of the public security organs in China is typically stated as follows: unified leadership (*tongyi lingdao*), different levels of management (*fenji guanli*), and integration of horizontal and vertical management (*tiaokuai jiehe*) with a greater emphasis on horizontal management (*yikuai weizhu*). *Tongyi lingdao* means that the national public security organs are under the leadership of the CCP and the government. *Fenji guanli* means that the MPS is under the leadership of the State Council; local public security organs at different levels are under the leadership of the local party committees and governments at the corresponding levels. *Tiaokuai jiehe* means that public security organs are under the leadership of public security organs at higher levels and of the party committee and the government at the corresponding levels. *Yikuai weizhu* means that the leader of the party committee and local governments is dominated. More specifically, the local party committee and governments control the personnel and expenditures; deciding, for example, the appointment of the chiefs of local public security organs. Local financial revenue differences influence the expenditure of the local public security organs. Problems also exist in the capital public security bureau. There has been quite a difference between the municipal public security bureau, the municipal sub-bureaus, and the sub-bureaus in Beijing (Wei, 2017).

The reason why dual leadership has been adopted is twofold: when the CCP learned the Soviet model and used vertical leadership, it caused multiple problems. Additionally, local governments have a greater awareness of actual circumstances and can accurately determine priorities in policing (Dai 2008; Tanner & Green, 2007). However, the present dual leadership system also leads to some issues; for example, to boost their image, local governments falsely report public security situations; the police participate in more non-policing activities under the direction of local governments; and the local governments disobey central directives (Tanner & Green, 2007; Xu, 2013).

Moreover, as the sole governing party, the CCP manages the whole country through various leading small groups or committees, such as the Leading Small Group for Education Work, the Financial and Economic Committee, and so on. The CCP has established the Political-Legal Commission (PLC), which is responsible for political and legal affairs and oversees all legal enforcement authorities, such as the police department, the courts, and the procuracy (see Scoggins, 2018). Its main responsibility is to guide, coordinate, and supervise these political-legal organs (Zhong & Dai, 2019). All the party committees of provinces, municipalities, and counties establish their respective political-legal committees.

Organization Components

Central Public Security Organ

The Central Public Security Organ is the MPS. According to Article 3 of the Organic Administration Regulation of Public Security Organs, the MPS is the organ that leads and commands the national public security work. Currently, the leaders consist of one minister, five vice ministers, one team leader of discipline inspection and supervision, one commissioner of anti-terrorism, and two assistant ministers.[2] The MPS consists of the following twenty-one units: the general office, information command center, research center, supervision and audit, personnel and training, propaganda, criminal investigation, economic crime investigation, public order administration, counterterrorism, food, and drug crime investigation, the secret service, railway public security, network security protection, prison and detention house administration, logistics, traffic administration, legal affairs, equipment finance, international cooperation, narcotics control, and scientific and technical information.[3]

Local Public Security Organs

As mentioned earlier, local public security organs at various levels are directed by higher-level organs, but the first priority is given to the party committees and governments at the same level, which provide financial resources and personnel arrangements. A general model of local public security organs from highest to lowest rank include the following: (1) the provincial level, which is called the public security department (*gong'an ting*) in twenty-three provinces and five autonomous regions and the public security bureau (*gong'an ju*) in the four centrally administrated municipalities;[4] (2) the prefectural level, which is set in prefecture-level cities (*diji shi*) and the autonomous prefectures (*zizhi zhou*), also referred to as the public security bureaus; (3) the county level, which exists in the county-level cities', counties', and autonomous counties' public security bureaus; and (4) the dispatched agencies (*paichu jigou*), which include public security sub-bureaus and police stations. Article 6 of the Organic Administration Regulation of Public Security Organs stipulates,

> The public security bureau of a districted city shall, when required by its work, establish public security sub-bureaus. The public security bureau of a city, county, or autonomous county shall, when required by its work, establish police stations.

Both the sub-bureau and the police station are dispatched agencies. Li (2010) argues that there is no legislative authority by which the sub-bureau sets up police stations. However, the practice is widespread. For example, based on the administrative region, there are sixteen public security sub-bureaus in the city of Wuhan in the Hubei province, and there are 223 police stations subordinate to the sub-bureaus (Liu & Liu, 2016).

Special Public Security Organs

Special public security organs are composed of five organs. First among these are railway public security organs, which hold responsibility for ensuring the safety of railway transportation, maintaining political stability and public security, fighting against enemy agents and criminal activities, protecting the safety of heads of the party and governments, and so on. These include eighteen local railway public security bureaus,[5] each of which holds jurisdiction over several offices. Under the Zhengzhou Railway Public Security Bureau, for example, there were 3,995 police officers in late 2017 and three agencies under its jurisdiction: the Zhengzhou Railway Public Security Department (forty-five police stations), the Luoyang Railway Public Security Department (thirty police stations), and Zhengzhou Railway Police Training School (Editorial Office of China Railway Zhengzhou Group Yearbook 2018).

Second among the five organs are the transportation public security organs, which are responsible for the shipping, maritime, and port public security works. Shipping public security organs include the Yangtze River Shipping Public Security Bureau and the Heilongjiang River Shipping Public Security Bureau. Maritime public security organs consist of the Tianjin, Shanghai, and Guangdong maritime public security bureaus. Port public security organs are made up of seventeen public security bureaus.[6] Third are the forestry public security organs, responsible for providing guidance to forestry public security forces, managing teams, cooperating with other departments, and steering the investigation of major and serious criminal cases related to forestry. The data show that the number of forestry public security organs has been increasing. There were only 5,058 organs throughout mainland China and 42,347 police officers in 1990 (Zhu, 1991, p. 93). In 2017, the number increased to 7,152 forestry public security organs and 62,000 police officers in thirty provincial-level administrative regions (except Shanghai) throughout mainland China (Hu, 2018, p. 149). In almost thirty years, the organizations and staff members increased by 41 percent and 46 percent, respectively. Fourth are the civil aviation public security organs, which are composed of seven public security bureaus subordinate to regional administration bureaus; each of these sets up several agencies in which security offices are established.[7] Their responsibilities are to draft rules about civil aviation security protection, gather intelligence, decide on and issue prewarning levels, deal with illegal interference in the civil aviation security crisis, and so on.[8] Fifth and last on the list are the anti-smuggling public security organs, whose main responsibilities include investigating smuggling cases, carrying out intelligence works, developing international cooperation on the fight against smuggling, and undertaking liaison works of the World Customs Organization.[9]

Special public security organs were co-subordinated to the MPS and other departments such as the Ministry of Transport and the Ministry of Forestry. In 2018, in compliance with the demand of "police is police, government is government, and enterprise is enterprise"—put forward in the *Adjustment Work Program of the Management System of the Public Security Organs* issued by the General Office of the Central Committee and the General Office of the State Council[10]—the leadership of special public security organs has been greatly transferred to the MPS. More specifically, the organs of railway, transportation, and forestry public security have been shifted to the sole leadership of the MPS. Although the adjustment has maintained the co-administration of civil aviation public security organs and anti-smuggling public security organs, the MPS has taken the dominant role.

Chinese People's Armed Police Force

As an integral part of the country's armed forces, the CPAPF made a great adjustment after Xi Jinping came to power in 2013. The adjustment has highlighted military characteristics and weakened police features. In January 2016, the Central Military Commission issued *Opinion on Deepening the Reform of National Defence and the Armed Forces*, in which it demanded consolidation and improvement of the party's absolute leadership over the armed forces and centralization of the power of leadership and command in the hands of the Central Committee and the Central Military Commission of the CCP.[11] Further, in December 2017, the Central Committee issued the *Decision on Adjusting the Leadership and Command System of CPAPF*, in which it clearly stated that the CPAPF is under the centralized and unified leadership of the Central Committee and the Central Military Commission.[12] To legitimize the adjustment, the Nineteenth Meeting of the Thirteen National People's Congress Standing Committee was held on June 20, 2020, and the revised draft of the law on the CPAPF was passed under its jurisdiction. The adjustment of the aforementioned decision has been definitely stipulated in the law, which also means that the local governments have lost command and mobilization of the CPAPF (Hsieh, 2019). Moreover, the CPAPF still assists the public security organs in implementing their arrest and pursue missions. Although some changes have been made, some issues remain unaddressed, such as the procedures and standards that armed police follow (Wu, Sun, & Fitchtelberg, 2011).

On March 21, 2018, the Central Committee issued *Scheme on Deepening the Reform of the Party and State Institutions*, in which it imposed a major reform on the CPAPF. Before the reform, there were eight forces: Internal Guard, Gold, Forestry, Hydropower, Transportation, Border Defence, Firefighting, and Safeguard. After the reform, six forces have been removed. Both the

Border Defence Forces and the Safeguard Forces have been transferred to the MPS. Both the Forestry and the Firefighting Forces have been transferred to the Ministry of Emergency Management. The Gold Forces have been placed under the Ministry of Natural Resources, and part of the enterprises subordinate to the Gold Forces have been incorporated into the China National Gold Group Corporation. The Hydropower Forces have been transformed into state-owned enterprises under the management of the state-owned Assets Supervision and Administration Commission of the State Council. Only two forces (Internal Guard and Transportation) still remain in the CPAPF. The mission of the Internal Guard Forces includes the following: serving as an armed guard for objects, targets, and major activities; guarding important parts of public facilities, nuclear facilities, enterprises, warehouses, water resources, water conservancy projects, electric power facilities, and communication hubs; providing a peripheral armed guard for prisons and detention houses; patrolling key areas or areas during special periods; and so on. Although the Armed Transportation Forces[13] remain in the CPAPF, they have been incorporated into the Armed Internal Guard Forces. In this scheme, the Coast Guard has been transferred from the State Oceanic Administration to the CPAPF. Moreover, the CPAPF also includes the Mobile Contingent, which is mainly responsible for handling terrorism, violent crimes, riots, and public security threats.

WORSENING POLICE-PUBLIC RELATIONS

Police–public relations experienced great changes during the past seven decades, shifting from a harmonious to a strained or even opposed relationship. These changes are closely linked to the rapidly developing social context. Although scholars differ on details in discussing the turning point of Chinese policing (Du, 1997; Zhong, 2009; Wu, Sun, & Hu, 2016), they reach a consensus on the fact that there used to be rather harmonious police–public relations under the guidance of the mass line, when the PRC was established. After reform and opening -up in the late 1970s, police–public relations started to deteriorate. Nowadays, police–public relationships have become worse, as maintaining social stability has become a major task of the police, and politics and other social elements have closely influenced relations (Du, 1997; Zhong, 2009).

Heavy Workload versus Low Police-to-Population Ratio

Citizens have expected police to respond to, help in, and provide rescue in all requests, whereas police have complained about overloaded work that involves both policing and non–policing tasks (Liu, Sun, & Liu, 2018). Compared with those of most Western countries, the Chinese police have a

rather low police–population ratio of about 1.38/1000 based on a 2007 statistic (Zhong, 2009; Wu, Sun, & Hu, 2016), which means that the Chinese
police have to undertake heavier workloads than their counterparts in other
countries.[14] Based on official records, from 2008 to 2012, 2,204 policemen
died on duty, the average age of policemen who died on duty was 42.8 years
old, and about 49.8 percent died due to being overworked.[15]

Based on the slogan of "Asking the police for help when you are in
trouble," in recent years more and more policemen have complained about
heavy workloads and the citizens' unreasonable requests, such as domestic
disputes, lost keys or dogs, and so on. One person even asked the police to
help him find a wife. Obviously, these requests have gone far beyond the
police's responsibilities.

What is more, as mentioned before, local police organs in China are
noticeably subject to the dual leadership of both local party committees and
governments and the police organs above them. Local governments exercise
strong control over police forces by determining policing priorities, allocating budgets, and conducting personnel management (Sun & Wu, 2010). It is
easy then to establish the idea that the police should end up supporting and
providing services to local governments and performing non–police duties,
such as birth control, economic disputes, handling petitioners, and other tasks
assigned by the local governments.

Declining Public Trust in the Police

Chinese public trust in the police has been declining since Reform and
Opening-up in the late 1970s. Public attitudes toward the police are influenced by a series of variables, including citizens' satisfaction with public
safety, the capability of crime control, people's quality of life, registration
identity, ethnicity, social status, and police misconduct (Cao & Hou, 2001;
Hu, Sun, & Wu, 2015; Jiang, Sun, & Wang, 2012; Sun, Hu, & Wu, 2012;
Sun, Wu, & Hu, 2013; Wu, Sun, & Hu, 2016; Zhang et al., 2014). Chinese
victims are dissatisfied with the police, for they have failed to recover property and proven unable to find or apprehend offenders (Hu, Sun, & Wu, 2015;
Wu & Sun, 2009). People's trust in the police has significant differences
between rural and urban residents, and villagers have displayed lower satisfaction with the police than urbanites (Sun, Wu, & Hu, 2013). What is more,
in the last two decades, the police were involved in the task of maintaining
social stability and hence were antagonistic to the public, which has intensified tensions between the police and the public.

To some people, the term "police" is addressed in a broad sense and as an
extended family, includes the public police and private security/police, sworn
officers, civilian staff members, and the para-police Chengguan[16] (Xu, Hu, &

Jiang, 2020; Xu & Jiang, 2019). Considering that auxiliary police officers, Chengguan para-police, and private security forces have not experienced strict and professional training, they are not equipped with professional skills to handle police-related cases lawfully and effectively (Zhong & Grabosky, 2009). In recent years, many news reports have established concerns regarding the misconduct of auxiliary police officers and private security personnel. Moreover, the firm street enforcement by the Chengguan has also enraged people, leaving bad impressions on the public.

Police Misconduct

Police misconduct is the most important factor that harms police–public relations in China (Du, 1997). As mentioned before, in the 1950s and 1960s, the mass line policy guided the police work in China, which demanded that police serve the people wholeheartedly, listen to them, and accept their supervision. After reform and opening -up and the reforms of police professionalization were carried out, police distanced themselves from citizens, and the market-oriented economy stimulated surging police misconduct in China (Du, 1997). The police are empowered with huge powers that can easily lead to abuse. Details about police misconduct are discussed in the next section, "Police Deviance." Police misconduct has eroded police authority and ultimately decreased public trust in the police.

Police's Mixed Perception of the Public

Police attitudes toward the citizenry influence police–public relations. Scholars found that Chinese police officers had mixed feelings about the public when judging from three dimensions, including citizens' cooperation, compliance with laws, and recognition and disrespect (Wu, Sun, & Hu, 2016). While the police negatively perceived citizens' level of cooperation, the public was law-abiding and recognized the police for their work. However, when dealing with petitions, local police have found that protesters who complain about unreasonable appeals or complain about benefits occupy a large proportion of the total petition cases (Chen, 2011).

Intervention of the Mass Media

The intervention of mass media has become a new challenge for police-public relations. Modern society is an information-driven society, and mass media plays an important role in spreading information and making up for shortages of insufficient information. Some petitioners and media outlets present their views, tell grievances, and show their anger via mass media, which broadly draws netizens' attention, guides their standpoints, and even arouses public anger about the police and local governments (Ni, Chen, & Wang, 2012). During this process, mass media actually reshapes police-public relations by guiding and shaping public opinions. The mass media is a double-edged sword, however, while it provides a platform for spreading information as well as services to supervise police activities, in some cases it has exaggerated police–public conflicts by only reporting a one-sided story (Ni, Chen, & Wang, 2012). Some petitioners have exerted pressure on the police and local governments to gain benefits and social support by shaping one-sided public opinions via mass media. In recent years, the police have realized the importance of guiding public feelings toward events shown on the network.

POLICE DEVIANCE

Police deviance occurs when police officers are involved in behaviors inconsistent with their legal authority, organizational authority, and standards of ethical conduct (Barker & Carter, 1986). It has always been a part of Chinese policing. Several prominent deviances are presented in the following paragraphs.

Types

Police Corruption

Corruption is a very common phenomenon in China. The existence of police corruption always draws criticism (Chan & He, 2017). In particular, the opening-up policy in 1978 dramatically changed the social structure and the role of civil servants (Deng, Zhang, & Leverentz, 2010) and led to the reinforcement of the rent-seeking concept. Liu (2013) found that corruption becomes increasingly severe and that more than half of it is repetitive; for example, there were 173 corrupt transactions over a period of 18 years in one case. Corruption also pervades the Chinese police. Numerous recent examples of serious police corruption can be found. Meng Hongwei, who was then vice–minister of the MPS and the first Chinese head of Interpol, was charged with bribery and sentenced to thirteen and a half years in jail on January 21, 2020. The Tianjin First Intermediate People's Court ascertained that he accepted about 14,460,000 yuan (about $2 million) in bribes.[17] Not just higher police officers but also grass-root officers have been involved with corruption. In January 2019, two police officers were brought to trial for embezzlement and taking bribes by a Ningdu county court, involving illegal gains about 1,354,700 yuan (near $200,000) between March and October 2015.[18] Some scholars tended to render the level of corruption as institutional. The police resort to fines and confiscation for minor offenses in gambling and prostitution cases (Jeffreys, 2010; Xu, 2013).

Protection of Illegal Activities

Illegal protection occurs when police accept money from vice operations or legitimate businesses that are operating in an illegal manner (Archbold, 2013). After analyzing the Chongqing crime crackdown, Wang (2014, 2016, 2017) argued that organized crime groups generally buy protection from local government officials, especially police officers. In the first half of 2019, seventy-six police officers were investigated in the province of Yunnan. Most acted as a protective umbrella for illicit groups.[19] Jin (2019) found that 43 percent of police officers sent news secretly, and 21 percent prevented other civil servants from investigating illegal activities.

Police Brutality

In police–citizen encounters, police brutality generally occurs when the police use verbal aggression or abuse and unlawfully use physical force (Archbold, 2013). For example, on June 10, 2016, one netizen posted a news story on a microblog. She mentioned that she and her younger sister passed by the Liutang gate on May 21 in the city of Shenzhen in Guangdong province. A police officer stopped them and checked their IDs. They asked the officer to show his officer card and were refused. The police officer dragged them into the police car by force, thereby disrupting public service, and drove them to the police station. On the way there, both parties had a conversation[20] in which the officer used abusive language, such as "You are a man," "Take off your clothes," "You idiot," and "You are bitchy." This sort of language is often offensive and degrading.

Apart from verbal abuse, it is common for the police to use excessive force. One such case that happened in the city of Taiyuan in the Shanxi province received much attention.[21] On December 13, 2014, four migrant workers who were working at a construction site came back from shopping and wanted to go through the site to return to their living areas. A security guard stopped the four workers because they were not wearing safety helmets and then clashed with them. Subsequently, the head of the security team called the police. The police officers were ready to take the worker, Li Mou, away when they arrived at the scene. Zhou Xiuyun, another worker, stopped the police officer, Wang Wenjun, and grabbed his neck. Wang seized her by the hair and made her sit on the ground, and Zhou grasped Wang's trouser pockets, which lasted nearly seven minutes. After Zhou refused Wang's order to let go, Wang pinned her head against the ground and made her lie there. Subsequently, he put his foot on her hair, which lasted about 23 minutes. When reinforcements arrived at the scene, Wang decided to lift her into the police car and bring her to the police station. Nearly one hour after arriving, Zhou was confirmed dead. The forensic science center authenticated that Zhou suffered from contusion of her larynx from blunt violence and died of acute respiratory failure syndrome. In a court verdict, the judge ruled that Wang's conduct exceeded the reasonable limit and caused Zhou's death.

Police Torture

Torture is as old as Chinese legal history. The earliest use of torture was in the Qin dynasty (221–207 BC) (Hsieh, 2014). To obtain the oral confession of a suspect, judicial officials were allowed to use torture at the time. The use of torture has become a serious problem (Ma, 2008). Police at basic-level police stations frequently use torture to swiftly solve crimes (Wu & Beken, 2010). After analyzing 141 cases, Zhong and Dai (2019) found that police torture was reported in 122 of them (86.5 percent). In a recent wrongful conviction, Wu Chunhong was charged with murder and sentenced to life imprisonment. On April 1, 2020, after being jailed for sixteen years, Wu Chunhong was released by the High People's Court of Henan province due to insufficient evidence.[22] Wu told her lawyer that she was tortured into making a confession. Belkin (2013) asked one police officer why the Chinese police are the most successful in the world. The officer said that it was not because the officers are smart but because they have obtained a confession in every case.

Causes

What causes police officers to be involved in deviance in China? Scholars have different views and have examined several causes of police deviance. The first cause is the individual factor. This factor, which includes the background, characteristics, and quality of an individual's education, becomes the focal aspect in explaining police deviance (Fu, 2005). Police officers' education level varies from area to area in China. At a basic police station, most officers have graduated from technical secondary school or have a high school degree (Liu, Sun, & Liu, 2018). The second cause is widespread power. Lee (2018) indicates that the positional power of senior police officers is greater than those of the state prosecutors, which has a bearing on operational decision-making and external oversight. In particular, during Zhou Yongkang's term, the secretary of the local PLC doubled as a police chief, which caused the power of public security organs to overwhelmingly exceed those of the procuracy and the court. The third cause is the institution factor. As analyzed previously, the police are under dual leadership. Local governments control their personnel and budget. Due to the unbalanced development of the provincial economies, the police are poorly financed by governments and forced to rely on extrabudgetary financing (Fu, 2005). The fourth cause is the politicization of the police. In a one-party state, the CCP mainly relies on the police to maintain social stability, and public security organs at all levels are firmly controlled by the CCP.

In a word, a lack of respect for the rule of law and a constitutional spirit of limited government are very common in China (Wong, 1998). Political imperatives and directives prevail over legal provisions and play a dominant role in Chinese social ordering (Fu, 1991, 2005). The political legitimacy of the CCP is based on keeping social stability. The worsening police–public relations in the PRC are a result of the weakening of the mass line and rising conflicts between police and the public. As Fu (2005) points out, the arbitrary political system is the root cause of police deviance. The police cannot truly respond to people's needs and be accountable to any institutions other than the CCP as long as the authoritarian state is preserved (Fu, 2005, p. 252). Therefore, the effects of police reform depend on political system reform. Both are synchronous.

NOTES

1. See https://laogairesearch.org/archives/最高人民法院付院长高克林同志在三月全国公安厅-2/?lang=zh-hant.

2. See https://www.mps.gov.cn.

3. See https://www.mps.gov.cn/n2254314/n2254315/index.html.

4. According to Article 30 of the Constitution of the PRC, the country is divided into provinces, autonomous regions, and municipalities. Provinces and autonomous regions are divided into autonomous prefectures, counties, autonomous counties, and cities. Counties and autonomous counties are divided into townships. Moreover, municipalities and other large cities are divided into districts and counties, and autonomous prefectures are divided into counties, autonomous counties, and cities.

5. These specifically include Beijing, Haerbin, Shenyang, Huhhot, Zhengzhou, Taiyuan, Jinan, Shanghai, Guangzhou, Wuhan, Nanning, Nanchang, Chengdu, Kunming, Xi'an, Lanzhou, Qingzang, and Urumqi railway public security bureaus.

6. These include bureaus of Dalian, Yingkou, Yantai, Qingdao, Rizhao, Lianyungang, Shanghai, Nantong, Zhangjiang, Ningbo, Shantou, Guangzhou, Zhanjiang, Hainan, and Shekou.

7. These include the Eastern China Regional Administration Bureau (ten security offices), North China Regional Administration Bureau (five security offices), Northeast Regional Administration Bureau (four security offices), Mid-South Regional Administration Bureau (nine security offices), Southwest Regional Administration Bureau (five security offices), Northwest Regional Administration Bureau (four security offices), and Xinjiang Administration Bureau (two security offices).

8. See http://www.caac.gov.cn/dev/gaj/.

9. See http://www.customs.gov.cn/customs/zsgk93/jgzn95/jgzn5/2011661/index .html.

10. See https://www.sohu.com/a/347592286_120044552.

11. See http://www.xinhuanet.com//mil/2016-01/01/c_1117646695.htm.

12. According to Article 3 of the 2009 Law of PAPF of PRC, the PAPF is under the leadership of the State Council and the Central Military Commission.

13. These forces are responsible for road, port, and urban construction works.

14. No exact count of the number of police agencies or officers in mainland China exists. In response to correspondents' questions in 2015, Huang Ming, the former deputy minister of the MPS, mentioned that there were more than 200 million police across the country.

15. See https://www.guancha.cn/society/2015_03_08_311430.shtml.

16. *Chengguan* are officers who are responsible for urban management and law enforcement. In a strict sense, they are not members of the Chinese police, but many people are confused because of their role in law enforcement.

17. See http://news.sina.com.cn/o/2020-01-21/doc-iihnzhha3938962.shtml.

18. See https://m.sohu.com/a/288309506_120053484.

19. See https://k.sina.com.cn/article_2946407714_af9e9d2201900hzs6.html.

20. See http://www.bjnews.com.cn/news/2016/06/10/406210.html.

21. See https://www.sohu.com/a/360294006_100168544.

22. See https://www.sohu.com/a/385100023_120045802.

REFERENCES

Archbold, Carol Ann. (2013). *Policing: A text/reader*. Publications.

Barker, Thomas, and David Carter. (1986). *Police deviance*. Anderson Publishing Company.

Belkin, Ira. (2013). China's Tortuous Path toward Ending Torture in Criminal Investigations. In *Comparative Perspectives on Criminal Justice in China*, edited by Mike McConville and Eva Pils, 91–117. Cheltenham, UK: Edward Elgar.

Cao, Liqun, and Charles, Hou. (2001). A Comparison of Confidence in the Police in China and the United States. *Journal of Criminal Justice* 29: 87–99.

Chan, Wing, Lun Wayne, and Holly Heng He. (2017). Media Representations of the Hong Kong and their Mainland Counterpart. *Police Journal: Theory, Practice and Principals*, 90(2): 173–188.

Chen, Baifeng. (2011). "无理上访与基层法治 [Unreasonable Petition and Rule of Law in Grassroots China]." *Peking University Law Journal*, 2: 227–247.

Dai, Mengyan. (2008). Policing in the People's Republic of China: A Review of Recent Literature. *Crime Law Social Change*, 50: 211–227.

Deng, Xiaogang, Lening Zhang, and Andrea Leverentz. (2010). Official Corruption during China's Economic Transition: Historical Patterns, Characteristics, and Government Reactions. *Journal of Contemporary Criminal Justice*, 26(1): 72–88.

Du, Jinfeng. (1997). "Police–public relations: A Chinese view." *Australian & New Zealand Journal of Criminology*, 30(1): 87–94.

Editorial Office of China Railway Zhengzhou Group Yearbook. (2018). 中国铁路郑州局集团有限公司年鉴 [China Railway Zhengzhou Group Yearbook]. Zhengzhou: China Railway Zhengzhou Group.

Fu, Hualing. (1991). Police Accountability: The Case of the People's Republic of China. *International Review of Police Development*, 14(3): 140–151.

Fu, Hualing. (2005). Zhou Yongkang and the Recent Police Reform in China. *Australian & New Zealand Journal of Criminology*, 38(2): 241–253.

Guo, Xuezhi. (2012). *China's Security State: Philosophy, Evolution, and Politics.* New York: Cambridge University Press.

Hu, Rong, Ivan Y. Sun, and Yuning Wu. (2015). Chinese Trust in the Police: The Impact of Political Efficacy and Participation. *Social Science Quarterly*, 4: 1012–26.

Hu, Xiaoxiao. (2018). 森林公安队伍建设 [The Team Construction of Forestry Forces]. In *China Forestry Yearbook*, edited by National Forestry and Grassland Administration, 149–151. Beijing: China Forestry Publishing House.

Hsieh, Kuo-Hsing. (2014). *The Exclusionary Rule of Evidence: Comparative Analysis and Proposals for Reform.* Farnham, UK: Routledge.

Hsieh, Yu-Lin. (2019). The Implication and Development of China PAPF's Reform. *Prospect & Exploration*, 17(2): 122–138.

Jeffreys, Elaine. (2010). Exposing Police Corruption and Malfeasance: China's Virgin Prostitute Cases. *China Journal*, 63: 127–149.

Jiang, Shanhe, Ivan Y. Sun, and Jin Wang. (2012). Citizens' Satisfaction with Police in Guangzhou, China. *Policing: An International Journal of Police Strategies & Management*, 35(4): 801–821.

Jin, Jiazhe. (2019). 扫黑除恶专项行动视域下公安民警涉黑腐败问题探究 [An Exploration of Corruption Problems of Police Officers Involving in Organized Crime in Specialized Struggles]. *Journal of Shanxi Politics and Law Institute of Administrators*, 32(4): 32–35.

Kornai, János. (1992). *The Socialist System: The Political Economy of Communism.* Princeton, NJ: Princeton University Press.

Lee, George Chak. (2018). Police Corruption: A Comparison between China and India. *Journal of Financial Crime*, 25(2): 248–276.

Li, Baoji. (2010). 关于公安分局的法学解析 [The Legal Analysis of Public Security Sub-bureau]. *Journal of Wuhan Public Security Cadre College* 1: 59–61.

Liu, Jusheng, and Nanhua Liu. (2016). 武汉公安年鉴 *2015* [Wuhan Public Security Yearbook 2015]. Wuhan: Wuhan Press.

Liu, Lin, Ivan Y. Sun, and Jianhong Liu. (2018). Police Officers' Attitudes toward Citizens in China. *International Criminal Justice Review*, 28(1): 45–61.

Liu, Qijun. (2013). 改革开放以来中国腐败状况实证分析 [Empirical Analysis of Chinese Corruption Situation since Reform and Opening-up]. *Journal of Political Science*, 6: 39–51.

Ma, Yue. (2008). The Chinese Police. In *Comparative Policing: The Struggle for Democratization*, edited by Maria Haberfeld and Ibrahim Cerrah, 13–60. Los Angeles: Publications.

Ni, Yinlin, Youyi Chen, and Shuping Wang. (2012). 涉警舆情危机的深层机制及对策 [Generating Mechanism and Solution to Policing-related Public Opinion Crisis]. *Journal of Chinese People's Public Security University (Social Sciences Edition)*, 1: 92–98.

Scoggins, E. Suzanne. (2018). Policing Modern China. *China Law and Society Review*, 3: 79–117.

Sun, Y. Ivan, and Yuning Wu. (2010). Chinese Policing in a Time of Transition, 1978–2008. *Journal of Contemporary Criminal Justice* 26(1): 20–35.

Sun, Y. Ivan, Rong Hu, and Yuning Wu. (2012). Social Capital, Political Participation, and Trust in the Police in Urban China. *Australian & New Zealand Journal of Criminology*, 45(1): 87–105.

Sun, Y. Ivan, Yuning Wu, and Rong Hu. (2013). Public Assessments of the Police in Rural and Urban China. *British Journal of Criminology*, 53: 643–664.

Tanner, Murray Scot, and Eric Green. (2007). Principals and Secret Agents: Central Versus and Local Control over Policing and Obstacles to "Rule of Law" in China. *China Quarterly*, 191: 644–670.

Wang, Peng. (2014). Extralegal Protection in China: How Guangxi Distorts China's Legal System and Facilitates the Rise of Unlawful Protectors. *British Journal of Criminology*, 54(5): 809–830.

Wang, Peng. (2016). Military Corruption in China: The Role of Guanxi in the Buying and Selling of Military Positions. *China Quarterly*, 228: 970–991.

Wang, Peng. (2017). *The Chinese Mafia: Organized Crime, Corruption, and Extralegal Protection*. Oxford, UK: Oxford University Press.

Wei, Hongyun. (2017). 对现阶段首都公安经费保障工作的若干思考 [Some Reflections on the Expenditure Guarantee of the Capital Public Security]. *Journal of Beijing Police College*, 2: 77–81.

Wong, Kam C. (1998). A Reflection on Police Abuse of Power in the People's Republic of China. *Police Quarterly*, 1(2): 87–112.

Wright, Teresa. (2015), *Party and State in Post-Mao China*. Malden, Cambridge: Polity Press.

Wu, Wei, and Tom Vander Beken. (2010). Police Torture in China and Its Causes: A Review of Literature. *Australian & New Zealand Journal of Criminology* 43(3): 557–579.

Wu, Yuning, and Ivan Y. Sun. (2009). Citizen Trust in Police: The Case of China. *Police Quarterly*, 12(2): 170–191.

Wu, Yuning, Ivan Y. Sun, and Aaron Fitchtelberg. (2011). Formalizing China's Armed Police: The 2009 PAP Law. *Crime Law Social Change*, 56: 243–263.

Wu, Yuning, Ivan Y. Sun, and Rong Hu. (2016). Public Trust in the Chinese Police: The Impact of Ethnicity, Class and *Hukou*. *Australian & New Zealand Journal of Criminology*, 49(2): 179–197.

Xu, Jianhua. (2013). Police Accountability and the Commodification of Policing in China. *British Journal of Criminology*, 53: 1,093–1,117.

Xu, Jianhua, and Anli Jiang. (2019). Police Civilianization and the Production of Underclass Violence: The Case of Para-police Chengguan and Street Vendors in Guangzhou, China. *British Journal of Criminology*, 59(1): 64–84.

Xu, Jianhua, Qipu Hu, and Anli Jiang. (2020). Authoritarian Capitalism and Policing Studies in China. In *Handbook of Public Policy and Public Administration in China*, edited by Xiaowei Zang, and Hon S. Chan, 391–406. Cheltenham, UK: Edward Elgar.

Xu, Tao, and Nan Yang. (2018). Chinese Policing: Its History from a Legal Perspective. In *Comparative Policing from a Legal Perspective*, edited by Monica den Boer, 363–379. Cheltenham, UK: Edward Elgar.

Zhang, Hongwei, Jihong Zhao, Ling Ren, and Ruohui Zhao. (2014). Social Bonds, Traditional Models and Juvenile Attitudes toward the Police in China. *Policing: An International Journal of Police Strategies & Management* 37(3): 596–611.

Zhong, Lena Y. (2009). Community Policing in China: Old Wine in New Bottles. *Police Practice and Research*, 10(2): 157–169.

Zhong, Lena Y, and Mengliang Dai. (2019). The Politics of Wrongful Convictions in China. *Journal of Contemporary China*, 28(116): 260–276.

Zhong, Lena Y, and Peter N. Grabosky. (2009). The Pluralization of Policing and the Rise of Private Policing in China. *Crime Law Social Change*, 52: 433–455.

Zhu, Qiu. (1991). 林业公安工作 [The Forestry Public Security Works]. In *China Forestry and Grassland Yearbook*, edited by State Forestry Administration, 80–84. Beijing: China Forestry Publishing House.

Chapter 10

The Police System in India

Issues and Challenges

Siddhartha Misra

India is host to a population of 1.3 billion and covers a land area of 3,287,263 square kilometers, with its massive size earning it the title of a "subcontinent." It consists of twenty-nine States and seven Union Territories and is host to multiple religions and cultures. Almost 70 percent of its population lives in villages. Due to its peculiar social, cultural, and economic circumstances, disputes are frequent and widespread. The high rate of crime constantly poses a problem for law, order, and internal security. The crime rate was reported to be 383.5 for every 100,000 people during 2018, a number much higher than the global average. With India's growing developmental needs, this statistic is alarming since the country cannot afford to have rampant crimes. There is a constant need for crime prevention and institutional control. The police system of India plays a crucial role in achieving the purpose. This paper shall provide an overview of India's police system, its legal framework, organization, authorities, independence, public image, and the relevant need for reforms.

INTRODUCTION

Peace is the ultimate aim of any social set up consisting of human beings. Therefore, the people constantly seek and devise the tools to ensure peace within the society. An instrument discovered over the ages for accomplishment of this purpose within a state is the Police. The police force comprises a group of people who maintain law and order in a country or town and is the proven means of preventing and controlling crimes while protecting individuals and their properties. The police's role becomes rather crucial in a country with peculiar social, economic, and political circumstances and diverse populations consisting of different casts, languages, religions, and creeds. India is a special example of the police system's functioning, and encompasses the successes and failures of the police in the prevention and control of crime, and in the maintenance of law and order.

It is a challenge to maintain law and order and keep the peace intact in a country that consists of 739 districts and 649,481 villages, with agriculture as the primary occupation. With almost 68 percent of the population living in villages, it remains largely an agricultural economy despite the hike in India's service sector over the last decade. With constant foreign invasions and subjugation of the territory, people have brought several undesirable problems to the nation. The country inherited a legacy of poverty, underdevelopment, unemployment, caste and communal divide, and constant political turmoil, most of which unfortunately exists to date.

At present, various social, cultural, and economic factors mean that disputes, conflicts, and crimes are common in India. Crimes including murder, kidnapping, rape, robbery, theft, grievous hurt, and extortion, and so forth, frequently occur throughout the country. Moreover, India also frequently witnesses cast and communal strife, with tensions that often lead to conflicts, protests, and riots. The high crime rate constantly poses serious national growth challenges and may tarnish the country's image before the international community. In view of its growing economy, India cannot afford to have unchecked and uncontrolled crimes. Thus, there is a constant need for crime prevention and crime control in India, and the Police play a crucial role in achieving this purpose.

Constitutional Framework of India

India or Bharat is a Union of States which holds governance over multiple territories. India chose to become a democratic and republican state after seeking independence in 1947. With twenty-eight States and nine Union Territories, it has a comprehensive Constitution that dictates the supreme law of the land. Numerous other laws exist for the criminal and civil administration of the country. India is a federal system marked by its characteristics, namely, supremacy of the Constitution, division of power between Union and States, the existence of an independent judiciary, and so forth, but its federalism leans in favor of a strong central government.

The Constitution makes India a state with both federal and unitary features. It creates a system of governance of the nation both at the central and state levels with a clear distribution of power and autonomy. The constitution contains three lists in its Seventh Schedule; Union List, State List, and Concurrent List. Each list has certain subjects on which the respective Central and State governments are eligible to base laws. Both the Parliament and the State legislatures can make laws on subjects mentioned in the Union List, the State List, and the Concurrent List.

Police are also a subject in the state list. This means that only the States can make laws concerning the police and the policing system in India itself. The police organization and its working are governed by regulations framed by state governments and need to be adhered to. Therefore, each state has developed its own police laws and police force and has incorporated the necessary rules in the Police Manual of States (Commonwealth Human Rights Initiative, n.d).

In India, each State and Union Territory has a separate police force. However, despite this difference, there are several common factors among the various police bodies. The police all over India are governed by the Police Act 1861. This naturally means that the police system across the country has many features in common. The major penal legislation, namely, the Indian Penal Code, the Code of Criminal Procedure, and the Indian Evidence Act, confer special powers upon the police and have an all-India application.

Moreover, all Indian Police Service systems recruit Police officers on the national level and deploy them in the states. These police officers make up the top brass of the police force and take their office at the pleasure of the Indian President. All these factors ensure coordination and cooperation regarding the Police System between the Center and States in India. Moreover, the Union Home Ministry has a major say in the policing system countrywide as it is the cadre controlling authority of the Indian Police Service (IPS) in States and Union Territories.

Even though "police" and "public order" are a State subject under the Constitution, the Constitution provides an important role to the Center as it can intervene in the states during certain situations and take steps concerning the police's functions. The Constitution imposes upon the Center a duty to protect every State against external aggression and internal disturbances and requires it to ensure that every State's Government is carried out in accordance with the provisions of the Constitution. Moreover, the Union Parliament has the power to make laws regarding the deployment of any armed force of the Union or any other force subject to the control of the Union. This includes the deployment of Para-Military Forces in any State and the granting of authorization to the Central Bureau of Investigation (CBI) to investigate criminal and civil matters across the country. Thus, the Indian Constitutional scheme makes a clear blueprint for maintaining law and order and internal security by organizing the institutional, legal framework for policing in the country.

HISTORICAL EVOLUTION OF POLICE SYSTEM

Early Hindu Period

Contrary to the general belief that policing in India is a British concept, the concept of rule of law and the administration of justice has been known to exist in India ever since the *Vedas,* the Hindu religious texts, including the Rigved, the Yajurved, the Samved, and the Atharvved, came to be recognized as the very epitome of *dharma* (religion or duty). The police officials had been denoted as *Jivagribhs* in *Rig Ved* and *Ugras* in the *Upanishads.* An effective police system flourished during the *Mauryan* period. The police was supervised by a *Dauvarika* (Doorkeeper) who was responsible for the peace outside palace compounds, while the *Antarvnashika* was responsible for peace inside the palace. Spies were used as a tool to keep the system intact and clean of criminals. The policing system envisaged by the philosopher *Kautilya* had two limbs that is, civilian departments entrusted with Police powers and the cadre of regular Police officers. According to *Arthshastra* formulations, the *Pradeshta* (commissioner) for rural areas, and the *Nagarakara* were officers in charge of a city who had the responsibility of detecting internal thieves inside fortified towns with the help of the *Sthaniks* and *Gopas* (Sharma, 2016). The traditions set by *Kautilya* were followed throughout history and all over India. This system was maintained by Gupta rulers, an ancient Indian dynasty that existed during the fourth century B.C., and their successors in northern and southern India (Aggarwal, 2000). The *Gupta* dynasty in ancient India was particularly known for its excellent law and order situation through a well-organized system of police (Padhi, 2007). The aforementioned discussion amply indicates that policing was not unknown to ancient India and a well-developed police system existed during succeeding kingdoms and dynasties governed by Hindu rulers. However, later invasions and occupations of India by foreign rulers meant destabilization of the existing administrative structure, of which the police were no exception.

Mughal Period

The *Mughals* belonged to the Muslim Turkic-Mongol dynasty and ruled India between the sixteenth and nineteenth centuries. They allowed the local police system to continue with slight alterations to differentiate it from the earlier systems. The police in India, during the *Mughal* period, was represented by a military officer and performed actions similar to the army (Chouhdary, 2009). During medieval India, the reign of *Sher Shah Suri* and *Akbar* were important from an administration perspective. *Sher Shah Suri* introduced an epoch, making reforms in the revenue and police administration by streamlining the *Zamindari*, a systemof landholding and revenue collection of an estate under a grant from the Mughal Emperors (Singh, 2002). He strengthened the spy system (Thorpe, 2005). His kingdom was distributed in Provinces consisting of Districts or *Sarkars*. The *Sarkars* further consisted of *Parganas,* which were groups of villages. There were *Shiqdars* in each *Sarkar*. The provinces were supervised under the Chief *Shiqdar* at the Center and above the *Shiqdars*, there were the Chief *Munsif* and Chief *Qazi*. The Chief *Shiqdar* was accountable for law and order in cities, while the *Gram Mukhiya* was entrusted with this responsibility in villages. However, the police system, in totality was bureaucratically centralized.

During the reign of *Akbar*, the police system was departmentalized further in the cities. The Governor of a province was called the *Subhedar* (MR, Ghanwat, 2017). The *Subedhar* was assisted by *Foujdars*, who were in charge of the districts. The *Foujdars* were assisted by *Thanadars* whose primary function was to use military force against robbers and to prevent social unrest in cities. *Chowkidars* carried out rural policing under the supervision of *Faujdars*. These *Chowkidars* were servants of the village community and were appointed by them. The *Mughal* Government, rather than taking the responsibility for rural peace and security, made villagers responsible for their own property and that of the travelers on the neighboring roads (Sarkar 2013). The chief of Police in the city was known as the *Kotwal*. In big cities, there were *Thanas* under the *Kotwals* who had army troops under them. The *Kotwals* used to hear charges against prisoners and punish them. The decision was appealable to the district *Kazi*. In the emperor's council, there was one Chief *Kazi* who was assisted by *Muhtasibs*. His role was to prevent immoral activities like rape, over pricing of essential commodities, and the sale of drugs and intoxicants. After *Akbar*'s death, the hands of local officials became less restrained. French traveler Bernier describes them as cruel and oppressive beyond imagination (Saini, 2001).

Justice and police were two weak points of the *Mughal* period. Due to the absence of a process for investigations in the *Mughal* period, the police system was prone to misuse. The police used to devise their own rules to extract information. The police system was very strict in all regards and in particular, the *Kotwal* kept people under his custody on the complaints of revenue collectors, *Subedars* for serious allegations, or whenever a *Kazi* sent a man for detention. It is believed that this system must have led to a large-scale wrongful confinement on flimsy grounds or due to vested interest. This police system, though suited to the needs of a simple agrarian community, could not sustain the strains of political disorder that followed in the wake of the disintegration of the *Mughal* Empire (Padhi, 2007).The police system during the Mughal rule apparently suffered from a number of flaws and shortcomings. It was not based upon any code or legislation and gave too much or even absolute discretion and authority to the persons entrusted with policing.

The apparent lack of a concept of rule of law may have given way to rampant arbitrariness and bias in the day-to-day administration of justice and often led to highly unjust consequences. The British gradually took over the reins from the Mughals and introduced their own system of administration across their territorial possessions.

British Period

The Police system in India, as we know today, took its basic shape during the British period. The British came to India primarily for commercial interests. However, the victory of East India Company in the battle of *Plassey* led to the political expansion of the British Empire. Since the focus of the Company was to collect revenue, they forcefully introduced the police reforms as and when a threat emerged to their interests. Warren Hastings, the first Governor General of India, noticed the defects in the then prevailing police system of the *Mughal* era. He abolished the *Faujdari* system and entrusted police functions to the judge of the civil court. The rural areas, however, continued to be regulated by *Zamindars*. By the time Hastings' tenure came to an end, the magistrates were given the power to try a small lot of cases. This reform marked the beginning of the joining of Executive and Judicial powers (Joginder, 2009).

Lord Cornwallis, the first British administrator, also attempted to improve the police system (Curry, 1971). He introduced drastic reforms in 1792 through a uniform pattern, which abolished the *Zamidari* and *Thanedari* systems (Kasture, 1966). He established four circuit courts at *Calcutta, Dacca, Murshidabad*, and *Patna*. The decisions of the civil courts were appealable to circuit courts. As per the regulations of 1793, police was under the exclusive control of the company where the Judge magistrates were in charge. The cities were headed by *Kotwals* who carried out supervision over *Daroghas,* who further had *Naiks* and *Chowkidars* as their subordinates.

The annexation of *Sindh,* in 1843, started a new phase in the police system regime. Sir Charles Napier assumed the charge and introduced the *Sindh* system which was later extended to Bombay and Madras. This model was based upon the Royal Irish Constabulary that was altogether more centralized and coercive than the subsequent British system (Verma, 2005). This system, regarded as military in form by Napier (Bano, 2013), comprised of a Superintendent of Police supervised by a Magistrate in each district and a *Talukdar* supervised by a *Mamlatdar* in each *Taluka*. The ultimate control in this system rested with the Governor General.

However, till the middle of nineteenth century, the police system was unsatisfactory and afflicted with authoritarianism (Verma, 2005). Following the surge in brutality by the authoritarian police under British rule, the

Madras government appointed the Torture Commission. The reports of the Commission recounted stories of brutality enacted by the revenue officers who performed police functions. The Mutiny of 1857, a watershed revolt that catalyzed a formal turn of power from the East India Company to the British Crown, had a major influence over policing structures and led to a lasting police bureaucracy (Kumar, 2017). Consequently, a Police Commission was appointed in 1860 for bringing reform and improvement in the Police Administration. The Commission was told to bear in mind that functions of the police are protective, repressive, or detective and that the line which separates the protective and repressive functions of a civil force from purely military functions, may not always, in India, be very clear.

The Commission assessed the working of the police and recommended changes to enhance efficiency while keeping the expenditure in check. Such recommendations became the basis for the enactment of the Indian Police Act, 1861 that brought uniformity and placed police under the control of Magistrate of provincial governments. The organization and discipline of police was similar to the Army and the interior force of police was headed by the Inspector General of Police in the State. However, due to defective supervision, failure to keep optimal staff and nonaccountability of superior officials, the system failed. A review of the existing structure and a search for alternatives resulted in the establishment of another Police Commission.

The Second Police Commission which was set up in 1902 highlighted the tyranny in the method of recruitment and training, the flaws in the constitution of the railway police and the dishonesty of investigating staff. It recommended major structural changes, mostly at the district level. The police, as they exist today, have roots in the foundation of the state and after passing through various phases of history, have evolved to their present status.

ESTABLISHMENT OF FORMAL POLICE SYSTEM

The Police Act of 1861, introduced during the colonial rule, set the ball rolling for the establishment of a uniform and pervasive police system in India. The basic structure of police organization as provided in the Act has withstood the test of time and forms the cornerstone of police administration even today (Parashar, 1997). The 1861 Act suited the needs of authoritarian British rulers and therefore, needed to be remodeled as per the desideratum of independent and democratic India.

Post independence, the Commission of 1977 highlighted how the current system was prone to misuse through political intervention and suggested the enactment of a Model Police Act. The Commission submitted eight reports between 1977 and 1981, but none of the recommendations were considered.

However, at the instance of a senior police official, Mr. Prakash Singh, the Indian Supreme Court in 1996 took cognizance of the ills existing within the Police System, a watershed event toward the reform of the Indian Police post-independence. The Supreme Court, in the case of *Prakash Singh v. Union of India* in 2006, ordered the Center and States to set up authorities to lay down guidelines for police functioning, evaluation of police performance, decisions on postings and transfers, and on receiving complaints of police misconduct (Anviti, 2017). The Court opined that its directions would be operational till a Model Police Act was prepared by the Central, and, or the State Governments and passed through the requisite legislations.

Based on the issued guidelines, the Model Police Act of 2006 was enacted, which was revised under the Model Police Bill of 2015 to correct the dilution of the functional autonomy of police by States in the guise of implementing the issued guidelines. A review of the status shows that as of August 1, 2016, only seventeen Indian states had passed the new laws while other states had merely passed executive orders (Trimukhe, 2019).

LEGAL FRAMEWORK OF POLICE SYSTEM

Under Indian Constitution, "Public Order" and "Police" are State subjects, thus, the regulation of police rests with the State Governments. The State is also responsible for the maintenance of courts, police prisons and prisoners. However, the authority of State Governments is overshadowed by the role played by the Union in regulation of police. Article 355 of the Constitution embodies the duty of the Union to protect States against external aggression and internal disturbances while ensuring that the States are governed in accordance with the Constitution. The Union is empowered to legislate on armed forces, their deployment, as well as on the regulation of arms, firearms, ammunitions, and explosives.

However, the State Governments can introduce amendments, respectively to the statutes applicable to the State(s), as both State and Center have concurrent powers in this regard. Since the regulation of Police, generally, is under the purview of State governments, the police force of each State is majorly divided into two segments: Civil Police and Armed Police. The role of Civil Police is to enforce law and to control crime while the Armed Police is deployed to assist Civil Police in extraordinary situations like violent disturbances and natural calamities. The Civil Police includes mainly the district police forces; having supervisory structures at the Range, Zone, and State Police Headquarters, and there also exist specialized branches to deal with crime, intelligence, and training problems.

The Armed Police, on the other hand, are divided into two groups: the District Armed Police and the Provincial Armed Constabulary. Moreover, at the level of State, there exist State investigation and intelligence institutions such as the Local Intelligence Unit (LIU), and Criminal Investigation Department (CID). The Central Government also undertakes the appointment for the posts of Indian Police Service (IPS) officers. While the IPS officers discharge their functions under the State government, their training, conditions of service and dismissal is in the hands of the Central Government.

The federal character of the Indian constitution also allows the Center to set up Central Police Organizations (CPO). These include Central Armed Forces like Border Security Force (BSF), Central Industrial Security Force (CISF), Central Reserve Police Force (CRPF), Indo-Tibetan Border Police (ITBP), National Security Guards (NSG), and Special Police Group (SPG). The Center also controls Central investigation and intelligence institutions like the Central Bureau of Investigation (CBI), and National Investigation Agency (NIA) among others. Thus, the Center extends its help to the State(s) in two ways: first, the personnel help by keeping the reserved military forces, and second, in terms of resources such as funds, intelligence reports, and infrastructural support, and so forth.

The Union also has the power to amend the legal instruments concerning the Police administration in India which include the Police Act 1861, Indian Penal Code 1862, the Code of Criminal Procedure 1973, and the Indian Evidence Act 1872.

Police Act, 1861

The Police Act of 1861, introduced during the British rule, lays down the basic structure and framework for the police system in India. "The Act" was passed to unify the entire police force under strict magisterial control in every province. The Act has been analyzed by various commissions to adjust it to the requirements of independent India. However, despite several steps taken to reform the system, the destination seems far. "The Act" places police force under the superintendence of the State Government, which can give such orders and directions as are necessary for the discharge of the executive and administrative functions performed by it. It establishes a system of dual control of police at district level and places the police forces under the District Superintendent of Police, but subject to the "general control and direction" of the District Magistrate.

"The Act" vests the powers of Magistrate to Inspector General of Police subject to the control and regulation by the State Government. It provides for disciplinary proceedings by senior officers to regulate subordinate officers, subject to the rule of reasonable opportunity laid down in article 311 of the

Constitution. These proceedings are quasi-judicial in nature, the result of which can be dismissal, suspension, or demotion in rank. Magistrates can conduct judicial proceedings which may result in conviction or punishment.

"The Act" provides for the deployment of additional force in disturbed areas and the costs for such deployment, as deemed necessary by the Magistrate, is borne by the inhabitants of the said area. It further provides for the appointment of special police officers from the residents of the neighborhood in three extraordinary events; namely unlawful assembly, riot, and disturbance of peace. A police officer is always considered on duty and the expression "subordinate police officers" means officers below the rank of the Deputy Superintendent of Police, under "the Act." The duties embodied in the Act include communication of intelligence affecting public peace and to prevent commission of offenses. "The Act" also mandates the maintenance of a general diary to keep a track of complaints and witnesses.

"The 1861 Act" conceived police to be a force rather than a service. It is often criticized for the supremacy of executive control and influence on the police. The pervasiveness of this influence over the rank and file including that of senior police officers, in ways that are not in keeping with police regulations, means that there is lesser obedience to the law, chain of command and established procedures (Daruwala, Devika, Maria Laura, Swati, and Janine 2005). This is often termed as the politicization of Indian police.

POLICE ORGANIZATION AND STRUCTURE

The appointment of Police officers of every State is done by the Union Public Service Commission (UPSC) and the State Public Service Commission (SPSC). The recruitment of the senior cadre of officers is done via the civil services exam conducted by the (UPSC) Central Government. These officers are designated as Indian Police Service (IPS) officers and are initially appointed at the rank of Assistant Superintendent of Police (ASP) in a state. They are eligible for attaining the highest post of Director General of Police in the state. The recruitment of Deputy Superintendent of Police (DSP) is done via an exam conducted by the State Public Services Commission. The officers recruited in this manner may get promoted till the rank of IPS officers. Recruitment of Subinspectors and DSP is done both through direct recruitment and promotion.

The senior supervising officers like the Director General of Police, Inspector General of Police, Deputy Inspector General of Police, Superintendents of Police, and Assistant Superintendents of Police belong to the Indian Police Service (IPS) (Pathi & Zonthansanga, 2013). The other senior officers are a part of State Cadre and are ultimately promoted to IPS designations depending upon their performance. The police force of a State is headed by the Director General of Police (DGP). His responsibilities include the administration of Police force along with advising the State Government in matters pertaining to the management of the State police. The Director General of Police is assisted by the Additional Director General of Police (Addl. DGP).

The next in the hierarchy is the Inspector General of Police (IGP) who oversees a Zone comprising of different Ranges. The Deputy Inspector General of Police (Dy. IGP) supervises a Range. The Senior Superintendent of Police (SSP) administers the police force of a larger District, whereas the Superintendent of Police (SP) assumes control of a District. The SP is assisted by the Additional Superintendent of Police (Addl. SP). A subdivision under a District is within the control of the Assistant/Deputy Superintendent of Police (ASP/Dy. SP). A Police Station is generally headed by the Inspector of Police or Subinspector of Police. The Subinspector of Police is assisted by the Assistant Subinspector of Police. The last in hierarchy are the Police Head Constable and Police Constable.

The District Police also has armed reserves which are deployed for escort duties. The State Armed Police however, take care of emergency situations. Armed Police is organized into one or two battalions with a Commanding Officer or Commandant in Charge. The rank of Commanding Officer is equivalent to the Superintendent of Police. A Battalion consists of six companies and each Company is headed by the Assistant Commandant or Subedar. A Company comprises three Platoons with the Subinspector/Inspector as the head and the Platoon is further divided into three Sections. A Section is headed by the Head Constable.

Police is a State subject, and its governance is subject to the regulations laid down in the Police Manuals of the State Police as well as different orders promulgated from time to time by the DGP, the chief of a state police force. The administrative superiors of the DGP are designated as the IAS (Indian Administrative Officers). The DGP is accountable for the administration and functioning of the police to the State government. There is a separate department for investigations called the Criminal Investigation Department (CID). It is divided into two branches: the criminal branch and the special branch. The criminal branch investigates specialized crimes like the counterfeiting of currency, professional cheating, activities of criminal gangs, crimes with interdistrict or interstate ramifications, and cases which are, for one reason or another, especially important (Draft Police Manual BPRD, n.d.). The Special Branch is concerned with the collection, collation, and dissemination of intelligence about various activities concerning law and order issues such as agitations, strikes, demonstrations, and riots and so forth.

Another branch of state police includes the Railway Police. Its focus is restricted to the crimes committed on railways and within the vicinity of railway establishments. State Transport Organization (STO) also comes within the ambit of the state police, which is headed by a person called Director who is an equivalent of the IGP for the transport police. He is assisted by both technical and nontechnical staff. Other departments of state police include transport police, guards and escorts etc. In some states, there is a rural police, which consists of watchmen responsible for patrolling and communicating issues pertaining to public unrest to the nearest police authorities.

GEOGRAPHICAL DIVISION OF POLICE

In India, to understand hierarchy within the Police System, it is important to consider the geographical division and subdivision within a State. A State is composed of different zones. The zones are further divided into different ranges. A Range includes different Districts. The Districts have subdivisions under them which are constituted by different police stations. Between the police station and the subdivision, there are police circles in some states.

Zones

The geographical area of a State is divided into different divisions or zones. As of 2018, there are 104 zones in India. The head of the zone is called the Inspector General of Police (IGP). The IGP is a two star officer who is also known as the Commissioner of Police in some states. He forms the connecting link of authority between the Director General of Police (DGP) and the district heads. The IGP exercises general and specific powers as delegated by DGP The IGP carries out the function of scrutinizing the reports received and sending reports about matters pertaining to administration, crime and law and order situations to the DGP He commands the subordinate officers and is also responsible for the transfer of officers up till the rank of Subinspector.

Range

The State government divides the states into different ranges in consultation with the DGP As of 2018, there are a total of 181 ranges in India (Data on Police Organisations 2019). A Range is headed by a Deputy IGP who, in consultation with the senior rank officers supervises the administration of Range field formations. The Dy. IGP reports directly to the Zonal IGP There are different branches within a Range, namely general force, law and order, crime, computer, and MIS.

The Dy. IGP monitors and supervises the subordinate field formations, scrutinizes the reports sent by the subordinate police divisions, and forwards the same to the Zonal IGP The Dy. IGP also conducts spot investigations in case of heinous crimes. Other reports maintained in a Range are in relation to administrative and financial matters, internal security including communal and terrorism-related matters, and instances of the use of police force, among others.

The Deputy Inspector General can exercise the power, general and specific, as delegated by the Zonal IGP He can transfer and officer up to the rank of Subinspector and office assistant within the Range. The Dy. IGP can also suspend an Inspector or a Reserve Inspector or a Subedar Major or a Subedar or officers of a lower rank on account of misconduct.

District

District policing is at the core of policing activities as it involves day-to-day regulation of the districts and there is accountability to the people, especially the vulnerable and the seniors. In 2018, India was reported to have 777 districts. A District is headed by the Superintendent of Police (SP). Districts are divided in subdivisions which are headed by Assistant/Deputy SP and Circles which are headed by Circle Officer (CO). The branches in districts include general ones like crime, force, accounts, administration, and establishment along with special units like reserve police lines.

The officers involved in the regulation of districts include SP, Additional SP, Assistant SP, Deputy SP, Inspector, and Subinspector. The role of the District Chief of Police is maintenance of peace and law and order, prevention and detection of crime, protection of lives, liberty and possessions of all sections of people and performance of all police functions in the district. The main functions of the SP are effective functioning of each unit through personnel and infrastructure management, promoting good public-police relations by maintaining integrity, shifting personnel for emergent situations except in the case of investigation teams, submission of monthly reports to the IG and allocation of work to the subordinate officers. The Assistant SP maintains budgetary control, ensures timely payment of salaries, and allowances and forwards monthly reports to SP. He also personally investigates and supervises important cases.

The District police is composed of the civil and armed police. The Reserved police line is another instrumental subset of the district police which has the responsibility of supplying resources for effective functioning of police administration. The Reserve Inspector (RI) heads the reserve line and is responsible for the safe custody of the clothing, accoutrements, arms, ammunition, tents, and stores in the lines and for the correctness of the register maintained for them. District police also has some specialized wings like District Special Branch, Fingerprint Bureau, and District Criminal Records Bureau and Forensic Units.

Commissioner System

In addition to the aforementioned policing systems, there also exists the Commissioner System of policing in India. The Commissioner system replaced the system of dual control established during the British regime, wherein the acts of the police were susceptible to control by the District Collector or the Magistrate. The dual system was conducive for the purpose of collecting land revenue, which was the main focus of the British. The system of dual control was inefficient for the complexity of the issues of law and order in cities, and therefore, the British Government introduced the Commissioner System in some parts of the country. The Commissioner system was first introduced in Calcutta (Kolkata) in 1855 and was later extended to Maharasthra, Madras (Chennai), and Hyderabad. The sixth report of the National Police Commission, issued in 1982, highlighted the need for the Commissioner System for cities with a population of half a million or more. With the introduction of the Model Police Act, 2006, the said recommendation was enacted with a revised limit of a million or above. According to the Bureau of Police Research and Development's (BPRD) report of 2019, sixty-three cities across fifteen States have the Commissioner System in India. Recently, in the North Indian State of Uttar Pradesh (UP), the government has introduced the Commissioner System in Kanpur and Noida, taking the total tally to sixty-five cities at present.

In the Commission System, there is unity of control over executive and police functions by the Commissioner of Police, who is of equivalent rank to the Dy. Inspector General of Police or above. The head of Police in such a system is the Commissioner of Police (CP), who may be assisted in his work by an Additional Deputy Commissioner or Special Commissioner of Police. There may also be a Joint Police Commissioner to head one or two districts. The head of Subdistricts is the Deputy Commissioner of Police. The Assistant Commissioner of Police is the head of subdivisions under districts and the Inspector of Police controls the Police Station. The Commissioner of Police has the powers of District Magistrate and any officer above or equal to the rank of the Assistant Commissioner of Police can exercise the power of Executive Magistrate. The scope of such power is guided by the Cr.P.C., subject to the amendments made by different state governments. However, the Commissioner of Police is directly accountable to the DGP and the State government for his actions.

Police Training

The training of police personnel is crucial for the effective rendition of duties and for inculcating the correct attitude toward the profession. The police training in India is done at the Central and the State Level. The Central Police organizations have their own specialized training schools as per professional requirements. The State level training institutes are of three types; namely apex, subordinate and specialized. Gazetted officers are trained at the apex institutes which also provide some specialized courses. The head of the apex institute is the Additional DGP who takes care of the administration, infrastructure, and quality of training. The subordinate level schools impart training to police constabulary, which is generally for a duration of nine months. Additional focus on leadership is given during the training of Subinspector or deputy inspector. The specialized training institutes cater to specific field establishments of police like traffic, motor driving, wireless, special branch etc. Apart from this, there are prepromotion courses prescribed as a mandate for promotion. Some specialized courses also focus on techniques of scientific investigation, dealing with insurgency, and VIP security, among others.

The Gore Committee on Police Training, in its 1971 report, noted that most of the instructors were serving police officers who had no training or experience in the art of teaching. Even the methods and infrastructure deployed for imparting training were insufficient. The Padmanabhaiah Committee (2000) and the Second Administrative Reforms Commission (2007) have noted that the entry level qualifications and training of constables do not qualify them for their role and therefore recommended to raise the qualification requirement. Considering the insufficient legal knowledge and inadequate forensic and cyber infrastructure, the Second ARC recommended that states should have specialized investigation units within the police force for better investigation of crimes (Vinayak, 2017). Though there is considerable increase in cybercrime, more than one in five police personnel frequently face the lack of the technology or expertise to investigate cybercrimes (Status of Policing in India Report, 2019).

The Comptroller and Auditor General (CAG) of India in the year 2016 reported that out of 71,711 recruitments at constable level, 67,669 constables have been trained. CAG report also highlighted the deficiencies in weapon training and the inadequacy of proper training infrastructure (Kushwah 2018). The report further reveals that the amount spent on police training is not sufficient as the percentage of total expenditure on police training in comparison to total police expenditure for 2017–2018 was merely 1.39 percent (Data on Police Organisations, 2019).The successive Governments, at Center and States, have taken numerous measures and initiatives for police training that have brought about considerable change in the way the police function now. However, given the size of the country and number of its population, there is a requirement of constant research and training of the police for bringing about efficiency in performance and to improve its cooperation with the people.

CONCLUSION

The organization of police in India is not in an ideal state. There is an acute dearth of police personnel in India and with 136.42 per a hundred thousand, it has one of the lowest police to population ratios in the world (Business Standard, n.d). Although it is the second most populous nation, it has merely 1,511 police persons for each 100,000 population. The national average of policemen on the ground is forty-two persons short of the sanctioned strength (India Justice Report, 2019).

Moreover, other than human infrastructure, the Indian police system also lacks physical and technological infrastructure. To deal with infrastructural issues, modernization of police forces (MPF) schemes were introduced, however, not much has progressed since then. There is shortage of modern equipment in Forensic Science Labs and shortage of technical staff. Police use outdated and unserviceable weapons, modernization funds remain unutilized, and one in ten police stations has no access to drinking water with one in five having no access to clean toilets.

Around 41 percent of police personnel reported that they failed to reach a crime scene on time, and 28 percent said that they could not escort an accused to court on time due to understaffing. (Hindu Data Team, 2019) Notably, around 70 percent of a department's allocation is used in meeting committed liabilities, such as payment of salaries, which leaves only around 30 percent for spending on everything else.

The constabulary and officers, respectively, makeup 85 and 15 percent of the Indian police. Constables are typically promoted once during their service, and normally retire as Head Constables. This leads to a lack of motivation for effective functioning. The police system is also plagued with political control. About 38 percent of the civil police reported that they always face political pressure in cases involving influential persons. Three out of five police personnel reported transfer as the most common consequence of not complying with such external pressures. Those who don't yield to such control suffer at the hands of the political heads. About 12 percent reported the most common consequence to be suspension or dismissal from service, while 5 percent also reported threat to their personal safety or physical assault. The number of deaths in prisons has increased in preceding years; the details of which are often concealed. The recent case of the Tuticorin Custodial Death is a testament to how prone the police system is to misuse (Gupta, 2020).

Apart from maintaining law and order, police personnel perform other functions such as traffic management, disaster rescue, and removal of encroachments, and so forth. These extra obligations lead to overburdening of the police force. Not only does this affect performance, but it also leads to stress and lack of motivation. There is a huge vacancy of Police personnel against the total sanctioned strength at national level. There is requirement of outsourcing of noncore police functions in a phased manner. However, it is interesting to note that despite the acute shortage of police personnel across the country, 63,061 police personnel are protecting 19, 225 VIPs, whereas the sanctioned strength for the same is 40,031.

Indubitably, the police are one of the most important instruments for maintaining law and order and for keeping internal security and peace in the Indian society. However, India, with its vast territory and huge population, coupled with its extremely diverse social set up, is highly prone to anti-social, criminal, subversive, and anti-national activities. Moreover, illiteracy, poverty, unemployment, and social strife make maintenance of law and order and keeping internal security a major challenge for the Central and State Governments. In such a scenario, the police present a great hope through prevention and control of crime and criminal tendencies and keep the society and nation peaceful and intact by maintaining internal security. However, the Police in India face many issues and challenges in its internal structure and functioning, and in protecting their image before the public. Police here still suffer from colonial legacy and, at most places, behave in a way suggestive of the existence of a police state.

The Second Administrative Reforms Commission highlighted the state and police partiality, corruption, brutality, and failure to register offenses to be the most important factors behind the unsatisfactory Public-Police relations (Second Administrative Reforms Commission, 2007). Generally, Public-Police relations are not in a happy state in India and the police have still not acquired an unblemished image of being the savior of people. The public still look at the police with suspicion and do not feel confident at the sight of police personnel. Unfortunately, there is a lack of trust for police among the masses and an average person wishes to avoid engagement and even the visual of police personnel. This is largely owed to the general attitude of police persons who still do not show a sympathetic and concerned attitude with the people. Rather, they behave arrogantly and even try to exploit and harass the common people. Moreover, the degree of political control and self-serving attitude within the police personnel remains a grave concern. Indian police, though, has come a long way since India's independence. Yet, a lot needs to be done, not only to bring efficiency and professionalism, but also to uplift its image and build confidence among the people.

REFERENCES

Aggarwal, Devi Dyal. *C.B.I. and Policing in India.* New Delhi: Kaveri Books, 2000.

Anviti, Chaturvedi. "Police Reforms in India." *P.R.S. Legislative Research, New Delhi* 4 (2017).

Choudhary, Rohit. *Policing: Reinvention Strategies in a Marketing Framework.* Sage Publications India, 2009.

CHRI. Government Compliance and Supreme Court Directives: An Assessment (2018, April 21). https://www.humanrightsinitiative.org/ download/1524467740Supreme %20Court%20directives%20on%20police%20reforms.pdf.

CHRI. Summary of Ribeiro Committee's Recommendations, October 1998. https:// humanrightsinitiative.org/publications/police/recommendations_ribeiro.pdf.

CHRI. The Padmanabhaiah Committee on Police Reforms A Critical Analysis of Some Important Recommendations. https://humanrightsinitiative.org/programs/aj /police/india/initiatives/analysis_padmanabhaiah.pdf.

Commonwealth Human Rights Initiative. Police Organisation in India http://www .humanrightsinitiative.org.

Curry, J. C. The Indian Police, London 1932. *P. Griffiths, To Guard My People: The History of the Indian Police, London* (1971): 409–411.

Daruwala, Maja, Devika Prasad, Maria Laura Canineu, Swati Mehta, and Janine Rauch. *Police Accountability: Too Important to Neglect, Too Urgent to Delay: The 2005 Report by the International Advisory Commission of the Commonwealth Human Rights Initiative Chaired by Sam Okudzeto.* CHRI, 2005.

Data on Police Organisations. India: Bureau of Police Research and Development (BPRD), 2019.https://bprd.nic.in/WriteReadData/userfiles/file/202001301028101 694907BPRDData2019-19forweb-2.pdf.

Draft Police Manual BPRD. Chapter 1: Indian Police: An introductory and Statistical Overview.

Ghanwat, M. R. "Police administration and public relations in Maharashtra." (2017).

Gupta, Nishtha.Tuticorin Custodial Death: Kin Say Father–son Duo Was Sexually Abused in Police Custody, Outrage in Tamil Nadu. *India Today,* News (7 June 2020).

https://www.indiatoday.in/india/story/tuticorin-custodial-death-kin-say-father-son -duo-was-sexually-abused-in-police-custody-outrage-in-tamil-nadu-1692411-2020 -06-25.

Hindu Data team. Are Police Stations in India Equipped with Basic Infrastructure and Adequate Staff? *Hindu* Data (4 December 2019). https://www.thehindu.com/data/ are-police-stations-in-india-equipped-with-basic-infrastructure-and-adequate-staff /article30162643.ece.

India Justice Report: Ranking States on Police, Judiciary, Prisons and Legal Aid. New Delhi: Tata Trusts, 2019.

Jeremiah, J., and Shanmukham, B. Utilisation of Forensic Services by the Investigating of Àcers in the U.T. of Puducherry. *Indian Police Journal*: 160.

Joginder, Singh. Inside Indian Police. (2009).

Kasture, *Thoughts on Police Reform 3*. National Police Academy, 1966.

Kumar, Aditya. In Blood and Color: The Madras Torture Commission Report as a Liberal Response to a Crisis in Racial Capitalism. PhD diss., Brown University, 2017.

Kushwah, V. S. Why India Needs Urgent Police Reforms. Observer Research Foundation, Expert Speak (4 December 2018). https://www.orfonline.org/expert -speak/why-india-needs-urgent-police-reforms-46003/#_edn6.

Padhi, Nagendra Kumar. *Police and the Weaker Sections*. A.P.H. Publishing, 2007.

Pai, Sudha, and Pattnaik, Sowesh. *Police, Its Work Processes and the Community: An Empirical Study of a District in Orissa*. Shodhgana, 2014.

Parashar, Rajinder. Police Administration: A Historical Survey. In Verinder, Grover (Ed.), *Political System and Constitution of India: Political Progress, Government* (pp. 652–675). Delhi: Deep and Deep Publications, 1997.

Pathi, Srinibas and Zonthansanga, David. *Police Administration in Mizoram 1987– 2005*. Shodhgana, 2013.

Saini, Kamal. *Police Investigations: Procedural Dimensions, Law, and Methods*. Delhi: Deep & Deep Publications, 2001.

Sarkar, Jadunath. *Mughal Administration* (Patna University Readership Lectures, 1920). Forgotten Books, 2013.

Sharma, Jolly. *Role of Police in the Administration of Criminal Justice System a Critical Study with Special Reference to Chandigarh*." 107th International Training Course Participants Papers.

Second Administrative Reforms Commission. Fifth Report "Public Order"(2007). https://darpg.gov.in/sites/default/files/public_order5.pdf.

Singh, Deepa, *Human Rights and Police Predicament*. Delhi: Bright Law House, 2002.

Singh, Dr. Deepa. *Human Rights and Police Predicament*. Delhi: Bright Law House, 2002.

Status of Policing in India Report. India: Common Cause &Lokniti, Centre for the Study Developing Societies (CSDS), 2019. https://www.tatatrusts.org/upload/pdf/ state-of-policing-in-india-report-2019.pdf.

Trimukhe, Shweta. Gender Mainstreaming in Police: A Study in the Police Training Centers of Maharashtra. PhD diss., 2019.

Verma, Arvind. *The Indian Police: A Critical Evaluation*. Daya Books, 2005.

Vinayak, Krishnan. Modernisation of Police Forces. PRS Blog, 2017.

Chapter 11

Policing and Law Enforcement in Indonesia

Sharyn Graham Davies

Indonesia has the world's fifth-largest police force, not surprising given the archipelagic nation is home to the world's fourth-largest population. Policing concentration is not evenly spread, however, with some provinces lightly policed while Papua is one of the most heavily policed places on the planet. Despite more than two decades of democratic reform in Indonesia, the police force remains plagued by inefficiencies and corruption. This chapter introduces Indonesia's police force, provides a history, discusses structure examines reform efforts and incorporates insights into how the police are incorporating women into their ranks.

INTRODUCTION

There are almost 600,000 police officers in Indonesia; roughly four percent of them are women. It is the fifth-largest police force in the world, policing a total population of 264 million people. In Indonesia, the national police force is referred to as Polri, a term derived from the Kepolisian Negara Republic Indonesia (The National Police of the Republic of Indonesia).

The police separated from the Indonesian military in 1999, one year after democratic rule was introduced in the country. Indonesia has a police-to-population ratio of one police officer for every 600 people. In the early 1980s, during President Suharto's authoritarian rule, the ratio was one officer for every 1,200 people (Jansen, 2008). The United Nations has suggested that the ideal ratio is around one officer for every 500 citizens (International Crisis Group, 2012, p. 4). Indonesia, on average, is nearing this ideal ratio but police are not evenly spread across the archipelago. The contested province of Papua is heavily policed with a ratio of one officer for every 100 citizens.

While the police force has grown considerably in size in the last two decades, inefficiencies remain. Inefficiencies are partly due to a lack of funding. Salaries for police are considered relatively high compared to other government jobs in Indonesia. However, with over 90 percent of the police budget spent on salaries, there is little money left for operational costs (Jansen, 2008). In fact, police officers often say that the reason they undertake corrupt acts is not necessarily for personal profit but rather to fill petrol in patrol cars and meet other essential expenses to allow them to perform their duties (Davies et al., 2015).

After the police split from the military in the early years of democratic reform, relations between the two services were particularly volatile (Malley, 2003). However, relations between security sectors seem to have improved, with each service having now developed a clearly defined role; police as responsible for enforcing on-the-ground domestic security (Jansen, 2008). There seems to be, however, an ongoing conflict between security forces in areas such as in the contested province of Papua.

Since 1998, when Indonesia ushered in an era of democratic rule, the police have benefited in numerous ways from reform efforts. Many of these reform efforts have been instigated by foreign entities that have contributed through substantial funding. Donor countries include the United States, Australia, Japan, the EU, and New Zealand. Reforms and attendant foreign donor funds have meant that Indonesia now has relatively well-trained and well-resourced special operation units. These units focus on things such as transnational crime including human trafficking, drug smuggling, money laundering, and terrorism. Another reform effort revolves around the development of a form of community policing. New Zealand and Japan have had a key focus on funding this type of reform.

Despite almost two decades of reform, though, the Indonesian police structure remains very hierarchical and militaristic. There are also ongoing issues of corruption, persistent human rights abuse, minimal levels of training, and extensive inefficiencies. An early International Crisis Group report illustrates these shortcomings, and there is no evidence to suggest that the situation has improved (International Crisis Group, 2012).

An ongoing issue regarding knowledge of policing in Indonesia is that there has been limited scholarly attention given to the police force. If one was inclined, material published in English, dedicated to understanding Indonesia's police force, could be read quite quickly (International Crisis Group, 2001, 2004, 2012; Meliala, 2001a, 2001b, 2002a, 2002b; Stasch, 2001; Prasetyo et al., 2005; Rahmawati & Azca, 2006; Villaveces-Izquierdo, 2010; Davies et al., 2013a, 2013b; Muradi, 2014; Buttle et al., 2015). Surprisingly, there is also little information about policing in Indonesia published in the local language (Dajoh & Ismail, 1997; Djamin, 1999; Markas

Besar Kepolisian Republik Indonesia, 1999; Bhakti, 2004). If one wants to extend their search and look up information regarding Indonesia's security sector, there is still a dearth of material regarding the topic (Kristiansen & Trijono, 2005; Jansen, 2008; Kingsley, 2010).

There is, therefore, a need for more research to be undertaken on Indonesia's police force. Without extensive research, it is difficult to understand in rich detail, the police organizational culture and its formal and informal departmental missions, its strategies, policies and procedures, and its styles of administration and policing. We also do not know much about the occupational culture, including values, norms, perspectives, and rules. Nor do we know much about how police culture influences police–community relations in Indonesia except for a few limited studies (Davies, 2013, 2014, 2015, 2016). We also know little about the history of police in Indonesia, as the following section shows.

HISTORY OF POLICE IN INDONESIA

It was with the Declaration of Independence in 1945 that the Indonesian police force first came into being (Meliala, 2001). The police were organized initially to assist in the fight for independence from the Dutch and Japanese occupation in the 1940s.

The police were first envisaged as being politically neutral, and as having operational and administrative independence. They were originally given equal status to the military. This autonomy lasted from around 1945 until President Suharto seized power in a military coup in 1966. Shortly thereafter, the police were merged with the military and by 1968 the police were effectively a paramilitary wing of the army, tasked with suppressing dissent against President Suharto. Usurpingly, as a paramilitary force, the police were structured like the army and they positioned citizens as the enemy. With this positioning, the use of brutal and deadly forms of extralegal violence against citizens was allowed and even encouraged (Jefferson, 1990). Public mistrust in the police grew, a mistrust that is still evident today. The police remained a highly centralized part of the military until the democratic reforms in Indonesia during 1998. In the post-1998 era, steps were taken to reform the police.

INDONESIAN POLICE REFORM

In 1999, Indonesia's police force was separated from the military and it was given increased political autonomy (Meliala, 2001b). One of the factors that helped with restoring police autonomy was the process of decentralization of power whereby national political structures were reconfigured to give local administrations more political authority (Djani, 2009). This process of decentralization gave greater autonomy to provincial police forces and loosened the national government control over the police (Stein & Lambang, 2005).

Increasing autonomy created its own problems for the police, however. For instance, the public continued to witness police abuse their power and continued to see the police as untrustworthy (Meliala, 2002b). One attempt at reform specifically aimed at promoting police legitimacy was sensitivity in policing (Meliala, 2001a). Meliala, a former police commissioner for Indonesia, proposed three dimensions to police sensitivity; individual police officers needed to be sensitive in their interactions with the public; police culture needed to change and promote sensitivity toward the public; and police organizational dynamics needed to promote a sensitive approach to policing. Meliala further recommended that the police adopt a community-orientated approach to policing in Indonesia.

There is much research that supports Meliala's push for this type of Indonesian police reform. For instance, there are studies showing the effectiveness of community-orientated approaches to policing in regional conflict zones (Braithwaite, Braithwaite, Cookson, & Dunn, 2010; Prasetyo et al., 2005). But despite efforts to implement a community-orientated approach to policing in Indonesia, the lack of public goodwill and poor police performance has continued to reduce community support for police. Further, persistent police corruption and the use of extralegal violence have remained significant barriers to Indonesian police reform. These barriers have additionally meant that citizens are unlikely to engage with the police, something that underpins effective law enforcement (Pino & Johnson, 2011). Quantitative public opinion surveys have shown that public trust in Indonesia's police is low, with only 33 percent of Indonesians saying that they held the police in a positive light (Kepala Kepolsian Negara Republik Indonesia, 2012). Corruption remains one of the most pressing issues within Indonesia's police force, as the next section reveals.

ISSUES OF CORRUPTION

In Indonesia, a national campaign against corruption has taken place since democratic reforms in 1998. Part of the impetus behind these reforms was the identification of corruption as a political and economic barrier to international investment in Indonesia (Martini, 2012). However, Indonesia has continued to score poorly on ratings of governance because of its high levels of corruption (Martini, 2012). For instance, Transparency International has a global corruption barometer which indicates that 36 percent of Indonesians have reported paying bribes for services (Hardoon & Heinrich, 2013). In contrast, only one percent of the Australians in the same study claimed to have paid a bribe (Hardoon & Heinrich, 2013). This finding indicates that corruption is embedded across Indonesia, and particularly, in the Indonesian police force. Indeed, corruption in Indonesia is a real problem across the criminal justice system (Winarta, 2009) and research has shown that one of the worst offenders are police representatives (Davies, 2016). For instance, on a scale of 1 to 5 (one being not corrupt and 5 extremely corrupt), the Indonesian police are rated at 4.5 and the judiciary is rated at 4.4 (Hardoon & Heinrich, 2013). These results indicate that the Indonesian criminal justice system, especially the police, are perceived as corrupt.

Police are gatekeepers to the criminal justice system and, as such, the Indonesian police give the judiciary many opportunities to engage in corrupt practices (Buttle, 2015). How the police are utilized often reflects on the political order of society (Reiner, 2000). As such, how police treat citizens is often perceived as a reflection of the justness and fairness of the state institutions constituting the criminal justice system (Tyler, 2004). If people have faith in a country's law and its criminal justice system, they will usually comply with police orders voluntarily. The legitimacy of Indonesia's police can therefore stand as a barometer, measuring the strength of Indonesia's political institutions and the social and economic wellbeing of citizens. Because the police are central to the success of relatively new democracies (Hinton & Newburn, 2009), including Indonesia, the issue of police corruption must be addressed to ensure the success of democratic rule. Corruption within Indonesia's police continues to flourish, despite several efforts to reform the institution (Davies, 2016). Given that corruption continues unabated, it is not surprising that the public perceptions of Indonesia's police force remain negative.

PUBLIC PERCEPTIONS OF POLICE

Public perceptions of police in Indonesia remain poor. Much of this perception is related to real instances of corruption, police brutality, and police inefficiency. In one study, drawing on seventeen in-depth interviews with people in Indonesia about their perceptions of police, Davies et al. (2015) showed that while people were often initially positive about the work of police; acknowledging the difficulties police face and recognizing that many officers work hard to keep their communities safe, all participants were highly critical of the police. Some people thought that just a few rogue cops were tarnishing the reputation of the entire police force, but this notion has been dismissed by a large body of research outside Indonesia (Caldero & Crank, 2011; Keppeler et al., 1998; Newburn, 1999; Punch, 2000; Punch & Gilmour, 2010). Other people believed that there was a predatory culture of money-motivated policing (Gerber & Mendelson, 2008) in Indonesia, driven by the requirement to repay academy entrance fees and the desire to get rich, both through bribing citizens and by letting the rich off serious offenses if they paid enough money.

For most people in Indonesia, their contact with police is in traffic law enforcement. Indeed, almost everyone in Indonesia has some interaction with traffic police, a situation that is also true elsewhere in the world (Blais & Dupont, 2005). For most Indonesians, their engagement with traffic police is not a positive experience. Interestingly, what shapes people's negative opinions of traffic police is not that they must pay a fine or even that they dislike the associated blatant corruption (bribery and corruption may be so ingrained that people tolerate the inevitability of bribes). What shapes people's negative opinions is that the bribes are unregulated and nonnegotiable. It is the constancy of bribes and their variability that produce the most overwhelmingly negative public perceptions of police in Indonesia.

The media are also partly complicit in Indonesia's poor policing track record. For instance, the Indonesian media either shows disinterest in reporting on the police or reports in sensationalist ways (Davies, 2015; Davies, 2016). Analyzing sixty-three articles that appeared in a local newspaper, Davies et al. (2015) found that the articles generally failed to criticize the police or promote police interests in any enduring way. They also found that articles reported on police in a benign way by simply describing characteristics of the incident, victim, and suspect, and discussing the status of an investigation or trial. This research suggests that media is largely disinterested in police and policing, and in a circular way, both these factors reflect and sculpt the public opinion regarding the police.

The media significantly shapes public perceptions of police, and the media has the potential to spark critical debate about policing in Indonesia. Reporting on police is important for a democratic nation and without critical reporting of police activities, people will remain largely disengaged from the police, allowing poor policing practices to persist. In addition to significant and critical media coverage, there are other ways that policing can be improved in Indonesia. For instance, research has suggested that a procedural justice approach to policing may increase both public trust in the institution and encourage more extensive reporting of policing across Indonesia, as the next section shows.

PROCEDURAL JUSTICE POLICING

One way that Indonesian police could improve public perceptions is by introducing a form of procedural justice policing. Research has shown that the Indonesian public would be highly receptive to procedural justice policing (Davies, 2014). Put simply, procedural justice policing involves quality treatment such as police treating people politely, quality decision-making involving police making fair decisions, and moral similitude where police accurately reflect social values (Tyler, 2008). Procedural justice policing is a move away from punitive policing, where people obey the law merely to avoid being punished. Zero tolerance policing comes out of this mold, as does the "three strikes and you're out" response to criminal justice. Yet, while punitive policing is ineffective in lowering crime rates (Tyler, 2007), it continues to dominate global policing approaches, and Indonesia is no exception.

Research has shown that people are most likely to obey the law when they feel there is a rightness to the law and when authorities are just in their execution of the law (Tyler, 2008). If police employ principles of procedural justice such as quality treatment, quality decision-making, and moral similitude when dealing with people, citizens are more likely to cooperate with police, comply with the law, and consider the police legitimate. There is widespread evidence of the positive link between procedural justice policing and cooperation with police (Tankebe, 2009; Murphy & Cherney, 2012). There is also evidence of a positive link between procedural justice policing and public compliance with the law (Jackson, 2012). Most of this research is based in the West with some notable exceptions (Tankebe, 2013; Reisig, 2013; Sun, 2013). Research in Indonesia has shown that support for the police increases when police use procedural policing (Davies, 2016).

With support from international donors such as Japan, the United States, Australia, and to a lesser degree, New Zealand, the Indonesian police force has slowly started to move away from a paramilitary understanding of law enforcement toward a community-policing model (Prasetyo et al., 2005). Effective policing requires the cooperation of citizens (Alpert, Dunham & Piquero, 1998) and community policing is a model geared toward developing public support (Hawdon & Ryan, 2003). As such, effective community policing needs to build positive public perceptions and develop police trustworthiness (Hawdon, 2008; Stoutland, 2001, cf. Acciaioli, 2001). The move toward community policing is a considerable improvement in comparison to how the country was policed during the military rule of the Suharto regime. However, evidence of how successful the police have been in adopting a community orientated approach to policing is ambiguous. Moreover, a specific move toward a procedural justice approach to policing has been suggested as a particularly fruitful way forward for the Indonesian police force (Davies, 2015). Alongside moves toward procedural justice policing, the inclusion of women within the police force is another clear way in which the police can improve both their image and their engagement with the public, as the following section shows.

WOMEN IN THE POLICE FORCE

For over six decades women have been included in Indonesia's police force, joining the force in 1948. Despite this long history, though, there are very few policewomen in contemporary Indonesia. In fact, less than 5 percent of the police force are women (Davies, Meliala, & Buttle, 2016). There are calls for women to make up 30 percent of the police force, in a similar way to the allocated quota for women in politics (Davies, 2012). To help meet this ideal quota, there have been several training initiatives (Human Rights Watch, 2014c). However, policewomen numbers continue to remain below 5 percent of the entire police force.

The majority of policewomen are assigned only a few roles. For instance, policewomen generally work in units assisting women and children or in administrative roles (cf Davies, 2010). One of the more recent initiatives developed by Indonesia's police force is to deploy policewomen in socially visible areas such as demonstrations, where policewomen oversee security and often hand out lollies in the hopes of calming protestors. Policewomen are also often involved in traffic coordination, both in physically directing traffic on the road and in reading traffic reports for various media networks.

Given the patriarchal nature of normative Indonesian society, and the police specifically, it is unsurprising that senior policemen reaffirm to the public that they, policemen, are ever-present and were a situation to arise that a policewoman could not handle, they would be willing and able to step in. For instance, if a policewoman was overwhelmed at a protest march, a policeman would be right behind to protect her.

In this initiative to increase the public role of policewomen, more stringent recruitment protocols have been developed for policewomen, as discussed below. Once selected, policewomen are often positioned as the public face of policing, with the notion that young, pretty, and pious policewomen support positive police–public relations. In fact, previous research has shown that, indeed, the public believes that policewomen are less corrupt than policemen, are more trustworthy, and have a greater ability than men to calm volatile situations (Davies, 2014). The strength of the value of beauty has meant that in recruiting policewomen, there is a strong focus on the physical appearance of the women.

While there are guidelines regarding men applying to the police force, there are even more strict guidelines for women (Davies, 2015a). To apply to be policewomen, women must be between seventeen and twenty-two years of age and never married. Once recruited, women are barred from marrying for two years and after marriage, a policewoman can only remain in the police force if her husband gives permission. Women recruits must pass a string of psychological tests and show that they are religiously pious.

Recruits must have passed high school and be willing to live anywhere across the archipelago. Recruits cannot need prescription glasses and they must be over 165 cm tall with an appropriate body mass index (BMI). To this end, the body measurements of the women are taken, and it is often policemen who measure women's hips and bust sizes. Recruits must also be judged as beautiful (see Saraswati, 2013). The women need to walk on a catwalk in front of the selection committee to be judged sufficiently beautiful (Davies, 2018). Women recruits also need to be virgins, which is discussed further below.

Women who successfully pass the recruitment stage then become police officers. One of the difficulties of the strict selection criteria for women is that the women who make it into the police force are then frequently positioned as too pretty, too pious, and too pure to perform any actual difficult police work (Davies, 2018).

While there is very little academic research on Indonesian police, there is even less on Indonesian policewomen. In fact, there was barely anything written regarding policewomen in Indonesia prior to 2013. But in 2013, the policewomen's profiles grew, to the point that some of the most-followed people on Twitter in Indonesia are policewomen (Davies & Hartono, 2015). With policewomen becoming social media icons, an increasing number of women were inspired to join the force, to the point that a police commissioner had to appear on television to tell viewers that becoming a policewoman was not an easy shortcut to becoming a celebrity.

Most women joining Indonesia's police force do so to serve their nation. The police also provide a steady and reliable income. Some women face resistance from their families during the joining process, given the often hard and dangerous work that family members perceive policing to involve. This perception is another reason why policewomen are often relegated to desk jobs; to appease family members with a guarantee that they will not be put in harm's way. Some women become officers because a friend joins or because they are not sure what they want to do with their life. For others, though, becoming a police officer is the culmination of a dream that they have had since they were young.

Once policewomen marry, which they can do after two years of service, they frequently resign from their job. For the women who continue with policing work, many struggle with the demands of being a wife and mother in paid employment. This struggle is particularly acute in Indonesia where it is enshrined in state ideology that a woman's priorities are to be a good wife and mother, and only after fulfilling these duties can a woman undertake work in the public sector. Some women find that being married to a policeman helps with this juggle because he understands the requirements of the job, especially the requirement of undertaking night shifts.

If women continue within the force as they get older, they become subject to discrimination. This discrimination extends from the recruitment procedures, where women are selected for their beauty; this beauty is then used as a reason to bar them from investigative police work. Without this experience of police work outside the office, women find it hard to secure promotion. Further, where women are recruited on the basis of beauty, which is equated with youth, their opportunities for varied police work, and thus promotion, diminish with age. Without a doubt, though, one of the most challenging aspects of policing for women in Indonesia is the requirement that they are virgins upon recruitment.

Indonesia, like many societies, places significant value on virginity for women. The idea that virginity is a hallmark of honor is prevalent. Virginity is a form of social and bodily capital through which a woman and her extended family can lay claims to social status and respectability. While virginity for men and women at marriage is valued, there is an expectation that men will likely have sexual experiences before marriage; for women, virginity is demanded (Bennett, 2005). Were a woman not to be a virgin at marriage, she would jeopardize both her marriage and the status of her family (Platt, 2012). Flowing from this value of virginity is the idea that policewomen showcase their self-control and honor by protecting their virginity up until their marriage. Virginity is used as a marker to the selection panel and implies that the applicant will be able to protect other citizens, especially women, just as she has been able to protect herself.

Women police recruits, just like women in Indonesia, are subject to high levels of sexual surveillance (Davies, 2015). This surveillance extends to a physical two-finger virginity test. The test has been a recruitment requirement since the 1960s, although it has not always been used, nor reported on. In 2014, though, Human Rights Watch publicized the practice, provoking the Indonesian police force to front up to the media on the issue of forced virginity testing. Human Rights Watch and other organizations loudly criticized the practice, noting that a two-finger virginity test was scientifically invalid and that it was blatantly sexist and discriminatory. In response, there were comments made by the police that the practice had been discontinued. However, research suggests that the practice is still ongoing (Davies, 2018).

Indonesian policewomen themselves have mixed reactions to the practice of virginity testing. Some women are emphatically against the practice, sharing stories of humiliation, pain, and trauma at having to undergo this practice. Other policewomen, though, offer support for the practice, noting how it is a rite of passage that marks their entry into an elite club of women who are able to protect and defend their morality and hence their nation (Davies, 2018). It is this notion of honor that provides an understanding into the policewomen's successful battle for the right to wear the Islamic head veil on duty (Davies,

2018). While it is admirable that the Indonesian police have acknowledged the importance of women being included in the police force, there is still much to do to ensure that policewomen are able to contribute fully to both the police force and society.

CONCLUSION

As one of the world's largest police forces, Indonesia has struggled to maintain an effective and efficient law enforcement sector. It seems, though, that despite its shortcomings, Indonesians have an attenuated approach to policing in the sense that, while they may be negatively disposed toward the current police system, they see a legitimate social role for a police force that is fair and just (Davies, 2014). This chapter ends, then, with a call for more research to be conducted on police in Indonesia. In particular, there is a need for more qualitative research on police. The majority of the policing ethnographies are based in Western nations (e.g., Westmarland, 2001; Behr, 2002) and there are few policing ethnographies outside the West (e.g., Sengupta 2010). Yet, we have much to learn and understand about policing in developing countries, many of which are reforming their police forces. There is also a need for more research regarding the public's perceptions of the police, especially with a qualitative lens (e.g., Brunson & Weitzner, 2011; Muniz, 2012). Exploring all avenues of policing will enable the development of better policing practices and grant a richer understanding of interactions between police and citizens, not only in Indonesia but globally as well.

REFERENCES

Acciaioli, Greg. (2001). "Grounds of conflict, idioms of harmony: Custom, religion, and nationalism in violence avoidance at the Lindu Plain, Central Sulawesi." *Indonesia* 72: 81–114.

Alpert, Geoffrey, Roger Dunham, and Alpert Piquero. (1998). "On the study of neighbourhoods and the police." *Community Policing: Contemporary Readings*: 309–326.

Amnesty International. (2012). *Shocking Police Brutality in Indonesia Revealed.* Retrieved 27 July 2020, http://www.amnesty.org.au/features/comments/28495.

Bhakti, Ikrar Nus. (2004). *Relasi TNI dan Polri dalam penanganan keamanan dalam negeri, 2000-2004.* Pusat Penelitian Politik, Lembaga Ilmu Pengetahuan Indonesia.

Blais, Etienne, and Benoit Dupont. (2005). "Assessing the capability of intensive police programmes to prevent severe road accidents: A systematic review." *British Journal of Criminology* 45(6): 914–937.

Braithwaite, John, Valerie Braithwaite, Michael Cookson, and Leah Dunn. (2010). *Anomie and Violence: Nontruth and Reconciliation in Indonesian Peacebuilding.* ANU Press.

Buttle, John W. (2003). "'What's good for them, is good for us': Outside Influences on the adoption of incapacitant sprays by the British Police." *International Journal of Police Science & Management* 5(2): 98–111.

Buttle, John W., Sharyn Graham Davies, and Adrianus E. Meliala. (2016). "A cultural constraints theory of police corruption: Understanding the persistence of police corruption in contemporary Indonesia." *Australian & New Zealand Journal of Criminology* 49(3) 437–454.

Caldero, M. A., and J. P. Crank. (2011). "Police ethics: The corruption of noble cause rev."

Crisp, D. (1990). "The police and the public." *Home Office Research Bulletin* 29: 15–17.

Dajoh, E. M. F., and S. Ismail. (1997). *Polisi Pamong Praja: Hari Ini dan Esok (Civil Service Police: Today and Tomorrow).* Jakarta: Kantor Kentraman dan Ketertiban Pemerintah DKI.

Davies, Sharyn Graham, Adrianus Meliala, and John Buttle. (2013). "Indonesia's secret police weapon: Perfectly coiffed hair and rose-pink cheeks underpin polri" s latest policing tactic." *Inside Indonesia*: 111.

Davies, Sharyn Graham, Adrianus Meliala, and John Buttle. (2013). "Ari' s audacity: How can you Be a straight cop when people just give You money inside. *Indonesia* 113 (July-September)."

Davies, Sharyn Graham, Adrianus Meliala, and John Buttle. (2016). "Gangnam style versus eye of the tiger: People, Police, and Procedural Justice in Indonesia." *Policing and Society* 26(4): 453–474.

Davies, Sharyn Graham, and Hanny Savitri Hartono. (2015). "The pretty imperative: handcuffing policewomen in Indonesia." *Intersections: Gender and Sexuality in Asia and the Pacific* 37.

Davies, Sharyn Graham, and J. W. Buttle. (2014). "Policing in Indonesia: Exploring Ways in Which the Legitimacy of the Police May Effect Economic Development and the Prosperity of the Indonesian State." *Wellington: Ministry of Foreign Affairs and Trade.*

Davies, Sharyn Graham, John Buttle, and Adrianus Meliala. (2015). "If you lose your goat: Public Perceptions of Police in Indonesia." *Journal of Social Science Research* 6(2): 1,036–1,046.

Davies, Sharyn Graham, Louise M. Stone, and John W. Buttle. 2015. "A disinterested press: Reporting Police in a Provincial Indonesian Newspaper." *Media Asia* 42(1–2): 47–60.

Davies, Sharyn Graham. (2010). *Gender Diversity in Indonesia: Sexuality, Islam, and Queer Selves.* Routledge.

Davies, Sharyn Graham. (2015). "Beautiful virgins: The hard road to becoming an Indonesian policewoman. *Asian Currents* (April). http://asaablog.tumblr.com/post /116987426401/beautiful-virgins-the-hard-road-to-becoming-an.

Davies, Sharyn Graham. (2018). "Skins of Morality: Bio-borders, Ephemeral citizenship and Policing Women in Indonesia." *Asian Studies Review* (1): 69–88.

Davies, Sharyn, Louise Stone, and John Buttle. (2016). "Covering cops: Critical reporting of Indonesian police corruption." *Pacific Journalism Review* 22(2): 185.

Djamin, A. L. (1999). *Menuju Polri Mandiri yang Profesional (The Limits of an Independent, Professional Police Force).* Jakarta: Yayasan Tenaga Kerja.

Djani, L. (2009). "Democratic decentralization and its enemy." In R. Rokim, R. Amri, E. Imran, N. M., and N. Razak (Eds.), *Indonesia Economic Almanac.* Jakarta: Pustaka Bisnis Indonesia.

Economist. (2010). "Cop killers: Indonesia's police." *Economist,* 397(8707): 55–56.

Flanagan, T., and M. S. Vaughn. (1995). "Public opinion about abuse of force." In *And Justice for All: Understanding and Controlling Police Abuse of Force,* Police Executive Research Forum, Washington, DC.

Garriott, William, ed. (2013). *Policing and Contemporary Governance: The Anthropology of Police in Practice.* Springer.

Gerber, Theodore P., and Sarah E. Mendelson. (2008). "Public experiences of police violence and corruption in contemporary Russia: A case of predatory policing?" *Law & Society Review* 42(1): 1–44.

Hawdon, James, and John Ryan. (2003). "Police–resident interactions and satisfaction with police: An empirical test of community policing assertions." *Criminal Justice Policy Review* 14(1): 55–74.

Hawdon, James. (2008). "Legitimacy, trust, social capital, and policing styles: A theoretical statement." *Police Quarterly* 11(2): 182–201.

Hills, Carol. (2014). "Indonesia has subjected policewomen to 'humiliating' virginity tests for decades." *Public Radio Iinternation,* http://www.pri.org/stories/2014-11-20/indonesia-has-subjected-policewomen-humiliating-virginity-tests-decades.

Human Rights Watch. (2014). "Indonesia: Hapus 'Tes Keperawanan' untuk Polwan [Indonesia: Stops 'Virginity Test' for Policewomen]." *Human Rights Watch.* https://www.hrw.org/id/news/2014/2011/2017/264612.

Indonesia, Kepala Kepolsian Negara Republik. (2012). "Policing leaders meeting report." *Indonesia's National Police. Jakarata.*

Indonesia, Markas Besar Kepolisian Republik. (1999). "Sejarah kepolisian di Indonesia [The history of police in Indonesia]." *Jakarta: Mabes Polri .*

Indonesia, Markas Besar Kepolisian Republik. (1999). "Sejarah kepolisian di Indonesia [The history of police in Indonesia]." *Jakarta: Mabes Polri .*

International Crisis Group. (2001). "Indonesia: National police reform." http://www.crisisgroup.org/en/regions/asia/south-east-asia/indonesia/013-indonesia-national-police-reform.aspx.

International Crisis Group. (2001). Indonesia: National Police Reform.

International Crisis Group. (2004). Indonesia: Rethinking Internal Security Strategy.

International Crisis Group. (2012). *Indonesia: The Deadly Cost of Poor Policing.* http://www.crisisgroup.org/en/regions/asia/south-east-asia/indonesia/218-indonesia-the-deadly-cost-of-poor-policing.aspx.

International Gay & Lesbian Human Rights Commission. (2010). "Indonesia: Police allow fundamentalists to disrupt another LGBT event."

Interpol. (2014). http://www.interpol.int/Member-countries/Asia-South-Pacific/Indonesia.

Iwama, Yoko. (2010). "International donors and the reform of Indonesian national police." *Workshop.*

Jackson, Jonathan, and Jason Sunshine. (2007). "Public confidence in policing: A neo-Durkheimian perspective." *British journal of criminology* 47(2): 214-233.

Jansen, David. (2008). "Relations among security and law enforcement institutions in Indonesia." *Contemporary Southeast Asia: A Journal of International and Strategic Affairs* 30(3): 429–454.

Jansen, David. (2010). "Snatching victory: When Indonesia' s National Police took on the Corruption Eradication Commission (KPK) over the Bank Century case, the KPK won." *Inside Indonesia, 100* (April–June). https://www.insideindonesia.org/weekly-articles/snatching-victory.

Jefferson, Tony. (1990). *The Case against Paramilitary Policing.* Milton Keynes: Open University Press.

Kappeler, Victor E., Richard D. Sluder, and Geoffrey P. Alpert. (1998). *Forces of Deviance: Understanding the Dark Side of Policing.* Vol. 2. Prospect Heights, IL: Waveland Press.

Kingsley, Jeremy Jacob. (2010). "Tuan Guru, community and conflict in Lombok, Indonesia." PhD diss.

Kristiansen, Stein, and Lambang Trijono. (2005). "Authority and law enforcement: Local government reforms and security systems in Indonesia." *Contemporary Southeast Asia: A Journal of International and Strategic Affairs* 27(2): 236–254.

Kristiansen, Stein, and Lambang Trijono. (2005). "Authority and law enforcement: Local government reforms and security systems in Indonesia." *Contemporary Southeast Asia: A Journal of International and Strategic Affairs* 27, no. 2: 236–254.

Media Activism. (2013). "West Papua: Indonesian police open fire on peaceful KNPB demo." *San Francisco Bay Area Independent Media Center.* http://www.indybay.org/newsitems/2013/11/28/18746975.php.

Meliala, Adrianus. (2001). "The notion of sensitivity in policing." *International Journal of the Sociology of Law* 29(2): 99–111.

Meliala, Adrianus. (2001b). "Police as military: Indonesia's experience." *Policing: An International Journal of Police Strategies & Management.*

Meliala, Adrianus. (2002a). "Local colours for Indonesian national police." *Policing and Society* 12(2): 153–161.

Meliala, Adrianus. (2010). *Trans-National Policing: "No Free Lunch Situation" to Indonesian Police.*

Meliala, Adrianus. (2002b). "Research note, policing, and society." *Policing and Society: An International Journal of Research and Policy* 12(2): 153–161.

Metropolitan Police. (2013). "Survey in the MPS: Londoners Views Count." *Total Policing,* (November): 1–3.

Morgan, Rod, and Tim Newburn. (1997). *The Future of Policing.* Oxford, UK: Clarendon Press.

Muradi. (2014). *Politics and Governance in Indonesia: The Police in the Era of Reformasi*. London: Routledge.

Murphy, Kristina, and Adrian Cherney. (2012). "Understanding cooperation with police in a diverse society." *British Journal of Criminology* 52(1): 181–201.

Murphy, Kristina. (2008). "Public satisfaction with police: The importance of procedural justice and police performance in police–citizen encounters."

Newburn, Tim, and Barry Webb. (1999). "Understanding and preventing police corruption: Lessons from the literature."

Oluwaniyi, Oluwatoyin O. (2011). "Police and the institution of corruption in Nigeria." *Policing & Society* 21(1): 67–83.

Paes-Machado, Eduardo, and Ceci Vilar Noronha. (2002). "Policing the Brazilian poor: Resistance to and acceptance of police brutality in urban popular classes (Salvador, Brazil)." *International Criminal Justice Review* 12(1): 53–76.

Pino, Nathan W., and Lee Michael Johnson. (2011). "Police deviance and community Relations in Trinidad and Tobago." *Policing: An International Journal of Police Strategies & Management*.

Prasetyo, E., B. Muqoddas, S. Marzuki, E. Riyadi, L. Arham, Imran, and Soekamid. (2005). "The role of the police in socio–political conflicts in Indonesia." *Pusham UII, The Asia Foundation, Yogyakarta*.

Punch, Maurice. (2000). "Police corruption and its prevention." *European Journal on Criminal Policy and Research* 8(3): 301–324.

Punch, Maurice, and Stan Gilmour. (2010). "Police corruption: Apples, barrels, and orchards: Maurice Punch investigates police and organisational deviance, followed by a response from Stan Gilmour." *Criminal Justice Matters* 79(1): 10–12.

Rahmawati, A. R. I. F. A. H., and Najib Azca. (2006). "Police reform from below: Examples from Indonesia's transition to democracy." *Democracy, Conflict, & Human Security: Further Readings, International IDEA, Report* 2: 53–67.

Sari Andajani, Dinar Lubis, and Sharyn Graham, Davies. (2015). Police raids on LGBT and the moral agenda: A media analysis'. *Jurnal Perempuan* 20(4): 97–107.

Sherman, Lawrence W., ed. (1974). *Police Corruption: A Sociological Perspective*. New York: Anchor Press/Doubleday.

Sims, Lorraine, and Andy Myhill. (2001). *Policing and the Public: Findings from the 2000 British Crime Survey*. Great Britain, Home Office, Research, Development and Statistics Directorate.

Stasch, Rupert. (2001). "Giving up homicide: Korowai experience of witches and police (West Papua)." *Oceania* 72(1): 33–52.

Stoutland, Sara E. (2001). "The multiple dimensions of trust in resident/police relations in Boston." *Journal of Research in Crime and Delinquency* 38(3): 226–256.

Sunshine, Jason, and Tom R. Tyler. (2003). "The role of procedural justice and legitimacy in shaping public support for policing." *Law & Society Review* 37(3): 513–548.

Tankebe, Justice, and Alison Liebling. (2013). "Legitimacy and criminal justice: An introduction." In *Legitimacy and Criminal Justice: An International Exploration*. Oxford, UK: Oxford University Press.

Tyler, Tom R., and E. Allan Lind. (1992). "A relational model of authority in groups." In *Advances in Experimental Social Psychology* 25: 115–191. Academic Press.

Tyler, Tom R., and Yuen Huo. (2002). *Trust in the Law: Encouraging Public Cooperation with the Police and Courts*. Russell Sage Foundation.

Tyler, Tom. R. (1990). *Why people obey the law*. New Haven, CT: Yale University Press

Villaveces-Izquierdo, Santiago. (2010). "Building internal and external constituencies for police reform: An Indonesian Case Study." *International Journal of Police Science & Management* 12(2): 183–194.

Waddington, Peter. (1999). *Policing Citizens: Authority and Rights*. New York: Psychology Press.

Chapter 12

The Challenges of the Royal Malaysia Police

Yik Koon Teh

First, this chapter will provide a brief introduction to the history, structure, and organization of the Royal Malaysia Police (RMP). Secondly, it will discuss the international collaboration of the RMP. As Malaysia is a Member State of the Association of Southeast Asian Nations (ASEAN), RMP is automatically a member of the ASEAN National Police or ASEANAPOL. ASEANAPOL has played an important role in preventing and solving cross border crimes and terrorism in the region. Finally, the chapter will discuss some of the challenges faced by the RMP since its establishment.

BRIEF HISTORY OF THE ROYAL MALAYSIA POLICE

The history of policing in Malaysia began during the period of the Malay sultanate in the fifteenth century, although it cannot be denied that a similar institution had already existed during the Buddhist Sri Vijaya rule in the seventh century and the Hindu Majapahit rule in the fourteenth century.[1] During the Malay sultanate period, the Sultan, or in his absence, the *Bendahara* (Chief Minister) had absolute power in meting out sentences while the *Temenggung* (equivalent to the Chief of Security) acted as the chief of police. Besides arresting criminals, the Temenggung was also tasked with building prisons and executing the punishment meted out by the Bendahara. Apart from the Temenggung, all the *Penghulu* (local chiefs) also maintained their own police or *mata-mata* (eyes of the state).[2] Their main tasks were tax collection, law enforcement, and maintenance of village security.

In the sixteenth century, Melaka, the oldest Malay sultanate, was colonized by the Portuguese. The Portuguese relied on the military to administer the state, and hence, all policing work was carried out by the Portuguese

207

soldiers.[3] As Melaka was already a cosmopolitan society, the Portuguese decided to use the *capitan*[4] system in their administration of the different ethnic groups. In the capitan system, each ethnic group was placed under a leader who performed the police institutional role.

In the seventeenth century, the Dutch captured Melaka from the Portuguese. Initially, the Dutch, which also relied on the military system, continued the capitan system. However, as the European population started to grow in Melaka, the Dutch established a police force called *Burgher Guard*. Dutch citizens living in Melaka were recruited to manage the Burgher Guard and the natives were employed as the lower ranks. The Burgher Guard was answerable to the Council of Justice whose members were chosen from the Dutch community in Melaka. The Penghulus also carried out the duties of the police during the Dutch rule.

In 1786, Captain Francis Light, a British subject, was sent to Penang Island by the British East India Company for trade purposes.[5] The Company, at the time, was controlling a vast area of India before the British Crown assumed direct control in 1874. Francis Light named the island the Prince of Wales Island. It was inhabited by a small group of Malay fishermen. Three years later, the population of the Island increased to 10,000 with many immigrants from other countries. Francis Light appealed to his superiors in India for assistance to maintain the security of the Island. At the time, there was no recognized body of law.[6] However, he did not receive any assistance. Instead, he was given the rank of Superintendent and was instructed to maintain the security of the Island himself.[7] Hence, he was forced to rely on the Bengali *sepoy* (soldiers) who came with him from India to carry out the task. However, the sepoys were undisciplined and could not carry out the task efficiently. A few riots took place, particularly between the foreigners, and Francis Light had to write to his superiors in India again to seek assistance to establish laws and a police force to maintain peace in the Island. Again, his request was ignored. Eventually, he appointed leaders among the Malays, Chinese, and Chulias (Southern Indians) who were given the title of Captain. Their roles were similar to those of a magistrate in adjudicating petty cases, while the serious cases were brought before the Superintendent. The Captains, who were each assisted by five peons, were also responsible for looking after the security of a few districts. The role of the peons was similar to that of a constable. In addition to their main role of law enforcement, they had other administrative roles, such as the control of the water supply, registration of births and deaths, fire prevention, and prison duties. However, the efficiency of the system in safeguarding the security of the Island was hampered by the inability of Francis Light to appoint a Captain among the European immigrants. The Europeans became ungovernable and unruly, as they knew they were not subjected to the rule of law. Francis Light had written to the East

India Company a few times for assistance to establish an official police force, but his requests were all ignored.

After the demise of Francis Light in 1794, Major Forbes Ross Macdonald took over the administration of the Island in 1796, but he left for India in 1797. In the late 1790s, Colonel Arthur Wellesley, who later became the Duke of Wellington, stopped by the Island on his way to the Philippines. He made a note on the security matters in the Island and pressed for an European magistrate to be appointed. In 1800, Sir George Leith arrived on the Island to take up the post of Lieutenant-Governor.[8] Four months later, John Dickens, an English barrister, was appointed the first judge and Magistrate of the Island.

In early 1804, Robert Townsend Farquhar arrived on the Island to replace Sir George Leith.[9] At the time, the police force was still weak and inefficient. This led to a total reorganization of the administration of the Island, which was given the status of a presidency. A Governor was appointed and a Council, answerable to the government in India, was established.

On March 25, 1807, the Island was granted the first Charter of Justice[10] by the British Crown. With this Charter, the Island was able to establish a proper court of judicature and a more efficient and effective police force as they could now carry out legal enforcement with a proper set of laws. This was the beginning of modern policing in Malaysia. A high sheriff, a deputy sheriff, and high constables were appointed among the Europeans, while petty constables were recruited among the Asians.[11] The Asians were issued with uniforms and paid a salary. However, the Europeans were not paid a salary as the services were considered part of their civic duties. This led to some dissatisfaction. Four of them who disrupted court functions were found guilty by the judge and were subsequently punished. Recruitment of Special Constables in the Island started in 1836[12] as the regular police was not effective in quelling the riots of the secret societies among the Malays and Chinese.[13]

In 1819, the British expanded their control to Singapore and in 1825, to Melaka. The British united Singapore, Melaka, and the Prince of Wales Island to form the Straits Settlements in 1826. The following year, the second Charter of Justice was issued. The charter was reported to be similar to the first charter and was only an extension of the jurisdiction of the court in the Island to Melaka and Singapore.[14] However, there was no move to unite the police from the three states.[15]

When the British took over Melaka from the Dutch, a Council meeting held in July 1827 created a police force and appointed a Superintendent of Police. W. T. Lewis became the first Superintendent or Chief Police Officer.[16] He was assisted by two European Constables, four headmen of the Burgher Guard, twenty-eight peons and twenty-one Penghulus.

In Singapore, after its acquisition by Thomas Stamford Raffles for Britain in 1819, he tried to set up an efficient police force, but did not succeed. By 1831, the force had only 18 men, but 10 years later the situation improved considerably with the Sitting Magistrate as the Superintendent, three European Constables, an Assistant Constable, 14 officers and 110 policemen.[17] When Thomas Dunman took over the posts of Superintendent of Police and Deputy Magistrate in 1843, he turned the police force into a disciplined and efficient organization. The Indian Police Act of 1856 allowed the local government in the Straits Settlements to appoint a Commissioner and a Deputy Commissioner of Police for each town or station.[18] This allowed the police force to be on a more regular footing.

In 1863, due to the unsatisfactory state of the police force, recruits were taken from India.[19] At around the same time, the first regular police uniform was introduced. In 1871, the Police Force Ordinance was introduced to the Straits Settlements where the whole police force of the colony was brought under the control of an Inspector General stationed in Singapore. The Inspector General was assisted by Superintendents, Assistant Superintendents, Inspectors, other officers, and Constables at each of the Settlements.[20] This was the beginning of the development of the Royal Federation of Malaya Police.

In 1873, a Malay prince, Raja Abdullah, who was a contender for the Perak throne, requested the British to send a Resident to Perak, in return for his recognition as the Sultan. The Pangkor Engagement or Pangkor Treaty was signed in 1874 and it accelerated British control into other states.[21] In the same year, the treaty was extended to Selangor and Negeri Sembilan. In 1895, Perak, Selangor, Negeri Sembilan, and Pahang became the Federated Malay States. Kedah, Perlis, Kelantan, Terengganu and Johor came under British control between 1909 and 1914. They formed the Unfederated Malay States.

The first official police force was reported to be established in Selangor.[22] In 1875, Harry Syers, a private in the infantry regiment, was appointed as the Superintendent of Police and Prisons in Selangor.[23] He reformed the existing inefficient police force and gave it the title of Selangor Military Police Force. The recruits were drilled and provided with arms and uniform. Similar reorganization of the police force took place in the other states, which had been almost entirely military in character. Although Syers managed to reorganize the Selangor police force into a more efficient organization, it was the Perak Armed Police that was reported to be outstanding. Built on the foundation laid by Captain Tristram Speedy, Captain Paul Swinburne developed the police force into "an organization recognizable as the ancestor of the Royal Federation of Malaya Police."[24]

When the Federated Malay States was formed in 1896, the police force from Perak, Selangor, Negeri Sembilan and Pahang were made contingents of the Federated Malay States Police.[25] They were given a common uniform and Syers was appointed the first Commissioner of Police. Each state was under a Chief Police Officer who was also a Deputy Commissioner or Assistant Commissioner. Syers, upon his death in 1897, was replaced by Captain H. L. Talbot. In 1899, Captain Talbot made the first attempt to bring the different police contingents into line with the issue of the Police General Orders from the Federal Headquarters.[26] However, it was the Police Force Enactment of 1903 that brought the whole force under the control of the Commissioner. This was the beginning of a new era for the police force. A new training scheme for probationers for the officer ranks was introduced and a Police Depot was established at Bluff Road to centralize the training[27] (the present Police Headquarters, commonly known as Bukit Aman).[28] The first commander of the Depot was Captain A. McD. Graham.

The Criminal Registry and its record of fingerprints (the introduction of forensic science), based on the Indian model, were established in 1904. Its first head was W. L. Conlay with at the rank of Assistant Commissioner.[29] He modified the system into a better one, which was extended to the Straits Settlements and the Unfederated Malay States.

In 1905, Raja Alang Iskandar, son and heir of the Perak Sultan, became the first Malay prince to join the police force, following Graham's idea that this was the best way to attract the Malays to join the service.[30] Raja Alang was made the Assistant Commissioner and posted to the Depot to be in charge of the recruitment of Malays.

In 1909, the first member of the Federated Malay States Police to be awarded the King's Police Medal was Sergeant Chong for his role in quelling the Chinese secret societies.[31] Some of the notable advancements which led to the structure of the present day police force were a better salary structure, changes in the method of recruitment of probationary officers from competitive examinations held by the Civil Service Commissions to that of appointment on interview and record, the expansion and restructuring of the Criminal Intelligence Branch, the introduction of traffic control training in the 1920s as the number of motor vehicles increased, and the formation of the Federated Malay States Police Band in 1932.[32]

In 1938, the titles of the gazetted officer ranks of the Federated Malay States were replaced with those used in the Straits Settlements and most parts of the British Empire; Commissioner of Police became Inspector General, Deputy Commissioner became Superintendent and Assistant Commissioner became Assistant Superintendent.[33] The Police Depot was moved from Bluff Road to Rifle Range Road in 1940.[34]

After the Japanese occupation from 1942 to 1945, the British named the police force Civil Affair Police Force. Administration of the police in the whole of Malaya was centralized under this Force.[35] In 1946, the Force was renamed Malayan Union Police Force.[36] It was renamed again in 1948 to Federation of Malaya Police Force.

Women were recruited into the police force during the Emergency period in 1948 when the Communist Party of Malaya tried to take over the country.[37] However, it was only in 1955 when a Women Police Force was formally established. Miss B. D. H. Wentworth, a British police officer, was seconded to the Unit to help with the training of the female recruits.

When Malaya gained independence from the British in 1957, the Federation of Malaya Police Force was granted the title of The Royal Federation of Malaya Police by the *Agong* (King).

Sarawak and Sabah joined Malaya to form Malaysia in 1963. The Sarawak Constabulary and North Borneo Armed Constabulary were absorbed into the Royal Malaysia Police.[38] However, Singapore left Malaysia to become independent in 1965. The Police Act came into force in 1967.

ORGANIZATION AND STRUCTURE OF THE ROYAL MALAYSIA POLICE

At present, the Royal Malaysia Police (RMP) consists of 137,574 police and civilian personnel headed by the Inspector General of Police.[39] The color of the police uniform is dark navy blue. Support groups that assist RMP in its duties include *Polis Tambahan* (Extra Police Constables), *Sukarelawan Polis* (Police Volunteer Reserves), *Polis Bantuan* (Auxiliary Police), Police Cadets and Civil Servants. It has seventeen police ranks within two main categories, which are Senior Police Officers and Junior/Lower Rank Police Officers and Constables.

Senior Police Officer ranks include, in a descending order:

* Inspector General of Police (IGP, 4 star),
* Deputy Inspector General of Police (DIG, 4 star),
* Commissioner of Police (CP, 3 star),
* Deputy Commissioner of Police (DCP, 2 star),
* Senior Assistant Commissioner of Police (SAC, 1 star),
* Assistant Commissioner of Police (ACP),
* Superintendent of Police (SUPT),
* Deputy Superintendent of Police (DSP),
* Assistant Superintendent of Police (ASP),
* Inspector (INSP),
* Probationary Inspector (P/I).

Junior Police Officers and Constables include, in a descending order:

- Subinspector (SI),
- Sergeant Major (SM),
- Sergeant (SGT),
- Corporal (CPL),
- Lance Corporal (L/CPL),
- Constable (CONST).

Overall, the structure of RMP consists of four levels, which are the Headquarters or Federal level at Bukit Aman in Kuala Lumpur, the State level, the District level, and the Station level.[40] The Headquarters is the administrative center for the police in the whole country and also the office of the Inspector General of Police and his Deputy. At the State level, there are fourteen Police Contingent Headquarters. In Sabah and Sarawak, the Contingents are headed by the Police Commissioners, while in the other states, the contingents are headed by State Police Chiefs. At the District level, there are 148 administrative districts throughout the country with their District Police Headquarters and District Police Chiefs. The rank of the District Police Chief is dependent on the size of the police district. At the Station level, there are 837 stations throughout the country and each station is headed by a Chief of Police Station, who holds a minimum rank of Sergeant, but not higher than Inspector.

RMP is divided into ten main departments. They are:

1. Management Department, which is responsible for the general management and administration of RMP;
2. Criminal Investigation Department, which is responsible for investigating criminal cases and arresting and prosecuting offenders;
3. Narcotics Crime Investigation Department, which is responsible for investigating and prosecuting cases related to drug trafficking and drug abuse;
4. Logistics and Technology Department, which is responsible for providing support services to RMP that include finance, communication and information technology, transportation, armaments, and management of assets and supplies;
5. Internal Security and Public Order Department, which is responsible for enhancing effective enforcement, maintaining public order, and national security. Its functions include land and maritime security and suppressing violence. As such, it must cooperate with other enforcement agencies, such as the Malaysian Armed Forces and Malaysian Maritime

Enforcement Agency. It has five branches, which are General Operations Force, Special Operations Force, Marine Operations Force, Federal
Reserve Unit and Air Operations Force;

6. Special Branch, which is responsible for the collection and processing of
   information and security intelligence;
7. Commercial Crime Investigation Department, which is responsible for
   investigating, arresting and prosecuting white collar criminals;
8. Integrity and Standards Compliance Department, which is responsible
   for strengthening the integrity of the police and ensuring that they perform their task in accordance with the standards that have been set;
9. Crime Prevention and Community Safety Department, which is responsible for strategizing and implementing initiatives for lowering crime rate
   and raising the level of perception of security among the public; and
10. Traffic Enforcement and Investigation Department, which is responsible
    for ensuring the safety and comfort of road users as well as investigating
    and taking action against irresponsible drivers.[41]

REGIONAL AND INTERNATIONAL COOPERATION

Malaysia, being situated in Southeast Asia, is one of the founders of the
Association of Southeast Asian Nations (ASEAN), which was established
in 1967. ASEAN has ten Member States, which are Brunei, Cambodia,
Indonesia, Lao PDR, Malaysia, Myanmar, Philippines, Singapore, Thailand
and Vietnam. The main aim of ASEAN is to "accelerate the economic
growth, social progress and cultural development in the region through joint
endeavors in the spirit of equality and partnership in order to strengthen the
foundation for a prosperous and peaceful community of Southeast Asian
Nations."[42] ASEAN also "promote regional peace and stability through abid-
ing respect for justice and the rule of law in the relationship among countries
of the region and adherence to the principles of the United Nations Charter."
ASEAN Member States have been enjoying regular and consistent warm-
working relationships with each other since its establishment. The closeness
can be seen from its motto "One Vision, One Identity, One Community."

ASEAN National Police (ASEANAPOL) was set up to facilitate cooperation among the police institutions of all the ASEAN Member States to
maintain regional security. Its main functions are cross-border cooperation on
intelligence and information sharing and exchange, and criminal investigations.[43] To facilitate these functions, the Member States agreed to build and
maintain an ASEANAPOL database, have regular joint training and capacity building, and develop scientific investigative tools, technical support,
and forensic science. The Royal Malaysia Police has constantly cooperated

with police forces from the other ASEAN Member States, particularly its neighboring countries that share its borders, such as Thailand, Singapore, Indonesia, and Brunei. Notable cooperation has been on transnational crimes and terrorism. One example is the case of Mas Selamat Kastari, a leader of Jemaah Islamiah, who was suspected of plotting to hijack a plane and crashing it into the Singapore airport.[44] He was captured by the Indonesian authorities in 2003 on immigration violation charges and was handed over to the Singapore authorities in 2006. He managed to escape from the high security prison in February 2008 by climbing through a ventilation shaft in a toilet and over a fence. He hid under an expressway and swam across the Tebrau Strait by keeping himself afloat with empty mineral water bottles to reach Johor, Malaysia. He was finally detained a year later in a joint operation by Malaysia and Singapore.

Internationally, Malaysia has been an active member of the International Criminal Police Organization (INTERPOL) since 1961. One example of Malaysia collaborating with INTERPOL is Operation Anchor in 2019. Operation Anchor was a multiagency exercise led by INTERPOL targeting maritime crime in Southeast Asia as the latter was an international maritime hub.[45] Law enforcement agencies that include the police, navy, coast guard, immigration, customs, and other maritime units in Indonesia, Malaysia, the Philippines, and Vietnam collaborated to locate and intercept individuals and groups responsible for cross-border crimes that included firearms and human trafficking, robbery at sea, hijacking, and kidnapping for ransom. Some of the exercises carried out were sea patrols, inspection of vessels, goods and crews, and screening of passengers and their passports. The collaboration effort resulted in several arrests and seizures.

MAJOR CHALLENGES FACED BY RMP

One of the most difficult challenges faced by the RMP thus far had been during the Emergency years of 1948–1960, when the Communist Party of Malaya (CPM) tried to establish a communist Malaya. CPM was established in 1930 with its origin in the Chinese immigrant society.[46] During the Japanese occupation of Malaya from 1942 to 1945, the Chinese immigrants were the most committed to fight against the Japanese, although Malays and Indians were also involved in the underground movements.[47] The Malayan Peoples Anti-Japanese Army (MPAJA), whose members were predominantly from the CPM, was formed with the assistance of the British. The MPAJA fought almost alone against the Japanese until the last few months of the war. The British took back control of Malaya after the Japanese occupation had ended. However, the communal relationship between the Malays and the

Chinese, particularly MPAJA, continued to be hostile. Issues, as listed by historians that led to such hostility, which started even before the Japanese occupation, include "long standing economic competition, increasing Chinese squatters in rural areas, the position of Malays as police and district officers, Malay resentment against MPAJA requisitions, and MPAJA reprisals against Malays who collaborated with the Japanese."[48] The mistrust and hostility became worse after the Japanese had surrendered, as many Malays believed that the Chinese would be taking over the country. Clashes between the two communities became more rampant.

In 1947, CPM, under the new leadership of hard-line Secretary-General Chin Peng, decided that it was time to seize power. All CPM activities were moved underground, and communist propaganda and violent actions were increased. Although CPM was mainly a Chinese party, there were some Malay members. When three European estate managers, among five people, were murdered, the government declared a State of Emergency throughout Malaya.[49] CPM was also declared an illegal organization. It then retreated into the deep jungle to set up its base. From there, they planned and launched guerrilla attacks. The government reacted by taking initiatives under the Briggs Plan, which was named after Lieutenant-General Sir Harold Briggs, the new director of operations in the Emergency. The initiatives included relocating Chinese squatters from areas that could be infiltrated by CPM, introduction of identity cards and curfews, carrying out psychological warfare and psychological operations, and effective intelligence gathering.[50] As the communist insurgency was a national problem, the police was given the main task to contain the problem, which included planning and strategizing, and "search and destroy operations" to eliminate the communists in the jungles, rural areas, and towns. For effective intelligence gathering, a Special Branch was created in the police. At the height of the communist insurgency in 1950, the strength of the police force was 161,281 (31,164 regular police, 44,117 special constables and 86,000 auxiliary police). By 1957, it was reported that the insurgency resulted in the death of the following number of civilians: 1,700 Chinese, 318 Malays, 226 Indians, 106 Europeans, 69 aborigines and 37 others.[51] At the end of the Emergency in 1960, the death toll was reported to be 1,865 members of the security forces, 1,346 members of the police force and 4,000 civilians. The wounded included 2,560 members of the security forces and 1,601 members of the police force. The number of civilians reported missing was 800. The highest casualties were among the Chinese civilians.

The first attempt to have a peace negotiation was in December 1955 in Baling; the Baling Peace Talk.[52] However, the attempt failed. CPM mounted a second wave of insurgency in 1968 but was again defeated by the police and the military.[53] In 1989, CPM finally laid down its arms. A Thai-brokered peace accord was signed between the party, represented by Chin Peng, Rashid Maidin and Abdullah C. D., and the Malaysian government in Hat Yai; the Hat Yai Peace Accord.[54]

Another major challenge in the history of Malaysia is the racial riot on May 13, 1969, which involved mainly three ethnic groups; Malay, Chinese and Indian. Briefly, in the 1969 election, the opposition political parties, which consisted of the Democratic Action Party (DAP), Gerakan and the People's Progressive Party, won more seats than the previous election although the ruling Alliance still retained its power. The Alliance's votes also dropped from 58.4 percent in 1964 to 48.8 percent.[55] These opposition parties, with non-Malay majority, had rejected the special position of the *Bumiputera* (Malay and indigenous people) enshrined in the Federal Constitution and propagated ethnic equality and cultural pluralism. On 13 May, Gerakan and DAP supporters held a victory rally that was reported to be noisy, provocative and abusive on the streets of Kuala Lumpur. A counter-rally by supporters of the United Malay National Organization (UMNO), the main political party in the Alliance, rapidly deteriorated into communal violence. A curfew had to be declared, the Constitution was suspended and a national emergency announced. After four days of bloody violence, the city was finally restored. The RMP, with the assistance of the military, played a major role in restoring public order. The death toll from this incident was 196 and 149 were wounded.

The Alliance, which became the *Barisan Nasional* (National Front) in 1973, was in power until 2018, when it was toppled for the first time by the opposition party, *Pakatan Harapan* (Alliance of Hope). However, in less than two years, Pakatan Harapan lost control of the government when the 94-year-old Prime Minister Mahathir Mohamad resigned from his post in February 2020. Without the majority, the Agong appointed the new coalition, *Perikatan Nasional* (National Alliance), which consisted of parties from the Barisan Nasional, as the new government.

Since the 1969 racial riot, ethnic relations in Malaysia have deteriorated further over the years. They have, in fact, become worse with the addition of religious extremism where the Malays are Muslims, and the other ethnic groups are mainly Buddhist, Hindu, Christian, and Sikh. Researchers, such as Teh,[56] have alleged that racial and religious issues have been played up by politicians from the Barisan Nasional, particularly UMNO, to direct attention away from their major corruption cases, such as the Bumiputera Malaysia Finance Limited (BMF), Maminco Sendirian Berhad, Perwaja Steel, 1 Malaysia Development Berhad (1MDB), *Tabung Haji* (Pilgrimage Funds) and the Federal Land Development Authority (FELDA), which had incurred losses in the billions if not trillions of Malaysian ringgit. When Pakatan Harapan managed to take control from Barisan Nasional after more than 60 years in power, the people were looking forward to institutional reforms in the country. Unfortunately, they were disappointed when Pakatan Harapan, which had been democratically elected by them, lost control of the government in less than two years and Barisan Nasional, under the Perikatan Nasional coalition, returned into power. This is the political situation that the RMP has worked under over the years. Under such a situation, the RMP has been accused of not being efficient in bringing down crime rate, police brutality, custodial deaths, discriminating against non-Bumiputeras, corruption, being politically controlled, and pandering to its political masters. In 2005, the Royal Commission to Enhance the Operation and Management of the RMP reported that

> the Malaysian police has been unsuccessful in projecting a positive image of itself to the people describing public confidence in the police as very low . . . PDRM (RMP) is generally viewed as inefficient, uncaring, unable to prevent or check crime and corruption to a significant degree. Concern regarding infringement and abuse of human rights are extensive and PDRM is not seen as being transparent or accountable to the public.[57]

The Royal Commission recommended the setting up of an Independent Police Complaints and Misconduct Commission (IPCMC) as the external oversight body to ensure good governance in RMP.[58] However, the recommendation of the Royal Commission was not taken up by the Barisan Nasional government as there was strong objection from the police force. Moreover, the Barisan Nasional government was worried of losing the police votes to the opposition parties in the coming election.[59] Instead, a watered-down Enforcement Agency Integrity Commission (EAIC), which could investigate but not take action, was implemented.[60] The negative perception and mistrust toward the RMP continued, perpetuated to a certain extent by the constant improvement in technology of the alternative media, such as online newspapers and blogs, where information and public experiences could reach a larger segment of the public at a faster rate.

When the Pakatan Harapan government took over the government in 2018, the Prime Minister's Department published the National Anti-Corruption Plan 2019–2023 (NACP) to try to curb corruption in the country, particularly after high-profile political corruption cases, such as 1MDB, where a former Prime Minister was involved, were exposed. In the NACP, it also reported that in a 2017 survey by Transparency International, 57 percent of the respondents perceived that police officers were corrupt.[61] The respondents also perceived the police to be the most corrupt government agency. Consequently, one of the strategies of the NACP was to introduce the IPCMC to address integrity issues and curb misconduct among the police. The Pakatan Harapan government tabled the IPCMC Bill in Parliament for the first reading in July 2019 and the second reading in October 2019, before being referred to a special committee for further review. It was to be tabled again in Parliament after the review, but the Pakatan Harapan government lost control of the government and the Perikatan Nasional coalition came into power in 2020. The latter had no interest in tabling the IPCMC. Instead, it was replaced with the Independent Police Conduct Commission (IPCC) Bill and was tabled in Parliament for the first reading in August 2020.

The Human Rights Commission of Malaysia (Suhakam), human rights NGO Suara Rakyat Malaysia or Suaram (Voice of Malaysian People), the Malaysian Bar and Human Rights Watch voiced their concerns about the IPCC. They believed that the IPCC did not capture the essence of the IPCMC Bill 2019 and the 2005 Royal Commission's recommendations. The IPCC lacks independence as commissioners could be police officers and government appointees, and it does not have the disciplinary powers to deal with police misconduct.[62] Suaram had commented that IPCC would be worse than the existing EAIC. Suaram also noted that, "Introducing a commission that is doomed to failure at a time when the RMP is struggling with allegations of serious misconduct that includes police brutality, custodial death and enforced disappearance will only further tarnish the reputation of the police force and affirm public mistrust of the police force" and that an accountable and professional police force would not fear any scrutiny by an independent commission.[63]

ARE THE ALLEGATIONS AGAINST THE ROYAL MALAYSIA POLICE FAIR?

While it cannot be denied that some members of the RMP have gone astray, Teh and Ahmad Ghazali stressed that the rules and regulations that the police force follow must be discussed in order to give a fair answer to the allegations against the RMP.[64] Under Article 4(1) of the Police Act 1967, it is stipulated that "the Force shall be under the command of an Inspector General who shall be a police officer and shall be responsible to the Minister for the control and direction of the Force and all other persons appointed or engaged for police duties, and who shall have all the powers conferred on a Commissioner or a Chief Police Officer." From the wordings of the Article, Teh and Ghazali argued that the Inspector General of Police (IGP) had the absolute power of command over the Force so long as they were within the bounds of the laws of the country. They also argued that the IGP was "responsible" to the Minister of Home Affairs, but not under the direct instruction of the Minister. The Police Act implicitly outlines the separation of power between the Ministry and the Force.

In order to redeem the negative image and perception of the police, it is, therefore, incumbent upon the leadership of the Force to address these issues without fear or favor. The majority of police personnel, who diligently discharge their duties with responsibility and integrity, should not be subjected to unfair public derision for the acts of a few undisciplined black sheep in the force. The officers, therefore, have the duty to ensure that the undisciplined few are strictly dealt with lest the image of the Force will continue to be tarnished. More importantly, officers must lead through example. The public must be convinced that this is happening, and the required measures are being taken. As such, the police force must be provided with credible leadership, which would be able to deal efficiently and effectively with the negative image and perception, and accusations leveled at the Force. This will help prevent the declining morale among the members of the Force. As leaders, the police officers owe it to their men, who bear the brunt of the negative public perception of the Force. As Teh and Ghazali noted, "The army is also apt to quote Field Marshall Sir William Slim, a Second World War Commander of the British Army in India, who famously noted that 'there are no bad soldiers, only bad officers' reflecting the importance of command responsibility over the performance of the subordinates. The police by analogy may adopt this maxim, too, that there are no bad constables, only bad officers."[65]

Is the police force solely to blame? If the table is turned around, what is the Malaysian police's perception of the public? A society is as good as the people in it.[66] Crime rate is a reflection of how good a society is. In the eyes of the police, they see the rampant bad behavior and attitude of the public every day. Ask any member of the police force and you will have a good story. For instance, many members of the public have no qualms committing simple offenses like beating the red light, jumping queues, using the emergency lanes during traffic jams, and double parking. There are some who will even try to bribe the police when they are caught, and yet they will complain that the police force is corrupt. These are tell-tale signs of the attitude and behavior of the Malaysian society. The public themselves have equal responsibility to ensure that rules and regulations are being followed. If everyone in the country is orderly, anyone who tries to break the rules will be more apprehensive. A society is as good as the people in it; the public and the police are both people in the society.

NOTES

1. Halal Bin Hj. Ismail, Samsudin Bin Ali, Abd. Latif Bin Yahaya, Selamat Bin Sainayune, and Ruziah Vinti Abdullah, *Sejarah Bergambar Institusi Polis di Malaysia (Pictorial History of the Police Institution in Malaysia)* (Kuala Lumpur:

Persatuan Muzium Negara [National Muzium Association], 1994), 1. The history of Royal Malaysia Police was mainly sourced from this book.

2. Patrick Morrah, "The History of the Malayan Police," *Journal of the Malayan Branch of the Royal Asiatic Society* 36, part 2, no. 202 (1968): 8. The history of Royal Malaysia Police was mainly sourced from this paper/book.

3. Halal, *Sejarah*, 3.

4. *Capitan* is a Spanish word and according to Morrah (*History*, 12), the system was introduced by the Portuguese. The local spelling for capitan is *kapitan*.

5. Halal, *Sejarah*, 7.

6. Soo Chye Tan, "A Note on Early Legislation in Penang." *Journal of the Malayan Branch of the Royal Asiatic Society* 23, part 1, no. 151 (1950): 100–107.

7. Halal, *Sejarah*, 7; Morrah, *History*, 15.

8. Morrah, "History," 21.

9. Morrah, 23.

10. Halal, *Sejarah*, 8; Morrah, *History*, 25.

11. Morrah, "History," 25.

12. Halal, *Sejarah*, 10.

13. Morrah, "History," 39–40.

14. L. A. Mills, Constance M. Turnbull, and D. K. Bassett, "British Malaya 1824-67," *Journal of the Malayan Branch of the Royal Asiatic Society* 33, part 3, no. 191 (1960): 84.

15. Morrah, "History," 28.

16. Morrah, 30–31.

17. Morrah, 34–35.

18. Morrah, 37.

19. Morrah, 38.

20. Morrah, 40.

21. T. N. Harper, *The End of Empire and the Making of Malaya* (Cambridge: Cambridge University Press, 1999), 18.

22. Morrah, "History," 52.

23. Morrah, 52–55.

24. Morrah, 61.

25. Morrah, 89.

26. Morrah, 96–98.

27. Morrah, 100.

28. *The Star*, "Brief History of the Royal Malaysia Police," May 17, 2005, https://www.thestar.com.my/news/nation/2005/05/17/brief-history-of-the-royal-malaysia-police/.

29. Morrah, "History," 104–106.

30. Morrah, 102–103.

31. Morrah, 114.

32. Morrah, 131–132, 136–138, 141.

33. Morrah, 144.

34. Morrah, 165.

35. Halal, *Sejarah*, 121.

36. Halal, 123–125.

37. Halal, 143.

38. Halal, 101, 111.

39. "Mengenai Polis Diraja Malaysia (About RMP)," The Official Portal of Royal Malaysia Police (RMP), accessed September 3, 2020, https://www.rmp.gov.my/infor -korporate/polis-diraja-malaysia.

40. "Mengenai Polis," *Struktur (Structure)*.

41. "Mengenai Polis," *Jabatan-jabatan (Departments)*.

42. "About ASEAN: Overview," Association of Southeast Asian Nations (ASEAN), accessed September 4, 2020, https://asean.org.

43. "Objective of ASEANAPOL," ASEANAPOL, accessed September 5, 2020, http://www.aseanapol.org.

44. *BBC News*, "Malaysia Hands Over Terror Suspect Kastari to Singapore," September 24, 2010, https://www.bbc.com/news/world-asia-pacific-11406014; *The Straits Times*, "Mas Selamat Hid Butter, Used Mineral Water Bottles in Escape: Malaysia Police," March 26, 2017, https://www.straitstimes.com/asia/se-asia/mas -selamat-hid-butter-used-mineral-water-bottles-in-escape-malaysia-police.

45. *INTERPOL*, "Multi-Agency Exercise Targets Maritime Crime in Southeast Asia," November 25, 2019, https://www.interpol.int/en/News-and-Events/News /2019/Multi-agency-exercise-targets-maritime-crime-in-Southeast-Asia.

46. Barbara Watson Andaya and Leonard Y. Andaya, *A History of Malaysia* (Basingstoke: Palgrave, 2001), 243.

47. Andaya, 261–264.

48. Andaya, 262.

49. Andaya, 271–274.

50. Halal, *Sejarah*, 128–129.

51. Chun Wai Wong, "Remembering Heroes and Villains," *The Star*, September 29, 2013, https://www.thestar.com.my/news/nation/2013/09/29/remembering-heroes -and-villains.

52. Halal, *Sejarah*, 138.

53. Halal, 163.

54. *Bangkok Post*, "Former Insurgents Celebrate 25 Years of Peace," December 4, 2014, https://www.bangkokpost.com/thailand/general/447082/former-insurgents -celebrate-25-years-of-peace.

55. Yik Koon Teh, *From BMF to 1MDB: A Criminological and Sociological Discussion* [Petaling Jaya: Strategic Information and Research Development Centre (SIRD), 2018], 6–8.

56. Teh, *From BMF*.

57. Yik Koon Teh, "The Best Police Force in the World Will Not Bring Down a High Crime Rate in a Materialistic World," *International Journal of Police Science & Management* 11, no. 1 (2009): 3.

58. Nadhrah A. Kadirand Kamaruzaman Jusoff, "Strategic Management and Improvement of the Malaysian Police from the Perspective of the Royal Commission Report," *Journal of Law and Conflict Resolution* 1, no. 4 (September 2009): 76, https://www.researchgate.net/publication/252974205_Strategic_management

_and_improvement_of_the_Malaysian_Police_from_the_perspective_of_the_Royal
_Commission_Report.

59. Faisal Asyraf and Zikri Kamarulzaman, "How Does the IPCMC Affect Police Votes?" *Malaysiakini*, August 23, 2020, https://zh.malaysiakini.com/news/539664.

60. *Malaysiakini*, "IPCMC Is Here – but Does It Have Bite?" July 19, 2019, https://www.malaysiakini.com/news/484490.

61. Prime Minister's Department. *National Anti-Corruption Plan 2019-2023* (Putrajaya: Prime Minister's Department, 2019).

62. *Malaysiakini*, "IPCC Bill: Suhakam Concerned over Lack of Independence, Conflict of Interest," August 27, 2020, https://www.malaysiakini.com/news/540302; *Malaysiakini*, "HRW Accuses PM of 'Spitting in Face' of Royal Commission on Police," August 28, 2020, https://www.malaysiakini.com/news/540441.

63. Zikri Kamarulzaman, "New IPCC is Significantly Watered-Down Version of IPCMC," *Malaysiakini*, August 26, 2020, https://www.malaysiakini.com/news/540153.

64. Yik Koon Teh and Ahmad Ghazali Abu Hassan, "Are the Malaysian Police the Aggressors or the Victims in Their Own Country?" *Beyond: Buletin Polis Selangor (Bulletin of the Selangor Police)* 1 (2013): 14–16.

65. Teh and Ahmad Ghazali, 15.

66. Teh, "The Best Police Force," 6.

REFERENCES

Andaya, Barbara Watson, and Leonard Y. Andaya. *A History of Malaysia*. Basingstoke: Palgrave, 2001.

ASEANAPOL. "Objective of ASEANAPOL." Retrieved September 5, 2020. http://www.aseanapol.org.

Association of Southeast Asian Nations (ASEAN). "About ASEAN: Overview." Retrieved September 4, 2020, https://asean.org.

Bangkok Post, "Former Insurgents Celebrate 25 Years of Peace." Retrieved December 4, 2014, https://www.bangkokpost.com/thailand/general/447082/former-insurgents-celebrate-25-years-of-peace.

BBC News. "Malaysia Hands Over Terror Suspect Kastari to Singapore." Retrieved September 24, 2010, https://www.bbc.com/news/world-asia-pacific-11406014.

Bernama. "Bukit Aman Confirms Receiving Info on Police Involvement in Gambling Protection Racket." *Sun Daily*. Retrieved August 11, 2020, https://www.thesundaily.my/local/bukit-aman-confirms-receiving-info-on-police-involvement-in-gambling-protection-racket-DA3417764.

Faisal Asyraf, and Zikri Kamarulzaman. "How Does the IPCMC Affect Police Votes?" *Malaysiakini*. Retrieved August 23, 2020, https://zh.malaysiakini.com/news/539664.

Halal Bin Hj, Ismail, Samsudin Bin Ali, Abd. Latif Bin Yahaya, Selamat Bin Sainayune, and Ruziah Vinti Abdullah. *Sejarah Bergambar Institusi Polis di Malaysia* [Pictorial History of the Police Institution in Malaysia]. Kuala Lumpur: Persatuan Muzium Negara (National Muzium Association), 1994.

Harper, T. N. *The End of Empire and the Making of Malaya.* Cambridge, UK: Cambridge University Press, 1999.

INTERPOL. "Multiagency Exercise Targets Maritime Crime in Southeast Asia." Retrieved November 25, 2019, https://www.interpol.int/en/News-and-Events/ News/2019/Multi-agency-exercise-targets-maritime-crime-in-Southeast-Asia.

Kua, Kia Soong. "Calls for End to Systemic Racism and Racial Discrimination." *Malaysiakini.* Retrieved June 9, 2020, https://www.malaysiakini.com/letters/529393.

Lee, Gwen. "Malaysia: Newest Case of Death in Custody Continues to be Unsettling." *Amnesty International Malaysia.* Retrieved December 20, 2017, https://www .amnesty.my/2017/12/20/malaysia-newest-case-of-death-in-custody-continues-to -be-unsettling/.

Malaysiakini. "IPCMC Is Here—but Does It Have Bite?" Retrieved July 19, 2019, https://www.malaysiakini.com/news/484490.

Malaysiakini. "IPCC Bill: Suhakam Concerned over Lack of Independence, Conflict of Interest," Retrieved August 27, 2020, https://www.malaysiakini.com/news/540302.

Malaysiakini. "HRW Accuses PM of 'Spitting in Face' of Royal Commission on Police," Retrieved August 28, 2020, https://www.malaysiakini.com/news/540441.

Mills, L. A., Constance M. Turnbull and D. K. Bassett. "British Malaya 1824– 67." *Journal of the Malayan Branch of the Royal Asiatic Society* 33, 191 (1960): 1–424.

Morrah, Patrick. "The History of the Malayan Police." *Journal of the Malayan Branch of the Royal Asiatic Society* 36, part 2, no. 202 (1968): 1–172.

Nadhrah, A. Kadirand Kamaruzaman Jusoff. "Strategic Management and Improvement of the Malaysian Police from the Perspective of the Royal Commission Report." *Journal of Law and Conflict Resolution* 1, no. 4 (September 2009): 72–78. https://www.researchgate.net/publication/252974205_Strategic_management_and _improvement_of_the_Malaysian_Police_from_the_perspective_of_the_Royal _Commission_Report.

Official Portal of Royal Malaysia Police (RMP). "Mengenai Polis Diraja Malaysia (About RMP)." Retrieved September 3, 2020, https://www.rmp.gov.my/infor-kor- porate/polis-diraja-malaysia.

Prime Minister's Department. *National Anti-Corruption Plan 2019–2023.* Putrajaya: Prime Minister's Department, 2019.

Saleh Mohammed. "Enforcement Officers: Harapkan Pagar, Pagar Makan Padi." *Malaysian Insight*, August 12, 2020. https://www.themalaysianinsight.com/s /266339, 10 September 2020.

Star. "Brief History of the Royal Malaysia Police." Retrieved May 17, 2005. https:// www.thestar.com.my/news/nation/2005/05/17/brief-history-of-the-royal-malaysia -police/.

Straits Times. "Mas Selamat Hid Butter, Used Mineral Water Bottles in Escape: Malaysia Police." Retrieved March 26, 2017, https://www.straitstimes.com/asia /se-asia/mas-selamat-hid-butter-used-mineral-water-bottles-in-escape-malaysia -police.

Straits Times. "Coronavirus: Jailed Malaysian Woman Decries 'Double Standards' in Sentencing of Zahid's Daughter." Retrieved May 6, 2020, https://www.straitstimes

.com/asia/se-asia/coronavirus-jailed-woman-decries-double-standards-in-sentenc-ing-of-zahids-daughter.

Tan, Soo Chye Tan. "A Note on Early Legislation in Penang." *Journal of the Malayan Branch of the Royal Asiatic Society* 23, part 1, no. 151 (1950): 100–107.

Teh, Yik Koon. "The Best Police Force in the World Will Not Bring Down a High Crime Rate in a Materialistic World." *International Journal of Police Science & Management* 11, no. 1 (2009): 1–7.

Teh, Yik Koon. *From BMF to 1MDB: A Criminological and Sociological Discussion.* Petaling Jaya: Strategic Information and Research Development Centre (SIRD), 2018.

Teh, Yik Koon, and Ahmad Ghazali Abu Hassan. "Are the Malaysian Police the Aggressors or the Victims in Their Own Country?" *Beyond: Buletin Polis Selangor (Bulletin of the Selangor Police)* 1 (2013): 14–16.

Wong, Chun Wai. "Remembering Heroes and Villains." *Star*, Retrieved September 29, 2013, https://www.thestar.com.my/news/nation/2013/09/29/remembering -heroes-and-villains.

Zikri Kamarulzaman. "New IPCC Is Significantly Watered-Down Version of IPCMC." *Malaysiakini*. Retrieved August 26, 2020, https://www.malaysiakini .com/news/540153.

Chapter 13

Law Enforcement and Policing in Australia

State and Federal Systems from the "Convict Night Watch" to "Problem-Oriented Policing"

Mark F. Briskey and Samuel M. Makinda

Australia, with a population of 25.5 million, had over 63,000 police personnel as of 2020 (PFA, 2020). This chapter examines and explains aspects of policing and law enforcement in Australia. In particular, it addresses the following questions. What are the origins of the Australian policing and law enforcement system? How is this system organized across the country? What is the nature of the relationship between indigenous Australians and the police and law enforcement system? What challenges has the system faced over the years and how has it addressed them?

This chapter explores the origins of Australia's policing system from the colonial period, through the Australian federation in 1901, to the present era. It provides a general overview of Australian policing, its early history, and convict settlement. The chapter explains how policing and law enforcement reflects the division of Australia into six states and two territories. The six states are New South Wales (NSW), with Sydney as the capital; Queensland, with Brisbane as the capital; South Australia (SA), with Adelaide as the capital; Tasmania, with Hobart as the capital; Victoria, with Melbourne as the capital; and Western Australia (WA), with Perth as the capital. The two territories are the Australian Capital Territory (ACT), with Canberra as both its capital and the national capital, and the Northern Territory, where Darwin is the capital. When we discuss policing and law enforcement in Australia, we need to bear in mind operations in the above jurisdictions, which have similarities as well as differences.

This chapter also points out the conflicted role of the law enforcement system with indigenous Australians. It touches upon several issues that have impacted the development of policing, including the brutality of the system toward Aborigines, the doctrine of *Terra Nullius* as well as the "White Australia" policy, which was in force from 1901 to 1975. This chapter has also devoted some attention to the examination of Australian police service's developmental challenges and responses to internal corruption and governance. In the past three decades, most Australian state police forces have been investigated by or been subjected to enquiries by the Royal Commission into their activities. These investigations have invariably resulted in cleaner, more accountable, and more responsive police entities.

A Royal Commission in Australia is an investigation, independent of the government, into a matter of significant public importance. There have been several Royal Commissions into Police Services in different states of Australia. This has meant that over time, police forces in Australia have had an outside judicial agency shine a light on their activities.

The remaining part of this chapter is divided into six sections. The first section explains briefly the origin of policing and law enforcement in Australia. This will be followed by a description of the organization of police services into the Australian Federal Police (AFP) and the state as well as territory police forces. Section three discusses the roles of other law enforcement agencies at the State and federal levels that assist the police. Section four shines light on the troubled relationship between the policing and law enforcement system on one hand, and indigenous Australians on the other. Section five explores some of the challenges the policing system has faced and how it has addressed them. We conclude by speculating about the future of policing and law enforcement in Australia.

ORIGINS OF AUSTRALIA'S POLICING AND LAW ENFORCEMENT

The origin of contemporary Australian policing is a product of Australia's colonial and frontier past with the original settlement of Australia as a place for British convicts. Australian policing was greatly influenced by models of British policing before the advent of modern policing in 1827 as well as that after the introduction of Peel's modern police. While some of these similarities may seem most evident in comparison with Britain and the frontier experiences of the United States, there are unique aspects to the organization and practice of policing in Australia that shall be explored.

Long-term colonization of Australia commenced with the British settlement of what is now Sydney by Governor Phillip as the repository of 775 convicts and 212 marines. The British did not recognize the indigenous inhabitants who had been in Australia for over 60,000 years and viewed them as primitive and without legal rights. The British believed in the doctrine of *terra nullius* in which the Australian landmass was said to be vacant of humanity. The doctrine was not fully rejected until a High Court decision in 1992. The maintenance of order in Australia at the outset was by the marines. The marines viewed the supervision of convicts as demeaning, while they themselves were guilty of crime in the fledgling colony. Six marines were executed for robbery while they also had moral misdemeanors in their relations to the female convicts (Tench, 1961; O'Brien, 1937).

These early problems were also compounded by occasional organized violence by the convicts. An uprising of predominantly Irish convicts, many of whom had been transported for their involvement in the Irish revolt, was violently suppressed in 1804 in what was sometimes referred to as the second battle of Vinegar Hill in the present-day Sydney suburb of Castle Hill. The marines were withdrawn and replaced by the New South Wales Corp, soon to be known as "Rum Regiment" due to this spirit becoming the acknowledged medium of exchange for a time less, than a year after the departure of Governor Philip. The officers of the Regiment acquired domination of early trade and agriculture in the colony and conducted the first and only coup in Australia's history with the removal of Governor Bligh of Bounty fame from his office. According to Historical Records (1971), the notoriety of the Regiment was commented on by the colony's second governor in a dispatch to England in 1796:

> They are sent to guard and to keep in obedience . . . and yet we find among those safeguards men capable of corrupting the heart of the best disposed, and often superior in every species of infamy to the most expert in wickedness among the convicts. (p. 574)

The early governors of the colony recognized the need to free the military from these duties and were themselves empowered to establish the architecture of justice for the new colony. The first people to undertake a police-like function were drawn from the ranks of the convicts and performed a role as a night watch and a "Rowboat Guard" instituted to protect Sydney Harbour (Hoban, 1988, p. 13). Henry Kable, the first chief constable of Sydney, had been a convict and sentenced to death, before he was transported to Australia. This practice of having convicts and free citizens policed by those who were convicts themselves, continued for some time. Sturma (1981) notes that as late as 1839, about 53 percent of police officers were ex-convicts.

Policing in the early colony was beset by struggles for power between the military and civil authorities and permeated by corruption and self-interest

(Bryett, Harrison, & Shaw, 1994). Although the colony was growing and expanding outwards from Sydney, the city harbored a reputation as one of the most crime-ridden towns in the British Empire, with one describing it in 1836 as worse than the most vice-ridden parts of London or Paris (Hartwell, 1955). As European settlement spread throughout the landmass of Australia and Tasmania, a range of new law and order problems emerged from that presented by convict runaways. Mobile groups of bandits, known in Australia as "bushrangers," robbed and preyed on settlers before escaping into the isolated fastness of the country. Often these "outlaws" were celebrated by a population with little liking for the police. Colonial era outlaws, such as "Ned Kelly," whose armed gang roamed across the Colonies of Victoria and New South Wales remain part of a popular anti-establishment folklore.

With the end of convict transportation to Australia, coupled with the impact of a growing "white" native-born population as well as an expanding free settler population and the Gold Rushes, policing evolved to suit new Australian conditions.

JURISDICTIONAL BOUNDARIES

As indicated earlier, policing and law enforcement agencies in Australia fall into National, State, or Territory jurisdictions. These jurisdictional boundaries have been modified over time through the enactment of police acts and regulations throughout the colonies and later States and Territories. As with many other countries around the word, the primary duties of Australian policing services are the prevention, detection, and investigation of crime and the maintenance of civil order. Depending on location, police in Australia may also perform a diverse range of other duties for their states, from the issuance of stock permits to court duties.

In 2020, Australian police forces were also involved in ensuring that Australians observed the restrictions relating to the coronavirus, COVID-19. All police services in Australia, except for the Australian Federal Police (AFP) and other federal entities, are controlled by state and territory governments, usually under a Minister of Police. Uniformed and plain clothes police in Australia carry sidearms, handcuffs, and other defensive and offensive equipment deemed necessary for their duties. There are also numerous specialized units within Australian policing from special operations/weapons units that undertake the resolution of sieges and other events to technical units involved in the covert installation of monitoring and listening devices on the premises, of serious offenders. There are then a panoply of these specialized units including specialized child sex offender units that investigate online and other offenders to witness security, forensics, family liaison, hostage negotiators to marine and airwing police.

A significant difference between the Australian model and the American model is the primary centralization of policing within State jurisdictions rather than on a municipal basis. Australia does not have a County, City, or localized policing function. In Australia, the State Police undertake all these functions, while the Federal Police, in a uniformed capacity, have a small community policing role in the Australian Capital Territory and several other small jurisdictions. The Federal Police's role in investigating terrorism, drug offenses and several other federal offenses means that from time to time, AFP and State Police in the course of investigating an offense will discover crimes outside of their strict jurisdiction. The law in Australia provides remedies for this with "application of laws" legislation that allows assessment or examination of multijurisdiction crimes in the course of an investigation. In the remaining part of this section, we discuss different State police forces as well as the roles of other federal agencies that assist police in law enforcement.

New South Wales Police

Sydney, the capital of New South Wales (NSW), was the site of the first European settlement in 1788 and the first police in Australia. The NSW Police is the largest police service in Australia, with over 23,000 sworn police officers and other enabling functions. The NSW police started employing policewomen in 1915. The first Aboriginal female was employed in 1973. From 2014 onward, policewomen have represented nearly 30 percent of the sworn police officers and 35 percent of the overall staff in the state (NSW Police, 2020).

Tasmania Police

Van Diemen's Land or Tasmania, as it became known later, began as a convict settlement. The origins of its policing date back to 1804 following the formation of a night watch and a special field police to pursue escaped convicts in 1826. Under Governor Arthur during the 1820s, Tasmania became the closest thing to a totalitarian state the British Empire had ever known. The Police were completely subservient to the whims of Governor Arthur whose management ensured they held no allegiance to either convicts or settlers and that he could expect a "dog like obedience and canine ferocity from them" (Hughes, 1986, p. 392). The Tasmanian Police were unified in 1899, just prior to federation, with other states in the newly formed nation of Australia in 1901. The induction of the first female officer in Tasmania occurred in 1917–1918 (Tasmania Police Museum, 2020).

Victoria Police

The Victoria Police, with 15,000 members, have their origins in several entities that undertook various law, order, and protection duties during the colonial era. Prior to the formal establishment and consolidation of the Victoria Police in 1853, there had been a Metropolitan police (Melbourne), mounted police, Gold Fields Police, Native Police Corps, Gold Escort police, water police, and border police. The colonial era Victoria Police were involved in some of the most significant events in Australian criminal justice history, including suppressing the Eureka Stockade rebellion in 1854 (Lancashire Infantry Museum, 2020) and the pursuit and capture of the "Ned Kelly" outlaw gang (Culture Victoria, 2016) in which three police were killed by the gang. Significantly, the Victoria police riots of 1923 over dissatisfaction with pensions and supervision led to looting, three deaths and the discharge of 634 members. The first two women were appointed to the Victoria Police in July 1917. Victoria appointed Christine Nixon, the first female Chief Commissioner of Police in April 2001.

Queensland Police

The Military Police originally enforced law and order in the convict settlement of Moreton Bay, which later became Brisbane, the capital of Queensland State. Like other convict settlements in Australia, the Moreton Bay settlement was subject to a harsh disciplinary environment in which corporal and capital punishment were frequently applied. Scotsman James Clunie, who commanded the settlement between 1830 and 1835, once sentenced a convict to 300 lashes for stealing a horse (Dukova, 2020). A separate water police existed from 1840 to1853, a Native Police or Mounted Aboriginal Police between 1848 and 1859, and a Border Police from 1839 to 1846. These forces were effectively para-military groups which did not undertake any preventative policing but were rather forces that undertook often violent retaliatory actions against indigenous Australians. In the process, the Queensland Police were a major force in the displacement and dispossession of indigenous Australians.

Just prior to the penal settlement being closed in 1842 and Queensland being opened to free settlers, Richard Bonnington, a former convict transported from Surrey in England was appointed commander of the Police in Brisbane. The Queensland Police were established in 1864, five years after the separation of the state from New South Wales, and they derived their original model of regulations and operation from the Victoria Police. One of their primary objectives was the eradication of banditry, or "bush ranging" as it is known in Australia, with mounted units and officers armed with both carbines and revolvers. Officers in remote areas of Queensland used both horses and camels as a means of transportation to undertake duties, while bicycles were introduced in the late 1890's for officers in Brisbane. The Brisbane Water Police obtained motorized patrol craft 1907. Queensland Police appointed its first women employees in 1931. The Queensland State Government appointed Katarina Carroll, the daughter of Croatian immigrants as Police Commissioner in July 2019.

The Queensland police modernized throughout the mid-twentieth century in forensic investigation methodologies, transportation and communications as well as police training with the first Police Librarian appointed in 1937 to manage the 5,000 law, crime, and forensic collection of the Central Police Library.

Western Australia Police

West Australia's (WA) history differs from that of the colonies on the eastern seaboard as WA was relatively a free colony with only a minimal number of convicts. Colonial WA included public order policing in the larger settlements of Perth and Fremantle in 1829 as well as a Mounted Police unit formed in 1834 to police the vast rural and frontier areas. Until 1912, leadership and management of the Police in WA were primarily undertaken by members of the gentry, public servants, and former military officers.

Like other Australian states the WA Police Force's early history of contact with indigenous Australians included a range of interactions from endemic racism to police involvement and complicity in mass murder. Up to 300 Aborigines were killed in 1926 during the Forrest River massacre. There were other incidents, such as at Mt. Barnett, where one police officer and five so-called native assistants shot and terrorized the local Aboriginal population forcing them to flee. Incidents such as these left an indelible stain on the WA police (Owen, 2016). The modern WA Police has undertaken considerable work to remedy the generational distrust and relationships between Police and the Aboriginal community. A number of initiatives involving indigenous community liaison officers, police cadetships for indigenous youth within their own community, recruitment of Aboriginal people into the police and the establishment of the first police station entirely staffed and operated by indigenous officers at Warakurna, have sought to remedy the relationship (ABC, 2020).

Police were also the recipients of violence in frontier Western Australia. One of the more significant incidents involved the murder of two senior police of the Gold Squad in the early 1920s involved in the investigation of offenses within the industry. Inspector Walsh and Detective Sergeant Pitman went missing on their bicycles during an investigation near Coolgardie, West Australia. Both were murdered their bodies dismembered, burned, and thrown in a disused mineshaft with two of the men involved in their murder convicted and executed (Conole, 2002).

Northern Territory Police

The history of the Northern Territory Police Service, with over 1200 members, is inextricably connected with South Australia from which the Northern Territory was formed. Up until 1869, when the Northern Territory Police was established, there was only a small part-time rural constabulary. As with other nineteenth-century Australian jurisdictions, the discovery of gold in 1872 increased the work and responsibilities of the fledgling police force. It was in 1872 that the first police fatality occurred with the loss of a mounted trooper to a salt-water crocodile. Police in the Territory were responsible for policing across vast areas of wilderness. Police investigations as well as rescue operations could not have been undertaken without the assistance of Aboriginal trackers. There were two Commissioners of Police in the Northern Territory with one responsible for the Territory of Northern Australia and the other for the Territory of Central Australia, but they amalgamated in 1931 to form the current Northern Territory Police service.

South Australia Police

South Australia's (SA) history is also different from those of other states because it was established by free settlers rather than convicts. Its current police force, with 6,000 members, was originally formed in 1838 as a response to concerns about felons entering the colony from other Australian jurisdictions. The inaugural force consisted of ten Mounted Constables and ten other Constables under the command of an Inspector. Until 1867, the SA Police also undertook the duties of the Fire Brigade and operated the Civil Ambulance service until 1954. South Australia was the first state in Australia to appoint female police officers in 1915.

Australian Federal Police

The Australian Federal Police (AFP) is Australia's national police service and is based in Canberra, but it has offices in the other eight capital cities. By 2020, the AFP had about 6,695 employees. The AFP, which has a large protective security component, is responsible for protecting Australian federal assets. The AFP's major function is the investigation of crime as well as performing the duties of community policing in the ACT, and external territories, including Norfolk Island in the Pacific and Cocos Islands in the

Indian Ocean. Under "application of laws" acts, it may also investigate state-based crime in the course of investigating federal matters. The AFP also has over twenty offices in Australian diplomatic missions around the globe, including Washington, D.C., in the United States, Bogota in Colombia, Jakarta in Indonesia, Beijing and Guangzhou in China, and throughout the Asia Pacific region. The AFP undertakes liaison duties to expedite criminal investigations for Australian State Police services and developing criminal justice development and training programs, including, for instance, the Jakarta Centre for Law Enforcement Cooperation in Semarang, Indonesia (AFP, 2020).

The AFP, for example, worked with Iranian Drug Control Headquarters to provide a more effective communication platform to enable the interdiction of Narco-Caravans from Afghanistan and Pakistan. It also established the inaugural anti-human trafficking program with the Bangladesh Police and UNDP to prevent the trafficking of women and children to servitude in India and the Middle East. The AFP also has a permanent representative at INTERPOL in Lyons, France, and a representative at EUROPOL.

The trigger for the Australian Federal Police Act 1979, under which the AFP was created, was the 1978 terrorist bombing of the Hilton Hotel in Sydney during the Commonwealth Heads of Government Regional Meeting. Thus, it was partly with a view to acquiring adequate counter-terrorism capabilities that the AFP came into existence.

Apart from the global and regional involvements mentioned earlier, the AFP has several working agreements with law enforcement and security agencies around the world, including partnerships with the U.S. Drug Enforcement Administration (DEA), U.S. Federal Bureau of Investigation, (FBI) and other agencies in combined anti-drug and counter-terrorism operations. Similarly, the AFP and the Royal Thai Police and other Thai agencies have overseen Thai officers undertake joint undercover operations in Australia and Thailand, resulting in substantial criminal intelligence and the interdiction and arrest of significant numbers of persons actively involved in criminal activities.

AFP and U.S. FBI officers, together with host government agencies, have also jointly investigated the role of Australian and foreign individuals involved in terrorist acts and conspiracies in Pakistan, Afghanistan, Indonesia, Malaysia, and several other countries after the September 11, 2001 and Bali 2002 terror attacks. AFP forensic and investigative officers also jointly investigated the Malaysian Airlines disaster in the Ukraine in 2014 after it had been shot down by Russian supported separatists. Similar to the U.S. Secret Service, AFP officers are also expected to protect the Australian Prime Minister and other VIP dignitaries posted to or visiting Australia.

OTHER AUSTRALIAN CRIMINAL JUSTICE AGENCIES

There are several other agencies, with significant law enforcement roles, that assist the Australian police forces at both federal and state or territory levels. At the federal level, these agencies include the Australian Border Force (ABF) and the Australian Criminal Intelligence Commission (ACIC). The ABF, which is a part of the Department of Home Affairs, was reconstituted into its present form in 2015 under the Australian Border Force Act 2015. It was a merger of the Australian Customs and Border Protection Service with the Department of Immigration and Border Protection. Its primary responsibility is to ensure the integrity of the Australian migration system. It does so through offshore and onshore border control enforcement, investigations into possible border breaches, and detention of illegal migrants.

The ACIC has also undergone a metamorphosis over the past four decades. One of its predecessors was the National Crime Authority (NCA), which was established in 1984 and lasted until 2002. The NCA was succeeded by the Australian Crime Commission (ACC), which was established under the Australian Crime Commission ACT 2002. Apart from the NCA, the ACC also superseded two other important agencies: the Australian Bureau of Criminal Intelligence and the Office of Strategic Crime Assessments. ACIC is also a part of the Department of Home Affairs and its primary functions are to investigate crimes, conduct research into criminal networks, and share information with other national law enforcement agencies.

Several members of the Australian Intelligence Community, including the Australian Secret Intelligence Service (ASIS), Australia's external intelligence agency, also have a remit for undertaking the collection of criminal intelligence by their officers at Australian Embassies and High Commissions concerning several transnational crimes that they undertake with the Australian Federal Police and foreign allies (ASIS, 2020). Similarly, the Australian Transaction Reports and Analysis Centre (AusTRAC) is an Australian government financial intelligence agency whose role is to monitor and report criminal financial transactions that include money laundering, organized crime, tax evasion, welfare fraud, and terrorism financing (AusTRAC, 2020). The Australian Cyber Security Centre (ACSC) and several state-based police units address the threat of the use of high technology to facilitate or directly conduct crime (ACSC, 2020).

Several Australian states also have legislatively created other entities that not only educate the public about corruption, but they also investigate corruption and criminal activities. These agencies were partly founded on the principle that educating the public about corruption is one of the most cost-effective ways of reducing it. For example, in New South Wales, there are two powerful permanent commissions that investigate corruption and organized crime. The first is the Independent Commission Against Corruption (ICAC), which was established in 1989. This is an independent agency of the NSW government whose primary responsibility is to eliminate corruption and enhance the integrity of public administration in the state. ICAC has the power to investigate Members of Parliament, civil servants, local councilors and even the academic staff of NSW universities. The second permanent commission in NSW is the Crime Commission, which is a statutory corporation that was reconstituted under the NSW Crime Commission Act 2012. Its functions are to reduce the incidence of organized crime, investigate terrorism-related offenses and other serious crime in NSW.

There are similar agencies in other states such as the Queensland Crime and Justice Commission formed in the wake of the 1987, "Commission of Inquiry into Possible Illegal Activities and Associated Police Misconduct," known as the Fitzgerald Inquiry.

POLICING AND INDIGENOUS AUSTRALIANS

Indigenous Australians constitute about 2 percent of the total population, but they comprise more than 27 percent of the national adult prison population. Whichever way one looks at the situation, indigenous Australians are over-represented in the criminal justice system. Despite many national inquiries into the rates of their imprisonment and deaths in custody in the past few decades, their problems have not gone away. One way of understanding the nature of the structural and systemic factors that have pitted the indigenous Australians against the criminal justice system is to examine how the first Australians have been treated since the advent of European colonization.

The collision of the European settlers with the indigenous population resulted in violent confrontations with a tragic record of massacres and brutalities visited upon the original inhabitants by police, military and settlers. According to Rusden (1883), the impunity with which the free settlers dealt violence to the Aborigines was noted in an early history of the Australian colonies:

> Governors had tempered, if they could not quell, the cruel blasts of persecution which raged over the land. But on disappearance of the Governor's active control, there arose a confidence that the Executive Government, dependent on the people's voice, would not dare, if even it should desire, to mete out equal justice to the two races. Dwellers in the outlying Districts denounced as impertinent any questionings as to the number, or the manner of the violent deaths of natives on their cattle stations. (p. 235)

There was violence on both sides when the Aborigines resisted, but there was a tragic record of shootings, poisonings, forcing Aboriginal people over cliffs and other massacres. The indigenous population was not protected or policed effectively with police either delivering this violence themselves or being complicit with other parties (Richards, 2008). In one response while being examined at the Select Committee on the Native Police Force of the Queensland Legislative Assembly as to what had occurred to the aboriginal community, Captain John Coley responded to the Committee chairman as follows:

Chairman: On the Kilcoy Station owned by Mr. Evan Mackenzie, there were two white men killed, and an imported bull; and their retaliation was very severe on the blacks—they destroyed hundreds of them. In what way?
Coley: By shooting and poisoning them.
Chairman: What with?
Coley: With strychnine and arsenic, in flour (Queensland Legislative Assembly, 1861, p. 19)

The term "dispersal" became a euphemism for the killing of the indigenous population in official records. Except for some significant matters, such as the case of two settlers who took part in the Myall Creek massacre of twenty-eight Aborigines being eventually convicted and hanged for their crimes, there was a remarkable indifference to the plight of the Aborigines or the crimes against them (National Museum of Australia, 2020).

Similar to other settler societies, such as the United States, and conducive with the doctrine of *Terra Nullius* and ad-mixtures of Social Darwinism, there was a strong belief that because the Aborigines were hunter gatherers, they did not produce any profit from the land through agriculture or pastoralism and, therefore, the seizure of the lands could be justified (Bryett, Harrison & Shaw, 1994). One newspaper referred to the indigenous inhabitants as: "Dogs and horses . . . irreclaimable brute[s] . . . the one argument a blackfellow understands is that delivered from a rifle or six shooter" (Grassby & Hill, 1988, p. 35).

Aggression against the Aborigines was, and remains, a theme in the development of Australia. Australian jurisdictions have undertaken several commissions of inquiry into the relationship between Police and indigenous Australians, including the 1987–1991 "Aboriginal Deaths in Custody." Lamentably, serious issues remain with police–indigenous relations, with a West Australian and Northern Territory police officer each charged separately with the murder of Aboriginal persons in 2019. As of December 2020, despite efforts by the "Black Lives Matter" movement, there remain major problems in Australia's manner of tackling issues surrounding its indigenous population.

CHALLENGES: MULTICULTURALISM AND DIVERSITY WITHIN AUSTRALIAN POLICE SERVICES

As we mentioned earlier, the police often reproduce the dominant values of the society that they themselves come from. In much of the first two hundred years of European settlement, the Australian society was hostile to Aborigines and did not regard them as citizens. The police were equally hostile to people of non-European heritage. For example, Chinese miners were violently attacked during the Gold Rush period in the second half of the nineteenth century and the police, in some instances, retreated from violent mobs wishing to free those arrested for violence against the Chinese (Preslaw, 1971, p. 255). Racism was explicitly evident in both the colonial period and after Australian Federation, when a "White Australia" Policy was the officially sanctioned position of the Government from 1901 to 1975 (National Archives of Australia, 2020). The *Bulletin*, an influential Australian magazine, published openly racist xeno-phobic tirades against the Chinese in Australia from the 1880s to 1890s and labeled the Chinese as corrupt, opium-addicted immoral people who should be ejected from Australia. One publication titled, *"The Mongolian Octopus—Its Grip on Australia"* featured a pull-out anti-Chinese poster that readers could then post in locations of their choice (The Bulletin, 1886).

However, Australian police forces have changed from being all-white to multicolor and multicultural entities, with nonwhite migrants also playing promi-nent roles. This is largely because Australia is now arguably one of the most successful multicultural countries in the world, with 28 percent of the population in 2016 having been born overseas. Thus, creating diverse police services that represent the communities they serve as well as being able to effectively police diversity is an important modern objective of Australian Police Services.

Earlier in this chapter it was shown that the first female police officers were inducted into the New South Wales and South Australian police in 1915. There have been improvements upon the recruitment of women into the police service with the rate expanding from just 1.8 percent in 1971 to over 28 percent in 2017 (ANZPAA, 2017). A great deal of this was driven by litigation and not through choice, with police executives avoiding their obligations until forced to do so (Sarre & Prenzler, 2018). Sexual harassment in some services has also been difficult to eradicate, with a 2015 Report into the Victoria Police identifying entrenched misogyny and sexism (Victorian Equal Opportunities and Human Rights Commission, 2015).

There has also been considerable effort since the mid-1980s to recruit more indigenous officers into Australian Police Services and to seek to redress the impact of the colonial period. Indigenous Australians were not allowed to vote until the late 1960s. New recruiting initiatives, the establishment of indigenous courts, as well as the earlier example of the all indigenous police station in Western Australia, are attempts to redress the weight of history and move beyond tokenism.

Australian Police Services also have addressed diversity in terms of recruitment and relations with the Lesbian, Gay, Bisexual, Transgender, Intersex and Queer (LGBTIQ) community. The establishment of LGBTIQ liaison teams, recruitment from the community, and the involvement of LGBTIQ police officers marching in such significant events as the Sydney Gay and Lesbian Mardi Gras have sought to redress the historical inequities. Similarly, the investigation of a number of "cold case" gay hate murders, such as the 2020 prosecution of an individual for the murder of 27-year-old American man Scott Johnson in 1988, seek to reassure the community that the perceived dismissive, and/or homophobic attitudes of the past were no longer tolerated (ABC, 2020). Similar work is also continuing with other minority groups in Australia as well as consolidating the gains made in diversifying the police force across the spectrum of gender, ethno-cultural, and sexuality representation as well as providing enhanced education of the police.

Education of Police

As in other professions, police services are known to improve their performance if their officers receive appropriate education. Australian police services recognized this during the 1990s (Sarre & Prenzler, 2016). The findings of several Royal Commissions also identified this link, including the Fitzgerald Commission of Inquiry, which examined the corrupt conduct of the Queensland Police in the late 1980s, noting:

> Police need more education to cope with their increasingly complex role. Officers should be encouraged to undertake higher education in colleges of advanced education and other tertiary institutions along with students from other disciplines. There should be a long term move to recruit more graduates (Fitzgerald, 1989, p. 365).

While Police still attend Police Academies, their education in Australia covers a much broader variety of subjects, with a few Police Academies co-located and integrated with universities. Officers also have opportunities to attend overseas programs offered by allied agencies such as courses in the United Kingdom and the FBI Academy in the United States.

Science and Technology's Impact on Australian Policing

Science and technology is a double-edged sword. While they have exponentially increased the effectiveness of Australian policing, they have also enabled criminals to operate more efficiently. Up until the 1980s, police services, such as the Queensland Police, were still using antiquated criminal records via complexly organized systems of index cards. Similarly, the identification of offenders relied on fingerprints, physical evidence, and physical surveillance, while the interview of suspects was undertaken via a typed or written record of the interview.

As of now, the police have access to sophisticated internal databases to record criminal intelligence, and access to an array of sophisticated electronic surveillance technology for intercepting communications as well as listening devices deployed upon criminal suspects. The advent of the recorded (audio and visual) interview of offenders has led to decisive prosecutions. It has also gone some way to eradicating police malpractices in the "verbals" of suspects with unsigned records of interview and unsigned confessions, which were previously presented to court as the true record of the police interaction and interview of the offender. A police "verbal" in the Australian context is the purposeful inclusion of damaging remarks and admissions by a suspect by police during an interview. The remarks included in the verbal are then presented as authentic in court and have caused the imprisonment of innocent persons. Several Australian Royal Commissions into policing have addressed the issue of police fabrication of evidence and corrupt conduct.

Public concerns about police access to data have been heightened in the wake of legislation designed to give police more powers to obtain evidence against terrorists, organized crime, and information "leaks" from government. The issue is contentious in Australia due to the *Telecommunications and Other Legislation Amendment (Assistance and Access) Act* 2018, which directed telecommunications companies to maintain records for two years to enable criminal justice agencies access for criminal investigations. Domestic intelligence and policing agencies have argued that access to this metadata might reveal the whereabouts of wanted persons or other information that could assist an investigation.

Notwithstanding several concerns about the privacy and individual rights of Australian citizens and technology, the impact of science and technology and its exponential growth have aided criminal investigations as well as contributing to make the process more efficient and aiding more effective oversight and detection of police corruption and malpractice.

CONCLUSION

This chapter has provided a broad picture that portrays policing and law enforcement in Australia as an evolving practice that often takes into account the changing norms of global governance, the emerging human rights regimes, and the perceptions of migrants who might have come from countries where there is no mutual trust between the police and the people. It has highlighted the way improvements in technology have helped law enforcement come up with newer ways of detecting criminals and their crimes. Some of the factors that have impacted policing in Australia are likely to do so in the next decade or so. Due to space constraints, we shall mention only two of these factors: changes in science and technology; and relations with indigenous Australians.

By science and technology, we include artificial intelligence and cyber issues. While we are not in a position to say what kind of technological breakthroughs we might witness in the next five or ten years, it can be argued that Australia's policing and law enforcement agencies have to prepare for technology-related crimes of the kind they have not seen before. Changes in technology are likely to give rise to new types of crimes or new ways of committing them, which might compel the Australian law enforcement agencies to design new methods of addressing the new dangers.

While the Australian policing and law enforcement system has improved its relations with indigenous Australians remarkably over the past five decades and is sensitive to some of their needs, it has a long way to go to earn the respect and trust of first Australians. Unfortunately, the policing and law enforcement agencies, by themselves, do not have all the tools to address many of the social, economic, health, governance and related problems that afflict indigenous Australians. These problems, including over-representation in the criminal justice system, need to be addressed by State and Federal Government in close consultation with indigenous leaders.

REFERENCES

Arizona State University. (2020). Center for Problem Oriented Policing. https://pop-center.asu.edu/content/about-us.

Australia New Zealand Police Advisory Agency (ANZPAA). (2020). *Police Workforce Compendium.* http://www.anzpaa.org.au/ArticleDocuments/180/ANZPAA%20Workforce%20Compendium.PDF.aspx?OverrideExpiry=Y.

Australian Broadcasting Corporation (ABC). (2020). *Police Cadet Zarelda Dickens Turning Heads and Fighting Crime in the Kimberley.* https://www.abc.net.au/news/2020-06-28/zarelda-dickens-kimberley-police-cadet/12393362.

Australian Broadcasting Corporation (ABC). (2020). *Warakurna Welcomes First All-Indigenous Police Station, Aiming to Repair a Community's Mistrust.* https://www.abc.net.au/news/2018-06-20/this-is-the-first-indigenous-run-police-station-in-australia/9861778.

Australian Broadcasting Corporation (ABC). (2020). *Four Other Gay Hate Crimes Being Investigated by NSW Police after Scott Johnson Murder Charge.* https://

www.abc.net.au/news/2020-05-16/scott-johnson-charge-four-other-sydney-gay -hate-murders/12247922.

Australian Cyber Security Centre (ACSC). (2020). https://www.cyber.gov.au/.

Australian Federal Police. (n.d.) AFP across the world. https://www.afp.gov.au/what -we-do/our-work-overseas/afp-across-world.

Australian Secret Intelligence Service. (ASIS). (2020). https://www.asis.gov.au/.

Australian Transaction Reports and Analysis Centre (AusTRAC). (2020). https:// www.austrac.gov.au/.

Bryett, K., Harrison, A., & Shaw, J. (1994). *The Role and Functions of the Police in Australia*. Butterworths.

Bulletin. (1886, 21 August). The Mongolian Octopus: Its grip on Australia. https:// www.nla.gov.au/stories/blog/exhibitions/2019/05/10/australia-for-the-white -man.

Conole, P. (2002). *Protect & Serve: A History of Policing in Western Australia*. Western Australian Police Historical Society.

Culture Victoria. (2016). *Ned Kelly*. https://cv.vic.gov.au/stories/a-diverse-state/ned -kelly/.

Culture Victoria. (2016b). *Suit of Armour Worn by Ned Kelly*. https://cv.vic.gov.au/ stories/a-diverse-state/ned-kelly/suit-of-armour-worn-by-ned-kelly/.

Duke of Lancashire Infantry Museum, *The Battle of the Eureka Stockade, 1854*. http:/ /www.lancashireinfantrymuseum.org.uk/the-battle-of-the-eureka-stockade/.

Dukova, A. (2020). *To Preserve and Protect: Policing Colonial Brisbane*. University of Queensland Press.

Fitzgerald, G. E. (1989). Report of a commission of inquiry into possible illegal activities and associated misconduct. *Brisbane, Queensland Government*.

Goldstein, H. (1990). *Problem-Oriented Policing*. McGraw Hill.

Grassby, A. J. (1988). *Six Australian Battlefields: The Black Resistance to Invasion and the White Struggle against Colonial Oppression*. Angus & Robertson Publishers.

Hartwell, R. M. (1955). The pastoral ascendancy, 1820–50. *Australia: A Social and Political History*, 46–97.

Watson, F. (1915). Historical records of Australia. Series I. Governors' despatches to and from England. Volume III, 1801–1802. Edited by Frederick Watson.

Hoban, L. (1988). Law and order in early Sydney. *NSW Police Review* 68(1).

Hughes, R. (1986). *The Fatal Shore*. Panther.

National Archives of Australia. (2020). *The Immigration Restriction Act, 1901*. https://www.naa.gov.au/explore-collection/immigration-and-citizenship/immigra- tion-restriction-act-1901.

National Museum of Australia. (2020). *Myall Creek Massacre*. https://www.nma.gov .au/defining-moments/resources/myall-creek-massacre.

New South Wales Police. (2020, July). History https://www.police.nsw.gov.au/about _us/history.

O'Brien, E. (1937). *The Foundation of Australia* (Vol. 23). Sheed & Ward.

Owen, C. (2016). *"Every Mother's Son Is Guilty": Policing the Kimberley Frontier of Western Australia 1882–1905*. Apollo Books.

Police Federation of Australia (PFA). (2020). https://pfa.org.au/.

Preslaw, G. O. (1971), Lambing Flats. In *History of the Australian Gold Rushes*, N. Keesing (ed). Lloyd O'Neill Pty Ltd.

Queensland Legislative Assembly. (1861). *Native Police Force. Report from the Select Committee on the Native Police Force and the Condition of the Aborigines Generally: together with The Proceedings of the Committee and Minutes of Evidence.* Fairfax and Belbridge, Brisbane. [Trove: National Library of Australia] https://nla.gov.au/nla.obj-52862431/view?partId=nla.obj-103375941#page/n36/mode/1up.

Richards, J. (2008). *The Secret War: A True History of Queensland's Native Police.* University of Queensland Press.

Rusden, G. W. (1883). *History of Australia,* Vol. 3. Chapman and Hall.

Sarre, R., & Prenzler, T. (2018). Ten key developments in modern policing: An Australian perspective. *Police Practice and Research*, 19(1): 3–16.

Sturma, M. (1981). Police and drunkards in Sydney, 1841–1851. *Australian Journal of Politics & History*, 27(1): 48–56.

Tasmania Police Museum. (2020, July). History of policing in Tasmania. https://6f4f42510cef420c83171da9318aaea3.filesusr.com/ugd/419dff_063852de978a44c4a2554e5121fe55df.pdf.

Tench, W. (1961). *Sydney's First Four Years.* Angus & Robertson.

Victorian Equal Opportunities and Human Rights Commission. (2015). *Independent Review into Sex Discrimination and Sexual Harassment, Including Predatory Behavior in Victoria Police.* VEO & HRC.

Chapter 14

Policing in New Zealand

Ross Hendy

New Zealand Police is the chief law enforcement and policing agency in New Zealand. Established in 1886, on the final disbandment of an armed constabulary, New Zealand Police is notable in that it is one of five routinely unarmed police forces in the OECD. While research on New Zealand Police is limited, influences from nineteenth-century British policing remain apparent. Today, NZP has broad policing and regulatory responsibilities, including public safety, order maintenance, criminal investigation and road policing, emergency/disaster response, coronial investigation, firearms regulation, and high policing activities relating to organized crime, national security, and counterterrorism. While it has been spared the misfortunes of systemic corruption, it has faced criticism for problems associated with organizational culture.

INTRODUCTION

This chapter contemplates how New Zealand's sole policing agency, the New Zealand Police *Nga Pirihimana O Aotearoa* (NZP), sits in comparison to others in the global environment. Two characteristics set NZP apart from its contemporaries. First, unlike other Anglo-American common-law countries, this national agency provides almost all policing and criminal law enforcement services from community policing to national security. And, unlike most policing agencies, NZP operates while routinely unarmed. Officers do not carry firearms on their person. Indeed, one intention of this chapter is to prompt policing scholars to compare New Zealand's policing system with those of decentralized systems (say that of Australia and the United States) to entice theoretical contemplation. Can the study of New Zealand's policing system provide opportunities to construct, or *reconstruct*, forms of system best practice?

Second, as many police agencies face calls for disarmament and defunding, insight may be gained from studying how the disarmament of policing in 1886 continues to shape contemporary policy and practice. In the present climate of increasing para-militarization and weaponization of police agencies across the globe, is the study of New Zealand's policing model a helpful addition to the discourse?

NEW ZEALAND'S PUBLIC POLICING SYSTEM

New Zealand's "policing assemblage" benefits from the country's single legal jurisdiction and constitutional arrangements. New Zealand's single public policing agency, New Zealand Police (NZP), has jurisdiction over three geographical domains: local, national, and international policing. NZP is one of six national agencies coalescing in the "justice sector"—the backbone of New Zealand's criminal justice system—whose primary function is *policing*. The other members include the Crown Law Office, the Department of Corrections, the Ministry of Justice (including courts), *Oranga Tamariki*—Ministry for Children, and the Serious Fraud Office, all of which have limited *policing* functions.

Other specialized and administrative policing agencies operate on a national model. New Zealand has separate enforcement or regulative agencies for aviation security, customs, immigration, fisheries, maritime, and military matters. Border policing is the responsibility of Biosecurity New Zealand, Immigration New Zealand, and the New Zealand Customs Service. Uniformed officers from these agencies have limited policing and enforcement powers. New Zealand's national security is presently the responsibility of the New Zealand Intelligence Community, namely the GCSB, SIS, and the NAB (New Zealand Intelligence Community, 2017). As officers of the Intelligence Community have no executive powers, NZP operates a national security criminal investigation unit for the investigation, arrest, and prosecution of national security matters (Butterworth, 2005; New Zealand Intelligence Community, 2017).

NEW ZEALAND POLICE FORCES

The history of NZP is well documented and researched but largely comes from an orthodox perspective from "cop-sided" and hegemonic perspectives (Bowling, Reiner, & Sheptycki, 2019).

Antipodean Context—Policing of Free and Penal Populations

The evolution of civil policing in New Zealand appears to have been hindered by the focus on quelling insurrection by Māori during the New Zealand Wars. Moreover, early policing was shaped by the challenges arising from the combination of colonial demands of the frontier and nation-building, establishing police for the safety of free settlers and controlling the penal population of incarcerated and freed convicts (Nettelbeck & Smandych, 2010; O'Brien, 1960). English colonization of Australia and New Zealand in the late eighteenth and early nineteenth-centuries were not consistent. Following the arrival of English explorer Captain James Cook in New Zealand in 1769, and Australia in 1770, the initial colonization of Australia was driven by Britain's policy of forced convict emigration (Finnane, 1994). Conversely, British colonization of South Australia and New Zealand were not convict-centric, rather, "free" settlers were encouraged to emigrate from Britain to profit from the natural resources abundant in the new frontiers (Clyne, 1987).

British approaches to native peoples across the colonies were similarly inconsistent. While Australian aboriginal tribes were thought "too weak and dispersed to offer significant resistance" (Hill, 1986, 29), the Māori tribal-groups of New Zealand and the Moriori of the Chatham Islands were seen as more formidable (Hill, 1986). Relations between Māori and the British Crown were later codified in 1840 through *Te Tiriti o Waitangi* (the Treaty of Waitangi) which recorded the cession by Māori chiefs to the British Crown. In exchange, Māori became British subjects and were afforded the protection of the Crown (King, 2004). No such arrangement was sought from the Aboriginal peoples of Australia (Clyne, 1987).

British Policing of the Colonies

The significance of Peel, Rowan and Mayne on the formation of Antipodean policing has been well demonstrated (Clyne, 1987; Hill, 1995; Killey, 2019; O'Brien, 1960). British-styled policing came to Australasia with the arrival of the "First Fleet" at Botany Bay, Australia in 1788. Among the convicts and settlers were the continent's first constables and night-watchmen (O'Brien, 1960). Population growth and crime pressures resulted in regular policing reform, including the marshaling of constables and night-watchmen of the First Fleet under the provost marshal in 1801, with control passing to magistrates in 1804, the establishment of the Sydney Police Act 1833 (NSW), and failed attempts during the remainder of the decade to adopt the reforms, espoused by Sir Robert Peel, which formed the basis for the London Metropolitan Police (O'Brien, 1960). Escaped and freed convicts from the penal colony at New South Wales settled sporadically in New Zealand: those who became involved with the trade of seals, whales, flax, and other commodities (King, 2004). The first British representative posted to New Zealand, James Busby, requested formal protection of naval ships and two British constables in 1835 from the Colonial Office (Carpenter, 2009). However, this was dismissed as a "whining request" (King, 2004, p. 155) at the time by the Governor at New South Wales. When the Treaty of Waitangi formally established the British colony of New Zealand (Belich, 1996; King, 2004), initial policing for the colony was provided by members of the New South Wales mounted police (Hill, 2012). Over the next 46 years, policing journeyed through several reforms: the creation of an armed police force, the formation of independent provincial police forces in 1853, and the establishment of an armed constabulary in 1867.

Provincial police forces in New Zealand unified in 1877 when they were merged with the armed constabulary. Before this time, the force was occupied with military conflict (such as the Māori Land Wars from 1845 to 1872) and civil and criminal conflict (such as problems associated with the Gold Rushes of the 1860s). The conflation of military and civil policing personnel was the antithesis of Peel's English policing reforms: his "new police" were to be independent of military authority (Bowling, Reiner, and Sheptycki 2019). However, legislative reforms later disestablished the armed constabulary and created a unified national police force of civilian constables under the enactment of the Police Force Act 1886. Hill (1986) argues that the style of policing in colonial New Zealand transformed from order imposition (such as that of the Irish Constabulary) to order maintenance (modeled on the British "new police"). At the same time, mounted police became responsible for the higher crimes of civil conflict and insurrection including the suppression of conflict arising from the Māori Land Wars, where the foot-based "civil" police concentrated on "low" crimes committed by the citizenry.

Disarmament and Civilianization

Colonial police forces were established as armed forces. Hill (1986) notes that the disarmament of the "civil" police officers in New Zealand occurred in 1878, before the disestablishment proper of the armed constabulary in 1886. At that time, the armed constabulary consisted of mounted officers and foot officers. Routine carriage of firearms by foot officers (those known as the "police branch") ceased at the same time as other provincial police forces were amalgamated into the armed constabulary. Discontinuation was not because of legislative change; the decision was one of policy. Likewise, the disestablishment of the armed constabulary of 1886 did not prohibit the use of firearms by officers, simply authorized the Governor to make, alter, or revoke such regulations respecting the training, arms and accoutrements, clothing, and equipment of such force.

The civilianization of policing was most likely to have been influenced by domestic political concerns and the reorganization of colonial affairs (King, 2004). Up until 1885 (the time of the Russian war scare) New Zealand had not faced any external threats to its security. While the armed constabulary had acted as the colony's "de facto standing army," changes were required to address the threat of invasion by foreign forces. Hill draws attention to the publication of Rowan and Mayne's British policing maxims in the *New Zealand Police Gazette 1880* (1986). Moreover, while there was no legislative prohibition of the use of firearms, customary practice mirrored that of British police forces where the use of firearms was discretionary.

While the police force was no longer called an "armed constabulary" it did, in fact, remain an armed force, with officers able to draw firearms if the circumstances permitted. Indeed, although officers ceased to carry firearms routinely, officers remained armed with other weapons. The change of name of the force coincided with the "professionalization" of police through the formal division of policing and military operations spelled out in the 1886 Act. Hill (1995) notes that from 1905, only senior officers and detectives were to be routinely issued with revolvers; all new constables would cease to be issued with firearms when enrolled. Firearms remained available to all officers, but only for use during emergencies.

Legacies from 1886

Prior to NZP's establishment in 1886, policing services were provided by a variety of public bodies including the *foreign* New South Wales mounted police from 1840, an armed constabulary, and provincial forces. Legislative reforms disestablished the armed constabulary and created a unified national police force of civilian constables under the enactment of the *Police Force Act 1886* (Hill, 1986). Legacies of these reorganizations continue to shape contemporary policing. First, NZP is a national police agency that serves as *the* public police department throughout New Zealand. Second, the symbolism of the replacement of the Armed Constabulary with a civilian police force in 1886 pervades the "national psyche" with the expectation that policing should be delivered without recourse to the use of or threat of use of firearms (Hendy, 2020).

The New Zealand Police *Nga Pirihimana O Aotearoa*

Today, the New Zealand Police *Nga Pirihimana O Aotearoa* (NZP) is a nonpublic service department of the New Zealand state sector (Govt.nz, 2020, p. 228). In addition to territorial policing responsibilities of public safety, order maintenance, criminal investigation, and road policing, NZP has responsibilities ranging from emergency/disaster response, coronial investigation, firearms regulation, and high policing activities relating to organized crime, national security, and counter-terrorism (New Zealand Police, 2005).

New Zealand Police: A Force, Service or Both

Nomenclature may seem a superficial starting point of analysis. The literature does, however, show us that there is a certain utility in contemplating how agencies portray their mandate to the public they police (e.g., Bowling, Reiner & Sheptycki, 2019). For example, agencies styled as a "service" ostensibly present themselves to the public as "providing a service" in contrast to exercising force (Mawby & Wright, 2008). In doing so, there is some alignment with the tenets of Wilson's service style (i.e., the consensual, helpful functions of the police; Bowling, Reiner, & Sheptycki, 2019, p. 182) in contrast to other self-defining "watchman" and "legalistic" styles (Wilson, 1968). The use of branding mottos "to protect and serve" or "to serve and protect" are ubiquitous in North American policing and symbolize an agency's strategic and operational intent. So, it is a reasonable question to ask how the omission of either moniker should be interpreted: is the agency a force, a service, neither, or indeed both?

The name and mandate of New Zealand's police agencies have changed over time. While NZP is an armed police agency, officers have not routinely carried weapons on their person since 1886. This is in direct contrast to the public police agencies of Australia which have all successively adopted open firearm carriage policies (e.g., Sarre, 1996; McCulloch, 2001). NZP ceased being styled as a "police force" from 1958. The "force" moniker was dropped from the agency's official name when the Police Act 1958 repealed the Police Force Act 1947. Butterworth (2005) notes that this change was neither debated in parliament nor discussed in official police reporting at the time. Instead, noting that it has been "explained as expressing a desire to break away from the old military associations and stress the civilian peacekeeping role of the police in a democratic society" (2005, p. 104).

Present "Service" Function

More recently, NZP's communications set out that it aspires to be a "police service" (New Zealand Police, 2019a) while promoting a "strategy-on-a-page" infographic of its present service provision as "our business" (New Zealand Police, 2020). At a more fundamental level, New Zealand's parliament most recently defined NZP's core functions in the Policing Act 2008 to include: keeping the peace; maintaining public safety; law enforcement; crime prevention community support and reassurance; national security; participation in policing activities outside New Zealand; and emergency management.

In addition, NZP provides many specialized policing services that are often performed by separate agencies in other jurisdictions and *on behalf of* other government agencies (see "Office of Constable" later in this chapter). For example, it is contracted by the Ministry of Transport to provide road policing law enforcement and conducts investigative enquiries on behalf of the Coronial service.

Governance

The NZP is headed by a Commissioner of Police (CoP), who serves as the chief executive of the police agency and serves as the de facto chief constable (Butterworth, 2005). The CoP has operational and disciplinary command over all police employees. Internal governance and policy setting occur at a national level. NZP simultaneously delivers local policing through semi-autonomous district commands and national services through national service centers and a national command through national headquarters. District and national commanders form a senior executive group to set national policy and operational priorities (Butterworth, 2005).

Governance presently aligns with the "Peelian" convention of "constitutional independence" which posits that the executive branch of government has no direct control of police agencies (Killey, 2019). Such a convention was first regulated in the Police Regulations 1992; prior to this, constabulary independence had been assumed under the constabulary oath office (Butterworth, 2005). Indeed, after unfounded concerns of undue influence by the Prime Minister during the 1999 diplomatic visit of the Chinese President (Stenning, 2007), further clarification was legislated in the Policing Act 2008. This spelled out that although the CoP is responsible to the Minister of Police for carrying out the functions of policing (s16(1)), the CoP must operate independently regarding the maintenance of order and enforcement of the law in relation to individuals or groups, the investigation and prosecution of offenses, and decisions about individual police employees (s16(2)). Recent scholarship points to the "mythology of police independence," commonly assumed under British-styled policing, that commissioners of police are influenced through *indirect* actions (Killey, 2019). For instance, as the CoP is appointed by the Governor-General on the advice of the executive branch of government, the CoP is attuned to the political ramifications of resisting government demands as the statutory position is limited to a maximum term of five years and may be terminated at the "pleasure of the Governor-General" (Policing Act 2008 s13).

Indirect ministerial control of NZP is evident. Having shed responsibilities for traffic control in the 1930s (Dunstall, 1999), NZP reluctantly, at the direction of the government, absorbed the Ministry of Transport's Traffic Safety Service in 1992 (Butterworth, 2005). While a case was made that such a maneuver would address increasing road deaths and fiscal efficiencies by combining both agencies, Butterworth notes that "in the final analysis . . . the amalgamation was a political decision, not one sought by either of the contracting parties; indeed, both had misgivings about it" (2005, p. 297). Successive governments have controlled the size of the organization through the allocation of funding of officer positions, a process of which usually occurs during the electioneering, and the control of police budgets (Butterworth, 2005).

Office of Constable

Key statutes suggest that New Zealand's parliament has, over time, provided the office of constable with supremacy as *the* primary policing and law enforcement officer. Constables do not outrank other law enforcement officers but have a more diverse collection of powers and privileges than other warranted officers. The Crimes Act 1961 empowers constables to make an arrest without warrant on the basis that the constable *finds* (s315(2)(a)) or *has good cause to suspect* (s315(2)(b)) a person is disturbing the peace or committing any offense punishable by imprisonment. Similarly, constables may conduct warrantless search and seizure, and assume the powers of other warranted law enforcement offices (see below). Constables also become agents of the coroner under the Coroners Act 2006 and have specific powers to use force, detain, or force entry under the Mental Health Act 1992. In essence, the constable has become a principal enforcement officer in New Zealand.

The "office of constable" was retained in the 1886 Act, which disbanded the armed constabulary and created the new civilianized police, and modeled on Peel's 1829 "citizen-in-uniform" with a constable's general powers and privileges afforded by common law (Hill, 1995). The recruitment of two Commissions from London's Metropolitan Police (1898–1909) further shaped NZP doctrine through professionalization, consistent practice, and reinforcing independence from political control (Dunstall, 1999). Indeed, constabulary independence today may be witnessed in the present constabulary oath of office where constables swear or affirm allegiance to the Sovereign, not the government. In practicality, this makes NZP and constables answerable to the Crown,[1] not the government, which also serves the Crown (Butterworth, 2005).

This office retains its primacy in operational matters today. While the rank of constable places the position at the bottom of NZP's organizational hierarchy, *all* sworn ranks from constable to commissioner hold the powers and privileges afforded by the office of constable. In addition to those privileges associated with warrantless powers of arrest and search, NZP maintains significant prosecutorial independence. Although some charging decisions for criminal prosecution require the consent of the Attorney-General (e.g., transnational crimes, terrorist acts, bribery, or corruption; Crown Law, 2013), NZP is not subordinate to or directed by prosecutors to the degree between police with US district attorneys or Scottish Procurator Fiscal (Stenning, 2011). NZP also directly prosecute minor to moderately serious criminal offenses, traffic prosecutions, and youth court prosecutions, and attend coroners' inquests. The most serious criminal offenses are prosecuted by independent warranted lawyers.

Other offices of enforcement, created under statute, do not have the same widespread general powers of arrest, search and seizure, entrusted to a constable. Some offices have limited powers such as a Conservation Warranted officer (Conservation Act 1987 s40) or a Biosecurity Inspector (Biosecurity Act 1993 s107) to "stop, detain, search, and seize." Indeed, some enforcement powers are available to *any person* (such as "citizen arrests" under the Crimes Act). However, a constable is also afforded many "nonconstabulary" enforcement powers and can use those statutory powers or assume the role of the office. For instance, constables are enforcement officers under the Land Transport Act 1998, fisheries officers under the Fisheries Act 1996, a fish and game ranger under the Conservation Act 1987, and have the powers of an aviation security officer under the Civil Aviation Act 1990.

Civilianization

While the disestablishment of the armed constabulary in 1886 signals one avenue of civilianization (i.e., civilians-in-uniform), the allocation of policing tasks performed by constables to non-constabulary officers poses a larger question about constabulary independence and constabulary-informed decision making.

Nonconstabulary specialists were appointed as members of police from the 1950s (Butterworth, 2005), but it was not until 1989 that NZP became the official employer of *nonsworn* civilian employees. While nonsworn staff had long fulfilled important nonpublic facing "support" roles (e.g., secretarial support, fingerprint analysis), management reviews from the 1980s began a trend for the civilianization of public-facing operational roles that did not necessarily require constabulary powers. Such roles that were previously filled by sworn officers became earmarked for civilianization and culminated in the Police Amendment Act 1989 (Butterworth, 2005). Further reorganization occurred under the Policing Act 2008 with the creation of the office of Authorized Officer (an office which confers limited role-specific constabulary powers) splitting NZP's workforce into three classes. As of June 2019, 71 percent comprised of sworn constabulary officers, 2 percent of sworn authorized officers and 27 percent of nonsworn civilian employees (New Zealand Police, 2019a).

By 2020, public-facing civilianized roles included station front-counter enquiries, vetting services, telephonic and electronic crime reporting, and emergency call handling. Parts of the operational command and control system too are partially civilianized with civilian dispatching staff making deployment decisions (e.g., Li et al., 2020).

Para-Militarization

The dilemmic nature of para-militarization of NZP confronts the ideology of Peel and the architects of New Zealand policing. The ethos behind the 1886 disarmament and disestablishment of the Armed Constabulary, in favor of a gentler, civilian-led force of "citizens-in-uniform," has become challenged by the professional necessity for NZP to hold a capability to overcome resistance (see Den Heyer, 2014; Phillips, 2018). The founding of the Armed Offenders Squad (AOS) in 1964, in response to fatal shootings of police officers in 1963–1964 (Butterworth, 2005), is a turning point in the path of para-militarization of NZP.

But there are two further notable controversies that have drawn attention to the *visibility* of NZP's para-militarization in the wider political and popular discourses. The first relates to NZP's response to nationwide civil disorder during the South African rugby team's tour of New Zealand during 1981. At the time, New Zealand was one of many commonwealth countries which had agreed to boycott South African sporting fixtures as an avenue to combat apartheid. The tour of South Africa's national rugby team, therefore, caused widespread conflict between sporting enthusiasts and those who opposed the tour. NZP's nationally coordinated use of planning, intelligence gathering, deployment of public-order policing units, and the resulting skirmish lines between police and the public, became a powerful and visible manifestation and demonstration of the police's capability to marshal the force, and indeed to use force to quell disorder in a militaristic nature (McCulloch, 2001; Phillips, 2018). It is also worthwhile to consider how the *appearance* of officers ("citizens-in-uniform") was recorded at the time Butterworth (2005, p. 228):

> With their helmets, visors, shields and batons, their members would always have looked threatening, and indeed their appearance was part of their psychological armour. However, they looked even more intimidating in the later stages of the tour, when they always wore their dark uniform greatcoats and heavy boots. These were in fact the only form of body armour available to them, especially against firebombs and fireworks, and they prevent many injuries, but they made the squads appear very menacing.

The complication of safeguarding health and safety while balancing the symbols of approachability and restraint continues to be a pressing issue for contemporary times. Many recent safeguarding initiatives have triggered concerns about the increasing militaristic appearance of police. While Phillips (2018) observes how the transition to semi-automatic side-arms in America is a step of militarism gone unnoticed, the increasing weaponization of NZP constables certainly has not. The introduction of OC spray, stab-resistance body armor, CEDs, Glock 17, and Bushmaster M4 firearms have each drawn criticism popularized by mainstream media, activists, and politicians. But perhaps a more compelling narrative in the discourse is the routine arming and carriage of firearms. The 2019–2020 trial of armed response teams (ART) poses as a more recent visual indicator of increased para-militarization. While there is a belief in the merit of routinely unarmed policing (Hendy, 2014), others posit that such a doctrine threatens officer safety and capability to adequately respond to the present environment. Others have noted that the belief that NZP operates routinely unarmed is a mythical misinterpretation (Shortt, 2020). The ART model replicated the British armed response vehicle model where routinely armed officers patrol and are deployable 24/7 (Waddington & Wright, 2008). Critics of the trial note that there was no operational mandate for such a trial, that deploying routinely armed officers would lead to further disproportionate policing of ethnic minorities, and as such these trials are "a step towards the Americanisation of law enforcement in New Zealand" (Rākete, 2019). Indeed, at the cessation of the trial, the new police commissioner determined that the operational utility was difficult to evaluate and subsequent changes to the deployment model would require community engagement (Coster, 2020).

With the rejection of the ART model, the centrality of the AOS remains in NZ's present deployment model (New Zealand Police, 2019b). It is expected that first responders, who have access to firearms secured in vehicles, provide a primary response and *if possible,* await the arrival of the secondary response from an AOS. Unlike SWAT/ARV units in other jurisdictions, AOS units are not operational 24/7; thus, deployment is dependent on the availability of squad members to stand to and deploy from central locations. A tertiary level of response is provided by the elite Special Tactics Group (formally the Anti-terrorist Squad) which provides a full-time capability to respond to significant terrorist or events which are out of the scope of the regional AOS (Butterworth, 2005).

There are some data available from NZP regarding police–citizen encounters and the use of "tactical options."[2] For the year ending December 2014, police officers (excluding Armed Offender Squad and Special Tactics Group officers) reported the use of 7,162 tactical options at 4,823 police–citizen encounters (New Zealand Police, 2015). While NZP also reported that 99.9 percent of "recorded face-to-face interactions with the public" did not involve reportable use of tactical options, mandatory reporting is not required for all uses of coercive force such as handcuffing or physical searches. Handcuffing, for instance, is only reportable if used in association with pain-compliance or used in combination with another tactic.

CULTURE, CONDUCT, AND CHANGE

While NZP has been spared the misfortunes of systemic corruption endemic in some Australian police forces (Butterworth, 2005), it has faced criticism for systemic malpractice and cultural bias associated with organizational culture (Rowe, 2009; Te Whaiti & Roguski, 1998). Two issues briefly discussed here consider race relations between Māori and NZP and the poor practice and malpractice associated with victims associated with adult sexual assault.

Cultural and Racial Relations

The disproportionate rate of Māori offending and imprisonment has long been topical in New Zealand's criminal justice discourse. While Anglo-American jurisdictions grapple with the highly visible disproportionate police practices of "stop and search" or "stop and frisk" as drivers of police–public disharmony (see Weitzer, 2014), NZP's role as gatekeepers to the criminal justice pipeline, through the apprehension and prosecution, has become a more pressing focus. Both Marshall (2009) and Den Heyer (2019) outline, more comprehensively than can be done here, the over-representation of Māori arrests, convictions, imprisonment, reconviction, and reimprisonment when compared to the population of non-Māori. Marshall's review of research exploring bias toward Māori and Pacific Islanders in the criminal justice system failed to identify conclusive evidence to support either differential involvement or discrimination in the New Zealand setting (Marshall, 2009).

Two pieces of cornerstone research completed in the late 1990s provide nuance to the complexity of Māori-Police relations. Some Māori micro-level perceptions of police strongly influenced a macro-level perspective that NZP was a racist institution with strong anti-Māori attitudes evidenced by racist abuse during arrest and disrespect for *tikanga Māori* (cultural protocol) (Te Whaiti & Roguski, 1998). Furthermore, respondents' perspectives linked contemporary practices of NZP with historical practices and agency predecessors. Conversely, research on police officers' attitudes toward Māori revealed racist attitudes toward Māori. Such views were held by a minority (about 25 percent), and there were also racist attitudes displayed toward Pacific Islanders and Asian people. Revealingly, officers who were Māori, held senior ranks, were more experienced or no longer working in the 'front line' were more likely to hold positive views toward Māori than those who were non-Māori, younger, lower-ranked and engaged in front-line work (Maxwell & Smith, 1998).

More recently, two contrasting events highlight the ongoing and now changing NZP institutional attitudes toward Māori. In 2007, paramilitary-styled AOS and STG units conducted a series of nationwide arrests under warrants issued under the Arms Act 1983 and Terrorism Suppression Act 2002. At the time, NZP held that the raids were in response to terrorist training camps, where political activists, including Māori nationalists, were weapons-training with illegal firearms and Molotov cocktails (Battersby, 2018; Small, 2011). While arrests of the principal suspects went without incident, certain tactical decisions—the establishment of police roadblocks—were found to be unlawful. Local residents were therefore unlawfully stopped, searched, and photographed. For the local residents, the positioning of the roadblocks was particularly distressing as they were positioned where Ngai Tūhoe (the local Māori tribe) had land confiscated by the Crown during the 1860s (Independent Police Conduct Authority, 2013). In recompense, CoP Bush (2014–2020) made two public announcements which signaled at attempt to redress the increasingly problematic Police–Māori relationship. First, was a public apology to Tūhoe in 2014 for the wrongdoing during the 2007 police operation (Mankelow, 2014). Second, was an acknowledgment that the agency had been "influenced by unconscious bias in their relations with Māori" and that this was represented in the disproportionate arrest and prosecution of Māori (Harley, 2015).

Sexual Misconduct and Malpractice

Two manifestations of improper conduct have added further blemishes to NZP's reputation. A 2004 Commission of Inquiry (CoI) established in response to sexual misconduct of officers during the 1980s identified areas of inappropriate culture and practice. The inquiry noted that sexual misconduct of the 1980s, which emerged in the mid-2000s, was poorly dealt with under insufficient adult sexual assault procedures but such misconduct was relatively rare (Bazley, 2007). Nevertheless, the CoI recommended changes to police practice, the monitoring of police misconduct, disciplinary practices and bolstering the police oversight agency. Specific recommendations were also given to implementing a code of conduct and developing policies on appropriate and inappropriate sexual conduct with members of the public. Of note, the CoI drew attention to the importance of improving the levels of diversity in the workforce, with regard to recruiting more women and members from ethnic minorities, as a fortifying mechanism to prevent further malpractice and undesirable manifestations of police culture (Bazley, 2007).

Some ten years after the implementation of a new code of contact, NZP became embroiled in a further controversy surrounding endemic bullying within the police workplace. Allegations this time centered around the bullying behavior of the members of NZP's executive, including a Deputy Commissioner. Further disclosures of bullying practices at operational levels prompted a formal review by the Independent Police Conduct Authority (notably bolstered on the recommendations of the 2007 Commission of Inquiry report). This review is still underway at the time of press.

Diversity

The CoI recommended that an increase in the diversity of NZP's workforce may prevent recurrence of malpractice and it is evident that NZP has taken active steps to increase diversity within its workforce (New Zealand Police, 2019a). The employment of female constabulary staff was first provisioned in 1938 (Dunstall, 1999), but it was not until 1990 that female constables were afforded pay equality (Butterworth, 2005). Butterworth (2005) notes that opportunities and conditions for females were significantly improved after the merger with the Traffic Safety Service in 1992. At the time of the CoI, females constituted 29.2 percent of the workforce and comprised 16.7 percent constabulary workforce and 65.8 percent the nonconstabulary workforce (New Zealand Police, 2008). This compared poorly against the aggregated 26.6 percent of Australian female constabulary members at 2008 (Prenzler and Sinclair, 2013) and 25 percent of England and Wales at 2009 (Prenzler, Fleming, and King, 2010). As of 2019, female employees constitute 34.2 percent of the workforce, 22.0 percent constabulary and 66.0 percent nonconstabulary employees (New Zealand Police, 2019a).

While the passive acceptance of Māori as constables can be traced back to the mid-1950s, Butterworth (2005) notes that active recruitment took place from the late 1960s. Recruitment was not extended to Pacific Islanders, except for Cook Islanders as they were provided New Zealand citizenship. Current NZP reporting notes that Māori are not proportionately represented (11.9 percent of the workforce but comprise of 14.9 percent of the population) (New Zealand Police, 2019a), nor are the other key ethnic groups targeted for representative parity (New Zealand Police, 2019a). Running parallel to the recruitment of Māori constables was the formation of the Māori Warden scheme in 1945. Separate to NZP, Māori Wardens volunteers are warranted under the Māori Community Development Act 1962. They hold limited law enforcement powers to control the access of liquor on marae, limited policing to control drunkenness of Māori in public places and licensed premises, and were encouraged to "assist in stamping out mischief before it becomes a crime and in the maintenance of order" (Fleras, 1981, p. 496).

SUMMARY

This chapter briefly surveyed the historical context of early policing in New Zealand, noting some of the pressures that shaped the establishment of a routinely unarmed national police agency. The following observations, discussed below, should entice further theorizing about how New Zealand's policing system can provide solutions to some of the pressing issues relevant to contemporary policing.

National and Centralized Police Agency

One of the hallmarks of New Zealand policing is the centralized national model that delivers national and local policing services relatively free of direct governmental control. The New Zealand system provides evidence for other common law jurisdictions that favor local or decentralized models, that national models can be responsive and accountable to local issues (e.g., McCardle & Webb, 2010). Therefore, policymakers should use the New Zealand model as an exemplar when weighing up the benefits of a generalist and nationalized systems, and the effectiveness of legislative mandates to operate independently from the government.

Specialization

Lessons from NZP's policy shift from a generalist to specialist approach, seen with the growth of specialist squads in the late 1950s and the increasing civilianization of policing activities, may lead to unintended consequences. First, the creation of a specialist capability inevitability creates demand for that capability, which in turn, leads to rationing of the capability (due to availability, cost, and policy). Perversely, rationing invariably causes generalists to "make do" at times when the specialist capability is not available (e.g., Hendy, 2020). Could the historical aversion to routinely arming NZP have created an environment that precipitated the necessity for the first paramilitary policing unit (the AOS) in the Five Eyes group of nations? Similarly, could the aversion toward the permanent establishment ART units precipitate the permanent routine arming of all the NZP constabulary by default?

Second, specialization affects those at organizational boundaries as those in smaller communities, farther from the central operations base, must wait for specialists to arrive. In some cases, where timeliness is not critical, delays may be acceptable. However, in time-critical events delays invariably lead to differential policing capabilities, forcing less capable generalists to respond to circumstances where specialists might be best suited to respond.

Third, the reorganization of policing services to accommodate greater cost efficiencies through civilianization may lead to a reenvisioned version of the armed constabulary disbanded some 110 years earlier. Organizing tasks according to those that require constabulary powers poses dilemmas for NZP that a reshaped workforce will become more representative of a para-militarized motorized constabulary responding to critical and violent events with civilian employees ("civilians-in-uniform") providing noncritical policing services.

NOTES

1. See Quentin-Baxter and McLean (2017) for a detailed explanation of this constitutional construct.
2. NZP define "tactical options" and report according to the following: "Handcuffs with pain compliance, or without pain compliance when used with another reportable tactical option; other restraints; OC spray bursts; empty hand tactics; baton strikes; dog bites or other dog-related deployment injuries; weapons or opportunity; sponge rounds; shows and discharges of a TASER and/or firearm" (New Zealand Police, 2015, p. 7).

REFERENCES

Battersby, John. (2018). Terrorism where terror is not: Australian and New Zealand terrorism compared. *Studies in Conflict & Terrorism* 41(1): 59–76.

Bazley, Margaret. (2007). *Commission of Inquiry into Police Conduct - Te Kōmihana Tirotiro Whanonga Pirihimana*. Commission of Inquiry into Police Conduct.

Belich, James. (1996). *Making Peoples: A History of the New Zealanders from Polynesian Settlement to the End of the Nineteenth Century*. Penguin.

Bowling, Benjamin, Robert Reiner, and James Sheptycki. (2019). *The Politics of the Police* (5th edition), edited by Benjamin Bowling, Robert Reiner, and James Sheptycki. Oxford: Oxford University Press.

Butterworth, Susan. (2005). *More Than Law and Order: Policing a Changing Society 1945–92, Vol. 5: The History of Policing in New Zealand*. University of Otago Press.

Carpenter, S. D. (2009). *Te wiremu, te puhipi, he wakaputanga me te tiriti, Henry Williams, James Busby, a Declaration, and the Treaty*. Waitangi Tribunal.

Clyne, Robert. (1987). *Colonial Blue: A History of the South Australian Police Force, 1836–1916*. Wakefield Press.

Coster, Andrew. (2020). Police commissioner: High threshold for routine use of armed police. In *Morning Report*, edited by Corin Dann. Radio New Zealand.

Crown Law. (2013). *Statutory Offences Requiring the Consent of the Attorney-General*. Wellington: Crown Law.

Den Heyer, Garth. (2014). Mayberry revisited: A review of the influence of police paramilitary units on policing. *Policing and Society* 24(3): 346–361.

Den Heyer, Garth. (2019). New Zealand police cultural Liaison officers: Their role in crime prevention and community policing. In *Policing and Minority Communities: Contemporary Issues and Global Perspectives*, edited by James F Albrecht, Garth Den Heyer, and Perry Stanislas. Springer.

Dunstall, Graeme. (1999). *A Policeman's Paradise? Policing a Stable Society 1918– 1945, Vol. 4: The History of Policing in New Zealand*. Dunmore Press.

Finnane, Mark. (1994). *Police and Government: Histories of Policing in Australia*. Oxford University Press.

Fleras, Augie. (1981). Maori Wardens and the Control of Liquor among the Maori of New Zealand. *Journal of the Polynesian Society* 90(4): 495–513.

Govt.nz. (2020). New Zealand police. New Zealand Government. Retrieved 5 August 2020. https://www.govt.nz/organisations/new-zealand-police/.

Harley, Alison. (2015). Commissioner: Police addressing bias in Maori relations. Retrieved 28 August 2020. https://www.scoop.co.nz/stories/PO1511/S00456/lisa -owen-interviews-police-commissioner-mike-bush.htm.

Hendy, Ross. (2014). Routinely armed and unarmed police: What can the Scandinavian Experience Teach Us? *Policing: A Journal of Policy and Practice* 8(2): 183–192. https://doi.org/10.1093/police/pau012.

Hendy, Ross. (2020). Effectiveness and efficiency: Oslo police officers' perspectives of the necessity and utility of temporarily routinely arming in response to a terrorist threat. *Policing and Society*.

Hill, Richard S. (1986). *The Colonial Frontier Tamed: New Zealand Policing in Transition, 1867–1886, Vol. 2: The History of Policing in New Zealand*. Wellington: Historical Publications Branch, Department of Internal Affairs.

Hill, Richard S. (1995). *The Iron Hand in the Velvet Glove: The Modernisation of Policing in New Zealand 1886–1917, Vol. 3: The History of Policing in New Zealand*. Dunmore Press.

Hill, Richard S. (2012). Police: The earliest police forces. Te Ara: the Encyclopaedia of New Zealand. Retrieved 2 March. http://www.teara.govt.nz/en/police/page-1.

Independent Police Conduct Authority. (2013). *Operation Eight: The Report of the Independent Police Conduct Authority*. Independent Police Conduct Authority.

Killey, Ian. (2019). *Police and Government in Australia: Who's in Charge and Who Should Be in Charge?* Australian Scholarly Publishing.

King, Michael. (2004). *The Penguin History of New Zealand*. Viking.

Li, Judy, Rhiannon Newcombe, Ross Hendy, and Darren Walton. (2020). A disproportional increase in lower priority mental health-related calls to New Zealand Police between 2009 and 2016. *Policing and Society* 30(5): 519–531.

Mankelow, Natalie. (2014). Police apologise to Tuhoe over raids. *rnz.co.nz*. Retrieved 28 August 2020. https://www.rnz.co.nz/news/national/251999/police-apologise-to -tuhoe-over-raids.

Marshall, Bronwyn. (2009). *Identifying and Responding to Bias in the Criminal Justice System: A Review of International and New Zealand Research*. Research Evaluation and Modelling Unit, Ministry of Justice.

Mawby, Rob C, and Alan Wright. (2008). The police organisation. In *Handbook of Policing*, edited by Tim Newburn, 224–252. Willan.

Maxwell, Gabrielle, and Catherine Smith. (1998). *Police Perceptions of Maori: A Report to the New Zealand Police and the Ministry of Maori Development: Te Puni Kokiri*. Institute of Criminology.

McCardle, Hamish, and Mike Webb. (2010). Inviting public conversations about policing: Experiences from New Zealand. *Policing: A Journal of Policy and Practice* 4(3): 211–217.

McCulloch, Jude. (2001). *Blue Army: Paramilitary Policing in Australia*. Melbourne University Press.

Nettelbeck, Amanda, and Russell Smandych. (2010). Policing indigenous peoples on two colonial frontiers: Australia's mounted police and Canada's north-west mounted police. *Australian & New Zealand Journal of Criminology* 43 (2): 356–375.

New Zealand Intelligence Community. (2017). New Zealand Intelligence Community (NZIC). Retrieved 21 August 2020. https://www.nzic.govt.nz.

New Zealand Police. (2005). *Policing with Confidence, the New Zealand Way: Strategic Plan 2010*. New Zealand Police.

New Zealand Police. (2008). *2007/08 Annual Report*. New Zealand Police.

New Zealand Police. (2015). *NZ Police Annual Tactical Options Research report #3: 1 January to 31 December 2014*. New Zealand Police (Wellington). http://www.police.govt.nz/sites/default/files/publications/annual-tactical-options-research-report-3.pdf.

New Zealand Police. (2019a). *Annual Report 2018/19*. New Zealand Police. Wellington: New Zealand Police.

New Zealand Police. (2019b). *Operating Procedures for Armed Response Teams*. New Zealand Police. Wellington: New Zealand Police.

New Zealand Police. (2020). *Our Business Tā Tātou Umanga*.

O'Brien, G. M. (1960). *The Australian Police Forces*.

Phillips, Scott W. (2018). *Police Militarization: Understanding the Perspectives of Police Chiefs, Administrators, and Tactical Officers*. Routledge.

Prenzler, Tim, Jenny Fleming, and Amanda L. King. (2010). Gender equity in Australian and New Zealand policing: A five-year review. *International Journal of Police Science & Management* 12(4): 584–595.

Prenzler, Tim, and Georgina Sinclair. (2013). "The status of women police officers: An international review." *International Journal of Law, Crime, and Justice* 41(2): 115–131.

Quentin-Baxter, Alison, and Janet McLean. (2017). *This Realm of New Zealand the Sovereign, the Governor-General, the Crown*. Auckland University Press.

Rākete, Emille. (2019). Armed police patrols are a dangerous response to a non-existent problem. *Spinoff*. Retrieved 20 August 2020. https://thespinoff.co.nz/atea/22-10-2019/armed-police-patrols-are-a-dangerous-response-to-a-non-existent-problem/.

Rowe, Michael. (2009). Notes on a Scandal: The official enquiry into deviance and corruption in New Zealand police. *Australian & New Zealand Journal of Criminology* 42(1): 123–128.

Shortt, Richard. (2020). NZ's police have been 'routinely armed' for nearly two decades. *Stuff*. Retrieved 20 August 2020. https://www.stuff.co.nz/stuff-nation /121792553/nzs-police-have-been-routinely-armed-for-nearly-two-decades.

Small, David. (2011). The uneasy relationship between national security and personal freedom: New Zealand and the War on Terror. *International Journal of Law in Context* 7(4): 467–486.

Stenning, Philip. (2007). "The idea of the political 'independence' of the police: International interpretations and experiences.'" In *Police and Government Relations: Who's Calling the Shots?* edited by M. Beare and T. Murray, 183–256. University of Toronto Press.

Stenning, Philip. (2011). "Governance of the police: Independence, accountability and interference." *Flinders Law Journal* 13(2): 241–267.

Te Whaiti, Pania, and Michael Roguski. (1998). *Māori Perceptions of the Police*. He Pārekereke/Victoria Link, Ltd.

Waddington, P. A. J., and Martin Wright. (2008). "Police use of force, firearms, and riot control." In *Handbook of Policing*, edited by Tim Newburn, 465–496. Willan Publishing.

Weitzer, Ronald. (2014). Police race relations. In *The Oxford Handbook of Police and Policing*, edited by Michael D Reisig and Robert J Kane. Oxford University Press.

Wilson, J. Q. (1968). *Varieties of Police Behavior*. Harvard University Press.

Part IV

THE AMERICAS AND
THE CARIBBEAN

Chapter 15

Police and Policing in the United States of America

Joselyne Chenane Nkogo

As formal agents of social control, police play an important and central role in the United States. In democratic societies such as the United States, police have the mandate to protect the public as well as perform other significant roles. The United States is a democracy and this means that the people control government agencies including law enforcement agencies (Walker and Katz 2018). Policing in democracies is done through consent where the citizens give up some of their rights in exchange for government services and protection. In other words, citizens give up their rights to use force against other people and punish them for crimes in exchange for the government doing it for them through police officers. This means citizens no longer have the right to take the law into their own hands. Police are commonly referred to as the gatekeepers of the American criminal justice system, which means citizens first encounter police officers before they can encounter other players in the criminal justice system.

Given that police patrol the streets and communities, a majority of the citizens are likely to encounter them, although they may never encounter other members of the criminal justice system such as judges. The police determine what cases will move forward in the criminal justice system and which ones will never enter the system, since they have discretion in their decision making. Finally, the police determine the workload for the rest of the criminal justice system—that is, if police arrest every person who violates or breaks the law, the workload in the courts and other criminal justice agencies will increase. In addition to being the most visible members of the American criminal justice system, police can legally use coercive force against citizens. However, recent fatal encounters between police and minority citizens have called into question the need for officers to use force, particularly in situations where citizens were not presenting a threat to the officer, yet fatal force was used. Scholars have described policing as having an impossible mandate, as they are not able to make everyone happy.

This chapter is divided into *four* parts. The first part chronicles the history of American policing. The second part covers the organizational structure of the US police. The third part discusses the function and role of the police and the final part discusses controversies, such as racial discrimination, in American policing.

HISTORY OF AMERICAN POLICING

The first modern police agencies in the United States were established in the 1830s and 1840s (Walker & Katz, 2018). Organized policing in the United States was born out of necessity. As the population grew, it became difficult to control people's behavior and hence there was a need to create a formal system of social control (Walker & Katz, 2018). The origins of modern American policing can be traced directly to the English model of policing. Aspects of community policing and crime prevention as well as the idea of sheriffs and constables ensued from English law enforcement (Uchida, 1993). However, from the onset, there were stark differences between the English model and the American policing model. The American police were more likely to use force, they were decentralized (i.e., they did not have a national organization) and were heavily controlled by local politicians (Walker & Katz, 2018). Moreover, police officers were hired by a local city councilman (or mayor) in exchange for money and political favors. The composition of pioneer police officers was also different as they were made up of uneducated new immigrants with no training. It is important to understand the history of the police in the United States as it will help set the ground to discuss modern American policing.

The English Model

The American criminal justice system has its cradle in the English common-law tradition. From the onset, the American police drew on and was heavily influenced by the English Model initiated by Sir Robert Peel. Sir Robert Peel, commonly referred to as the father of modern policing, was a member of Parliament in England who had a deep desire to change the quality of policing in England. By the early 1900s, the old system of law enforcement collapsed under the impact of urbanization and industrialization. The city of London experienced unprecedented poverty, disorder, ethnic conflict and crime (Walker & Katz, 2012). Sir Robert Peel was instrumental in helping to pass the Metropolitan Police Act (1829), which facilitated the creation of the London Metro Police—the first full-time police organization as we think of policing today. He was also responsible for the design and structure of the London Metropolitan Police (Walker & Katz, 2018). Prior to the London Metro Police, the watchmen were responsible for maintaining order and catching criminals, however, Sir Peel introduced the concept of crime prevention (Walker & Katz, 2018). The Bobbies, as they were commonly referred to, were assigned to areas referred to as the "beats" of the city to patrol, in order to know the people in their neighborhoods and prevent crime and disorder (Walker & Katz, 2018).

Policing in Colonial America

In Colonial America (seventeenth and eighteenth centuries), policing followed the English system. Pioneer English colonists in America created their own law enforcement agency borrowed from their English heritage (Uchida 1993; Walker & Katz, 2018). English heritage in the early forms of American policing was seen in the tradition of limited local police authority and decentralized and fragmented police systems (Walker & Katz, 2012). Policing in the early colonies took two forms—it was either informal or communal (the watch) or private-for-profit policing, also known as "The Big Stick" (Porter, 2013). Three institutions that were adopted from the English model for American colonies were the *sheriff, constables,* and *watch.* The county sheriffs, appointed by the governor, became the most important law enforcement agents in America (Uchida, 1993). They had broad roles including law enforcement, collecting taxes, supervising elections, maintaining bridges and roads, serving subpoenas, and other miscellaneous duties (Walker & Katz, 2018). Given that sheriffs received higher fees based on the taxes they collected, apprehending criminals was not their main concern. As such, law enforcement was a low priority for sheriffs.

Constables also had the responsibility of enforcing the law and carrying out certain legal duties. At first, constables were elected, however, the constable position gradually evolved into a semiprofessional appointed office. According to Walker and Katz (2018), in larger cities such as Boston and New York, the office of the constable became a desirable and often lucrative office. Night watches (or the watch) closely resembled the modern-police in their roles. The watchmen patrolled cities to report fires, crime, and disorder. They also raised a hue and cry, maintained street lamps, and arrested or detained suspicious individuals (Uchida, 1993). Initially, there were only night watches, however, as towns grew larger, day watches were added. The city of Boston (Massachusetts) created its first watch in 1636, New York in 1658 and Philadelphia in 1700 (Porter, 2013). Given that the watch system was mostly reactive in nature, that is, they responded to crime and criminal behavior when called upon by the public (Uchida, 1993), the night watch was not a particularly effective crime control device (Porter, 2013). Watchmen often slept or drank on duty. Although all men were expected to serve as watchmen; many men tried to avoid this responsibility by using different means such as paying others to serve in their place. Moreover, many "volunteers" were simply attempting to evade military service or they were performing watch duties as a form of punishment (Porter, 2013). Subsequently, the watch evolved into a paid professional position (Walker & Katz, 2018). Another interesting aspect of policing in colonial times, unique to American law enforcement, was the slave patrol.

The first formal slave patrol was created in the Carolina colonies in 1704 (Porter, 2013). Slave patrols were prominent in the Southern states where slavery existed. Their role was to guard against slave revolts and capture runaway slaves, among other duties (Walker & Katz, 2018). As noted by Porter (2013), "After the Civil War, these vigilante-style organizations evolved into modern Southern police departments, primarily as a means of controlling freed slaves who were now laborers working in an agricultural caste system, and enforcing 'Jim Crow' segregation laws; designed to deny freed slaves equal rights and access to the political system" (p. 2). As an illustration, the Charleston, South Carolina, slave patrol had about 100 officers in 1837, larger than any city police force at the time (Walker & Katz, 2018). It is important to note that slave patrols were not completely disbanded after slavery ended. When slavery ended, several groups merged with former slave patrols to maintain control over African Americans. Other groups such as federal military, the state militia, and the Ku Klux Klan took over the responsibilities of the slave patrols and were known to be more violent than their predecessors. As time went by, these groups began to operate in a similar fashion to the newly established police departments in the United States (Archbold, 2012).

Although the early forms of policing (e.g., the watch, constables) continued well after the American Revolution (1765), there was an urgent need for change. As historian Samuel Walker and his colleague (2012) succinctly noted "Colonial law enforcement was inefficient, corrupt, and affected by political interference. Contrary to popular myth, there was never a 'golden age' of efficiency, effectiveness, and integrity in American policing" (p. 27). The first centralized municipal police department emerged in the United States in the 1830s. In 1838, the city of Boston established the first American police force, followed by New York City in 1845, Albany, New York and Chicago, Illinois in 1851, New Orleans and Cincinnati in 1853, Philadelphia in 1855, and Newark, New Jersey and Baltimore, Maryland in 1857. By the 1880s all major U.S. cities had municipal police forces in place (Porter, 2013).

Modern American Police

Many police departments were expanded versions of existing night watch systems (e.g., Boston police department) or slave patrols in Southern states. These departments contained vestiges of the English model as well as local influence. Policing scholars have noted that the development of local, centralized bureaucratic police forces throughout the United States was a result of necessity. Similar to England, the rapid urbanization of many American cities along with industrialization and immigration put pressure on the old and informal systems of law enforcement (Walker & Katz, 2018). Crime and disorder went up as the population grew, particularly in the newly established urban areas, which meant that the watch and constables were no longer an adequate form of social control (Porter 2013). Some scholars have noted that with urbanization, there was an increase in mob violence, particularly violence directed at immigrants and African Americans by white youths. There was also an increase in public disorder, mostly public drunkenness and sometimes prostitution, which was now more visible and less easy to control in growing urban centers than it had been in rural villages (Porter, 2013; Walker, 1996).

Eras of American Policing

Like every aspect of the American society, modern policing has undergone changes since its inception. Policing scholars have generally classified policing into *three eras*—political, professional/reform, and community. A unique feature that distinguished early American policing from the London Metro police was that the latter had minimum political interference while the former was rife with political influence. As Walker and Katz (2012) stated, "The London police became highly professional, while the American police were completely unprofessional. The difference was that the Commissioners of the London Metropolitan Police were free from political interference and were able to maintain high personnel standards. As a result, London Bobbies eventually won public respect. By contrast, the lack of adequate supervision in America tolerated police misconduct, and the result was public disrespect. From the very start, in short, police in the two countries went in different directions" (p. 30).

The political era of American policing lasted from the 1840s and ended in the early 1900's (Archbold, 2012). This era was characterized by close ties between police and politics. During the political era police departments had no personnel standards, which meant police officers were selected entirely on the basis of their political connections. In most departments, recruits received no formal preservice training (Walker & Katz, 2012). Instead, the recruits were handed a badge, a baton, and a copy of department rules (if there was one) and were then sent out to patrol the streets. Additionally, police officers in the political era did not have job security, which meant that they could be hired and fired at will. Local politicians rewarded their friends by offering jobs as police officers and this presented several challenges such as supporting the interests of elected officials (Walker & Katz, 2012). Although the Pendleton Act (1883) was meant to protect government employees (e.g., police officers) from political interference, it was difficult to dismiss incompetent employees (Hooper, 2014). Unfortunately, corruption and political meddling continued to be an issue until the 1920s when the push for police reforms became hard to ignore, which gave rise to the professional/reform era.

The reform era, otherwise known as the professional era, began in the 1930s and ended in the 1970s. American policing underwent significant changes in the twentieth century. Historians and policing scholars have attributed the dramatic changes in American policing to the introduction of modern technology as well as the organized movement for police professionalism (Walker & Katz, 2012). The infiltration of modern technology into policing had a significant impact on American policing. For example, the introduction of patrol cars, the two-way radio, and the telephone revolutionized patrol work, the nature of police–citizen interactions, and police management (Walker & Katz, 2012). The gross corruption and inefficiencies of police officers during the political era was an impetus for police reforms, which were initiated most notably by reformers such as August Vollmer—who served as Chief of Police in Berkeley, California, from 1905 to 1932 (Walker & Katz, 2012) and his protégé, O. W. Wilson. Chief Vollmer, has commonly been referred to as the father of American police professionalism because of his efforts on police reforms. Of his many contributions to policing, he is famous for advocating for higher education for police officers, hiring college graduates, and organizing the first college-level police science courses at the University of California in 1916 (Walker & Katz, 2012). Vollmer also wrote the 1931 Wickersham Commission Report on Police. The Wickersham Commission report examined the rising crime rates in the United States and the inability of the police to control the crimes (Archbold, 2012). A key recommendation of the report was that police could more effectively address the rising crime problem by focusing on crime control rather than social services (Archbold, 2012).

A primary goal of the reform movement during the 1900s was to professionalize American policing. This could be achieved by setting personnel standards for police officers, implementing better police training, and adopting various types of technology (e.g., use of two-way radios) to assist police officers in their day to day activities (Archbold, 2012). The professionalization of the police in the United States gave rise to centralized bureaucracies focused primarily on crime control (Archbold, 2012). Prior to the reform era, policing was not considered a profession; however, the reformers defined policing as a profession. This meant that police were, for the first time, defined as public servants with a professional obligation to serve and protect communities (Walker & Katz, 2012). Another goal of the reform movement was to remove politics from policing. Other notable contributions of the reformers include: appointing qualified chief executives and the creation of specialized police units devoted to traffic, juveniles, and vice crimes (Walker & Katz, 2012). Before the creation of specialized units, American police departments had only patrol and detective units. The first female police officer in the United States, Lola Baldwin, was hired in 1905 by the Portland (Oregon) police department as a juvenile specialist (Walker & Katz, 2012).

The reform era was followed by what policing scholars have commonly termed as the era of community policing. As stated previously, the goal of the reform era of American policing was to make the police a professional body. Although this goal was based on good intentions, several unforeseen challenges between the police and the communities they served arose (Archbold, 2012). As an illustration, the relationship between the police and the public deteriorated with the introduction of motorized patrols and a focus on crime fighting (Archbold, 2012). With the advent of motorized patrols, the number of face-to-face contacts between the police and citizens reduced police–citizen interactions, making them more impersonal and strained. Some scholars have observed that the growing rift between police and citizens contributed to the development of a police subculture, which emphasized a distrust of citizens, the media, and police administrators (Archbold, 2012). Thus, the unforeseen challenges of police reform paved the way for a new era of policing— the era of community policing. A major goal of the community policing era was to rebuild the relationship between the police and citizens that had been weakened in the 1960s (Archbold, 2012). The community policing model began in the early 1970s and continued through the 1990s and early 2000. Community policing became popular among policing scholars in the 1990s and received additional support with the passage of the 1994 Violent Crime Control and Law Enforcement Act (Archbold, 2012). This legislation was meant to encourage the implementation of community policing throughout the United States.

In summary, each of the three eras of policing was characterized by unique features. The political era was rife with political interference with no personnel standards for police officers. During the reform/professional era, the focus was on making the police a professional body and eliminating politics from policing. The community policing era, on the other hand, emphasized fostering better police–citizen relations.

The reforms that were introduced during the reform era yielded unforeseen challenges that strained the relationship between the police and the public,

leading to a deep distrust between the two entities. As such, community policing, defined as "a philosophy that promotes organizational strategies, which
support the systemic use of partnerships and problem-solving techniques to
proactively address the immediate conditions that give rise to public safety
issues such as crime, social disorder, and fear of crime" (Office of Community
Oriented Policing Services) was a response to the deteriorating relationship
between the police and citizens. However, a growing number of scholars have
argued that there is a fourth era of policing. Some have called this fourth era
the "information era" (Hooper, 2014), while others have named this era the
era of homeland security (Oliver, 2006). American policing has continued
to evolve and innovate since the introduction of community policing in the
1970s. Although a detailed discussion of these strategies is beyond the scope
of this chapter, it is important to note that other policing strategies such as
problem oriented policing, hot spots policing, and predictive policing have
also been introduced to help curb the problem of crime and disorder in the
United States.

STRUCTURE AND FUNCTIONS OF
THE AMERICAN POLICE

The American police is organized in a quasi-military design. This means
that the structure of the American police in many regards (not all) resembles
that of the military. For example, the police wear uniforms, use military-
style designations (e.g., sergeant, captain), and have a hierarchical command
structure similar to the military (Walker & Katz, 2018). Police are part of the
executive branch of the U.S. government and they represent the government
at all levels—local, county, state, and federal. They serve under mayors,
county commissioners, governors, and the President. The police are also
influenced by the U.S. government through constitutional and legislative
restrictions, government oversight, funding decisions, hiring and firing of
administration. As scholars have described it, American law enforcement
is highly fragmented—that is, there is no formal, centralized system for
coordinating or regulating all these agencies (Walker & Katz, 2012). There
are thousands of local, state, and federal police agencies across the United
States. There are approximately 18,000 law enforcement agencies in the
United States. Out of the 18,000 agencies, there are 12,500 local police
departments, about 3,000 sheriff's departments, 50 state police departments,
about 1,700 special police agencies, and 73 federal agencies (Walker &
Katz, 2018). Each of these agencies is tasked with different roles and responsibilities and has different structures. Needless to say, the structure and
organization of the United States police is complicated. Under local police

agencies there are municipal police, county police, and county sheriffs. State police agencies are made up of state police and bureaus of criminal investigation, while at the federal level, there are federal law enforcement agencies and military law enforcement agencies. There are also special district police such as public school officers, transit police, and college and university police. Furthermore, there are Native American tribal police. In addition to the government law enforcement agencies, there are also private security firms and security personnel.

A huge majority of law enforcement personnel serve under local and state police. To put this in context, there are approximately 785,000 full time sworn police officers in local and state agencies. According to Walker and Katz (2018), the number of local and state police officers has increased significantly—there are about 35 percent more full-time police officers now relative to 1987. A Bureau of Justice Statistics (BJS) report shows that in 2016, local police departments employed about 468,000 full-time sworn officers (Hyland & Davies, 2019). The BJS report further illustrates that more than two-thirds (71 percent) of the local police departments served populations of less than 10,000 residents; about 1 in 8 local police officers, and about 1 in 10 first-line supervisors, were female; about 1 in 4 local police officers, and about 1 in 5 first-line supervisors, were black or Hispanic; the majority of departments serving 100,000 or more residents had specialized units with personnel assigned full-time to address child abuse, drug enforcement, and gangs; and an estimated 2.5 percent of full-time local police officers (11,870) served as school resource officers (Hyland & Davies, 2019).

Prominent among local law enforcement agencies are municipal or city police departments, which make up over 70 percent of law enforcement agencies and employ over 60 percent of the officer workforce (Walker & Katz, 2012). As mentioned earlier, police are the most visible branch of the American criminal justice system. As such, police and police departments are heavily influenced by their environments (e.g., location, demographic composition of the population). The external environment has a more significant impact on municipal/city police departments. For instance, police departments within large and diverse cities handle a higher number of serious crimes relative to smaller/rural police departments. Moreover, urban police departments are expected to deal with a wide range of emergencies and additional duties such as order maintenance (Walker & Katz, 2012). The largest police departments in the United States are located in New York (New York City Police Department), Illinois (Chicago Police Department, California (Los Angeles Police Department, Los Angeles County Sheriff's Department), Texas (Houston Police Department), and Pennsylvania (Philadelphia Police Department). While the population of the ensuing cities represents about 7 percent of the American population, these cities experience approximately 23 percent of all violent crimes in the U.S. and about 34 percent of all robberies (Walker & Katz, 2012).

Interestingly, while the largest police departments represent a small fraction of all police departments in the United States, they employ about 13 percent of all sworn police officers (Walker & Katz, 2012). In other words, these police departments employ the largest number of police officers relative to the majority of police departments across the United States. This is significant because the majority of police departments employ less than 100 full-time sworn officers; yet, the New York City police department has approximately 36,000 full-time police officers, which is more than three times the number employed by any other police department. The second largest police department, Chicago, had about 11,965 sworn officers as of 2016 (Hyland & Davies, 2019). However, the majority of municipal police departments are in small towns. About half (50.4 percent) of the municipal police departments employ less than ten sworn police officers (Walker & Katz, 2018). Law enforcement looks different in small and rural police departments when compared to urban police departments. An assessment of calls to the police in rural areas has shown that the bulk of the calls are for traffic problems, public disturbances, family problems, and stray dogs (Walker & Katz, 2012).

Function of Police in the United States

The mission of police in the United States is to *serve and protect*. In order for the police to accomplish the mission of serving and protecting the public, they have to wear many hats. Simply put, the functions and roles of the police in the United States are multifaceted and vary across police departments. Scholars have generally classified the duties of the American police into five categories: law enforcement, peacekeeping/order maintenance, crime prevention, protecting citizens' civil rights, and service delivery (Worrall & Schmalleger, 2017). The law enforcement role of the police involves the enforcement of traffic, criminal and civil laws. Police intervene when the law has been violated and they identify and/or apprehend the guilty suspect(s). The police cannot enforce all laws and as such, enforcement is at their discretion. While most people think of the law enforcement role of the police, the police have other responsibilities. Only a handful of calls to the police are for law enforcement; the rest of the calls are for law enforcement involving. Peacekeeping/order maintenance involves sanctioning behavior that disturbs or threatens to disturb the public peace. For example, citizens may call the police when they spot a drunk driver.

Another core function of the police is crime prevention. Police are expected to deter crime and disorder in communities, and it has been argued that police can deter crime via patrol. Those in support of this idea have posited that the mere presence of police officers in the field would deter would be criminals from committing crime. Additionally, the police are responsible for protecting the civil rights of Americans. Police protect the right to free speech and assembly during peaceful protests. The service delivery role of the police encompasses a wide variety of noncrime activities such as helping motorists, finding and returning stray animals. The bulk of policing activities in the United States fall under the umbrella of service delivery. Often times there is a clash between the roles of police officers. On the one hand, the police are expected to enforce the law by performing duties such as arresting and apprehending criminals. On the other hand, the police perform mundane tasks such as responding to calls to assist individuals with mental illnesses or address complaints against noise. For example, the police are expected to protect citizens' right to free speech during peaceful protests, however, when the protests turn violent, the police shift their role to law enforcement.

RACE AND POLICE IN THE UNITED STATES

In March 1991, Rodney King, an African American man from Los Angeles (LA) California, was brutally beaten by the LA police for allegedly evading arrest. A bystander filmed the incident and sent the video to a local news channel. Subsequently, riots broke out in LA after several of the officers that were involved in the beating of Mr. King were acquitted of the crime. The Rodney King case highlighted and brought to the fore the plight and experiences of many minority citizens with respect to the police. Prior to Mr. King's case, there had been allegations of police brutality and use of excessive force but perhaps the evidence was lacking. However, the film showing Mr. King being beaten by fourteen police officers revealed what was likely happening in police–minority citizen encounters (perhaps with less severity), but had scarcely been seen by the general public. The relationship between American police and minority communities has historically been frayed and characterized by distrust. The tension between police and the African American community as well as other minority communities can be traced back to early policing in the United States.

During the era of slavery, the control of minorities was a key feature of early policing in the United States. Some states had slave patrols, groups of three to six white men who enforced laws related to slavery. They were organized to prevent revolts and escapes. Congress later gave slave patrols nationwide jurisdiction to capture runaway slaves. Police drove "paddy rollers" or "paddy wagons" to transport slaves. After the Civil War and the abolishment of slavery, slave patrols were converted into city and county police forces. Officers enforced the law, including Jim Crow laws (Walker & Katz, 2018). American policing has come a long way yet there is still more to be done, particularly on the topic of building trust and mending the relationship between police agencies and individuals/communities of color. Indeed, the recent fatal encounters between police and minority citizens such as George Floyd, Breana Taylor, and Michael Brown, among others, underscores the need for reconciliation and ensuring equitable justice. Blue ribbon commissions and collaboration between several stakeholders have been formed in an effort to mend the relationship between police and communities of color.

For example, in the wake of multiple fatal shootings of people of color and the ensuing riots in places such as Dallas, Ferguson, and Baltimore, President Obama, on December 18, 2014, signed an executive order establishing the Task Force on 21st Century Policing (President's Task Force on 21st Century Policing). The President charged the Task Force with identifying the best practices for promoting effective crime reduction while building public trust. The Task Force outlined *six* major pillars—building trust and legitimacy, policy oversight, technology and social media, community policing and crime reduction, training and education, and officer wellness and safety—for mending police–citizen relations. Pillar one—building trust and legitimacy—delineates the importance of trust in enhancing perceptions of police legitimacy and building positive relations between the police and the communities they serve. Policing scholars have consistently posited that normative concerns pertaining to procedural justice (fair process) and distributive justice (fair outcomes) are essential ingredients in rebuilding the public's trust (Tyler, 1990).

CONCLUSION

In sum, police play an important and central role in the American criminal justice system. Although the English model had a huge influence on American policing, there are key distinctions between the two systems. Unlike the English system, the American police has a decentralized structure. Decentralization means that there is no single national police force in the United States, rather, there are federal, state, and local police organizations distributed throughout the United States. Historically, the American police has had strained relationships with minority communities; however, recent events involving the fatal encounters between the police and minority citizens have revealed an urgent need to address these issues.

REFERENCE

Archbold, Carol A. *Policing: A Text/Reader*. Sage, 2012.
Hooper, Michael K. Acknowledging existence of a fourth era of policing: The information era. *Journal of Forensic Research and Crime Studies* 1 (2014): 1–4.

Hyland, Shelley S., and Elizabeth Davis. Local police departments, 2016: Personnel. *Bureau of Justice Statistics, U.S. Department of Justice* (2019). Retrieved 20 December 2020, https://www.bjs.gov/content/pub/pdf/lpd16p.pdf.

Oliver, Willard M. The fourth era of policing: Homeland security. *International Review of Law Computers & Technology* 20, no. 1–2 (2006): 49–62.

Potter, Gary. The history of policing in the United States. Retrieved 20 December 2020, Academia.edu.

Tyler, Tom. *Why People Obey the Law: Procedural Justice, Legitimacy, and Compliance*. Yale University Press, 1990.

Uchida, Craig D. The development of the American police: An historical overview. *Critical Issues in Policing* (1993): 16–32.

Walker, Samuel. *The Police in America: An Introduction.* McGraw-Hill, 1996.

Walker, Samuel, and Katz, Charles M. *Police in America.* McGraw-Hill, 2012.

Walker, Samuel, and Katz, Charles M. *Police in America.* McGraw-Hill, 2018.

Weitzer, Ron. Is American policing at a crossroads. *Criminologist: The Official Newsletter of the American Society of Criminology*, 4, no. 4 (2015): 1–5.

Worrall, John, and Schmalleger Frank. *Policing.* Pearson, 2017.

Chapter 16

The Police of Honduras

Mark Ungar

Perhaps no modern law enforcement agency has faced a wider gap between criminal violence and their capacity to address it than Honduras' police force. Since 2010, the country has ranked in the top three homicides rates around the globe. The rate has climbed from 40 per 100,000 people in 2000 to 62 by 2010 and then to the world's highest at approximately 85 during 2013—a rate surpassing even countries embroiled in civil war, such as Iraq and Afghanistan. It then declined to a range of fifty-five to sixty-five after 2017, which still ranks among the highest—and is far greater than the global average of nine. This violence stems from a perfect storm of criminality. One source is the omnipresent power of the two highly armed and organized gangs known as the *maras*: *Mara Salvatrucha* (also known at MS-13) and *Barrio 18* (also known at 18th Street). Established by teens that were deported from the United States, the two maras have a physical control that rivals the government, and criminal operations that rival those of transnational cartels. As one news report concluded, the penetration of the maras in Honduras "is as unquestioned as the Earth rotating the Sun or the laws of gravity" (*El Heraldo*, 2016). The second source is the inundation of narcotrafficking, centered on the relocation of operational hubs of major cocaine cartels to Honduras after the attack on them by concerted campaigns in Mexico and Colombia. Over the past decade, between 40 and 90 percent of U.S.-bound cocaine transited through the country. Amid underfunded state institutions and a weak rule of law, powerful criminal actors have corrupted the country's security forces.

This chapter discusses how Honduran government and the security forces of Honduras have confronted these threats, focusing on the three periods that best define the chronological evolution of the police since its establishment in 1997. For each period, the article examines the central reform that began during that time and the range of obstacles that it faced, such as ineffectiveness, corruption, disorganization, politization, and contradictory policy. The first is from 1997 to 2003, when the new police force was being constructed while the country grappled with growing criminality. In this period, the article examines the major reforms at the time—community policing and anti-gang crackdowns. The second period begins with the political crisis that triggered during 2009, leading to a period of major reforms amid deepening division. The major reforms in that period were an overhaul of the entire criminal justice system and police education. The third and current era began in 2017, amid growing autocracy and repression. For that period, the article discusses the 2019 arms control law, which is one of the few reforms that occurred in this period. Collectively, the ongoing challenges and pressures in Honduras embody the larger struggle in Latin America against crime during the democratic era.

PERIOD 1: 1997–2009

Although its 1982 Constitution brought elected governments to Honduras and helped it escape the civil wars engulfing the rest of Central America during the Cold War era, the country was heavily militarized and repressive during that time, due, in part, to acting as a military base for the United States. Its Public Security Force (FSP: Fuerza de Seguridad Pública), under the control of the armed forces, along with the secret police, the National Office of Investigation (DNI: Dirección Nacional de Investigaciones); and death squads like Battalion 316 were involved in disappearances, extrajudicial executions, drug trafficking, and other crimes. Democratization in the 1990s, however, finally began to bring change. In 1993, the DNI was eliminated and a Public Ministry (MP) was established. The executive-branch Security Secretariat (Secretaría de Seguridad) was created in 1997, and the 1998 Organic Law of the National Police (LOPN: Ley Orgánica de la Policía Nacional) officially formed a new civilian police force to replace the FSP, with standards and structures similar to those created by neighboring countries' peace accords. All police units operated under the Secretaría after the reform and were usually separated into three main subsecretariats: Prevention, which oversaw the main police force, the Policía Nacional, which focused on Intelligence and kept a check over the operation of other bodies, and a third unit that specialized in education and training.

Since then, however, the police has undergone constant restructuring, sometimes nearly every year. As of 2020, there are sixteen separate police agencies under the Secretaría. Those units fall into five main categories. The first are the two intelligence agencies: the Office of Police Intelligence (DIPOL: Dirección de Inteligencia Policial), which formulates strategies through the acquisition of intelligence and the Police Office of Investigations (DPI: Dirección Policial de Investigaciones) formed in 2015 to bring focus, professionalism, and resources to the fight against organized and violent crime. The DPI works closely with the Technical Criminal Investigation Agency, (ATIC: Agencia Técnica de Investigación Criminal) the investigative unit of the Ministerio Público (MP), which is the nation's prosecutorial branch.

Two agencies coordinate community policing and relations: the Office of Interinstitutional and Community Affairs (DNPSC: Dirección de Asuntos Interinstitucional y Comunitarios) and the National Office of Prevention and Community Security (DNPP: Dirección Nacional de Prevención y Seguridad Comunitaria). They are the latest iterations of a long series of community policing units. A third group is the technical agencies, inclusive of the DPT Dirección Policial de Telemática, which is responsible for maintenance of the police's telecommunication and informational systems; and the Police Statistics System (SEPOL: Sistema Estadístico Policial en Línea), which gathers, analyzes, and publicizes independent and ongoing analysis of crime data.

The Special Units Office (DNFE: Dirección Nacional de Unidades Especiales) oversees the Special Response Squad (TIGRES: Unidad de Toma Integral Gubernamental de Respuesta Especial de Seguridad), the Special Operations Command (COBRAS: Comando de Operaciones Especiales), the Anti-Riot Unit (Unidad Antimotines), and the Unidad Aero Policial. This is the area of policing that has attracted the greatest concern because of the lack of transparency and the often-unaccountable exercise of deadly force by these units. Additional units associated with the DNFE include the anti-narcotics unit (DNPA: Dirección Nacional Policial Antidrogas), the Border Unit (DNSP: Dirección Nacional de Servicios Policiales Fronterizos), and the unit protecting top ranking official and foreign dignitaries (DNPSE: Dirección Nacional de Protección y Servicios Especiales)

The final set of police bodies are the three academic institutes, which operate under the National Office of Police Education (DNEP: Dirección Nacional de Educación Policial). The oldest is the National Police Academy (ANAPO: Academia Nacional de Policía), created in 1985 to train the police's top officials. More recent is the Technical Training Institute (ITP: Instituto Técnico de Policía), funded by the Inter-American Development Bank to train lower-levels officers, with far higher standards and a more comprehensive curriculum than its predecessor. In particular, it is centered on community-oriented policing, with courses on subjects such as human rights and sociology. Its first class graduated in December 2015. Another new addition is the National Police University (UNPH: Universidad

Nacional de la Policía de Honduras), established to provide high-level and specialized courses for the upper ranks.

This constant restructuring has been characterized earlier all by institutional proliferation. As crime stubbornly rose and criminal policy faltered, the first response by Honduran administrations was to create more security forces—such as the Tigres, Cobras, and anti-extortion agencies—with greater levels of autonomy. At several points, there were up to fifteen anti-gang units. In interviews, every Security Minister has complained about their lack of control over the range of regular and special forces nominally under their command. Once established, a new unit could take advantage of high crime and malleable officials to expand their realm of operations. The Cobras were originally an anti-guerrilla force, for example, but since then have been used to quell prison uprisings, coordinate anti-gang activities, disperse illegal land occupations, and bolster security in high-crime zones. Perhaps the greatest culmination of this trend was the 2013 formation of a military police, known as Military Police of Public Order (PMOP: Policía Militar de Orden Público). Formed originally to patrol the streets, the PMOP became increasingly involved in organized crime investigation and public order raids, and, after 2017, in direct physical repression of political protesters. Such power among all units has been further embedded though the National Interinstitutional Security Force (FUSINA: Fuerza de Seguridad Interinstitucional Nacional), which coordinates the overlapping responsibilities of the police, PMOP, Intelligence Police, MP, and national court system.

Such proliferation in structure and mission undermined the key principle of accountability in the agencies that were created to uphold it. Among those agencies have been the Office of Professional Responsibility (OPR) which conducts internal reviews of police misconduct, and the National Council of Interior Security (CONASIN: Consejo Nacional de Seguridad Interior), comprised of NGOs as well as state agencies as the primary channel for civil society participation on security issues. Another agency established by the LOPN was the Internal Affairs Unit (UAI: Unidad de Asuntos Internos), empowered to investigate wrongdoing by any police officer and to detain them if necessary. Outside the security apparatus, a Human Rights Commission conducts reports on police abuses and criminal policy, while *fiscales* are also authorized to investigate abuses—but, like the succession of internal accountability agencies, neither has been effective at reigning in police power or abuse.

Community Policing and Anti-Maras Law

As soon as Honduras adopted democracy, it got pulled in opposite directions on security issues, the biggest challenge it faced. One direction was the international shift in police reform toward community policing, in which citizens were integrated into policing policy and activity. But a growing crime rate, spurred by the fast spread of the *maras*, also led to pressures to adopt the kinds of harsh police repression that community policing was trying to reduce.

Community policing in Honduras has been ongoing, but with varying levels of political support and citizen acceptance. It can be divided into three main categories. The first is comprised of national initiatives, starting with the 2002 Safer Communities program (CMS: Comunidad Más Segura), in which initiatives like foot patrols, citizen councils, and seminars on social issues such as drugs were created in over thirty high-crime neighborhoods (*colonias*) throughout the country. In its first year in operation, with 126 police officials working in seven cities, the program claimed to have "benefited" 264,000 people (*La Prensa*, 8 January 2004). A second category are programs originating at the local level. For example, the high-crime city of Choloma developed a program in which residents and the range of social services met regularly to tackle the sources of violence, such as decrepit schools and discrimination against women. In San Pedro Sula, anti-violence groups and community centers focused on identifying and suppressing the causes of violence to significantly reduce crime in many *colonias*. In nearby Rivera Hernandez, one of the highest crime districts in the world, a new commissioner committed to community policing worked with church leaders to develop community reconciliation. The third and most recent area of community policing has been new training for the police itself, with the ITP tutoring police cadets and the National Community Policing Training Manual, *Modelo Nacional de Servicio de Policía Comunitaria*, retraining serving officers under a community policing paradigm.

As in neighboring countries also afflicted by the maras, community policing in Honduras has been continually undermined by repressive policing backed up by harsh laws. In Honduras, this mano dura (iron fist) approach began under the Presidency of Ricardo Maduro, whose son was killed by criminals, with the 2003 Law of Illicit Association (commonly known as the Anti-Maras Law), which doubled the punishments against suspected mareros, and the Presidential decree 123-2002, which allowed searches without a judicial warrant in residences where illicit activity was suspected. Along with other laws, a weak judiciary, and police proliferation, this approach encouraged officers to make mass arrests based on circumstantial evidence. In some cases, local police used community policing as a front for extrajudicial killing of suspected *mareros*.

Another challenge for both community policing and the police itself was the privatization of security. The Security Ministry's Registry reports 1,497 firms registered between 2000 and 2019, which employ between 60,000 (according to the head of ASEMSIPH, the Association of Private Security

Companies in Honduras; author interview, Salomón Sevilla, November 15, 2019) to 100,000 guards (*Once Noticias*, November 5, 2018; *La Prensa*, June 10, 2018), a size three to five times larger than the police force. The estimated firearms in the sector are between 70,000 (according to the Comisión Especial de Depuración y Transformación) and 400,000 (Violence Observatory, IUDPAS)—of which only 80,000 are registered. But this number does not include unregistered firms, which are estimated to be three times more numerous than registered ones, and does not account for the country's estimated 700 irregular armed groups—such as landowners' militias and death squads—which collectively may have up to 500,000 arms (*Proceso Digital*, 26 March 2018). Compounding the uncertainty brought by such a large unregulated force are the working conditions of its personnel. A typical private guard earns about U.S.$280 per month, which is less than the average 2020 minimum wage for all comparative sectors, such as construction, of U.S.$370. This official minimum wage is for an eight-hour day, but many private guards work up to twelve hours, under temporary contracts, and with no unions. Together, these conditions are a time bomb for corruption and violence: thousands of guards with weapons of all kinds working on insufficient wages in areas of high crime.

PERIOD 2: 2009–2017

Honduran politics has been shaped almost entirely by a crisis that began in June 2009, when the military removed President Manuel Zelaya of the Liberal Party for laying the groundwork to be reelected, which was forbidden by the constitution. In protest of his ouster, the great majority of international security assistance—which funded community policing, training, anti-violence and other programs—was withheld. Juan Orlando Hernández, the head of Congress (akin to the Speaker), was then elected President in 2013 after a bitter contest with Zelaya's wife, Xiomara Castro. The basis of his victory was his then-popular formation of the military police (PMOP: Policía Militar de Orden Público) to reign in the country's spiraling crime. Once in office, Hernández pushed through his nominees for Supreme Court, who then struck down the constitutional prohibition of Presidential reelection—allowing him to run again in 2017. Additionally, a corruption scandal in 2015 involving the social security system implicated the President and spurred protests that almost toppled him. A resulting swell of opposition led to the growth of the Anticorruption party, which aimed to end the political monopoly of the National and Liberal parties. At the same time, the United States began to pressure the country to reform, centered on a plan known as the Biden Billion, to fund reforms in security, economic development, and governance.

Because high crime led to citizen distrust that imperiled the reelection prospects the President was more open to reform. In 2017, just 28.7 percent of Hondurans had confidence in the police—the lowest in Latin America and well below the second lowest score of 35 percent in neighboring Guatemala. More worryingly, Honduras scored the highest in response to the question, "Do the police participate in crime?" A total of 63.1 percent of the survey participants answered affirmatively, higher than any other Latin American country (Criterio, 2017).

This belated effort at reform exposed deeply embedded weaknesses in policing. Most prevalent was the lack of preparation, training, and support of police on the ground. Throughout the country, police stations lacked basic equipment like cars and computers, as well as safety support, from communications to bulletproof vests, which made officers reluctant to proactively stop crime. Poor management aggravated these deficiencies. There was little oversight, officers were rotated frequently, schedules were disrupted by unexpected directives from the top, and there was little-to-no monitoring of weapons. Local stations were poorly run and rife with disorganization, ad hoc decisions, favoritism, and abuse. Police administration was so dysfunctional that the Security Ministry had to conduct a survey in 2013 to see how many police agents they actually had. It revealed that there were far fewer than the official number of 13,000: more than 3,000 didn't show up for work; 1,224 were not reported by their superiors; and over 800 were fake, created for others to collect their salaries.

That survey also revealed the corruption at the heart of poor and abusive policing. As one officer summed up in 2016, the force itself is "a long chain of corruption." As elsewhere, such corruption takes on many forms, from traffic-stop shakedowns to budget embezzlement, and is virtually engrained into the state. As reported by the Associated Press and confirmed by NGOs, half of the extortion rackets that plague nearly every urban neighborhood—and the harassment, intimidation, and extortion accompanying them—are run by the police. Efforts to check such corruption are weak, further encouraging it. In particular, channels for reporting corruption do not function because those to whom it is reported are often complicit. The succession of attempts to address corruption and rights abuse floundered, from the 2003 firing of the UAI chief after she charged officers with extrajudicial killing to the evisceration of a 2014 committee to purge the police. The only successful effort was the purge commission from 2015 to 2017, which led to the dismissal of over 5,000 officers for abuse and corruption. Headed by the Security Minister, a head of the Catholic Church, and a leader of the nongovernmental sector, this was one of the most important advances in recent years. But since that commission stemmed from political pressures at the time, its achievements unraveled as those pressures lifted and thousands of former disgruntled officers began to use the knowledge, skills and weapons they had acquired to collude with criminals. In October 2018, for example, the Attorney General announced the arrest of sixteen current and former officials on organized crime charges. In this and other cases, authorities also uncovered officers on active duty who were supposed to have been dismissed—including a detective who continued to receive his salary despite having been removed for alleged links to drug trafficking.

Much corruption is rooted in the police's links to the powerful web of organized crime whose infiltration of the state extends from local officials to the Presidential Cabinet. For example, at the very top, the last President's son and wife were convicted and sentenced for corruption and drug trafficking. A United States court also convicted both a former police chief and current President Hernández's brother for cocaine trafficking (U.S. Department of Justice, 2020). Collaboration among these groups as well as with the state constantly fuels their growing wealth and power. Traffickers in arms, narcotics, pharmaceuticals, people, forestry products, and other contraband are learning to share their physical, financial, and electronic resources—and investing much of their earnings into the licit market. Illegal logging operations clear runways for drug flights, and ranching and agricultural businesses like those of the Valle Valle and Maradiaga families are a cover for criminal operations. Contraband flows across the borders through the dozens of border blind spots, even though the country's three integrated surveillance systems have drones designed to monitoring all national frontiers. In many border areas, local citizens are often pulled into the illicit activities. Along the northeast border with Guatemala, for example, extreme poverty and displacement of farming communities by export agriculture has led many of its labor force into the illegal market. Further fueling organized crime, ironically, was the anti-mara crackdown after 2003, in which the police broke up large urban cells and arrested anyone with tattoos or clothing associated with the maras. In response, MS-13 and 18th shed those visible markings and divided into smaller groups that spread throughout the country into small towns and rural areas. They also started to integrate into the country's economic and political life, by buying assets in the legal economy like carwashes and motels, and even sending members to the police academy. This strategy put them in a perfect position when the cartels moved in after 2009, and they took on pivotal roles such as intimidating police and recruiting locals as cocaine consumers throughout the country. Without the investigative ability or citizen trust to track these shifts in criminality, the police failed to predict, understand or document it.

Criminal Justice

The other major reform started in this period was of the criminal justice system. Though central to citizen security and justice, the entire criminal justice process is rife with delay and dysfunction. Currently, only between 3 and 5 percent of homicide cases lead to a trial and conviction, due primarily to a lack of investigators and investigative capacity. Criminal investigation is poor at all stages, beginning with a failure to protect crime scenes, inability to collect evidence, and other steps which cause most crime reports to be incomplete or insufficient even after delays of six months or more. Nearly half of the reports that are submitted are rejected by prosecutors, and judges estimate that 40 percent of cases they receive are dismissed because of poor investigation. A study of the 400,000 person city of Comayagua, for example, found that there were just six prosecutors and three judges in a municipality with a homicide rate of 79 per 100,000 people. Of the nearly 400 murders there between 2010 and 2012, only 34 led to a completed police investigation, and only three to a trial and conviction (Inter-American Commission of Human Rights, 2015). Like the police, criminal justice lacks sufficient resources and training. The Prosecutor's Office (Fiscalía) is unable to handle all the reports it gets and is unable to investigate more than a quarter of cases. Some detectives even say that they have been stuck at headquarters because no vehicle is available to take them to a crime scene. Even in the rare cases where evidence is collected, a lack of photo, vehicular, ballistics, and chemical toxicology labs can halt investigation, since many cases depend on preservation and testing of DNA and other material evidence. Similarly, the Witness Protection Program does not function. The protection offered to witnesses is normally limited to six months on average, while a trial can last up to two and a half years. Worse, some people in the program have been turned over to their assailants by officials charged with protecting them. Overall, only 33 out of every 100 cases are investigated, and of the cases that do arrive, there are delays of 18 to 36 months (author interview, Irina Pineda, MP, April 19, 2017), with an average of 30 months. The current total of delayed processes is 180,000.

Statistics for marginalized sectors—such as women, the LBBT population, the Afro-Honduran community (known as the Garifunas)—are even more dismal. According to the Special Prosecutor for Women, there were 407 femicides just in 2009, but between 2008 and 2010, only 221 cases were brought to criminal court, with only 58 leading to conviction (Morales, 2011). Of the 10,367 domestic violence cases reported in 2018, 70 percent did not lead to a charge (*El Heraldo*, March 30, 2019). Currently, a Honduran woman loses her life in the country every fifteen hours—making Honduras one of the most dangerous countries for women (Nazario, 2019). The courts also fail to fully investigate white collar, financial and corruption crimes. While many *fiscales* work on corruption, about nine out of every ten cases of corruption the *Fiscalía* handles are rejected for lack of evidence or transferred to other agencies (author interview, Rigoberto Cuellar, Adjunct Attorney General; Tegucigalpa, Honduras, September 2014). One reason is that individual *fiscales* and judges are frequently subject to threats, attacks, and assassinations. Along with being overwhelmed with cases, such risks lead to frequent turnover of court personnel, which derails criminal investigations.

Because of these conditions, criminal justice reforms began in this period. In 2015, the establishment of the two investigation agencies, DPI and ATIC, introduced effective strategies like the use of mobile forensics labs that began to gradually bring down crime through better investigation and cooperation with prosecutors. In 2016, the country's formation of a national circuit of special jurisdiction courts on extortion and corruption made Honduras the second country in Latin America, after Peru, to have jurisdictional bodies specifically for public corruption. Another major reform was the National Plan for the Eradication of Judicial Default, established in 2016 to identify and address the sources of the judiciary's deficiencies. With an annual allocation in the national budget that always fall short of the 3.0 percent established constitutionally, the result has been chronic scarcity of human, material and technological resources. Other problems identified by this Plan have been contradictory, insufficient or overly formal procedural mechanisms; overly heavy workloads on new personnel; and abuse of due process rights in most criminal justice procedures. The third reform was expansion of community justice though Mobile Peace Courts and judicial facilitators. As of 2019, there were 305 Mobile Peace Courts in municipalities across the country; and 1,900 judicial facilitators working in 15 departments. But nearly every criminal justice official, from local judges to the Chief Justice (author interview, Rolando Argueta, November 12, 2019), acknowledged that even if such efforts are fully implemented it would take years before they could speed up the gears of justice. More worryingly, judges are subject to political pressures by the political parties that nominated them, which increasingly means being under the thumb of the National Party, whose uninterrupted time in power since 2009 (author interview, *Jueces por la Democracia*, November 7, 2019) has allowed it to increasingly control the judicial branch. Such politization can be seen in the lack of prosecution over killings connected with the 2017 election.

PERIOD 3: 2017 TO THE PRESENT

Despite the reforms and reduction in violent crime, deepening political polarization turned the 2017 election into a powder keg, set off immediately by its contested result. The President was widely accused of fraud after his main opponent, Salvador Nasralla of the Anti-Corruption party, took a lead by a percentage statistically impossible to overcome with uncounted ballots. But after a nearly 24-hour blackout, the electoral Council tallying the votes announced that Hernández had won by a small percentage. The widespread allegations led every election monitor including the Organization of American States, to call for a recount or a fresh election. The government refused, generating months of political violence marked by crackdowns by military and other security officers that included mass arrests, a clampdown on freedoms of the press and assembly, and the killings of thirty and thirty-five people, mainly by the PMOP (Kinosian, 2018). About twenty of those killings were during protests (in which the ballistics lab confirmed that the bullets came from the heavy caliber weapons owned by public security forces) and the others were extrajudicial executions. To date, there have been no formal investigations or accusations of officials who carried out the killings.

After Hernández was inaugurated for a second term in January 2018, the political repression continued. In cities throughout the country, those suspected of being opposed to the government have been harassed and threatened. This includes former party activists who criticized the electoral fraud, government employees seen as disloyal, and local activists advocating for environment issues or the rights of the Garifunas. Significant role of the security forces has grown, with widespread actions of surveillance, threats, torture, and killings to support a government facing widespread resistance and unrest. The President's stronger domination of the judiciary and the Congress has allowed both the corruption as well as the state violence to deepen. An example of this trend was the formation of an international commission, known by its Spanish acronym, MACCIH (Misión de Apoyo contra la Corrupción y la Impunidad en Honduras), to identify and root out corruption in the country—only the second time such an agency was established. Like the police reforms in the earlier period, the government agreed to the commission as part of its effort to recoup international support after the disputed election. And like the security changes, those reforms faltered once the pressure eased. Soon after MACCIH began its work, in fact, the government passed laws to neutralize its powers to investigate and indict public officials. And in 2020, the government decided to end MACCIH completely by refusing to extend its mandate.

Arms Control

Political violence and autocracy since late 2017 has sped up under COVID-19, with the PMOP and other security units using excessive force to enforce the lockdown. Amid the overlapping political and health crisis, there have been few efforts at security reform. The one exception is the 2019 Arms Control Law (Ley de Control de Armas de Fuego, Municiones, Explosivos y Materiales Relacionados), which reduced the number of weapons that citizens can have, established a new national registration structure, and created clearer guidelines for the Armería, the state-run store from which all arms are bought and sold. Though one of the biggest steps toward arms reform in the region since the advent of democracy, the law exposes the long-term institutional and political obstacles to the police and security reforms discussed earlier.

The first challenge, as with other reforms, is information. Absences in local reporting, data manipulation by security agencies, and other methodological problems that have long afflicted criminal justice in Latin America also undermine arms control. Although it is the most basic figure, the total number of weapons in circulation in Honduras is unclear, ranging from 400,000 to 1.2 million. The percentage of this total that is illegal, as well as the total of each type of weapon, is also uncertain. According to the UNDP, up to 650,000 are illegal and there are up to 500,000 illegal types of arms in civilian hands, but estimates by the UNAH Observatory on Violence put that number at over a million. Another basic statistic lacking consensus is the percentage of homicides in Honduras committed with firearms. Every NGO estimates that between 70 and 80 percent of homicides are committee with firearms, while the Security Minister's response to a request claimed the percent ranged between 30 and 45 percent.

The new law's registration structure should help clarify numbers, but it runs into another common problem: a lack of institutional and procedural development. As with the proliferation of police units discussed earlier, the law's ambitious institutional expansion is not matched by a detailed or realistic way to fund, monitor or evaluate development. The law creates three new units to oversee it: the Weapons Control Unit, the Control Section for Specialized Weapons Services Fire and Ammunition, and the Section for Control and Specialized Services of Explosives and Related Materials. But there are no budgets or frameworks, nor are there any plans to associate them with established bodies. In addition, Congress plans to establish forty-four ballistics laboratories and licensing centers around the country in order to maximize citizen registration, which will be financed by the income generated from the law's implementation. But there has been no published plan, schedule, or budget (http://congresonacional.hn/, 20 September 2018). Similarly, there is a lack of analysis of the three main registration processes: the Single Window (*Ventanilla Única*), through which a weapon license is obtained; the National Arms Registry (RNA) offices; and the Ballistic Registration System. There is no procedural planning to bring access, transparency, analysis, or efficiency to any of these processes. In particular, there is a lack of incentives to register weapons, without which there will be no lasting reduction. Strategies that cheat the system, such as registering weapons under the names of family members are also rampant, and are not targeted by these reforms. In addition, there is no plan to shut down the flourishing production of "artisanal" arms, which are the sixth most common weapons in homicides, or the brisk sales done in pawn shops and through social networks like Facebook.

Ballistics testing, a critical step in the criminal justice process, is done by the General Office of Forensic Medicine (DGMF: Dirección General de Medicina Forense), which uses the Integrated Ballistic Identification System (IBIS) to analyze the arms material found in crime scenes. The unique and indelible microscopic marks etched inside a gun's barrel during manufacturing are transferred to a bullet or cartridge when the gun is fired. When bullets are seized at crime scenes, IBIS converts them into digital images and then searches a database for other rounds that have similar markings and are likely to have been fired from the same weapon. Matches then become the prosecutors' main evidence, since they can use them to track both individual suspects and broader patterns of gun use. In Honduras, the average repeated use of a weapon is between three to six crimes until it is confiscated, making this analysis critical to crime fighting. Despite its pivotal role, the DGMF suffers from debilitating deficiencies. Its lab lacks basic biosecurity equipment, such as clothing and eye protection, and with only five full-time technicians, it is only able to operate at 35 percent capacity, only a third of its true potential. It has also been politicized, which has led to the firing of top officials. Amid such conditions, the DGMF review about 2,000 weapons annually—far fewer in comparison to neighboring countries—and with a backlog of 5,000 cases. Less than 20 percent of the weapons that arrive at the laboratory are registered in the RNA. This mean that 80 percent are not properly registered or digitized, obviating the possibility of making "hits." Delays also afflict cases even if there are hits. Between June 2013 and November 2017, only 5–10 percent of the cases involving DGMF evidence were prosecuted. The DGMF, in addition, has little control over the weapons under the exclusive control of the PN and the Armed Forces. Most alarmingly, the whole system shut down in May 2019, because the government did not pay the annual licensing fee for IBIS.

An additional problem is the common sale of military weapons to organized crime. In fact, there is little accountability over the enormous quantity of weapons held by the government, most of it acquired through $105 million in purchases from thirty countries between 2009 and 2018 (*La Prensa*, November 13, 2019), with a record high of U.S.$35.5 million in 2017 and 2018. Although the Defense Minister said that it is "impossible" that any of these weapons could end up in the hand of criminals (interview, General Fredy Santiago Díaz Zelaya, November 14, 2019), the loss has been common and no one has been held liable. One such example is when Military-grade heavy-caliber weapons were seized during the arrest of the head of the MS-13 hitmen in September 2019. Police chiefs in the northern region have claimed that ammunition trafficking forms one of the strongest links between military officers and the gangs. However, the criminal justice reforms that began in 2015 have made progress against such criminality. One of the first successes of the DPI was the dismantling of the arms trafficking networks, which included operations such as one in September 2019 that captured members of the arms trafficking "El Negro" gang. But such efforts will need to go much deeper to root out the embedded nature of arms trafficking. As with other organized crime networks described earlier, the illegal arms market involves elaborate supply chains that connect transnational networks with current and former security officers, ranchers, merchants, private security firms, and others. These individuals are closely integrated with both the state and other criminal syndicates.

REFERENCES

Alianza para La Paz y la Justicia. *Combatiento la Impunidad en Comayagua: Éxitos y Obstáculos (2014)*, May 2014.

Criterio Staff Writer, Policía hondureña la peor de Latinoamérica, según encuestas de percepción, Retrieved 23 March 2017, https://criterio.hn/2017/03/23/.

El Heraldo Staff Writer. Mapa: ¿Cómo están distribuidas las maras y pandillas en Honduras?, El Heraldo, March 28, 2016.

Inter-American Commission of Human Rights. *Situation of Human Rights in Honduras*. December 2015.

Kinosian, Sarah. Families fear no justice for victims as 31 die in Honduras post-election violence, *Guardian*, January 2, 2018.

La Prensa Staff Writer. A un año de su implementación, January 8, 2004.

Morales, Tacuazina. *Honduras: Escalada de Feminicidios* (2011)

Nazario, Sonia, "Someone Is Always Trying to Kill You" *New York Times*, April 5, 2019.

News Service on Women in Latin America and the Caribbean, March 14, 2011.

U.S. Department of Justice, Former chief of Honduran National Police charged with drug trafficking and weapons offenses, Retrieved 30 April 2020, https://www.justice.gov/usao-sdny/pr/former-chief-honduran-national-police-charged-drug-trafficking-and-weapons-offenses.

Chapter 17

Reconsidering the Security in Nicaragua

A National Police Reform

Skarlleth Martínez Prado

The Nicaraguan National Police (further referred to as National Police) has had an interesting historical development. Born during the Sandinista Revolution in 1979, it survived the democratization process in the 1990s and became one of the foremost institutions in the country's political context. The National Police has been recognized internationally as one of the best in Latin America. To guarantee the security of the communities, Community-Based Policing (COP) has been practiced on the basis of prevention policies, which has resulted in the lowest homicide rate in the region. However, the role of the National Police is being threatened by the political context in which it operates, as it fails to fulfill its function of safety for the public, and instead only serves a subsector of the population. The previously mentioned argument is elucidated by the police's interactions with the community it serves and its increasing participation in social conflicts during the last seven years.

This chapter addresses the institutional trajectory of the National Police outlining the evolution of its interaction and relations with the community, how police patrols are carried out and their public perceptions, and the role of the National Police in the central government. After the wave of political violence in April 2018, political activists have spoken about the need to reconsider the policies and strategies which guide the institution in an effort to protect human rights, especially in times of social uprisings within the current political context. The arguments presented in this chapter represent a contribution toward that debate.

HISTORICAL BACKGROUND

Although it could be stated that the democratic reform of the defense and security sector in Nicaragua is one of the most emblematic experiences in Latin America due to its intensity and speed, it should be kept in mind that in the case of the National Police, there was no breakdown with its organizational past. Throughout its existence, the police institution has developed a Community-Based Policing (COP) model that it calls "preventive, proactive and community-based" (Policía Nacional de Nicaragua, 2011, p. 5). The Nicaraguan COP model is distinguished from its peers in Central America since it has its origins in the Sandinista revolution.[1] While the National Civil Police (PNC) of Guatemala and El Salvador emerged from the respective peace agreements—signed after intense lobbying between the guerrilla organizations and the authoritarian governments of the time—the National Police was founded after the triumph of the Sandinista Liberation Front (FSLN by its acronyms in Spanish) in 1979, and it has no connection with its predecessor, the now-dissolved National Guard of Anastasio Somoza's dictatorship. Before the Sandinista Revolution, Nicaragua did not have an institution that assumed an independent police force's function.

The Sandinista National Police was founded on September 5, 1979, and it is attached to the Ministry of Interior. Throughout the 1980s the police created the community model, which organized the communities in support of revolutionary goals, establishing a model of two parts: the Committees for the Defense of the Revolution and the heads of the sector. The Committees transformed themselves into neighborhood watch organizations and were then linked to the National Police after the approval of the 1996 organic law, while the heads of the sectors have been a critical piece of community policing since the institution's inception. This COP program consists of dividing the entire country into synoptic sectors, each assigned to a responsible officer. In this way, each of the 153 municipalities, the smallest administrative division in the country, is organized into numerous operating sectors for the same number of chiefs, who are the most essential links in the police–community relationship (Policía Nacional de Nicaragua, 2011, p. 13).

The political transition that began in 1990 with the electoral defeat of the revolutionary government and the rise of a new political regime, marked the end of the long military conflict that had afflicted the country during the 1980s. During the first years of the transition and pacification, the country experienced new forms of violence that were expressed, above all, through conflicts and political violence, and took the form of massive protests, institutional takeovers, strikes, land takeovers, rearming of ex-combatants, and misuse of weaponry (Cuadra, 2013, p. 110).

Consequently, the National Police faced an identity crisis due to frictions with the authorities of the Ministry of the Interior, who had been appointed by the new government. The result was a dilemma that divided the police headquarters among those who had a position adducing loyalty to the institution's partisan origins; and others, who said that the police's responsibility is due to society and it should act accordingly (Cuadra, 2002, p. 197). This was the first phase of the process of redefinition, professionalization, and institutional consolidation of the police institution.

INSTITUTIONAL FRAMEWORK ESTABLISHMENT

The police are not immune to reforms and social change. The first step toward police reform in Nicaragua was the renewal of the National Police headquarters and the strengthening of the institutional legal framework. As a result, the Organic Law of the National Police was enacted in 1992, because of negotiations between the new government and the police officers. This law includes the terms of the institutional identity and the nature and structure of police functions. In 1995, the existence of the police force was established in the Constitution through a series of reforms. In 1996, the National Assembly approved the National Police Law, known as Law 228, which clearly establishes the mission of the apparatus as the preservation of the integrity, safety, and life of all citizens, as well as prevention and prosecution of crime, and preservation of internal public and social order.

Law 228 defines the police functions and fundamental principles of action; the organic structure and its dependencies; the competencies and powers for each one of the controls, specialties, and organs; further defines the police career, disciplinary regime, hierarchies, and procedures for institutional changes. Furthermore, it reaffirms the constitutional mandate that the National Police "will be subject to civil authority that will be exercised by the President of the Republic through the corresponding ministry," which is the aforementioned Interior Ministry (Asamblea Nacional de Nicaragua, 2005, sec. Título V).

The second step can be identified as occurring between 1997 and 2006. It was a 10-year process that the same institution termed the "process of modernization and professionalization." The Police Academy, which was in recess due to the country's political changes, was reopened. The Academy suspended operations for new admissions from 1990 to 1994. There was a new introduction of programs regarding human rights, which became one of the main aspects of the training at all levels. Also, new specialties were reorganized and created. During this time, the Social Crime Prevention Committees were formed, which had coordination at the local and territorial levels for joint preventive actions with social organizations.

The important elements at this stage were the promotions and retreats, which were carried out in accordance with the provisions of the Police Law. In other words, the officers rose in rank and responsibility depending on experience and the merits they were achieving. The directors changed every five years and went into retirement, which remained a good practice in the police institution during that period (Asamblea Nacional de Nicaragua, 1996, sec. IX).

The transformations of the Nicaraguan political system have also affected the judiciary. The justice system is comprised of the Public Ministry or Prosecutor's Office, the Office of the Attorney General of the Republic, the Government Ministry to whom the National Police and the Penitentiary System are subordinated, the Supreme Court of Justice, the courts and tribunals, the Office of the Ombudsman Public, and the Institute of Legal Medicine. Many of these institutions are quite new since they were created during the late 1990s and 2000s.

The modernization process has been long and has involved the completion and update of the country's legal framework with the approval of laws and new judiciary codes.[2] However, as in most Central American countries, the influence of politics on the security and justice system is one of the main challenges in Nicaragua. The judiciary system is placed in a position susceptible to political influences by the executive branch.

BEGINNING OF THE INSTITUTIONAL BACKSLIDING

Daniel Ortega, the Sandinista leader that governed the country from 1979 to 1990, returned to the presidency in 2007. Ortega remained in power after winning the reelections in 2011 and 2016. Since 2007, the new administration has influenced and changed all the institutions, and one of the first effects was at the discursive level. The President became the commander-in-chief of the National Police in order to highlight its "Sandinista roots" and its historical link with the revolution. This was evident in the police publications (police magazine and statistic yearbook) and through public interventions of its top leaders, including its director; the first commissioner, Aminta Granera.

However, the effects transcend to the legal level. The exclusion of the Government Ministry as the administrative intermediary between the police and the President as well as the new title of "Supreme Chief" characterizes the changes within the new law. During the first seven years of Ortega's administration (2007–2014), the National Police's role continued to be defined by Law 228 of 1996. However, this changed in mid-2014 with the enactment of Law 872; the Organization, Functions, Career, and Special Social Security Regime Law of the National Police. Thus, the police passed from being subject "to the civil authority which will be exercised by the President of the Republic through the Government Ministry" (Asamblea Nacional de Nicaragua, 1996, sec. Capítulo V) to submitting "to the civil authority which will be exercised by the President of the Republic, in his capacity as Supreme Chief of the National Police" (Asamblea Nacional de Nicaragua, 2014, sec. Capítulo II). The same thing happened with the Nicaraguan National Army.

This legal reform affected the Community-Based Policing (COP) model. Ortega's administration established the Citizen Power Councils (CPCs), organizations created as a counterpart to the police for community prevention and for any type of police coordination at the local level, making the work of the Social Crime Prevention Committee redundant. This new association from the CPCs within the state apparatus partially replaced the conglomerating and organizational role that both NGOs and the Crime Prevention Committees had assumed within the COP model; roles which had contributed to its politicization. This was the starting point of a citizen control and surveillance system, which has been extremely important in the actions of repression and political violence since 2007. Ortega installed them outside the law in the framework of the COP model. Among these organizations, the CPCs stand out, which were replaced later by the Family Assemblies.

Prior to 2007, the National Police had maintained an open and active collaboration with a variety of civil society organizations that have worked toward the provision of helping services to youth in neighborhoods. Regarding doctrinal values and institutional policy, the National Police has been a pioneer in Central America; organizing a series of security and protection services for specific interest groups which are usually subject to more physical and psychological violence, and which are also usually in a situation of greater social and economic vulnerability. For example, with the enactment of Law 228 of the National Police, the Special Police Stations for Women and Children were formalized as a subspecialty of the Department of Criminal Investigations. Similarly, the Youth Affairs Division was established, which worked to promote youth care programs in risky areas as well as to demobilize activities for members of various youth gangs. This differs from police operations in El Salvador, Guatemala, and Honduras, which severely repressed gang members and were based on heavy-handed approaches: anti-gang laws, the broom plan, zero-tolerance plan, and heavy-handed plan (Rodgers, Muggah, & Stevenson, 2009; Seelke, 2010).

In 2011, the document "Systematization of the proactive community policing model in Nicaragua," prepared by the National Police, highlights that the application of the model has not been homogeneous within departmental delegations and districts, specialties, and units of the Police due to the different styles of work and levels of discretion granted to the police chiefs. The aforementioned oversight has resulted in a negative impact on the implementation

of the COP model. Since that moment, it can be observed that the police conduct has been shaped by new ideas coming from the government. It reflects
the bias and preferences of the police institution toward some people in the
community. The institution does not allow equal treatment and protection of
their basic rights and avoids the exercise of legitimate rights of assembly and
association, jeopardizing equal access to justice. These situations detract from
the credibility, effectiveness, and efficiency of the National Police.

In the second period of Ortega's government, his administration reformed
the Political Constitution of Nicaragua, allowing him to consolidate his
political power in the country to reflect his political control during the 1980s.
Ortega now controls the government, public officials, media; the great private
company that was a fundamental ally during these last eleven years; and ultimately the army, which was the only institution that presented some independence in the country. The reform to the Law 872, backed by the reform of the
Political Constitution in 2014, establishes the indefinite permanence of the
positions of the National Police leadership, whose appointments and duration
are at the discretion of the President and not based on merit. The risks of this
new relationship of police-president were confirmed. With the legal backup,
members of the army and the National Police may occupy positions in the
sphere of the executive branch. Even though it is pointed out that they are of
a temporary nature, adducing reasons of national security, this has opened the
door to the militarization of the positions of public administration.

The most controversial aspects of the reform were the changes made to the
defense and security sectors and to the property sector in regard to the construction of the interoceanic canal, which subsequently had an impact on the
April 2018 protests. According to the reforms, the executive branch assumes
new roles (after the disappearance of the figures of the Ministry of Defense
and Ministry of Government as intermediaries between the executive and the
military and police institutions). This transfer of power and responsibilities
runs a high risk of becoming perverted or of becoming a factor of care over
these institutions, where the privilege of use of force is deposited. Second,
the reform to the Constitution and the approval of Law 800; the Law of the
Legal Regime of the Grand Canal Project and the establishment of the Grand
Canal Authority on July 3, 2012, legalizes the purchases and concessions
of land or resources for the construction and exploitation of an interoceanic
canal, allowing the expropriation of any property even when the owner does
not agree with it.

Therefore, a new wave of social conflict and political violence has
reemerged where the main actors are citizens and members of social organizations, supporters of the government, as well as the police (BBC News,
2014; Tittor, 2018). A closer look at the government's strategies and
responses toward the critics of the canal demonstrates its hostility toward

social movements outside of the government's sphere. Attempts to co-opt the debate and repress criticism are the current strategy but within a broader context of secrecy and obfuscation. The problem with the reforms is that they allowed discretion to rise to unacceptable levels, as individual relationships between members of the leadership and the presidency were fostered, degenerating into what is basically known as clientelism, which holds no benefit for the police institution, nor for Nicaraguan society at large.

SECURITY CONDITIONS IN NICARAGUA: FROM THE SAFEST TO THE MOST VIOLENT COUNTRY

For several years Nicaragua was considered the safest country in Central America due to its lowest crime rate, according to data related to the homicide rate per 100,000 population. Different organizations and academics (Cuadra 2013; Rodgers, Muggah, & Stevenson, 2009; Schrader, 2017; UNDP, 2014) applauded these results and began searching for the unique variable that made Nicaragua different from the rest of the Central American countries. Since 2000, there has been a growing trend in the homicide rate. This indicator shows a decrease from 12.5 to 7 homicides per 100,000 population between 2011 and 2017. Some police reports and the UNDP report indicate that there are localities where this indicator shows critical behavior in relation to activities linked to transnational organized crime (PNUD, 2011).

Nicaragua's achievement was related to the National Police COP model's practices which have been implemented since the revolution and have placed emphasis on prevention and played a historic role that has supplemented COP policing with several programs. Success in fostering a culture of non-violence, regardless of ideology or government in power, includes different actors as the main foundation. While the police and military in El Salvador and Honduras have been implicated and prosecuted for death-squad killings of hundreds of men in the Maras or youth gangs, Nicaragua's death squads disappeared decades ago. This was one of the main features that characterized the Nicaraguan model as successful, and the National Police as one of the best performers and as a trusted institution in Latin America, together with the Carabineros from Chile (Yagoub, 2017). Notwithstanding this finding, Nicaraguans placed crime and violence in third or fourth place of importance among the main problems of the country based on the citizens' perceptions (IEEPP, 2016a).

Nevertheless, using the homicide rate as the only indicator to measure security between countries and the effectiveness of policies is very limited, since it does not factor into account other problems that are much more rooted in culture, and that affect citizens differently such as sexual violence, violence against women, injuries and political violence. Regarding sexual crimes, rape is a growing crime that affects mainly women and girls. Violence against women is a serious problem inside their homes, but violence on public roads is also frequent and mainly affects girls, adolescents, and young adults. Its most common forms of expression are those that are usually known as "street harassment," which also include physical assault and sexual abuse. Meanwhile the injuries in the neighborhood and street fights are caused by problems regarding coexistence such as "intolerance, lack of work, loss of listening ability, financial problems, communication difficulties and other behaviors such as alcohol consumption" (IEEPP, 2016b).

Since 2018, political violence has increased and has shaped citizen security concerns to other levels. "Now it is impossible to talk about citizen security without talking about political violence" (Cuadra, 2020a). Nicaragua's security conditions have been closely related to the evolution of the country's sociopolitical context, which is characterized by repression and the imposition of a state of exception, which limits or eliminates human rights.

The political violence has given rise to the current insecurity factors in the country. Before 2018, the most important challenges or risks to security were linked to common crime, organized crime, and certain expressions of political violence that had already been on the rise since 2013. After April 2018, the levels of violence and the risk of being a victim of violence have increased, especially from the government, which has affected the perception of insecurity among citizens. In the face of violence, there is government silence and official statements blatantly deny the truth. There is silence on the abuses and imprisonment as well as the harassment of mobs that intimidate. This has created a distortion of reality due to the government not publishing official statistics of the violence in the country, and the independent voices are being bullied into silence.

However, it is possible to highlight the main risk factors for citizen security in Nicaragua, which are related to repressive police that has neglected its missions and functions; the presence of paramilitary groups that act with impunity; a huge presence of firearms and weapons of war and the release of those deprived of liberty for common crimes (Cuadra, 2020b). With no accountability for the violence, abuse of power and authority, and the use of force, violence has been on the rise across the country.

UPRISINGS AND DEMONSTRATIONS: THE FALL OF AN INSTITUTION

Political violence has become the Achilles heel of the National Police. After President Daniel Ortega came to power in 2007, the violence and police abuses against the protests increased. Between 2007 and 2011, there is no precise data on the number of violent episodes; however, some journalistic reports indicate that the most serious acts of violence have occurred during the 2008 and 2011 electoral campaigns (Cuadra, 2013). This new violent pattern of police abuses and the participation of paramilitary forces was more evident after the complaint filed by the Nicaraguan Center for Human Rights (CENIDH by its acronyms in Spanish) and the Center for Justice and International Law (CEJIL) at the Inter-American Commission on Human Rights (IACHR) in its 149th session on October 2013. The majority of cases of human rights violations were related to physical assaults and ill-treatment at the time of arrest, repression of social protests, and breach of the duty to protect the physical integrity of citizens who demand their rights against assault from the pro-shock forces of the government (CENIDH, 2013).

Despite the evidence, the authorities claimed these to be isolated events with a relation to common crimes. Since 2013, a new wave of protests and social mobilization formed to demand solutions to the many problems that have been accumulating for years and still remain unresolved to date. None of the different governments were able to recognize the situation in all its magnitude. Throughout history, various paramilitary groups were formed from people related to the government in order to infiltrate the demonstrations to provoke riots, groups that are not controlled by the National Police. The institution constantly said that the complaints were baseless, which ended up dragging the police institution to commit the most heinous acts of human rights violations during the protests that began in April 2018.

The protests began with a reform in the social security system, announced on April 16, which President Ortega tried to promote in the face of strong rejection. The reform functioned as the great trigger for the discontent which had accumulated over the years. Different social sectors united in the protests that broke out on April 18, 2018: students, businessmen, peasants, and even leaders of the Church. Since then, Nicaragua has been experiencing a socio-political crisis that has led to a wave of violence and government repression with serious consequences for the rights and security of its citizens. It left more than 325 people dead, thousands injured, and tens of thousands forced into involuntary displacement and exile (IACHR, 2018).

According to reports from civil society, 777 people were arrested and prosecuted, of which at least 500 were deprived of their liberty; 300 health professionals have been dismissed; 144 Nicaraguan National Autonomous University (UNAN by its acronyms in Spanish) students have been expelled; and over 70 journalists and media workers have been forced into exile. The United Nations High Commissioner for Refugees (UNHCR) stated that about 62,000 Nicaraguans have fled to neighboring countries; 55,000 of them seeking refuge in Costa Rica (GIEI, 2018).

The National Police's involvement was focused on discouraging participation in demonstrations. Consequently, the government's repressive response to the protests has led to a serious human rights crisis where a quick solution is not yet in sight, despite all the joint efforts made with the international community. The UNHCR concludes that the State of Nicaragua has violated the rights of its citizens, including rights to life, personal integrity, health, personal liberty, assembly, freedom of expression, and access to justice. Until now, there exist concerns about the murders, suspected extrajudicial executions, mistreatment, acts of torture, and arbitrary detentions perpetrated against the country's mostly young population. After the politicization, the National Police became a repressive and criminal apparatus, which exercised powers outside the scope of the law. To the protests and civic mobilizations that started in April 2018, the police and the government responded by using deadly force and military weapons against the protesters.

These results clearly show that the police are unable to satisfactorily fulfill their main constitutional functions, including the control of public order. The incidents from 2018 made evident the existence of several problems in the satisfactory fulfillment of its main constitutional and legal functions, including the prevention and investigation of crimes and the control of public order. This process requires changes and transformations aimed at solving urgent issues, with a medium and long-term perspective that points to a significant institutional reconfiguration.

There is a consensus on both the unsatisfying results of recent responses and the urgent need for more radical reform. Many parties in opposition to the current system have been proposing a new refoundation of the institution. The performance and behavior of the police officers have shown the political manipulation and subordination of the police to the FSLN party, which undermines the professionalism of officers. This further reduces police capacity to combat crime effectively, which manifests in a lack of confidence by the public. It is necessary to initiate a larger reflection on its mission, its functions, and its resources. The fundamental challenge is how to create a democratic and trustworthy National Police. Police violence and misconduct are so widespread and rooted in institutional practice that public confidence in the police is low and decreasing. This led to the Nicaraguan society demanding a new police force that is truly based on respect for human rights, democratic principles, and the nonrepetition of these events.

A NEW POLICE, A NEW PERSPECTIVE

Nicaragua is a postconflict country, where the National Police established itself as an institution that emerged from the revolution and was able to survive all of the democratization processes during the 1990s. However, the historical link with the FSLN party was never broken. On the contrary, the bonds were reinforced again, regardless of whether it was framed in a political logic that differed from the principles of the revolution. Despite attempts at previous reforms, the police have conserved the rigid bureaucracy, lack of transparency, and propensity for abuse. This institutional and social context poses huge obstacles to any police reform efforts. These challenges are heightened by the context of high crime levels and extreme social anxiety.

The National Police does not enjoy a high level of social legitimacy. This negative perception of the police as an organization is due to the prevalence of corruption and the persistence of human rights violations. Deep down, the police in Nicaragua tend to pay greater heed to the demands of the government in comparison to the needs of citizens. This is a prelude to the debate on reform or refoundation. The National Police's background would never allow democratic legitimacy and a healthy police–citizen relationship, and for this reason, a refoundation of the National Police is seen as a genuine way to democratize the institution. The main vision should lead to trust-building processes and should update the police–community strategies based on the respect and guarantee of human rights. The purpose is not to make the police more effective or more efficient; it is to reinvent the whole institution so it would be in tune with the principles of democratic governance.

The refoundation should include different strategies such as police purging and the establishment of outside supervision of police conduct; a detailed revision of the police training, curricula, and professionalization; and improved police relationship with the community. The frequent need to purge police forces is an indicator of the weakness of recruitment mechanisms and of existing disciplinary procedures for combating corruption and abuse. This context makes the introduction of internal and external mechanisms of control of police abuse one of the frequent pillars of police reform.

One of the key factors that will define the police success in the future is the professional training of its members. There are still no rigorous external evaluations of Latin American countries, or even comparisons of the quality of education received by police officers in Latin America (Casas, González, & Mesías, 2018), and Nicaragua is no exception. The police schools are closed entities, and little is known of their curricula and internal testing.

Improved police relationship with the community is the strongest area of this police refoundation, and at the same time, it represents a big challenge. While the COP model was an important improvement in the security in Nicaragua, the police leadership created distortions on its implementation. In the mid-2010s, the COP model was deformed by political influence, lack of professionalism; and a centralized, top-down, biased, and rigid system. The fact that the legal order not only supported but also maintained the separation between militants and opposition members to the ruling party—for the time that Ortega has been in power—and the fact that the police were obligated to maintain that order, has established a pattern for police behavior and attitudes toward opponents that persists to this day. The pattern includes the idea that opponents have fewer civil rights, and the task of the police is to keep them under control rather than to protect them.

To be successful, a police refoundation requires committed political leadership and the assignment of sufficient resources to the process of institutional transformation. The recent community safety imperatives, along with law enforcement challenges, national emergency conditions, penal reform repercussions, and wider implications for rule of law, security, and justice reform is still needed, and the support from the International community is necessary, now more than ever. Given the institutional shortcomings and adverse social context, it is hard to foresee this happening in Nicaragua without the intervention of the international community.

In general, the refoundation should be based on a national security reform strategy, as the police is not the only institution that requires a revision on its mission and performance. This process also needs to include other instances, especially in the system of administration of justice, whose incapacity is evident in the high levels of impunity with respect to cases of serious human rights violations or those with high social impact (Arias, Rosada Granados, & Sain, 2012). Thus, it is noted that the lack of independence in the court does not come from the lack of regulatory precepts, but rather from the pressure of different interest groups to distort the functioning of the judicial system. The Nicaraguan Justice System, far from fulfilling its obligation to protect, has become another piece of the human rights violation scheme, through the criminalization of the citizens that participated in the protests.

This refoundation process can be strengthened by the involvement of multiple actors: the police force itself, civil society, and the government, in order to gain legitimacy. The legitimacy of security is crucial for democracy. This process should decrease the resistance of the police toward accountability processes. To address this, it is important to have a change in political power. A case in which the public is pressuring the government to hold the police accountable can finally give these institutions the ability to act (Ungar 2017). This would also generate a new culture of citizen-focused security.

NOTES

1. On July 17, 1979, Anastasio Somoza Debayle, the beleaguered president of Nicaragua, gave up the struggle against the popular insurrection which was fighting to topple a nearly 40-year-old dynastic dictatorship, and fled the country. Political power

was immediately seized by the spearhead organization of the armed resistance, the Frente Sandinista de Liberación Nacional (FSLN). From 1979 to 1990, the Sandinista movement would totally dominate Nicaragua, taking over the economic, political, social, military, cultural and educational structures of the country (Lipski, 1997). In this period, the Contra War waged between the FSLN-led government of Nicaragua and the United States-backed Contras from 1981–1990.

2. Some important laws were approved, such as the new Code of Criminal Procedure and the Penal Code, as well as the Law against Organized Crime and the law that sanctions violence against women. In addition, specialized units against organized crime were created in different institutions such as the Public Ministry and the National Police.

REFERENCES

Arias, Patricia, Héctor Roberto Rosada Granados, and Marcelo Fabián Sain. (2012). *Reformas policiales en América Latina: principios y lineamientos progresistas.* Friedrich-Ebert-Stiftung, Programa de Cooperación en Seguridad Regional [u.a.].

Asamblea Nacional de Nicaragua. (1996). *Ley 228, Ley de la Policía Nacional.*

Asamblea Nacional de Nicaragua. (2005). *Ley de Reforma Parcial de la Constitución Política de Nicaragua con reformas de 1995, 2000 y 2005.* https://pdba.georgetown.edu/Constitutions/Nica/nica05.html.

Asamblea Nacional de Nicaragua. (2014). *Ley 872, Ley de Organización, Funciones, Carrera y Régimen Especial de Seguridad Social de la Policía Nacional.* http://legislacion.asamblea.gob.ni/Normaweb.nsf/b92aaea87dac762406257265005d21f7/0f03308df36e772206257d0800829eb4.

BBC News. (2014). Nicaraguans protest over canal plan. *BBC News*, December 10, 2014, sec. Latin America & Caribbean. https://www.bbc.com/news/world-latin-america-30426100.

Casas, Kevin, Paola González, and Liliana Mesías. (2018). Police transformation in Latin America by 2030. *Inter-American Development Bank (IADB)*, November, 35, 2020.

CENIDH. (2013). Derechos Humanos en Nicaragua: Informe 2013. Centro Nicaragüense de Derechos Humanos (CENIDH). https://cenidh.org/recursos/33/.

Cuadra, Elvira. (2002). Nuevas dimensiones de la seguridad ciudadana en Nicaragua. In *Seguridad ciudadana, ¿espejismo o realidad?*, 1a ed., 189–203. Facultad Latinoamericana de Ciencias Sociales (FLACSO). https://pdba.georgetown.edu/Security/citizensecurity/ecuador/evaluaciones/docflacso.pdf.

Cuadra, Elvira. (2013). Nicaragua: Una excepción en la seguridad de Centroamérica. In *A Dónde Vamos?: Análisis de políticas públicas de seguridad ciudadana en América Latina*, 103–27.

Cuadra, Elvira. (2020a). El gobierno es más peligroso para los nicaragüenses que la delincuencia común, asegura Elvira Cuadra. https://www.laprensa.com.ni/2020/07

/26/nacionales/2700645-el-gobierno-es-mas-peligroso-para-los-nicaraguenses-que
-la-delincuencia-comun-asegura-elvira-cuadra.

Cuadra, Elvira. (2020b). Asesinatos incrementaron en el primer semestre del año
en comparación con el 2019, según estudio. *La Prensa* (blog), August 12, 2020.
https://www.laprensa.com.ni/2020/08/12/politica/2707774-asesinatos-incremen-
taron-en-el-primer-semestre-del-ano-en-comparacion-con-el-2019-segun-estudio.

GIEI. (2018). Informe sobre los hechos de violencia ocurridos entre el 18 de abril
y el 30 de mayo de 2018. Text. Reporte sobre Nicaragua. Managua: Grupo
Interdisciplinario de Expertos Independientes (GIEI); Comisión Interamericana
de Derechos Humanos (CIDH). https://www.oas.org/en/iachr/media_center/
PReleases/2019/101.asp.

IACHR. (2018). Gross human rights violations in the context of social protests in
Nicaragua. Country Report. OEA/Ser.L/V/II. Washington, D.C.: Inter-American
Commission on Human Rights (IACHR). https://doi.org/10.1163/2210-7975_HRD
-9962-20180042.

IEEPP. (2016a). VIII Encuesta de Percepciones Sobre La Seguridad Ciudadana. 2016.
https://docplayer.es/35979030-Viii-encuesta-de-percepciones-sobre-la-seguridad
-ciudadana.html.

IEEPP. (2016b). XII Informe de Gestión de la Seguridad Democrática. Instituto de
Estudios Estratégicos y Políticas Públicas (IEEPP). https://es.scribd.com/docu-
ment/417879994/XII-Informe-de-Gestion-de-La-Seguridad-Instituto-de-Estudios
-Estrategicos-y-Politicas-Publicas-Nicaragua.

PNUD, ed. (2011). *Informe nacional sobre desarrollo humano 2011: las juventudes
construyendo Nicaragua.* PNUD Nicaragua.

Policía Nacional de Nicaragua. (2011). Sistematización del modelo policial comuni-
tario proactivo de Nicaragua. Policía Nacional de Nicaragua. https://www.policia
.gob.ni/cedoc/sector/revistas/sistematizacion.pdf.

Rodgers, Dennis, Robert Muggah, and Chris Stevenson. (2009). Gangs of Central
America: Causes, costs, and interventions. *Small Arms Survey*, May, 44.

Schrader, Stuart. (2017). "Nicaragua: Central America's security exception." *NACLA
Report on the Americas* 49(3): 360–65. https://doi.org/10.1080/10714839.2017
.1373969.

Seelke, C. R. (2010). *Gangs in Central America.* CRS Report for Congress. DIANE
Publishing Company. https://books.google.com/books?id=csZE5JU2XjEC.

Tittor, Anne. (2018). Conflicts about Nicaragua's Interoceanic Canal Project:
Framing, counterframing, and government strategies. *Cahiers Des Amériques
Latines*, no. 87 (September): 117–40. https://doi.org/10.4000/cal.8561.

UNDP. (2014). Human Development Report for Latin America 2013–2014. United
Nations Development Programme (UNDP). 2014. https://www.undp.org/content/
undp/en/home/librarypage/hdr/human-development-report-for-latin-america-2013
-2014.html.

Ungar, Mark. (2017). Talking policy: Mark Ungar on rule of law in Latin America—
World Policy." *World Policy* (blog)." July 14, 2017. http://worldpolicy.org/2017
/07/14/talking-policy-mark-ungar-on-rule-of-law-in-latin-america/.

United Nations Office on Drugs and Crime (UNODC). (2000). Homicide rates. Data UNODC, https://public.tableau.com/views/Homiciderates_15826327950430 /Homicide-rates?:embed=y&:showVizHome=no&:host_url=https%3A%2F %2Fpublic.tableau.com%2F&:embed_code_version=3&:tabs=no&:toolbar=yes& :animate_transition=yes&:display_static_image=no&:display_spinner=no&:dis- play_overlay=yes&:display_count=yes&:loadOrderID=0.

Yagoub, Mimi. (2017). From Chile to Mexico: Best and worst of LatAm police. *InSight Crime*, September 13, 2017, sec. Analysis. https://www.insightcrime.org/ news/analysis/best-worst-latam-police/.

Chapter 18

The Evolution of Policing in Jamaica

Lorna E. Grant

The Jamaica Constabulary Force (JCF) is the police force of Jamaica. Its mission is "to serve, protect and reassure the people of Jamaica through the delivery of impartial and professional services aimed at: Maintenance of Law and Order, Protection of Life and Property, Prevention and Detection of Crime, and Preservation of Peace." "We serve, we protect, we reassure with courtesy, integrity and proper respect for the rights of all."

Jamaica, like many other Caribbean countries with a colonial past, was influenced by the British system of policing based on its colonial past. In Jamaica, policing dates back to 1716, when night watchmen guarded the cities of Port Royal, Kingston, and the parishes of Saint Andrew and Saint Catherine. In establishing the first permanent police force, William Ramsey, in 1835, was appointed the first Inspector General of the police force. However, since 1835, Jamaica has experienced different eras in policing. This chapter provides a comprehensive overview of the foundation of policing in Jamaica. It focuses on the different changes the Jamaica police force has undergone and is inclusive of its history, structure, administration, legislation, reform, innovation, training, and style of policing. Additionally, attention is given to police corruption, police and society, police brutality, and Jamaica's ranking in the world regarding the police's mode of operation. In conclusion, policy recommendations are included on how the police force can better serve Jamaica's people and guests.

HISTORY OF POLICING IN JAMAICA

Preindependent Era of Policing

Jamaica was a British colony from 1655 to 1962, after which it gained independence as a nation. Along the way, during 1670, Spain, which had some control of the island, formally relinquished its control to the British. Preceding Jamaica's independence in 1962, safety programs focused on the security of the colonial state, its governmental administration, and the business-related interests of the privileged (Harriot, 2000, 2002, 2009). Nevertheless, policing in Jamaica dates back to 1716 when night watch-men guarded the cities of Port Royal, Kingston, and the parishes of Saint Andrew and Saint Catherine. In establishing the first permanent police force, William Ramsey, in 1835, was appointed the first Inspector General of the police force. Under the leadership of William Ramsay, the organization had responsibility for the security of the island until 1865, when the historic Morant Bay Rebellion happened. The Morant Bay Rebellion showed how fragile Jamaica's police were in maintaining peace and law in the country. This led to the creation of an unconventional police force, formally known as the Jamaica Constabulary Force (JCF), which, to date, holds the responsibil-ity for law and order.

The JCF was established in 1867, while still under the British, with 984 sworn officers. Its first Inspector General was appointed by the British Governor over the island. Its mission was to confront challenges and concerns posed by local uprisings which threatened the economic and political classes. Following British policing procedures, the JCF was created to be paramili-tary, reflecting the British approach at the time to Irish unrest (Government of Jamaica [GoJ] 1935, Art. 3 s2 [b] [December 19, 1935]).

Post-Independent Era of Policing

In the postindependent era of policing, residents experienced a different style of policing. Paramilitary-style of policing was the practice, especially in urban areas with crime-prone communities. Jamaica, although being independent, continued to practice the policing style inherited from Britain. In the early post-independence period, democratic practices and democratiz-ing institutions were challenging for a newly independent nation. Although, being a recent colony of Britain, the official style of policing was more indic-ative of the Irish model of policing, which was "policing by control" rather than of the English model which was "policing by consent" (Harriott, 2000). Harriott defines this as "Political Policing" (Amnesty International (AI), July 24, 2014; Harriot, 2000, 2001, 2009a; Leslie, 2010).

Jamaica Constabulary Force Era of Policing

The Jamaica Constabulary Force (JCF) is the official police force of Jamaica and is under the authority of The Ministry of National Security. As defined by Jamaica's penal code, "The JCF is responsible for the maintenance of law and order, the prevention and detection of crime, the investigation of alleged crimes, the protection of life and property and the enforcement of all criminal laws." Additionally, the JCF has the responsibility to provide general assistance to the public. The JCF's mission is "to serve, protect and reassure with courtesy, integrity, and respect for the rights of all." The Citizens' Charter, states "the JCF endeavors to serve its citizens in general service and through the impartial, transparent enforcement of law and order" (Jamaica Gleaner, August 31, 2008). Although the JCF was established in 1867, as the official police force of Jamaica, there was another security entity known as the Island Special Constabulary Force (ISCF) which was a reserve to the arm of the JCF with its administrative structure.

The Island Special Constabulary Force

In 1904, the Special Constabulary was established under the Constables Special Law of 1904 (Ministry of Justice, January 1, 2008). The law made provision for two Justices of the Peace to appoint individuals residing in each parish, who were willing to be appointed Special Constables to act in that role. Special Constables were expected to assist the JCF in the preservation of peace and order. Unlike the JCF, the Special Constables were not given formal training, and there was no hierarchical structure. They were appointed under the orders of the Justice of the Peace, therefore, they were obligated to comply with the law that guided Justices of the Peace unless or until an officer or subofficer of the JCF was present to take command.

Law 18 of 1950, a new act of Jamaica Parliament, established the Island Special Constabulary Force as a permanent organization (U.S. Department of State's Country Reports on Human Rights Practices for 2009). In 1994, the Government of Jamaica approved a merger of the JCF and the ISCF, but this official process was not realized until May 2014 (U.S. Department of State's Country Reports on Human Rights Practices for 2010. Sec. 1d, Jamaica Information Service, March 4, 2014).

STRUCTURE OF THE JCF

Currently, there are approximately 12,000 sworn officers (Jamaica Constabulary Force, 2020). There are five divisions in the JCF. Division one covers four parishes, namely Trelawney, St. James, Westmoreland, and Hanover. Division two covers St. Ann, St. Mary, and Portland. Division three is Clarendon, Manchester, and St. Elizabeth, while Division four is St. Andrew Central, St. Andrew South, Kingston Western, Kingston Central, and

Kingston Eastern. Finally, Division five has St. Andrew North, St. Catherine South, St. Catherine North, and St. Thomas.

Training Division

There are two locations where Jamaica's Constabulary Force officers are trained: Twickenham Park, Spanish Town, St. Catherine, and Harman Barracks Training Wing in Kingston. In 1976, the training division attached to the Mobile Reserve Division in Artillery and fieldcraft was located in Port Royal until relocation to Twickenham Park. With this new location, JCF was able to accommodate all the forms of training to include basic, in-service, and higher training for officers. In 1982, the institution was renamed the Jamaica Police Academy (JPA). Later, in 2014, per a strategic review of the Jamaica Constabulary Force, the National Police College of Jamaica (NPC) was created. This united the efforts of all the training units (the Jamaica Police Academy, the Jamaica Constabulary Staff College (JCSC), the Caribbean Search Centre, the Firearm and Tactical Training Unit, and the Police Driving School) of the Jamaica Constabulary at the Twickenham campus into one unit.

Although located on the same campus, these units functioned independently. There was also a period of rebranding and reorganizing the JCF's existing facilities into novel entities, namely Faculty of Leadership and Professional Development (FLPD), Faculty of Recruit and Probationer Training (FRPT), Faculty of Operations Management, and Skills Training (FOMST), as well as other divisions. The National Police College of Jamaica now offers training to Private Security companies, the Department of Correctional Service, Passport Immigration and Customs Agency, Jamaica Customs Agency, and Fire Brigade Services. These services are extended to regional counterparts in Montserrat, Bermuda, Antigua, and the Cayman Islands (History of NPCJ, 2020).

The minimum length of basic training is six months. Training is delivered in modules and recruits sit four written examinations and twelve practical tests. They are also required to visit selected police stations and parish courts. Upon completion of basic training, there is a passing-out exercise where officers are transferred to two years of probationary training at different divisions under the supervision of the Divisional Training Subofficer. On completion of 18 months of service, they return to the Jamaica Police Academy for an additional 5 weeks of training before going back to their respective divisions to complete the probationary period. A Specialized Operations Branch (formerly Mobile Reserve) is trained in para-military styles of training (Jamaica Constabulary Force).

Specialized Units

The JCF comprised several specialized units. These units include the Anti-Corruption Branch, the Major Organized Crime and Anti-Corruption Agency (MOCA), the Narcotics Division, the Serious and Organized Crime Branch, the Criminal Investigations Branch, The Major Investigation Taskforce (MIT), the Center of Investigation for Sexual Offences and Child Abuse (CISOCA), and The Professional Standards Branch (PSB).

THE INTERNAL AFFAIRS COMPLAINTS DIVISION

The Division pays attention to issues relating to internal investigations and prepares files for the Police Public Complaints Authority (PPCA) with the possibility of getting to the Director of Public Prosecutions (DPP) for a ruling. It also responds to unsatisfactory conduct such as poor service, complaints of abuse, domestic violence, and negligence of responsibility (Jamaica Information Service) (March 18, 2006).

The Internal Affairs Bureau of Special Investigation

This was instituted by an Executive Order of the Government. It directs its attention to the use of force relating to firearms, and corruption in the public sector. Included in their scope of duty is the criminal and administrative investigation, reviewing administrative processes involving the use of firearms, and concerns of the members of the JCF (Jamaica Information Service) (March 18, 2006).

The Corporate Planning Division

This Division has the primary duty of The Corporate Planning, Research, and Development Division to reform and modernize the program of the JCF. The Statistics and Information Management Unit operates out of the Planning, Research, and Development Branch. (Jamaica Information Service) (March 18, 2006).

Other units include the Legal Affairs Department, which handles case preparation, which includes assisting legal counsel with components of their portfolio of responsibility, and which is directed by Attorneys-at-Law who are members of JCF (Jamaica Information Service, March 18, 2006); the Performance Monitoring and Auditing Bureau, which has the responsibility of auditing and monitoring to ensure that procedures are followed, and that the best practices are identified for replication across the Force; and the

National Intelligence Bureau (NIB), which renders intelligence to the officer corps and operational units in the constabulary force, specializing in security intelligence at local and international levels. The NIB and Operation Kingfish merged to form NIB Kingfish to strengthen aspects of the Special Branch, which it replaced. The Bureau was instituted to administer the new approaches utilized by the JCF to increase accountability and effectiveness and establish intelligence-led policing. The formation of a Professional Standards Branch and a Performance Monitoring and Auditing Bureau (PMAB) was an addition to this Bureau (Jamaica Constable Force).

THE COMMUNITY SAFETY AND SECURITY BRANCH

This Branch develops greater partnerships and relationships with neighborhoods toward rebuilding communities plagued by crime and violence to enhance safety. Initiatives to accomplish this include: (a) The Preemptive Violence Interruption Strategy (PVIS), which is aimed at avoiding vigilante justice that aggravates the crime dilemma. Police officers in this unit utilize one-on-one intervention with residents and involve colleagues in investigating difficult cases; (b) "Proximity Policing," a philosophy and strategy of policing on-demand with public consent, which is effective in hotspot areas. Proximity Policing also assists with stabilizing potentially volatile situations, having a presence in the community, and building relationships with residents. Safe Schools Program, Neighborhood Watch, Farmers' Watch, and Business Watch programs are all in this department. This unit was specially designed to get stakeholders, police, and citizens to develop a positive relationship through working collectively (Jamaica Information Service, January 29, 2015).

Reform and Initiatives in the Jamaica Constabulary Force

Harriott (2000) argued that for more than 150 years, the JCF functioned as a colonial institution with a primary purpose of maintaining order and control by applying paramilitary tactics on residents. Furthermore, he maintained that the organization did not act as one serving citizens, despite its motto, "to serve and protect" (Harriott, 2000). Traditionally the JCF was centralized, predominately male, authoritarian. It promoted experienced officers instead of educated officers, with little emphasis on training (Harriott, 2000).

Changing the traditional practices and procedures within the JCF was paramount to effectively fight crime, provide better security for citizens, and improve efficiency in how members undertook their responsibilities. There were efforts to reform the JCF in the 1980s and 1990s, but these were met with much resistance from the sectors of the JCF. Nevertheless, there were incremental changes in organizational structure, personnel, divisions and units, modes of delivering service, and the ways officers undertook their responsibilities.

Although there was partial reform, the prevalence of criminality in Jamaica drew attention at the local, national, and international levels with calls for more improvement. There was a general lack of confidence in the police by residents due to increased incidences of police brutality. Reports in the media were devastating, resulting in more mistrust between the police and citizens. Lack of trust and confidence in the JCF deterred citizens from giving evidence that could assist with investigations and the conviction of criminals. This hampered security and helped in undermining the country's capability to create and sustain a financial system that could maintain satisfactory levels of well-being for most of the residents. With the worsening situation, the consensus was that the JCF needed change.

After years of unsatisfactory performance, and complaints against members of JCF, in 2007, the Ministry of National Security (MNS) under which the JCF reports, appointed a strategic evaluation of the JCF. A Justice System Reform Project (JJSR) was convened. National and international experts were commissioned to do a strategic review of the organization. The directive was to establish a new concept for the security governance of Jamaica, by reviewing the governance, management structures, key infrastructure, standards, and performance of the JCF (Ministry of National Security, 2007).

From the review, several policy recommendations for reform were presented and implemented. They included the enhancement of accountability mechanisms governing operations; developing professionalism, efficiency, and enhanced competence of the entire organization; the establishment of appropriate standards in recruitment, training, and professional development to ensure adherence to internationally accepted best practices; improvement of public confidence in policing, and review of the legislative and administrative framework governing the JCF, including the Jamaica Constabulary Force Act (Ministry of National Security, 2007).

Other areas of focus were improving the investigative capabilities of the police as there had been a longstanding lack of capacity to investigate a large volume of cases. This meant developing forensic expertise and having related resources. Abuse of citizens who come into conflict with the law was another pivotal area of concern. So too was encouraging the contributions of police to successful prosecutions. This meant an intensification of the investigative authorities of the police, therefore, legal reform was essential to benefit from new scientific and technological advances, such as the use of DNA testing.

The task force recommended that independent forensic laboratories eliminate the perception that their facilities were under the instructions of the Director of Public Prosecutions. It was further recommended that cases should be prioritized to avoid delays in obtaining forensic reports while adopting the practice of excluding illegally attained evidence. An additional recommendation was for more collaboration with other pertinent agencies to enhance ID parades, the reorganization of the procedure for the delivery of medical certificates. (Ministry of National Security, 2007).

Regarding the inadequacy of police contribution to prosecutions, there were challenges with the identification of witnesses and failure of witnesses to attend court which resulted in cases being delayed. Police Court-Liaison Officers would give their assistance when needed along with civilian staff members. Communication between the police and prosecutors posed a challenge, requiring that such occurred electronically outside the regular working hours to help in advancing cases. The idea pursued was that if there is a uniform checklist outlining the case and evidence against the accused by the police as Crown briefs, cases would not be delayed in the system.

From the strategic review, more funds were given to fight crime, specialized units were created, and there was a new mode of operations for officers. For example, in relating to citizen's statements or grievances, they were not given prompt consideration. Likewise, reports of domestic disputes related to women were considered disreputable (Ministry of National Security, 2007). To help in crime-fighting, in 2009, with the assistance of funding from the Department for International Development, $50 million was injected into the JCF budget to support the Reform Program. The funds went into the purchase of four mobile labs, a Police College, the training of over 700 personnel in "leadership and accountability" capacity building; the purchasing of two buses and equipment (computers, office furniture, crime scene tents, fingerprint processing equipment, Computer-Aided Design (CAD) systems, projectors, forensic equipment, etc.) for the Serious and Organized Crime Division and Performance Management Appraisal System (PMAS) (Jamaica Information Service, February 23, 2015).

Overall, the recommendations of the task force confirmed the notion that a reform of the JCF will play an important role in increasing the efficiency of the criminal justice system, building the confidence of the citizenry, reducing the delay in cases, and responding to concerns of residents. There were also changes in police management. For example, how officers could be dismissed from their jobs; as the termination of officers for any reason was rare. For an officer to be terminated, the violation had to be extremely egregious. Likewise, the resignations of officers were seldom accepted (Ministry of National Security, 2007). Quoting Active Voice:

> Resignations from the police force were not as easily granted as they are now, some constables, it was reported, actually misbehaved to be sacked, and thus get

a chance to leave. It was then reported that many men who got out of the force in this and other ways were prevented from leaving the island by the action of officers of the Criminal Investigation Branch CIB. (February 19, 2008)

The new Constabulary Force Act provides specific guidelines about registrations. Subofficers and constables must give six months' notice of their intent to leave the force. Failure to do so would result in either a $250,000 fine or three months in prison. In 2010, it was reported by the Jamaica Gleaner that in less than 5 years, 900 policemen and women resigned (Jamaica Gleaner, March 21, 2010). The Economic and Social Survey of Jamaica as of December 31, 2016, reported that 549 officers left the Force and 71.4 percent were due for resignation. The absence from work in the JCF was a normal occurrence.

Police Corruption and Misconduct

Globally, corruption has been found in police departments. This can be external (bribery, extortion, stealing money, drugs, and weapons, accepting money in exchange for not enforcing the law), as well as internal corruption (from ignoring criminal activities of other police officers to protecting criminals such as drug dealers). Jamaica's police force is not immune to corrupting influences. The perception of police corruption tarnishes the public image of law enforcement. Sherman (1978) argued that when police are involved in corruption, it distracts from the recognized goals of the organization and may lead to "the use of organizational power to encourage and create crime rather than to deter it" (Sherman, 1978).

Jamaica like many other countries has incarcerated police officers if found to be involved in corruption. For example, in 2019, The Jamaica Gleaner headline read, "Police Inspector, Constables Arrested for Corruption" (Jamaica Gleaner, September 13, 2019) and in 2020, "Constable Garth Davis was sentenced to life in prison" and "Christopher Smith sentenced to six years and 10 months for the shooting of Omar Marshall" in 2009 (Radio Jamaica, January 8, 2020). In 2019, Jamaica pollster Bill Johnson found that over 50 percent of Jamaica's police was perceived to be corrupt. Corruption was so bad in the police force that it prompted the Minister of National Security to threaten to revamp the Early Retirement Scheme for police officers as a strategy of purging corrupt members of JCF.

Indeed, with the formation of the Major Organized Crime and Anti-Corruption (MOCA) Task Force 2012, more police officers found themselves in conflict with the law. For example, in 2017, MOCA arrested twenty-four policemen, of which seventeen were involved in corruption. Five of the seventeen arrests were for breaches of the Dangerous Drugs Act. The Office of the Director of Public Prosecutions (DPP) highlighted that there had been a decrease in cases involving police officers from eighty-two in 2008 to twenty-five in 2016 and fourteen in 2015. In 2018, the number of corruption files obtained by the DPP's office compared to 2017 against the JCF continued to be on the decline. Even though there was a reduction in cases against police officers, there were still challenges in the JCF. The officer-in-charge of the Independent Commission of Investigations (INDECOM) acknowledged that the "code of silence" was a fixture of the JCF, which indicates that many cases may go unreported. Terrence Williams, head of INDECOM, expressed it bluntly when he said, "The code of silence in the JCF is on steroids." (Jamaica Observer, July 16, 2020)

The JCF's Internal Disciplinary Arm, the Inspectorate of Constabulary (IOC), another division established in the restructuring of the organization, noted 628 complaints against JCF in 2018, an increase from 606 in 2016 (Jamaica Gleaner March 2018). Related news headlines included: "Constable Marlon Campbell Charged for Attempting to Pervert the Course of Justice CPA" (Jamaica Observer, Thursday, July 16, 2020: Constable Euwitt on Robbery and Aggravation Charges Offered Bail (MOCA July 13, 2020)). Although there is wide publicity of corruption in JCF, most of its members are law-abiding, loyal Jamaicans who work conscientiously to serve the citizenry. With the introduction of the Independent Commission of Investigations (INDECOM), another new division recommended by the strategic review, the JCF has experienced a more positive review from citizens regarding corruption in the agency (Jamaica Observer, February 14, 2019).

Police and Society

Despite improvements in public perceptions of the police, there are still news headlines about police killings and recently, post–George Floyd's killing in the United States, there are frequent calls for the rebuilding of trust between police and citizens in Jamaica. While some citizens believe that they are victimized by the police, the police insist that they care about law and order. Contrary to their motto "To Protect and Serve," officers, at times, fail to embrace the word "serve." Citizens understand the dangers and challenge police encounters, although the law must be applied when necessary. Amnesty International (April 2001) maintained that when police officers are not held to account for their actions, police brutality thrives. Research shows that when police help in solving community problems, their legitimacy is embraced; hence, voluntary cooperation helps to solve crimes (Tyler, 1990/2006).

With each negative headline, there is always a call for reform and the rebuilding of trust between the police and citizens. One strategy that was used to rebuild the trust was the introduction of the Community Relations

Division of the JCF. Intermittently, however, there is a positive headline of police–citizen interaction.

Police–community relations are primary in Jamaica's policing future. In the late 1990s, the force began to shift from being a reactive, paramilitary policing entity to embracing community-based policing. Nevertheless, it was not until 2008 that the approach was fully embraced and actively operationalized for a cultural shift within and outside the JCF.

The Community Safety and Security Branch

The CSSB has a Community Policing Unit, and all officers are expected to embrace the philosophy. With the full operation of the unit, Jamaica saw a reduction in crime; however, the approach's paramilitary policing was not replaced, but merely supplemented. Numerous published research, including the JCF's research, determined that the parenting style of policing was a deterrent to building positive relationships in communities, with community policing being essential to preventing crime. A call to strengthening community policing followed.

Research conducted by the Overseas Development Institute, a UK-based independent think tank on international development and humanitarian issues highlighted that "community policing in Jamaica has been shaped by many contextual factors, including, in particular, high levels of violent crime, which have been fueled by socioeconomic problems." The heightened violence encouraged the continuation of paramilitary styles of policing that emerged from histories of slavery and colonialism and has perpetuated a deep mistrust of the police among many community members, especially in the urban communities most affected by crime. High levels of violent crime and perceptions of police corruption have weakened police–community relations and meant that reliance on informal security structures has become ingrained in local cultures of protection. (Overseas Development Institute [ODI], May 2014).

Subsequently, the JCF's corporate strategy mandated community policing in its crime-fighting efforts. The message on the official website of the JCF read "the traditional style of policing used in Jamaica and many other countries for many years is not suitable to deliver modern policing and community safety services." The website further stated: "The demands of our modern age require that the police act in partnership with the public and with other public, private, and voluntary sector organizations to deliver collaborative services that address crime, fear of crime, and other safety issues which concern communities. Community policing is central to the concept of community safety" (Jamaica Gleaner, February 12, 2015).

Given a dire need for resident's support, cooperation, and assistance in solving crime, community policing strategies were strengthened in 2018. The

Commissioner of Police, Major General Antony Anderson, acknowledged at the time, that it was not possible for police to solve or prevent crime without the community's help. Along with the effort, he stated that a system would be introduced that would allow complaints to be heard and would render feedback on time, to increase the quality of police service (Jamaica Information Service, May 24, 2018).

Strategies used to strengthen community relations included: The training of police officers to effectively respond to citizen's complaints, improving community-based networks to reinforce crime-prevention, using civilian information of crime, and integrating dynamic neighborhood programs. This holistic approach was intended to build better relationships with communities, address issues such as civilian control, and enforce public order by police. Toward building trust and citizen satisfaction, police were obligated to engage the public. This was through community walks, understanding the community's priorities and preferences, engaging all segments of society, and utilizing community social development programs to elicit citizens' help in solving crime. Noted by Superintendent Michael Slack in 2018, "It is important for policing agencies to ensure 'visible' accountability in all aspects of service delivery and member conduct, via both internal and external processes to engage the public through the use of tools such as community walk-throughs, understanding the priorities and preferences of different segments of society and community social development programs to get the support of the people to solve the crime" (Jamaica Information Service, May 24, 2018).

Policing Culture

Jamaica Constable Force, like most other organizations, has developed a unique organizational culture. This culture which encompasses values, beliefs, and practices is passed on to the recruits who oftentimes embrace it. With this culture, the Jamaican public perceives police culture to be organizationally centered with minimum consideration for the public. JCF was viewed as an organization that has low accountability, is resistant to change, male-dominated, and lacks the trust and respect of citizens. However, in divisions where there were effective leaders and management, complaints were less about the organization's culture, but more about organizational structure.

Before the restructuring, fear, intimidation, lack of responsibility, dogmatism, reluctance to change, favoritism, lack of transparency, lack of strategies to engage officers, objection to alternative views, and reliance on rules and guides dictated JCF functioning.

The behavior exhibited by rank-and-file members discouraged self-discipline and principle-based behavior, rather it promoted externally enforced discipline. Traditionally, authority and power were not normally shared, but the restructuring of the organization made a difference. New divisions were created, which allowed for less time in navigating the chain of command, the identification and processing of corruption, more transparency, along with the evaluation, promotion, and accountability of officers in all divisions.

Despite efforts to address the dominant culture, JCF still has strong subcultures that have manifested themselves in groupings and affiliations such as senior and middle management and rank and file officers, with each group having its unique subculture. There are small groups of officers who share the same backgrounds, skills, and perceptions; and are closely knitted. Indubitably, this impacts communications, the manifestation of power, and authority in relationships (Jamaica Gleaner, February 12, 2015).

CONCLUSION

Despite the numerous positive gains by police in Jamaica in recent years, tensions still exist between police and society. Given the nature of policing, public support is desirable. Citizens having a positive attitude toward police help with fighting crime and support policies and programs to protect residents. The integration of the community in policing is fundamental to effective policing. Brain (2016, p. 47), maintained, that when communication is ignored, it is to the peril of individual officers or agencies. This means that if the police do not interact with residents, especially in crime-prone neighborhoods, it will be more difficult to solve crimes and enact legislation. Crime is a societal problem that requires a societal response.

A problem-solving approach is necessary to identify the causes of crimes in communities and to resolve them. Moreover, police must be seen as good moral citizens displaying integrity for citizens to change their negative perceptions of them and to choose to engage with them. The police must also be viewed as effective and sufficiently resourced to perform or these vulnerabilities can fracture community relations. Further, the JCF must continue to adapt modern policing techniques as they evolve or fall behind in their efforts to reduce crime.

RECOMMENDATIONS

1. *Rebuilding Communities to foster better relationships between police and citizens.* It is important to rebuild communities with stakeholders' input. Community members must work with the police to ensure the restoration of peace and tranquility in communities. This can be accomplished through police engaging residents in town hall meetings and community activities such as sports, mentorship programs, and summer

camps to improve relations between the police and citizens. That is where the rebuilding of respect, trust, and confidence begins with police becoming a part of solutions.

2. *Developing strategies and programs to enhance police effectiveness.* The JCF must evaluate their current strategy of policing with the view of developing new strategies to effectively combat crime without abusing law-abiding citizens in crime-prone areas. For example, the utilization of the Geographic Information System. As noted by Diamond (2004, pg. 42), crime-mapping technology has given law enforcement agencies the intelligence needed to effectively deploy officers to prevent crime.

3. *Building the capacity of the Jamaica Constable Force Training College.* The Ministry of Security and the JCF should take steps to strengthen the capacity of the Training College to offer new training courses that will allow police to be more effective.

4. *Recruiting people with integrity and good moral standards.* Although recruits must pass an entrance examination, a test on an antecedent investigation, a physical test, a medical evaluation, and psychological screening, before basic training and should also have critical and analytical skills, it is important to realize that the integrity and morals candidates bring to the organization are of vital importance. Greater care in recruiting officers with integrity and high morals should help to combat police corruption.

REFERENCES

Active Voice. (February 19, 2008). Jamaica Constabulary Force under pressure. Retrieved June 1. 2020, https://anniepaul.net/category/police-corruption/.

Amnesty International (AI). (July 24, 2014). Jamaica must act with full transparency on allegations of human rights violations. (AMR 38/003/2014). Retrieved May 9, 2015, https://www.amnesty.org/download/Documents/4000/amr380032014en.pdf.

Centre for the Investigation of Sexual Offences and Child. Accessed June 15, 2020 https://evaw-global-database.unwomen.org/en/.

Communities and Transforming Policing Cultures: A Desk Study of Community Policing in Jamaica. Retrieved June 1. 2020, https://www.odi.org/publications/8426-securing-communities-and-transforming-policing-cultures-desk-study-community-policing-jamaica.

Constabulary Force Act. Retrieved March 12, 2020, https://www.refworld.org/docid/4d2abae22.html.

Criminal Investigations Branch-Jamaica Constable Force. Retrieved June 1, 2020. https://www.jcf.gov.jm/portfolio-item/criminal- investigations-branch.

Government of Jamaica (GoJ), (1935), Art. 3 s2(b). (December 19, 1935). Constabulary Force Act Retrieved June 22, 2020 https://moj.gov.jm/laws/constabulary-force-act.

Harriott, Anthony. (2002). Crime trends in the Caribbean and responses. *United Nations Office on Drugs and Crime.*

Harriott, Anthony. (2009). *Controlling Violent Crime: Models and Policy Options.* Gracekennedy Foundation.

History of NPCJ. (2020). Retrieved June 1, 2020, http://npcj.edu.jm/en/about/history.

Island Special Constabulary Force (ISCF). https://en.wikipedia.org/wiki/Island_Special_Constabulary_Force.

Jamaica Constable Force. https://www.mns.gov.jm/jamaica-constabulary-force.

Jamaica Constable Force, Narcotic Division, Jamaica Constable Force. Retrieved June 4, 2020, https://www.jcf.gov.jm/portfolio-item/narcotics-division Jamaica.

Jamaica Constabulary Force. Community Safety and Security Branch. 1st ed. *Manual for Community Policing Services Delivery.* Retrieved March 12, 2020, https://www.refworld.org/docid/4d2abae22.html 1935 (amended 2002).

Jamaica Constabulary Force. (2020). Office of Commissioner of Police, Retrieved March 12, 2020, https://www.govserv.org/JM/Kingston/177006552362668/Jamaica-Constabulary-Force.

Jamaica Gleaner. (March 21, 2010). Cops quit close to 900 policemen and women resigns in less than five years. Retrieved June 1, 2020, http://jamaica-gleaner.com/gleaner/20100321/news/news1.html.

Jamaica Gleaner. (August 31, 2008). Police Citizens' Charter. Retrieved June 1, 2020. http://old.jamaica-gleaner.com/gleaner/20080831/letters/letters2.html.

Jamaica Gleaner. (February 12, 2015). Community policing in Jamaica. http://jamaica-gleaner.com/article/western-focus/20150214/community-policing-jamaica.

Jamaica Gleaner. (March 2018). Corruption cases against cops decline but…INDECOM concerned that code of silence could allow corrupt police to go unpunished. Retrieved May 31, 2020. http://jamaica-gleaner.com/article/lead-stories/20180318/corruption-cases-against -cops- decline-indecom-concerned-code-silence.

Jamaica Gleaner. (September 13, 2019). Police inspector, constables arrested for corruption. Retrieved May 31, 2020, http://jamaica-gleaner.com/article/news/20190913/police-inspector-constables-arrested-corruption.

Jamaica Information Service. (October 26, 2017). The Law Reform (Zones of Special Operations) (Special Security and Community Development Measures) Law. Retrieved May 31, 2020, https://jis.gov.jm/information/get-the-facts/law-reform-zones-special-operations-special-security-community-development-measures-law/.

Jamaica Information Service. (February 23, 2015). $50 Million for JCF Reform Programme. Retrieved May 1, 2020, https://jis.gov.jm/50-million-jcf-reform-programme/.

Jamaica Information Service. (January 29, 2015). Get the facts: Community Safety and Security Branch (CSSB) practicing smart policing. Retrieved May 1, 2020, https://www.odi.org/publications/8426-securing-communities-and-transforming-policing-cultures-desk-study-community-policing-jamaica.

Jamaica Information Service. (February 15, 2018). Laws to be "Strengthened to Fight Crime," Retrieved June 1, 2020, jis.gov.jm/laws-strengthened-fight-crime/.

Jamaica Information Service. (February 16, 2009). Major Investigations Task Force to expand operations beyond corporate area. Retrieved June 1, 2020, https://jis.gov .jm/major- investigations-task-force-to-expand-operations-beyond-corporate-area/.

Jamaica Information Service. (May 24, 2018.) JCF strengthening community policing strategies. Retrieved June 15, 2020, https://jis.gov.jm/jcf-strengthening-community -policing-strategies/.

Jamaica Information Service. (March 4, 2014). Cabinet approves merger of JCF and ISCF. Retrieved June 1, 2020, https://jis.gov.jm/cabinet-approves-merger-jcf-iscf/.

Jamaica Information Service. (March 18, 2006). Professional Standards Branch getting support from Jamaicans to rid JCF of corrupt cops. Retrieved June 1, 2020, https://jis.gov.jm/professional-standards-branch-getting-more-support-from -jamaicans-to-rid-jcf-of-corrupt-cops-2/.

Jamaica Observer. (February 15, 2018). Throne Speech: Police Service Act to replace Constabulary Force Act. Retrieved June 6, 2020, http://www.jamaicaobserver.com /latestnews/%23ThroneSpeech:__Police_Service_Act_to_replace_Constabulary _Force_Act?profile=1228.

Jamaica Observer. (February 14, 2019). Corruption haunts police force. Retrieved May 31, 2020, www.jamaicaobserver.com/news/corruption-haunts.

Jamaica Observer. (July 16, 2020). Constable Marlon Campbell charged for attempt-ing to pervert the course of justice. Retrieved May 1, 2020, http://www.jamaicaob-server.com/latestnews/Constable_Marlon_Campbell_charged?profile=0.

Leslie, Glaister. (2010). Confronting the don: The political economy of gang violence in Jamaica. Retrieved May 1, 2020. http://smallarmssurvey.org/fileadmin/docs/B -Occasional-papers/SAS-OP26-Jamaica- gangs.pdf.

Major organised crime and anti-corruption agency: No one. Retrieved June 13, 2020, https://moca.gov.jm.

Ministry of National Security. (2008). A new era of policing in Jamaica: Transforming the JCF. *Report of the JCF Strategic Review Panel*. Retrieved March 12, 2020. https://www.refworld.org/docid/4d2abae22.html.

Ministry of Justice. (January 1, 2008). Constables (Special) Act. Retrieved March 12, 2020, https://moj.gov.jm/laws/constables-special-act.

Major Organised Crime and Anti-Corruption Agency (MOCA). (July 13, 2020). Constable Euwitt on robbery and aggravation charges offered bail. Retrieved June 1, 2020, https://moca.gov.jm/news-release-constable-euwitt-on-robbery-and -aggravation-charges- offered-bail/.

Narcotic Division, Jamaica Constable Force. https://www.jcf.gov.jm/portfolio-item/ narcotics-division.

Nationwide News. (October 2, 2014). New NIB director. Retrieved May 31, 2020, https://nationwideradiojm.com/new-nib-.

Overseas Development Institute (ODI). (May 2014). Victoria Chambers. Securing.

Police Service (Amendment) Act. (2007). Retrieved March 18, http://www.ttparlia-ment.org/legislations/a2007-13.pdf.

Radio Jamaica, (January 8, 2020). Police officer sentenced to life in prison for 2009 murder. Retrieved June 1, 2020, http://radiojamaicanewsonline.com/local/police -officer-sentenced-to- life-in-prison-for-2009-murder.

Sherman, Lawrence W. (1978). *Scandal and Reform: Police Corruption.* University of California Press.

Transnational Crime and Narcotics Division to be renamed Narcotics Division. February 23, 2015. Retrieved March 12, 2020. http://jamaica-gleaner.com/article/20150223/transnational-crime-and-narcotics-division-be-renamed-narcotics-division.

Tyler, Perry. (1990/2006). Police brutality. Retrieved March 12, 2020, https://www.bing.com/images/search?q=police+brutality+-+tyler+1990%2f2006+tyler%2c+t.%2c+2006+)&qpvt=police+brutality+-+Tyler+1990%2f2006Tyler%2c+T.%2c+2006)&form=IGRE&first=1&scenario=ImageHoverTitle.

United States (U.S.) Department of State's Country Reports on Human Rights Practices for 2009. Jamaica: Structure and Hierarchy of Jamaica.

Chapter 19

The Organization and Functioning of Police Forces in Brazil

Leandro Piquet Carneiro

MAPPING BRAZILIAN LAW
ENFORCEMENT INSTITUTIONS

The Brazilian criminal justice system encompasses the three levels of the Federation, articulates different organs from the Executive and the Judiciary branches, and is organized into three main fronts: public security (police forces), prosecution and justice, and correction system. The Constitution promulgated in 1988, after the military regime of 1964–1985, defined the current organization of the criminal justice system in Brazil. Following the country's civil law, the existing police forces derive their authority from the national Constitution through the following bodies: a federal police force, federal highway police, federal railway police, federal prison police, state civil police, state military police, and state prison police. In addition, the municipalities are responsible for creating local municipal guards, bodies with only limited police powers. Civil and military police forces are state-level institutions regulated by state laws and constitutions. Since Brazil is a federal republic formed by the Union of twenty-six federal states and the Federal District, fifty-four state police forces are responsible for policing and performing crime control and investigation activities. At the local level, 60 percent of the 5,000 municipalities (993 municipalities) have a municipal guard (IBGE, 2012). Brazilian federalism is quite distinct from the United States, and states are not allowed to pass any penal legislation or change the organization of police forces. Municipal governments, although recognized as part of the Federation, did not have a constitutional mandate to institute a security police organ. The Municipal Guard typically provides security services on local government facilities. Still, in recent years, the Municipal Guards considerably expanded its role in law enforcement activities. A new federal law from 2014 authorized it to carry out preventive patrolling activities, a significant change from the original Constitutional design. This change was primarily motivated by mayors and local administrations in the face of the overwhelming pressure of violence and rising crime rates in Brazil (Pereira Filho, Alves, & Souza, 2018; IPEA, 2019).[1] The social demand for a more adequate and effective response to public security problems led to this significant institutional adaptation.

In addition to these agencies, the Office of the Public Prosecutor (OPP) achieved the competence to promote, by its authority, criminal investigations.[2] The Federal OPP is notably diligent on political corruption cases, and the state's OPPs are responsible for the investigation of serious organized crime. Both Federal and state's OPPs are vested in the external control of police activities. As a result, criminal offenses committed by police officers and the constitutional rights of prisoners in direct custody of the police authorities are monitored and investigated by the Federal and local OPPs. There is no formal subordination of the police forces to the OPP at the national or state levels. However, if the prosecutor verifies any disciplinary faults, the prosecutor reports to the superiors about the offending police officer and proposes the appropriate legal sanctions.

The Brazilian criminal justice system is gradually changing from an inquisitorial to a more adversarial model under the 1988 Constitutional rule. However, judges and magistrates play a substantial role in the criminal justice system, especially in the investigation process and sentencing proceedings (Lopes Jr., 2018). In Brazil, the criminal courts are organized into National and State levels. Federal Courts and Federal Regional Courts deal with interjurisdictional crimes and crimes against the Union. At the state level, judges and States Courts of Justice administrate most of the criminal cases in the country. Public Defender's Office at the national and state levels handles the every-day adjudication of the criminal justice system, providing legal assistance to indigent defendants.

The National Penal Execution Law regulates the correction system managed by the National Council for Criminal and Penitentiary Policy, the National Penitentiary Department, and a new prison police force created in 2019 by a Constitutional Amendment[3] with the mission to escort inmates and secure state and federal prisons.[4] These institutions advise the Ministry of Justice and propose the criminal policy guidelines for the national correctional system. The idea of resocialization of offenders normatively inspired the design of the correctional system. Overcrowded facilities where 773,000 prisoners occupy 461,000 prison spots[5] and the national spread of gang prisons turn the prison system into a significant threat to law enforcement agencies.

National Police Forces

The four federal police forces are the judicial police (Departamento de Polícia Federal), highway police (Polícia Rodoviária Federal), the railway police (with only legal existence), and the prison police (Polícia Penitenciária Nacional). The Federal Police operational focus is on the illicit trafficking of drugs, other transnational crimes, and, mostly, political corruption. Maritime, air, and border policing are among its constitutional attributions. The "Delegados de Polícia," a police officer with a law degree and five months of training at the National Police Academy, take up the higher positions at the federal police department. Investigators and forensic specialists enter the force in a different career path that does not allowed them to become high-rank police officers. This twofold career path is a common characteristic of the Brazilian law enforcement system, both at the national and state levels.

The Federal Highway Police is the road safety police authority responsible for carrying out patrol activities along federal highways against drug trafficking and other types of crime. Although the 1988 Constitution established the Federal Railway Police, the Congress did not vote the legislation needed to regulate the organization of this police force, and, as a result, there is no public institution in Brazil dedicated to policing the railways. A union-like association advocates, without success, for the right to deliver security services to the federal railway authority, and to be recognized as a police force. The Federal Prison Police is the newest law enforcement agency created in the country—only in 2019—to overview two thousand inmates at the federal prison system.

The National Secretary of Public Security (SENASP) is responsible for promoting the integration of law enforcement agencies in the country for planning, monitoring, and evaluating the federal government public security policies. Since its creation in 1997, SENASP amplified its policy and operational capacity, stimulating and providing technical assistance to national and state police forces and even supporting the municipal initiatives in public security. SENASP manages the National Public Security Information System (INFOSEG) and the National Coordination System for Public Security (SUSP), a program that promotes the coordination between local and national law enforcement institutions. The ambitious idea behind SUSP is the search for a national integrated managing model for public security.

The states and municipalities that join the National Coordination System sign a protocol of intentions with the Ministry of Justice and Public Security, creating an integrated management office at the state level with representatives from the national and state police forces and municipal guards. A National Steering Committee monitors and evaluates the proposed policies and supports it through the National Public Security Fund, created in 2000, shortly after the first National Public Security Plan.

Finally, it is necessary to consider the National Public Security Force (FNSP), created in November 2004, and inspired by the United Nations (UN) peacekeeping forces. The National Force did not operate permanently; it borrowed its police officers from other law enforcement agencies and depends exclusively on the cooperation between Federal states. The states voluntarily join the program and decide, according to states' operational capacity, the number and when to send their officers to join the National Security Force. The Minister of Justice and Public Security, at the request of the state governor, orders the mobilization and deployment of the National Force. Every year a new group of 150 to 200 police officers sent by the states is trained according to the operational standards of the National Force. After a brief training period, they return to their home states and remain available for future deployment.

STATE LEVEL POLICE FORCES

The Brazilian "military police" is a gendarme style police force. Its organization evolved throughout the twentieth century largely inspired by Europeans and Latin American police forces like the Gendarmerie Nationale from France,[6] the Guarda Nacional Republicana from Portugal, the Gendarmeria Nacional Argentina, and other National Police Forces from Latin America. Military police forces are responsible for patrolling, responding to emergency calls, and preventing crime. They are de-facto subordinate to the state governments and are usually under the public security secretary authority. There are currently twelve ranks, from private to colonel, mirroring the Brazilian Army organization, except for the General position, which does not exist in the police. The commander-in-chief of the military police in the states has the rank of colonel. According to the Constitution, the military police is an auxiliary force of the Army and could be deployed in the face of external military conflict or civil war. Even though this constitutional provision has not been used by any government so far, in practical terms, this legal disposition is compatible with the gendarme nature of the military police force, as a standard provision in the face of international and domestic civil conflicts. What is necessary to highlight is that there is no direct or hierarchical link between the Army and the military police forces, except when national sovereignty is at stake.

To illustrate this point, consider the military regime and the 1967 Brazilian Constitution. Even then, under the rule of five consecutive Army Generals appointed as Presidents, the military police were largely preserved as state-level law enforcement agencies responding to governors and commanded by local police officers. This legal aspect reveals a bitter controversy among researchers and advocacy organizations that stand for the police "demilitarization." This is addressed further on in this chapter. The ranks at the military police correspond to the Brazilian Army. Police officers with command authority enter the force after a two-to-four-year training at a military police academy and start the career at the rank of lieutenant. The highest rank is colonel. Police officers in charge of patrol are enlisted after a three-to-twelve-month training as privates and could reach first-class sergeant position. Briefly, officers at the military police follow two separate career pathways: command positions are reserved for high ranking officers while low ranking officers are not eligible for leadership positions.

The other state-level police force that plays a major role in the Brazilian criminal justice system is the civil police, the judiciary-investigative branch of the local criminal justice system. Along with the military police, they formed two separate and independent institutions, with different careers, attributions, and organizations at the law enforcement system. A "Delegado de Polícia" heads the civil police departments and the police stations at the local level. The police officer selected by a public tender to hold this position must have a law degree and complete a short training period at a local police training center.[7]

The civil police chief does not need to have any previous experience with ordinary police work. This was due to scarcity of local judiciary representatives or town judges at the depopulated Brazilian interior (Viana, 1949).[8] In the past, the civil police chief was a public servant who was literate in law and was available to provide essential legal services to enhance the law enforcement activities (Holloway, 1993). Currently, the civil police chief manages police stations, plans, controls, and coordinates the judiciary police activities such as the investigation of criminal activities, arrests, execution of orders issued by judges, and initiation of investigations. They are not responsible for patrol or other police emergency services as those are the responsibility of the Military Police.

Even though the career patterns of the Civil Police differ from one state to another, there is a common distinction between the police chief (Delegado) and the lower ranking police officers who conduct investigations, serve as clerks, and do forensic work. None of these officers are eligible to become a police chief (Delegado) by merit or promotion unless they get legal training at a law school and go through public concours for the position of the police chief. Thus, they follow a different and parallel career track separate from the police chief track. In some states, the forensic unit forms an independent Scientific Police, but in most states, these activities are performed by the Civil Police.

THREATS AND EMERGING ISSUES

The problems facing law enforcement agencies in Brazil are many and complex. The first and more pervasive one is the diffuse presence of organized crime in Brazil, manifested through many illegal activities such as arms and drug trafficking, bank robbery, biopiracy, smuggling, product falsification, and human trafficking. National border patrols have not been successful in controlling these evolving challenges. Brazil is among the largest cocaine users globally (Abdalla et al., 2014; Bastos & Bertoni, 2014). The county's extensive border with Colombia, Peru, and Bolivia, the three most notable global cocaine exporters, and the traffic routes through Paraguay make border management a significant operational challenge. This puts tremendous pressure on Brazilian law enforcement institutions. There is also an extensive presence of organized crime within the legitimate business and official government activities, including financial transactions, state bureaucracy, police services, and local politics (Carneiro, 2010). To understand why the country entered this corridor of problems, it is important to consider both the historical characteristics that led the criminal justice system to adopt its current institutional design and the political choices made in the transition to Democracy in the 1980s.

THE INHERED CHOICES

The Brazilian criminal justice system consolidated its current structure gradually during its historical evolution. The role of state-level institutions and the tensions between national and local elites were key players. National security policy coordination agencies, such as the SENASP and SUS, are relatively new and have only limited influence at the local level. Despite the rise in federal participation, the main players in security policies are still the state governments. Historically, the political disputes between the national executive and the local elites, and the pressure presented by the social and economic realities of a conservative society based on slavery, drove the process of creating local police forces in Brazil.

The solution was to decentralize the administration of the law enforcement institutions but, at the same time, keep the national Executive branch and the Congress as the policymakers with veto power over states' choices. The institutional design of the law enforcement system was nationally conceived and encrusted at all national constitutions after Brazil's independence in 1822. States can administer the system but they cannot decide how to organize it to fit local necessities adequately.

As a result of this historical process, Brazil has a fragmented policing system. The first crime response officer is generally a military police officer, who must report the crime to a judicial police officer, who, in turn, initiates the criminal indictment process. After the civil police investigation, the public prosecutor conducts the felony prosecution before a judge, following an inquisitorial rite of criminal justice. This fragmented police system is a controversial aspect of the Brazilian criminal justice system. Legal reform initiatives have proposed the unification of both police forces under a civilian organization. Critics of the current institutional arrangement point to the inherent inefficiency produced by two different institutions, with deep antagonism, forced to cooperate to prevent and solve crimes. Split between two competing organization, ordinary police services, such as patrol, emergency response, proactive policing and criminal investigation, are hardly connected, ineffective, and consumes a considerable amount of scarce public resources.

A second recalcitrant issue is the organization of the military police as a gendarme force and the community-police relations. For most critics of the actual institutional arrangement, Brazil has not overcome the negative influence of the military regime on police forces. It is a shared common political doctrine that "the country has not yet managed to bring the principles of justice, peace, development and equity to important sections of the population" (Souza, 2015). The military police is often portrayed as an organization intrinsically ill-suited to serve society. Militaries, analysts fear, are averse to any form of external control and transparency and tend to patronize civilians (Zaverrucha, 2005). They call for the demilitarization of the military police and a merger of the same with the civil police (Bicudo, 2000). In the last three decades, the National Congress evaluated more than 130 bills and Amendments to the Constitution with a view to changing the organization of the state's police forces. They all failed. The pressure of corporatism—not only from the military police but also from the civil police—defeated the most ambitious attempts at legislative reform.

The plea that Brazil is facing a trend toward the militarization of public security has gained momentum at the national political debate. A capital aspect of this debate has been the new legislation (passed in 1999 and 2001)[9] that regulated the assistance of the Armed Forces at the Law and Order Guarantee Operations (GLO). These special operations—episodic and temporary—are strictly regulated and require the support of other constitutional bodies. The National Army is unable to start a GLO based on its own accord. The President could employ the Armed Forces in a GLO either directly on its initiative or at the request of the heads of the other constitutional bodies such as the Presidents of the Supreme Federal Court, the Federal Senate, or the House of Representatives. Although the GLO are under civilian control, they are not to be confused with other such initiatives in Latin America of public security militarization.

While the intended macro-institutional reforms of the criminal justice system discussed earlier are not taking place, it is essential to look closely at the public policies that help to reconfigure how the police forces operate in the country. Since the 2000s, more innovative and consistent public security policies have appeared in some states. The state of São Paulo, the most populous in Brazil, is an outlier in this regard. The incarceration rate in São Paulo is above the national average with 508 inmates per 100 thousand inhabitants.[10] It also has the lowest national homicide rate at 9.5 homicides per 100 thousand population. The State of São Paulo went from one of the most violent states of Brazil in 2000 to the least violent in 2010. São Paulo is not the only good example. Even in the complex criminal scenario of Rio de Janeiro, with extensive areas controlled by drug trafficking and militias, the "Pacification Police" experience from 2008 to 2013 produced a 63.6 percent reduction in the number of homicides (Lessing, 2018, 26). Although this policy survived for a short time, it contributed to breaking the inertia produced by decades of wrong and ill implemented policies that have given the organized crime the role of providers of security services in these areas. In the State of Pernambuco in the Northeast of the country, a new management system inspired by the New York's COMPSTAT, named Pact for Life produced a homicide reduction of 24 percent from 2007 to 2012. It is doubtful that these policies can endure and produce improvements in the performance of law enforcement agencies in Brazil. Together with the new national coordination structures described earlier (SENASP, SUSP, and FNSP), these examples had positively impacted the debate on crime control policies and performed a shared base of successful experiences.

Another question to be addressed is the controversy about incarceration. Brazil has an incarceration rate of 323 prisoners per 100 thousand inhabitants, the seventeenth in the world with the fourth-largest prison population size from the United States, China, and Russia. The current Brazilian prison system is characterized by overcrowding, lack of prisoner legal assistance, and insufficient medical and psychological services, gang control, rampant abuse of inmates by correctional officers, and corruption. All of this is part of the daily life of Brazilian prisons. As pointed out before, only a small fraction of the penitentiary system is under Federal responsibility,[11] while the state prisons holds almost 760,000 inmates. The differences between the states are significant. Still, the difficulties in managing this prison population are immense, even for the wealthiest states in the south and southeast of the country. The correctional system is undoubtedly an area where the local and national governments move slowly toward any noticeable improvement. Underfunded and negligently managed by an unqualified bureaucracy, it is currently the most vulnerable component of the criminal justice system. For the public, the correctional system is an opaque phenomenon, which contributes to keeping it out of the priority of local governments.

One emerging issue connected to the previous discussion of the correctional system is the black incarceration problem. Blacks are more likely to suffer a violent death from gangs and police violence and are also incarcerated at a higher rate (Sinhoreto & Morais, 2018). Research on race and criminality grew considerably during the last decade and spotted the significant differences in victimization risks between blacks and whites in Brazil. In a review of literature, Trindade and Lima (2017) pointed out that young black men from disadvantaged neighborhoods in large Brazilian cities are among those with a higher risk of homicide victimization. Epidemiological studies have also offered strong evidence of racial differentiation in criminal victimization: blacks comprised 69 percent of homicide victims in 2009, yet, they represented 45 percent of the Brazilian population. In addition, homicide among blacks increased by 28.6 percent from 2000 to 2009 (Soares Filho, 2011). Income and education do not mitigate for victimization for blacks as well as they do for the white population. Blacks with higher income and lower levels of education experienced increased victimization risk from 2000 to 2009. During the same time, the risk decreased for the white population for both socioeconomic groups.

Racial bias in police violence is similarly a critical issue at the national debate about the status of the criminal justice system. Reliable data about police violence is scarce to date. One of the most comprehensive reports about the problem was published in 2017 by the police ombudsman from the State of São Paulo.[12] The report analyzes 639 police records of 756 cases of civilians killed by the police and finds evidence of excessive use of force by police officers in 74 percent of the cases. Approximately 50 percent of those killed by the police that year were young men between eighteen and twenty-five years of age and 65 percent of them were black. It is not clear how the Brazilian society will enhance police accountability. The answers provided by the society in this debate could help reshape the institutional culture of police departments and its "blue wall of silence" codes, historically associated with racism against the black population.

THE WEAKENING OF THE CRIMINAL JUSTICE SYSTEM

The policies formulated in response to the crime wave that reached Brazil in the new democratic age after 1985 were inadequate for several reasons. First, the crime problem was framed as a secondary issue at the country's redemocratization agenda. The defense of human rights was a major concern for a society emerging from more than 20 years of an authoritarian government. Political leaders and public opinion were overly sensitive to the argument that Brazil was criminally violent as it was not yet a full democracy. The current belief was that the crime escalation in the years between 1980 and 1990 was a clear indication of the social and political failure of the overthrown authoritarian regime. Crime was not a problem in itself; this was the common thinking of the time, but a mere reflection of the structural and political characteristics of the Brazilian society. A brand-new Democracy would be the antidote that would gradually make Brazil a less violent society. Second, the very role of criminal justice institutions in controlling and restraining crime was politically discredited and weakened (Carneiro, 2016). The fact that Brazil was in a fast process of becoming one of the most violent countries in the world was out of the vision of the leaders who guided the redemocratization movement.

It took more than two decades to realize that only with strong law enforcement institutions is it possible to move forward with effective crime control policies. Yet, to understand the functioning of the criminal justice system, it is necessary to address some of its structural characteristics. Brazil, like other countries in Latin America, has a relatively small and ineffective criminal justice system, judging by the high level of crime and violence observed. In general, Latin American countries have a low level of incarceration and police per capita (Soares & Naritomi, 2010). Globally, these countries form a homogeneous cluster with similar crime control policies. Prison sentences are applied less frequently than expected, given the level of violent crime in these countries, and the availability of police officers follows the same trend.

In a country characterized by high levels of inequality and poverty and structural deficiencies in providing basic services such as health and education, it is often difficult to prioritize public security policies and to position them for adequate funding. The mainstream argument was that extended social policies should take precedence over dissuasive crime control policies. This oblique political thinking only fans discontent that precipitates violence at a time when the country needs a rapid improvement in income distribution, poverty reduction, inflation control, and enhanced open access to education.[13] The contrast between improved social conditions and increased crime rates defines the unique position of Brazil among the most violent countries in the world.

In contrast to common anticipation, the Brazilian society gradually opted for less punitive criminal legislation in the face of an unexpected rise in crime rates. Also, major political players weakened the role of the police and criminal justice in controlling crime and violence by defunding the defense and the public security sectors. The consequence of these choices was and continues to be quite heavy for the society: the homicide rate increased 110 percent between 1985 and 2019 (the first year of the current democratic term),[14] prison gangs became a national phenomenon, and the police forces are among the worst-rated institutions in the country.[15]

It is notable that Brazil is among the 5 percent most violent countries in the world, with a homicide rate that is nearly three times the world average rate. What is particularly unclear in the Brazilian case is the combination of wealth and violence. Among the other top 5 percent of the most violent countries (Liberia, Russia, Somalia, Venezuela, Guatemala, El Salvador, Angola, South Africa, Sierra Leone, and Colombia), only the oil-exporting countries (Russia and Venezuela)[16] have higher per capita income than Brazil. The country is the wealthier member of a low-income cluster of violent countries. A deeper investigation of the characteristics and possible areas of improvement of the criminal justice system and its agencies could help to answer this puzzle.

NOTES

1. The national homicide rate in 2017 was 28.5 per 1,000 thousand inhabitants and dropped to 20.1 in 2017. Homicide rates are considerable higher in important capital cities like Manaus (55.9 per 100,000 inhabitants); Salvador (63.5); Fortaleza (87.9); Belém (74.3); Rio de Janeiro (35.6), among other capitals. These figures put Brazilian some Brazilian cities among the most violent cities in the Americas Region. Sources: Monitor da Violência G1 and IPEA 2019. http://especiais.g1 .globo.com/monitor-da-violencia/2018/mortes-violentas-no-brasil/?_ga=2.62510572 .1711685417.1581424139-28686389.1558827135#/dados-anuais.

2. After a long litigation process, the Brazilian Supreme Court recognized in 2015 the constitutional prerogatives of the Public Prosecutor to directly carry out investigative activities for the purposes of prosecution.

3. Presidência da República do Brasil, EMENDA CONSTITUCIONAL Nº 104, DE 4 DE DEZEMBRO DE 2019.

4. Those under eighteen years and the mentally ill are criminally unsuitable according to Brazilian legislation. Underaged offenders are sentenced to so-called "socioeducational" correctional facilities.

5. Survey conducted by the Departamento Nacional Penitenciário, 2019.

6. At the beginning of the twentieth century, the São Paulo Public Force, currently the Military Police of the State of São Paulo, hired, in March 1906, a training program from French Army Unit that carried out police activities in Paris. This military unit carried out an extensive training program for the military police of São Paulo from 1906 to 1914 and from 1919 to 1924.

7. Each state defines the training time required to become a police chief. Usually from five to seven months.

8. After its Independence in 1822, Brazil adopted for sixty-seven years a representative parliamentary constitutional monarchy regime. The monarchy was overthrown by a civil-military coup in 1889 and adopted the actual presidentialism system. Another

important historical landmark in Brazil history is the 1930 Revolution (a second civil-military coup) that ended the first republic period (1889–1930). The dictatorship of Getúlio Vargas ended in 1946, and a new democratic period lasts until 1964 when a military dictatorship overturned democratically elected leaders and ruled the country until 1985 when a civilian president was elected by the Congress. A new Constitutional Assembly voted the actual Brazilian constitution in 1988. The actual shape of the Brazilian law enforcement institutions came mostly from the post-1930 period.

9. These special operations are regulated by the Federal Constitution, in its article 142, by the Complementary Law 97/1999, and by Decree 3897/2001.

10. Fórum Brasileiro da Segurança Pública, Anuário Brasileiro da Segurança Pública. Available at: https://forumseguranca.org.br/anuario-brasileiro-seguranca -publica/.

11. According to the National Penitentiary Department (DEPEN) only five Federal penitentiaries are operative at the moment with the capacity to accommodate a maximum of 1,200 inmates (Departamento Penitenciário Nacional, 2020)

12. "The use of Lethal Force by Police in São Paulo and Police Victimization" available at: http://www.ssp.sp.gov.br/ouvidoria/.

13. The twelve-year period from the first government of Fernando Henrique Cardoso (1994) to the first government of Dilma Roussef (ended in 2014).

14. Instituto de Pesquisa Aplicada e Fórum Brasileiro de Segurança Pública https://www.ipea.gov.br/atlasviolencia/dados-series/20.

15. Survey conducted by Datafolha in April 2019. Available at https://g1.globo .com/politica/noticia/2019/04/11/datafolha-aponta-que-51percent-dos-brasileiros -tem-medo-da-policia-e-47percent-confiam-nos-policiais.ghtml.

16. Our World in Data, 2015 data (last available estimation for Venezuela). Available at: https://ourworldindata.org/grapher/gdp-per-capita-worldbank?region =World.

REFERENCES

Abdalla, Renata Rigacci, Clarice S. Madruga, Marcelo Ribeiro, Ilana Pinsky, Raul Caetano, and Ronaldo Laranjeira. (2014). Prevalence of cocaine use in Brazil: Data from the II Brazilian national alcohol and drugs survey (BNADS). *Addictive Behaviors* 39(1): 297–301.

Bastos, Francisco Inácio, and Neilane Bertoni. (2014). *Pesquisa nacional sobre o uso de crack*. FIOCRUZ.

Bicudo, Hélio. (2000). A unificação das polícias no Brasil. *Estudos Avançados* 14(40): 91–106.

Carneiro, L. Piquet. (2010). Ameaça do crime organizado à segurança pública. *Interesse Nacional* 3(10).

Carneiro, L. Piquet, and Fabio R. Bechara. (2016). O impacto no Brasil dos mercados ilícitos globais e do crime transnacional. In *Criminalidade Organizada: Investigação, Direito e Ciência* (1st edition). Almedina, pp. 69–104.

Departamento Penitenciário Nacional. (2020). Levantamento nacional de informações penitenciárias (INFOPEN). Brasília, Governo Federal. http://dados.gov.br /dataset/infopen-levantamento-nacional-de-informacoes-penitenciarias1/resource /320b7326-3f9b-40ba-9c86-5acc10cfbb5e.

Holloway, Thomaz. (1993). *Policing Rio de Janeiro Repression and Resistance in a Nineteenth-Century City*. Stanford University Press.

Instituto Brasileiro de Geografia e Estatística. (2012). Pesquisa de informações básicas municipais. In *Instituto Brasileiro de Geografia e Estatística. Rio de Janeiro.* Retrieved September 15, 2020 http;//www.ibge.gov.br/home/estatistica/economia/ perfilmunic/2012.

IPEA Instituto de Pesquisa Econômica Aplicada. (2019). *Atlas da Violência: Retratos dos Municípios Brasileiros.* IPEA (Instituto de Pesquisa Econômica Aplicada).

Lessing, B. (2018). *Making Peace in a Drug War*. Cambridge University Press.

Lopes, Aury Jr., (2018). *Direito Processual Penal* (15th edition). Saraiva.

Pereira Filho, O. Alves, M. Sousa, and P. F. Alves. (2018). Avaliação de impacto das guardas municipais sobre a criminalidade com o uso de tratamentos binários, multivalorados e contínuos. *Revista Brasileira De Economia* 72(4): 515–544.

Sinhoreto, Jacqueline, and Danilo de, Souza Morais. (2018). Violência e racismo: Novas faces de uma afinidade reiterada. *Revista Estudos Sociales* 64: 15–26. http://www.scielo.org.co/scielo.php?script=sci_arttext&pid=S0123 -885X2018000200015&lng=en&nrm=iso.

Soares Filho, Adauto Martins. (2011). Vitimização por homicídios segundo características de raça no Brasil. Rev. *Saúde Pública* 45(4): 745–755. http://www.scielo .br/scielo.php?script=sci_arttext&pid=S0034-89102011000400015&lng=en&nrm =iso.

Soares, Rodrigo R., and J. Naritomi. (2010). Understanding high crime rates in Latin America: The role of social and policy factors. NBER Chapters, in *The Economics of Crime: Lessons for and from Latin America*. National Bureau of Economic Research, Inc., pp. 19–55.

Souza, Luís Antônio F. (2015). Dispositivo militarizado da segurança pública. Tendências recentes e problemas no Brasil. *Sociedade e estado* 30(1): 207–223. http:// www.scielo.br/scielo.php?script=sci_arttext&pid=S0102-69922015000100207 &lng=en&nrm=iso.

Trindade, A., and R. S. de Lima. (2018). Estatisticas oficiais e crime no Brasil. *Boletim Informativo Bibliográfico* 84(2): 81–106. https://www.anpocs.com/index .php/bib-pt/bib-84/11101-estatisticas-oficiais-violencia-e-crime-no-brasil/file.

Viana, Oliveira. (1949). *Instituicões políticas brasileiras fundamentos sociais do estado*. Jose Olympio Editora.

Zaverrucha, J. (2005). *FHC, Forças Armadas e polícia: Entre o autoritarismo e a democracia, 1999–2002.* Record.

Chapter 20

Policing in Uruguay

History, Modernization, and Features

Diego Sanjurjo, Nicolás Trajtenberg, and Federico del Castillo

This chapter gives a general overview of policing in Uruguay with a particular focus on the Uruguayan National Police, the most important security actor in the country. To this end, we examine the history of the police force from its origins in 1829 to its recent modernization efforts in the twenty-first century. Also reviewed are its current institutional arrangements, strategies, capacities, and relations with the public. In this respect, the Uruguayan police is often considered an outlier in Latin America due to a series of institutional and operational reforms that were praised on multiple occasions by international organizations. However, along with recent modernization efforts came a drastic increase in crime and violence, which has called these efforts into question and left the direction of future changes in the air.

INTRODUCTION

Along with Chile and Costa Rica, Uruguay is arguably one of the very few countries in Latin America with a police force that resembles or conforms to Bayley's (1995) democratic policing criteria. That is, a police organization that is accountable to the law rather than to the government, protects human rights, is constrained in the use of force, and has the protection of citizens as its highest priority. Its exceptional situation in a region marked by the presence of corrupt and nondemocratic policing is largely due to a successful democratic transition and to its ability to maintain something close to a monopoly on violence (Prado, Trebilcock, & Hartford, 2012; Cruz, 2016).

The Uruguayan National Police (UNP) is the most important security actor in Uruguay and is a unified, nationwide, civilian, and professional police force. It was founded in 1829 with the birth of the Republic, but its history dates back to the eighteenth century and the colonial period. Since then, its development has been driven by political and social circumstances, as well as by the need to curb rising crime and increase its legitimacy in the eyes of the public. After being in an alarming state of decay during most of the twentieth century, the UNP underwent a series of profound structural changes to modernize the force and adopt a security paradigm consistent with that of a professional and democratic police organization.

These improvements, however, cannot hide the fact that the UNP faces considerable difficulties in providing its citizens with basic safety. As nearly all police forces in Latin America, it is still not well trained and prepared to deal with the increasing complexities of the criminal world and the rapidly developing series of dynamic illicit markets (Bergman, 2018; Dammert, 2019). As a result, the rates of homicide and violent robbery have dramatically increased in Uruguay since the 1990s, generating a strong demand for private security and compromising what used to be a safe country in an overall dangerous and violent region.

The literature on policing in Uruguay is fairly limited. Beyond a report on police reform by the Ministry of Interior (Bonomi et al., 2018), a handful of authors have analyzed its institutional development (González, 2003; Vila, 2012, 2016), its education system (Timote Correa, 2015, 2017) and policing strategies (Castillo, 2019; Castillo, Fraiman, & Rogers, 2014). In recent years, national and foreign authors have embraced field experimentation and evaluated a number of specific policing practices and instruments (Cid, 2019; Mitchell et al., 2018; Munyo & Rossi, 2019; Ariel et al., 2020; Bogliaccini, Monogan, & Pereira, 2019; Chainey, Serrano-Berthet, & Veneri, 2020).

This chapter seeks to provide the first general overview of policing in Uruguay, with a focus on the Uruguayan National Police, while also considering policing activities by other public actors. The next section will draw a sketch of the country and its security context. A third section will present its institutional framework, while a fourth and fifth section will analyze the history and modernization of the police force. The sixth section will review its main features and strategies, while the seventh section will discuss the public trust and legitimacy that it enjoys. The chapter ends with an eighth section on private policing and conclusions.

COUNTRY OVERVIEW AND SECURITY CONTEXT

Uruguay, officially the Oriental Republic of Uruguay, is situated in the eastern part of the Southern Cone of South America. It borders Argentina to its west and Brazil to its north and east, with the *Río de la Plata* to the south and the Atlantic Ocean to its southeast. Geographically, Uruguay is the second smallest nation in South America after Suriname and is home to an estimated 3.3 million people, the smallest population of all independent countries in the subregion. The republic is subdivided into nineteen departments and eighty-nine municipalities, with 40 percent of its population—1.4 million—living in the metropolitan area of Montevideo, its capital and largest city. The country's population presents an advanced demographic transition with a relatively mature age structure and rates of fertility and mortality comparable to those in European countries, even though proportions change significantly in the lowest socioeconomic strata.

The first Constitution was adopted in 1830 after its independence, establishing Uruguay as a unitary and representative republic with a centralized form of government. The country completed its organization at the end of the nineteenth century and consolidated its democracy soon afterwards. Its period of splendor would take place during the first half of the twentieth century. In a region marked by profound social inequalities and political instability, Uruguay became known for its high standard of living, advanced social policies, and democratic traditions. Nevertheless, economic downturns in the middle of the century led to a phase of social and economic deterioration with severe consequences for its political and democratic institutions. Political upheavals ended in a civic-military dictatorship that lasted between 1973 and 1985. The return to democracy implied the restoration of civil and political liberties and the beginning of a new historic period.

Modern Uruguay is a democratic constitutional republic with a presidential system and a relatively robust state, strong political parties, and a participative citizenry. Security, justice, defense, education, and health are all administered nationwide, in the form of a unitary state. Likewise, Uruguay's party system is among the most stable in Latin America and one of the only few with high levels of institutionalization (Mainwaring, 2018). In terms of democratic quality, Uruguay is not only ranked first in the region but is also at a comparable level to first world countries. For instance, Freedom House (2020) grants it a score of 98/100 regarding political rights and civil liberties, above developed countries like France, Germany, or Spain. The country is also currently ranked twenty-first in the world in the Corruption Perceptions Index (Transparency International, 2019), nineteenth in the World Press Freedom Index (Reporters without Borders, 2020), and twenty-second in the Rule of Law Index (World Justice Project, 2020).

Regarding development indicators, it is still far away from OECD (Organization for Economic Co-operation and Development) countries but is nevertheless considered a nation with high human development. Thus, it is currently in fifty-ninth place on the Human Development Index,[1] with only Argentina and Chile receiving higher scores in Latin America (UNDP, 2019). In this sense, the last decades have been especially fruitful. Uruguay is currently the most equitable country in the region (measured by the GINI coefficient) and has the highest GDP per capita. The latter increased fivefold between 2003 and 2018, as the percentage of inhabitants living under the national poverty line went from 32.5 in 2006 to 8.8 in 2019, even though there are still significant setbacks in the north of the country and among children (Uruguay-INE, 2020; World Bank, n.d.).

Unfortunately, the country tells a very different story when it comes to public security. Despite political stability and socioeconomic prosperity, indicators of crime, and particularly violent crime, have grown steadily in the last three decades. Hence, criminal rates per 100,000 inhabitants multiplied between 1990 and 2019, going from 1743.2 to 4,145.4 in the case of thefts, from 82.3 to 809.6 in the case of robberies,—locally known as *rapiñas*—and from 6.6 to 11.1 in terms of homicides. Impunity is high as well and this includes homicides, as the murder clearance rate is below 50 percent and a crime victimization survey of 2017 suggests that only 28 percent of all incidents are reported (Uruguay-MI, 2017b, 2020b, 2020a). Likewise, rates of domestic violence complaints have grown significantly, going from 204.4 in 2005 to 1,139.2 in 2018,[2] while the femicide rate has been measured since 2012 and has oscillated between 1.0 in 2014 to 1.7 in 2018 (Uruguay-MI, 2019a).

As a result—and contrary to common belief—modern Uruguay does not have low but rather medium levels of crime, as it went from traditionally being one of the safest countries in the region to having the fourth highest homicide rate in South America after Venezuela, Colombia, and Brazil (UNODC, n.d.). This juncture is also mirrored by a strong sense of fear regarding insecurity on the part of Uruguayans. The latest crime victimization survey finds that 52 percent of respondents define the country as insecure (Uruguay-MI, 2017b), whereas public opinion surveys suggest that insecurity became the most pressing problem in 2009 and this remained unchanged until the advent of the coronavirus pandemic in March 2020 (CIFRA, 2018, 2020).

As in the rest of the world, homicides in Uruguay affect disproportionately young males. In 2019, 88 percent of the victims were male, and 43 percent were between thirteen and twenty-eight years old. Furthermore, between 50 and 60 percent of all homicides are thought to be related to conflicts among criminals, drug trafficking, and organized crime. In the case of female victims, 47 percent died at the hands of their intimate partner or previous partner in 2018. It is also worth mentioning that the percentage of homicides committed with guns went from forty-nine in 2012 to sixty-one in 2019, a development that is common in the region and usually related to the greater presence of organized crime (Uruguay-MI, 2019a, 2020b).

Montevideo concentrates an important share of the criminal activity that takes place in the country, including 46 percent of all burglaries, 79 percent of all robberies, and 55 percent of all homicides. The capital shows the same worrisome trend as the rest, reaching a homicide rate record of 16.1 per 100,000 inhabitants in 2018 (Uruguay-MI, 2020a, 2020b). Moreover, violent crimes show a recognizable spatial concentration and distribute unevenly across the territory of Montevideo. Hence, more than 50 percent of all homicides and violent robberies are concentrated in only nine neighborhoods (Jaitman & Ajzenman, 2016; Uruguay-MI, 2020b).

Finally, and as in most of Latin America (Vilalta & Fondevila, 2019), the prison population experienced major growth in the last few decades, going from 2,956 inmates in 1990 to 11,755 in 2020. The latter indicates an incarceration rate of 337 per 100,000 inhabitants, the second highest in South America and the twenty-ninth in the world (Uruguay-CPP, 2019; World Prison Brief, n.d.). Prison violence is also common, with homicide rates being ten times higher within prisons than among the regular population (Vigna & Sosa, 2019). Taken together, the higher levels of crime on people and property produce a heavy burden on Uruguay's economy. The loss amounted to 1.592 million US dollars in 2015, a sum that was equivalent to 2.23 percent of the national GDP (Jaitman & Torre, 2017).

Overall, such a dramatic rise in crime seems paradoxical, considering the significant improvement of social indicators. The first notorious increase coincides with the consequences of the economic crisis of the late 1990s, that is, with periods of high unemployment and negative GDP growth rates. However, the socioeconomic indicators began to improve drastically in 2004, however, crime and violence did not subside but continued growing steadily. Other authors have tried to provide explanations for a paradox that can also be found in other parts of Latin America (e.g., Soares & Naritomi, 2010; PNUD, 2013; Bergman, 2018) and it is not the purpose of this chapter to make a local contribution. Nevertheless, the economic crisis accelerated and deepened a series of much subtler social processes that transpired during the second half of the twentieth century; above all was the increasing inequality among qualified and nonqualified workers, the explosive growth of slums in the outskirts of Montevideo, and the greater presence of illegal markets and organized criminal groups. From this perspective, the rise in crime seems to be the final manifestation of a long process of social fragmentation (Katzman et al., 2004). The following sections will examine the reaction of the country's public security actors.

SECURITY GOVERNANCE AND GOVERNABILITY

The Uruguayan State has exclusive competence over the preservation of public order and security. Their maintenance corresponds to the Executive Power through the Ministry of Interior, which constitutes the governing body of security policies within national borders. Its mission is to govern, execute, control, and evaluate the policies, plans, and programs related to public security, guaranteeing the free exercise of fundamental rights and freedoms.

The Uruguayan National Police falls within the jurisdiction of the Ministry of Interior and according to the Organic Police Law n° 19.315 of 2015, it constitutes a unified and nationwide security force of a civilian and professional nature. It is divided into nineteen headquarters, one for each department of the Republic. Since most Uruguayans live in the capital and it concentrates a large share of the country's criminal activity, the Montevideo Police Headquarters (MPH) is the largest and plays the leading role at the national level. It is divided into four operational jurisdictions and twenty-five sectionals.

Furthermore, the Armed Forces are constitutionally subordinated to the Executive Power through the Ministry of Defense and are formed by the Army, the Navy, and the Air Force. Unlike in other countries, the Uruguayan Armed Forces are generally not involved in the prevention, control, investigation, or fight against crime. Instead, and by the National Defense Macro Law 18.650 of 2010, the Armed Forces are exclusively dedicated to a set of civil and military activities aimed at preserving the sovereignty and independence of the country, the integrity of the territory and its strategic resources, as well as the peace of the Republic.

Accordingly, the Armed Forces are responsible for providing security against external threats, while the National Police is tasked with providing internal security, surveillance, and order inside the country's borders. Such a division is common among consolidated Western democracies and has been reinforced in many Latin American countries since the military dictatorships of the twentieth century. Exceptions apply, however. The surveillance and control of coastal areas and the shores of navigable rivers and lakes is the responsibility of the National Naval Prefecture, a division of the National Navy. Likewise, the other branches of the Armed Forces have taken on a series of tasks to support the police on an exceptional basis. This includes surveillance tasks in border areas, providing external perimeter security in prison facilities, and the performance of aerial police functions in cooperation with the National Police (Rodríguez Cuitiño, 2018).

HISTORY OF THE NATIONAL POLICE

The Uruguayan National Police (UNP) was founded along with the Republic, but its history dates back to the colonial period and specifically to 1730 when the Governor of the *Río de la Plata* inaugurated the first city council of Montevideo with a mayor and a sheriff.[3] When city councils were abolished in 1827, each department was appointed a police chief, who constituted the maximum political authority within each territory. These were party figures and faithful representatives of the partisan government. They had little knowledge about defense or security but acted as articulators between the political power and their subordinates. The UNP was founded shortly before the adoption of the first Constitution with the approval of the 1829 Law of the Police, Its Unification, and Services.

The first century of the new Republic was marked by recurrent coups and civil wars that constantly changed the nature, organization, and operation of the bodies in charge of security. From the start, the police authorities of the capital were better organized and more influential than those in the rest of the country. Hence, they tended to fall on retired military generals with a political orientation that was in line with the national government. In 1868, the watchmen in charge of the capital's night time surveillance were turned into the night time patrol police service. This service was then eliminated in 1888 to constitute what is known today as the MPH, with several police stations that are still operational.

In the countryside, police headquarters were also divided into police stations with a police chief in charge, but norms and regulations were incomplete and there was no legislation that provided a consistent organizational model. The weapons, equipment, vehicles, and levels of training were limited and precarious, increasing the asymmetries with Montevideo. Until the creation of the National Directorate of Police Education in 1943, police commissioners from the capital were trained through a semi-tertiary education that lasted two years, while commissioners from the countryside were determined by seniority and trained under standards that responded to basic school levels. On their part, junior officers nationwide—called *subalternos*—were only required to have completed primary school, but this requirement was not always met either (Timote Correa, 2017).

The deficiencies of the UNP became evident in the second half of the twentieth century, with the advent of social and political upheavals that the force was unprepared to handle. The 1960s were marked by a dramatic social, economic, and political crisis, which preceded the emergence of a left-wing urban guerrilla group called the Tupamaros, as well as student uprisings and the radicalization of striking workers. The government eventually hardened its stance and adopted an authoritarian profile, which led to extraordinary levels of violence and paved the way for what historians have called the "democratic road to the coup d'état" (Rico, 2008). This implied the growing influence and participation of the Armed Forces in internal security and politics, but also a series of radical reforms to the UNP that would have a long-lasting impact on its nature, operations, legitimacy, and institutional culture.

These reforms began at the end of the 1960s but deepened during the civic-military dictatorship, which is said to have had three distinct phases (Caetano, 2019). The different authorities first tried to establish order at all costs through state terrorism and repression (1973–1976), then attempted to reorganize and refund Uruguayan democracy (1976–1980), and finally prepared for the democratic transition (1980–1985). Alejandro Vila (2012) suggests that some of the reforms that took place within the police force during those decades correspond to a modernization process that was long overdue, while others respond to the political purposes of those phases.

Accordingly, a first reform wave implied the transition from a premodern organization—signaled by a lack of norms and standards—to one with a bureaucratic-authoritarian order. Hence, the Organic Police Law of 1971 and its regulatory decrees unified all police headquarters under the command of the UNP. They established a new structure for the organization and developed principles and norms that governed its operations and the conduct of its members. A progressive and much needed decentralization took place as well, which was accompanied by the gradual creation of specialized units and posts, and by the development of a new rank structure and standardized public office career for all police personnel at the national level, including prison and administrative staff.

These reforms also had a darker side, however, as the military gained power and influence within the ranks. The suppression and constraint that Uruguayan society experienced during those years required extreme discipline by army and police officers. In some cases, military regulations were applied within the police through a military rank structure of promotion and a severe code of conduct with rigorous and excessive penalties. Political discretion increased and, as of 1976, the leadership of the Ministry of Interior was occupied by military generals and colonels. The Armed Forces eventually penetrated the organization at every level and the UNP adopted the goals of the National Security Doctrine (see below), as its recently developed police intelligence bodies worked together with the Armed Forces to suppress political opposition.

Reforms also happened during the last years of the dictatorship. Both in Montevideo and the countryside, police jurisdictions were reorganized under new efficiency criteria. Moreover, criminal data was limited and dispersed until the end of the 1970s, so an important effort was made to gather and systematize information across the country, which eventually allowed the creation and use of criminal statistics. At last, every ministry developed its own planning agency, which was supposed to set goals for the administration and improve its working methods.

Overall, the military intervention and the requirements of the organization brought an unprecedented number of changes to the police in a very short period of time. The militarization of the force was accompanied by its modernization and professionalization. With the unification of all headquarters, the emergence of police units with national projection, and the establishment of a single training school, the UNP became truly national. The democratic transition would bring a whole new set of challenges to an organization that was very different from the one that existed before the breakdown.

POLICE MODERNIZATION

The transition of the UNP to the twenty-first century was marked by a conceptual and operational change in the way of understanding security. As in other parts of South America, the end of the civic-military dictatorship implied the gradual decline of what came to be known as the National Security Doctrine. This was the regional variant of the national security state and focused on the need to exercise military control of the state in order to defend it from internal and external threats (Leal Buitrago, 2003). Several security paradigms developed in its place, with public safety and community safety—aka citizen security—as the most relevant. While the first implies concerted crime fighting efforts by security institutions, the second corresponds to the Spanish term *seguridad ciudadana* and places a greater emphasis on community interaction and social cohesion (ICPC, 2010, pp. 3–4; Abizanda et al., 2012).

These conceptual changes, as well as the need to demilitarize and depoliticize police institutions, have generally guided the police reforms that have taken place in most Latin American countries since the 1990s. Nearly all democratic transitions were incomplete, however, and came accompanied by the formation and expansion of organized crime and illegal markets. Crime and violence grew significantly under these circumstances and imposed the need to create new civilian police forces or strengthen and modernize existing ones. Unfortunately, so far police reforms in Latin America display more challenges than results and have only brought a semblance of democratic policing to the region (Dammert, 2019; Macaulay, 2012; Ungar, 2011).

The Uruguayan National Police regained the leading role in the provision of security after the return to democracy in 1985 and adopted a public safety approach. This conception began to change at the end of the 1990s, fueled by regional and global discussions on community safety, citizen security, and human security (Vila, 2012). The local development of a citizen security paradigm can be divided into three periods. The first involved pilot efforts to advance crime prevention strategies (1998–2004), the second included key structural reforms to professionalize the force (2005–2012), and the last entailed the use of evidence-based strategies combined with policy innovations (2013-2020).

The first period can be defined as experimental. Between 1998 and 2004, the Ministry of Interior developed several pilot strategies, such as traditional community policing, domestic violence approaches, and broad social crime prevention programs. A key actor in this new strategy was the Inter-American Development Bank (IDB), which financed the Citizen Security Program and supported pilot strategies in Montevideo and Canelones (Alda, Buvinić, & Lamas, 2006; OVE, 2014). In this case, crime prevention was mainly associated with social and community prevention frameworks, which involved the combination of community policing with local social services (Uruguay-OPP-DGE, 2014). All in all, the Citizen Security Program struggled with obstacles that inhibited it from going beyond pilot strategies, but it introduced the UNP to new ways of doing police work and inspired future efforts.

A second, transitional period (2005–2012) involved the implementation of several changes to take the UNP to a new level of modernization. First, the Ministry of Interior began a progressive civilianization process, which resulted in the creation of new top-level management directions run by the civil bureaucracy. Police management was gradually centralized as well, procuring better coordination and more fluid relations between politicians and police authorities. The creation of the Republican Guard in 2010 responded to this logic as well, since it resulted from the combination of two former special units within the MPH. This is a quasi-military special force that has national jurisdiction and reports directly to the Minister of Interior. Finally, several important administrative changes were made to increase police oversight and improve the working conditions of the force. They included, among others, introducing management commitments, improving weapons and equipment, installing biometric control systems, GPS tracking, and gas control devices, as well as increasing wages and reducing work hours (Vila, 2016; Paternain, 2017; Bonomi et al., 2018).

This last issue was related to what had become—and still is—a structural problem of the force, namely, that wages are low and police agents seek to increase earnings by providing security services in the private sector. This is legally permitted when off-duty, in what is locally known as the "Service 222." By 2010, it was estimated that 11,000 police officers—over 70 percent of the force—were working as private security guards and half of them did around five extra hours per day (Uruguay-MI, 2017a). As wages increased, this possibility was gradually reduced, even though many police agents still operate informally in the private sector, which is referred to as "223" (Vila, 2016, p. 265).

In any case, this period of transition can be seen as the beginning of a broader police reform that took place during the third period (2013–2020), characterized by a series of comprehensive measures taken at different levels. A first keystone was the approval of a new Organic Police Law n° 19.315 in 2015, which crystallized the abandonment of the National Security Doctrine, replacing its traditional military profile and defining the UNP as a civilian police force committed to the preservation of public order, the prevention of crimes and the defense of Human Rights. The new law also centralized the command of the UNP in the National Police Direction—itself under the direct command of the Minister of Interior—and no longer in the MPH, where it had been effectively conducted until then.

Police education was reformed as well. With the support of the IDB, the Ministry of Interior began to develop international alliances in 2012 with prestigious policing experts and institutions. With their assistance, police officers were trained in evidence-based policing strategies, crime analysis, and criminal investigation (see section 6). In 2016, the success of these pilot training courses led the UNP to develop a broad educational police reform that demilitarized police education, trained cadets in evidence-based field practices and incorporated new areas of knowledge to the educational curricula, such as statistics, crime analysis, crime mapping, criminology, and anthropology of crime (Timote Correa, 2015).

Another major intervention was focused on the MPH. Its strategic reform divided Montevideo and neighboring areas into four jurisdictions or zones, each with its own operations center to oversee police stations and handle criminal investigations and service calls. Until then, the service calls were handled at the precinct-level, while criminal investigations in Montevideo were centralized in the Direction of Investigations. Its dismantling was a focal step for the UNP since this Direction was a place where political and police authorities perceived a major source of corruption. A fifth jurisdiction was also created for operational support and as a sort of policing lab where new tactics and strategies could be empirically evaluated. The new organizational model was to be replicated in all other police headquarters over the following years.

Crime-analysis was also significantly strengthened. The Direction of Tactic Information (DIT), which operated under the MPH, began to develop crime mapping and statistical crime reports to present and better understand crime patterns and trends (Castillo, 2018). These reports were sent to each jurisdiction and police station, resulting in the organization of operational deployments based on evidence and data. These practices went through a process of progressive sophistication that yielded positive results, which eased its standardization and implementation throughout the entire force. The DIT eventually acquired national jurisdiction and was renamed the Direction of Crime Analysis (DiAC, for its Spanish initials).

Finally, reforms were accompanied by a significant investment in policing technology. Perhaps the most well-known was the extension of a CCTV system for video surveillance, which now covers large parts of the metropolitan areas throughout the country (Munyo & Rossi, 2019), but technological improvements also materialized in other areas. Some examples are the development of a nationwide information system that allows real-time crime reporting and geolocation, the implementation of a terrestrial trunked radio (TETRA) communications system that enables encrypted communications and GPS tracking of vehicles and officers, the incorporation of ankle monitoring systems to control domestic violence perpetrators, and the installment of tablet computers in police vehicles to improve in-place crime reporting and reduce nonreported incidents.

All in all, these changes implied a departure from the way policing was understood in Uruguay in the 1990s, as well as a step toward a modern police organization that is able to perform in a context marked by a more complex and dynamic criminal world. As discussed in the next section, crime prevention and community-oriented practices were prioritized during these years (Malone & Dammert, 2020), but it would be wrong to claim that the Uruguayan police has adopted a citizen security paradigm since the commitment to a new policing philosophy is so far only an aspiration.

FEATURES AND STRATEGIES

Between civilian and police personnel, the UNP was hiring over 32,500 workers in 2020, 24,000 of whom were executive personnel, actively working in crime prevention, deterrence, investigation, and repression. The actual police officer rate stands at 679 per every 100,000 inhabitants, the highest rate in Latin America and considerably higher than the median rate of the European Union (326) (PNUD, 2013, p. 113; Eurostat, 2018). Moreover, police salaries have been raised significantly in recent years and almost doubled since 2000. Thus, the monthly salary of the lowest police rank in 2019 was USD 865 (Uruguay-MI, 2019c), which is probably well ranked among Latin American police salaries. The average salary that year was approximately USD 980; however, which is still six times lower than the average salary of a police officer in the United States (DePietro, 2020).

Furthermore, the bulk of the Uruguayan police force follows operational practices that resemble the standard model of policing (Weisburd & Eck,

2004). That is, a "one-size-fits-all" strategy based on routine preventive patrols, rapid response to service calls, and retrospective investigation. Consequently, local police authorities usually attempt to fight rising crime by increasing the number of police officers on the streets and their public visibility, and by enforcing saturation patrols and intensive arrests (Bogliaccini, Monogan, & Pereira, 2019; CID, 2019). There are no alternatives to these practices in the countryside, but they also dominate urban landscapes, with perhaps the sole exceptions of Montevideo and Maldonado. Even in these cities, however, this is still the prevailing policing model in the force.

The UNP appears to have been transitioning between policing philosophies. As described in the last section, the past decade was an era of reform marked by an impulse to modernize the force and embrace the citizen security paradigm. The IDB was a fundamental source of influence and was somehow involved in most parts of the force's modernization. This effort corresponds to the interest of the international organization in promoting such a paradigm in Latin America, which usually translates into financial and logistical support for police reforms and crime prevention policies and programs (Alda, Buvinić, & Lamas, 2006; OVE, 2014). Even though most of these endeavors were incapable of empirically demonstrating positive effects (OVE, 2010), those that did appear to have positive outcomes moved authorities to hierarchize crime prevention within police agencies and prioritize preventive strategies to address crime and delinquency.

Some of the most significant changes experienced by the National Police were related to criminal investigations and emergency response. On one hand, elite investigative units were created at the beginning of the last decade and trained in advanced techniques and protocols with the help of foreign experts, while significant investment in technology helped forensics scientists to process evidence and work in crime scenes. On the other, all police response services throughout the country were split into jurisdictions or zones as of 2013, which allowed a better adaptation to local contexts. Territorial decentralization was accompanied by an investment in technology, new vehicles, and equipment, which also contributed to a more efficient deployment (Bonomi et al., 2018).

In terms of crime prevention, the first experiences of the UNP were developed in 1998 and associated with traditional community policing (Cordner, 2014). These took place mostly in Montevideo and the city of Canelones and helped prevent issues such as drug and alcohol consumption, school violence, traffic accidents, and illegal street racing. They involved training police officers to lead community policing projects, promote citizen participation in crime prevention efforts, and build Pilot Prevention Centers to detect and report situations of domestic violence (Uruguay-OPP-DGE, 2014). Actions were too fragmentary and heterogeneous, however, and the program lacked a defined work plan with clear goals. Hence, it ultimately faced the same challenges encountered by other community policing programs in Latin American and was no longer operational by 2015 (Frühling, 2012; Ungar & Arias, 2012).

Nevertheless, the flagship program of the police reform was a criminal deterrence model called the High Operative Dedication Program (PADO, for its Spanish initials) (Bonomi et al., 2018). This is a large-scale hotspot policing endeavor that is still operational and was implemented for the first time in 2016 at the fifth jurisdiction of Montevideo—the policing lab— and then expanded to adjacent parts of the capital, as well to the cities of Canelones and San José. The PADO was led by the DiAC and developed in conjunction with the IDB and international experts. It can be considered the result of a long process of professionalization by the UNP in resource management, crime analysis, and crime mapping (Castillo, 2018). The evaluations of the program have shown a significant reduction in robberies in deployment areas (Chainey, Serrano-Berthet, & Veneri, 2020), which has moved authorities to prioritize its development over other policing approaches.

Unfortunately, while innovations in criminal investigation, emergency response, and criminal deterrence seem to have survived the test of time, the same cannot be said in terms of crime prevention. As community policing programs and the PADO were implemented, another pilot program of problem-oriented policing (POP) (Goldstein, 1979) was being tested in the twenty-fifth police sectional of Montevideo. This program was operational between 2012 and 2017 but suffered a similar fate as the community policing programs. A series of obstacles—largely linked to organizational resistance, inadequate leadership, and lack of resources—prevented its consolidation and development (Castillo, 2019). Despite the initial failure, POP did experience an expansion in 2019 in the form of a new pilot strategy that is still operational and continues with the support of the IDB and foreign experts.

In synthesis, even though preventive policing efforts have gained some recognition in recent times, they are still far from gaining the same status, support, and development within the UNP as criminal investigations and response and deterrence strategies (Castillo, 2020). Despite commendable efforts to reconceptualize the police–community relationship, the Uruguayan experience is in line with those who claim that there are still no true community policing programs in Latin America, as these have only been episodic and have not lead to any major cultural changes within police institutions (Frühling, 2012; Dias Felix, & Hilgers, 2020). Thus, the standard policing model prevails in Uruguay and will continue doing so for the foreseeable future.

POLICE AUTHORITY

When citizens do not trust or believe in the legitimacy of the police, there is less cooperation and compliance with the law, as well as greater chances of involvement in crime and violence (Tyler, 1990). Sadly, almost all police institutions in Latin America share high levels of citizen distrust as a result of their authoritarian past, poor effectiveness, widespread corruption, and excessive use of force (PNUD, 2013; Corbacho, Philipp, & Ruiz-Vega, 2015; Malone & Dammert, 2020). Likewise, low levels of legitimacy have been associated with greater support for vigilantism (Nivette, 2016) and the involvement of the military in the fight against crime (Pion-Berlin & Carreras, 2017).

Although data and research on the matter is scarce in Uruguay, public opinion surveys suggest that public trust in the police is among medium levels and higher than in most of the region. Thus, according to *Corporación Latinobarómetro* (2018, p. 50), only 35 percent of Latin Americans trusted the police in 2017, whereas in Uruguay, this percentage rose to fifty-nine, the highest among nineteen countries. Similar to what usually happens in large cities, institutional trust seems to be lower in the capital, as a survey by CAF (2014, pp. 230–32) found that police trust fell to 34 percent among Montevideo residents. Similar results were captured by Uruguay's latest crime victimization survey, which found that 60 percent of respondents had confidence in the police, whereas 51 percent was satisfied with the way in which the police had handled their complaint and 71 percent with the treatment given to the complainant (Uruguay-MI, 2017b). Finally, the anticipated emergency response time looks particularly promising, as only 3.5 percent of respondents believed that it could be 3 hours or longer, the same percentage as in the United States (Cohen, Lupu, & Zechmeister, 2017).

In a local study of more than 4,000 15-year-old adolescents from Montevideo and Zurich (Switzerland), Trajtenberg and Eisner (2014) found that low levels of police legitimacy in Montevideo were associated with violent behavior, even after controlling for socioeconomic confounders and other key criminological mechanisms such as morality, self-control, or rational choice (Trajtenberg, 2017). Surprisingly, the perceptions of police legitimacy were significantly higher among Uruguayan adolescents than among Swiss, but the association of low levels of police legitimacy with youth violence was stronger in Zurich than in Montevideo.

Furthermore, abuse and the unnecessary use of force are considered common elements of policing practices in the region (Cruz, 2016; Dammert, 2019). According to the LAPOP survey of 2008, 4.2 percent of Uruguayan respondents reported to having suffered physical or verbal abuse by the police in the last 12 months, placing the country in eleventh place among twenty countries (Cruz, 2009). However, in the survey from 2016 and 2017, only 2.9 percent of Uruguayans acknowledged that they had been asked for a bribe by a police officer in the last 12 months, way below the regional average of 12 percent (Cohen, Lupu, & Zechmeister, 2017). Similarly, in a region where, on average, 44 percent of respondents think that it is possible to bribe police officers, in Uruguay, this percentage stands at 21, the second lowest after Chile (Corporación Latinobarómetro, 2017). At last, Cruz (2016) finds that Uruguay is one of the very few countries in Latin America—together with Chile and Panama—that show no significant empirical evidence of what he considers state-sponsored violence. This includes torture and extrajudicial executions, extortion, and kidnappings by government actors, or state collusion with criminal organizations, among others.[4]

Again, only one local study[5] has focused on police abuse, applying a survey to roughly 400 adolescents and young adults from Montevideo (Mosteriro et al., 2016). Results showed that police detentions were concentrated among young males from poor neighborhoods. Also, 13 percent claimed to have suffered physical abuse, but only 5 percent of these had made a report, generally because they thought it would be useless. It is also apparently more common for police abuse to take place in police stations than on the street, and more in poor neighborhoods than in other parts of the city. Accordingly, 77 percent of respondents believed that police officers treat young people from poor neighborhoods worse than those from wealthy neighborhoods.

To sum up, the UNP continues to be an outlier in a region where police-community relations are characterized by high levels of mistrust, weak legitimacy, unnecessary use of force, corruption, and even explicit and direct involvement in criminal activities. In contrast, almost two thirds of Uruguayans trust a police force that comes close to the democratic policing criteria (Bayley, 1995), even in the backdrop of rising crime and violence.

CONCLUSION

As this chapter has shown, the Uruguayan National Police has undergone several significant reforms since its foundation almost 200 years ago. The structural changes of the twentieth century took place during a civic-military dictatorship that militarized the force but also transformed it into a truly national and professional organization. After the return to democracy, and particularly since the end of the 1990s, all governments have made efforts to modernize the UNP and improve its conditions to act in a deteriorating security context that is marked by the expansion of illicit markets and the growing presence of organized crime. While some of these reforms were driven by political motives, most had the quest for effectiveness and efficiency at their core, as well as the need to improve police legitimacy and appear successful in the eyes of the public.

Over the last two decades, the UNP adopted a mixed policing philosophy. With the public security paradigm of the 1990s and a standard model of policing in place, the agency took several steps toward a citizen security paradigm that prioritized crime prevention and community-oriented practices. However, the latter is far from being consolidated and a mixture of both paradigms prevails. The IDB played a fundamental role in this regard, supporting the modernization of many Latin American police forces and promoting the adoption of progressive technologies and programs. Beyond being one of the few police organizations in the region that conforms to democratic policing criteria (Bayley, 1995), the Uruguayan police stands out in the region today for its technological advancements and its experimentation with evidence-based practices.

This does not mean that it is yet well trained or equipped to deal with the criminal challenges that the country faces. Despite Uruguay's relatively robust state, and even though reforms appear to be going in the right direction, the high incidence of violent crime and the noticeable limitations of its human and material resources suggest that the UNP cannot entirely escape from the typical policing challenges of weak states (Goldsmith, 2002). As in most parts of the region, the pursuance of ambitious organizational reforms is frequently hampered by a backdrop of rising insecurity and by the public fears and political pressures that come with it. In this environment, policy makers frequently feel that they have to choose between prioritizing effectiveness or community-oriented policing, oscillating between cycles of hard and soft policing (Macaulay, 2012; Malone & Dammert, 2020). It remains to be seen if the arrival of a new government and new police authorities in 2020 may result in the continuation of this transition, in its reversal, or a change of direction.

NOTES

1. The Human Development Index is a summary measure of average achievement in key dimensions of human development: a long and healthy life, being knowledgeable and have a decent standard of living (UNDP, 2015).

2. Rises in domestic violence complaints should be taken with caution, as these may reflect a decrease in the dark figure of this crime. That is, an increase in the willingness to report victimization.

3. cf.: González (2003), Vila (2012), Timote Correa (2017) and Uruguay-MI-JF (n.d.).

4. It is worth mentioning that Cruz (2016) also considers "zero tolerance" policies as state violence. Among the practices that he includes in this category are extending

the scope of police powers, increasing the severity of sentences and unleashing massive police operations, all of which arguably apply to the Uruguayan case as well.

5. Results of this study should be considered with caution, given that analysis are based on comparisons without statistical tests and without control of relevant third factors, such as crime rates, etc.

REFERENCES

Abizanda, Beatriz, Joan Serra Hoffman, Lina Marmolejo, and Suzanne Duryea. (2012). *Citizen Security: Conceptual Framework and Empirical Evidence*. Inter-American Development Bank.

Alda, Erik, Mayra Buvinić, and Jorge Lamas. (2006). "Neighbourhood peacekeeping: The Inter-American Development Bank's Violence Reduction Programs in Colombia and Uruguay." *Civil Wars* 8(2): 197–214. https://doi.org/10.1080/13698240600877346.

Arias, Patricia. (2009). *Seguridad Privada En América Latina: El Lucro y Los Dilemas de Una Regulación Deficitaria*. FLACSO.

Ariel, Barak, Renée J. Mitchell, Justice Tankebe, Maria Emilia Firpo, Ricardo Fraiman, and Jordan M. Hyatt. (2020). Using wearable technology to increase police legitimacy in Uruguay: The case of body-worn cameras." *Law & Social Inquiry* 45(1): 52–80. https://doi.org/10.1017/lsi.2019.13.

Bayley, David H. (1995). A foreign policy for democratic policing. *Policing and Society* 5(2): 79–93. https://doi.org/10.1080/10439463.1995.9964713.

Bergman, Marcelo. (2018). *More Money, More Crime: Prosperity and Rising Crime in Latin America*. Oxford University Press.

Bogliaccini, Juan Ariel, James Edward Monogan, Juan Ignacio Pereira. (2019). Tackling druglords in an incipient market: Police raids and drug crime in Uruguay. Washington, D.C.: 115th American Political Science Association's Annual Meeting and Exhibition. https://bit.ly/2UxNKJO.

Bonomi, Eduardo, Alejandro Cid, Spencer Chainey, Federico del Castillo, Ricardo Fraiman, François Jacottet, Mario Layera, et al. (2018). *¿Cómo Evitar El Delito Urbano? El Programa de Alta Dedicación Operativa En La Nueva Policía Uruguaya*. Banco Interamericano de Desarrollo, Ministerio del Interior de la República Oriental del Uruguay.

Caetano, Gerardo. (2019). *Historia Mínima de Uruguay*. El Colegio de México.

CAF (Corporación Andina de Fomento). (2014). *Por Una América Latina Más Segura: Una Nueva Perspectiva Para Prevenir y Controlar El Delito*. Panamericana Formas e Impresos S.A.

Castillo, Federico del. (2018). Génesis, Desarrollo y Profesionalización Del Análisis Criminal En La Policía Nacional. In *¿Cómo Evitar El Delito Urbano? El Programa de Alta Dedicación Operativa En La Nueva Policía Uruguaya*. Banco Interamericano de Desarrollo, Ministerio del Interior de la República Oriental del Uruguay.

Castillo, Federico del. (2019). Obstacles to problem-oriented policing in Montevideo. *Policing* 42(3): 334–46. https://doi.org/10.1108/PIJPSM-02-2018-0025.

Castillo, Federico del. (2020). ¿Uruguay Tiene Una Policía Preventiva? La Situación de La Prevención Del Delito En La Reforma Policial Uruguaya.

Castillo, Federico del, Ricardo Fraiman, and Colin Rogers. (2014). The utility of community policing: Insights from England and Wales and Uruguay." *Australasian Policing* 6(2): 19–22.

Chainey, Spencer P, Rodrigo Serrano-Berthet, and Federico Veneri. (2020). The impact of a hot spot policing program in Montevideo, Uruguay: An evaluation using a quasi-experimental difference-in-difference negative binomial approach. *Police Practice and Research*: 1–16. https://doi.org/10.1080/15614263.2020 .1749619.

Cid, Alejandro. (2019). Saturation policing and robberies: Quasi-experimental evidence about the effect of sudden and quick operations. *Justice Evaluation Journal* 2(2): 164–80. https://doi.org/10.1080/24751979.2019.1629827.

CIFRA. (2018). Inseguridad: El problema más grave, que afecta más a jóvenes y mujeres." https://bit.ly/2X0n5Hn.

CIFRA. (2020). "Principal problema del país, el económico." https://bit.ly/3jUeS1c.

Cohen, Mollie J., Noam Lupu, and Elizabeth J. Zechmeister (Eds.). (2017). *The Political Culture of Democracy in the Americas, 2016/17: A Comparative Study of Democracy and Governance*. AmericasBarometer. LAPOP, USAID and Vanderbilt University.

Corbacho, Ana, Julia Philipp, and Mauricio Ruiz-Vega. (2015). Crime and erosion of trust: Evidence for Latin America. *World Development* 70: 400–15.

Cordner, Gary. (2014). Community policing. In *The Oxford Handbook of Police and Policing*, edited by Michael D. Reisig and Robert J Kane, 148–71. Oxford University Press.

Corporación Latinobarómetro. (2017). *Informe Latinobarómetro 2017*. Corporación Latinobarómetro.

Corporación Latinobarómetro. (2018). Informe Latinobarómetro 2018. Corporación Latinobarómetro.

Cruz, José Miguel. (2009). Police abuse in Latin America. *Americas Barometer Insights*. Vol. 11. AmericasBarometer. LAPOP, USAID and Vanderbilt University.

Cruz, José Miguel. (2016). State and criminal violence in Latin America. *Crime, Law and Social Change* 66(4): 375–96. https://doi.org/10.1007/s10611-016-9631-9.

Cruz, José Miguel, and Gema Kloppe-Santamaría. (2019). Determinants of support for extralegal violence in Latin America and the Caribbean. *Latin American Research Review* 54(1): 50–68. https://doi.org/10.25222/larr.212.

Dammert, Lucía. (2019). Challenges of police reform in Latin America. In *Routledge Handbook of Law and Society in Latin America*, edited by Rachel Sieder, Karina Ansolabehere, and Tatiana Alfonso, 1–26. Routledge.

DePietro, Andrew. (2020). Here's how much money police officers earn in every state. *Forbes*. https://bit.ly/2EgFclT.

Dias Felix, Annabelle, and Tina Hilgers. (2020). Community oriented policing theory and practice: Global policy diffusion or local appropriation? *Policing and Society*: 1–9. https://doi.org/10.1080/10439463.2020.1776280.

Eurostat. (2018). Police, court, and prison personnel statistics. 2018. https://bit.ly /30AX9D0.

Freedom House. (2020). Freedom in the world 2020: A leaderless struggle for democracy. Washington, DC: Freedom House. https://bit.ly/30Esvst.

Frühling, Hugo. (2012). A realistic look at Latin American community policing programmes." *Policing and Society* 22(1): 76–88. https://doi.org/10.1080/10439463 .2011.636816.

Goldsmith, Andrew. (2002). Policing weak states: Citizen safety and state responsibility. *Policing and Society* 13(1): 3–21. https://doi.org/10.1080/1043946032000050553.

Goldstein, Herman. (1979). Improving policing: A problem-oriented approach. *Crime & Delinquency* 25(2): 236–58.

González, José Luis G. (2003). La Policía En Los Estados de Derecho Latinoamericanos: El Caso Uruguay. In *La Policía En Los Estados de Derecho Latinoamericanos: Un Proyecto Internacional de Investigación*, edited by Kai Ambos, Juan-Luis Gómez Colomer, and Richard Vogler, 501–35. Instituto Max-Planck para Derecho Penal Extranjero.

ICPC. (2010). International report on crime prevention and community safety: Trends and perspectives, 2010. International Centre for the Prevention of Crime (ICPC).

Jaitman, Laura, and Nicolas Ajzenman. (2016). Crime concentration and hot spot dynamics in Latin America. IDB Working Paper Series N° IDB-WP-699. Inter-American Development Bank. https://bit.ly/2CGlTSo.

Jaitman, Laura, and Iván Torre. (2017). Un Enfoque Sistemático Para Medir El Costo Del Crimen En 17 Países de América Latina y El Caribe. In *Los Costos Del Crimen y de La Violencia: Nueva Evidencia y Hallazgos En América Latina y El Caribe*, edited by Laura Jaitman, 21–32. Washington, DC: Banco Interamericano de Desarrollo (BID).

Karp, Aaron. (2018). Estimating global civilian held firearms numbers. *Small Arms Survey - Briefing Papers*. Small Arms Survey.

Katzman, Ruben, Soledad Avila, Ximena Baraibar, Gabriel Corbo, Fernando Filgueira, Fernando Errandorena, Magdalena Furtado, Denisse Gelber, Alejandro Retamaso, and Federico Rodríguez. (2004). La Ciudad Fragmentada: Respuesta de Los Sectores Populares Urbanos a Las Transformaciones Del Mercado y Del Territorio En Montevideo. 2. Documento de Trabajo Del IPES - Monitor Social Del Uruguay. Universidad Católica del Uruguay.

Leal Buitrago, Francisco. (2003). La Doctrina de Seguridad Nacional: Materialización de La Guerra Fría En América Del Sur. *Revista de Estudios Sociales* (15): 74–87.

Macaulay, Fiona. (2012). Cycles of police reform in Latin America. In *Policing in Africa*, edited by David J. Francis, 165–90. Palgrave Macmillan. https://doi.org/10 .1057/9781137010582.

Mainwaring, Scott. (2018). Party system institutionalization in contemporary Latin America. In *Party Systems in Latin America: Institutionalization, Decay, and Collapse*, edited by Scott Mainwaring, 34–70. Cambridge University Press.

Malone, Mary Fran T., and Lucía Dammert. (2020). The police and the public: Policing practices and public trust in Latin America. *Policing and Society* 0 (0): 1–16. https://doi.org/10.1080/10439463.2020.1744600.

Mitchell, Renée J., Barak Ariel, Maria Emilia Firpo, Ricardo Fraiman, Federico del Castillo, Jordan M. Hyatt, Cristobal Weinborn, and Hagit Brants Sabo. (2018). Measuring the effect of body-worn cameras on complaints in Latin America: The case of traffic police in Uruguay. *Policing* 41 (4): 510–24. https://doi.org/10.1108/PIJPSM-01-2018-0004.

Mosteriro, Mariana, Tamara Samudio, Rafael Paternain, Ignacio Salamano, Guillermo Zoppolo, Mauro Tomasini, Tamara Samudio, Fernando Lagos, Gabriela Bouisa, and Henderson. Juanena. (2016). Adolescentes, Jóvenes y Violencia Policial En Montevideo: Una Aproximación Descriptiva. Ciencias Sociales y Políticas Sociales Nº 6. Facultad de Ciencias Sociales, Universidad de la República (Uruguay).

Munyo, Ignacio, and Martín A. Rossi. (2019). Police-monitored cameras and crime. *Scandinavian Journal of Economics*. https://doi.org/10.1111/sjoe.12375.

Nivette, Amy. (2016). Institutional ineffectiveness, illegitimacy, and public support for vigilantism in Latin America. *Criminology* 54(1):142–75.

Pion-Berlin, David, and Miguel Carreras. (2017). Armed forces, police and crime-fighting in Latin America. *Journal of Politics in Latin America* 9 (3): 3–26.

OVE (Oficina de Evaluación y Supervisión). (2010). Prevención Del Delito y La Violencia En América Latina y El Caribe: Evidencia de Las Intervenciones Del BID. RE-378. Banco Interamericano de Desarrollo.

OVE (Oficina de Evaluación y Supervisión). (2014). Respuesta Del BID a Los Principales Desafíos de Seguridad Ciudadana, 1998–2012." Banco Interamericano de Desarrollo. http://publications.iadb.org/bitstream/handle/11319/6378/cv2014Cover_Spanish.pdf?sequence=2.

Paternain, Rafael. (2017). Políticas de policía y gobiernos de izquierda. El caso de Uruguay. *Delito y Sociedad* 2(44): 161–200. https://doi.org/10.14409/dys.v2i44.7627.

PNUD (Programa de las Naciones Unidas para el Desarrollo). (2013). *Informe Regional de Desarrollo Humano 2013-2014. Seguridad Ciudadana Con Rostro Humano: Diagnóstico y Propuestas Para América Latina*. PNUD.

Prado, Mariana Mota, Michael Trebilcock, and Patrick Hartford. (2012). *Police Reform in Violent Democracies in Latin America. Hague Journal on the Rule of Law* 4. https://doi.org/10.1017/S1876404512000164.

Reporters Without Borders. (2020). 2020 World Press Freedom Index. Reporters Without Borders. https://bit.ly/32OfMpV.

Rico, Álvaro, ed. (2008). *Historia Reciente, Historia En Discusión*. Tradinco-Cruz del Sur.

Rodríguez Cuitiño, María Del Rosario. (2018). La Lucha Contra El Crimen Organizado y El Terrorismo En Uruguay: Un Desafío a Enfrentar. *Revista de Estudios En Seguridad Internacional* 4(1): 55–71. https://doi.org/10.18847/1.7.4.

Sanjurjo, Diego. (2017). The role of defensive firearm use in the governance of security in Latin America. *Theoretical Criminology* 21(3): 324–41. https://doi.org/10.1177/1362480616654002.

Sanjurjo, Diego. (2020). *Gun control policies in Latin America*. International Series on Public Policy. Palgrave Macmillan.

Soares, Rodrigo R, and Joana Naritomi. (2010). Understanding high crime rates in Latin America: The role of social and policy factors. In *The Economics of Crime: Lessons for and from Latin America*, edited by Rafael Di Tella, Sebastián Edwards, and Ernesto Schargrodsky, 19–55. University of Chicago Press.

Timote Correa, and Guillermo Andrés. (2015). La Enseñanza En La Formación Policial Uruguaya. Exploración Para La Conformación de Un Campo de Investigaciones. Universidad de la República.

Timote Correa, and Guillermo Andrés. (2017). Aspectos Normativos de La Enseñanza Policial En El Uruguay. Notas Para Pensar La Formación Policial Uruguaya. *Revista Policía Y Seguridad Pública* 7(1): 401–32. https://doi.org/10.5377/rpsp.v7i1.4315.

Trajtenberg, Nicolás. (2017). A matter of costs and benefits? The role of morality, legitimacy, and self-control as moderators of the link between rationality and youth delinquency in Uruguay. PhD diss, Cambridge University.

Trajtenberg, Nicolás and Manuel Eisner. (2014). *Towards a more effective violence prevention policy in Uruguay*. ANEP. Editorial Susana Aliano Casales.

Transparency International. (2019). Corruption Perceptions Index 2019. Transparency International. https://bit.ly/2ZWx5TU.

Tyler, Tom R. (1990). *Why people obey the law*. Yale University Press.

UNDP (United National Development Program). (2019). *Human Development Report 2019: Beyond income, beyond averages, beyond today: Inequalities in human development in the 21st century*. UNDP.

Ungar, Mark. (2007). The Privatization of Citizen Security in Latin America: From Elite Guards to Neighborhood Vigilantes. *Social Justice* 34(3/4): 20–37.

Ungar, Mark. (2011). *Policing democracy: Overcoming obstacles to citizen security in Latin America*. John Hopkins University Press. https://doi.org/10.1353/book.60322.

Ungar, Mark, and Enrique Desmond Arias. (2012). Reassessing community-oriented policing in Latin America. *Policing and Society* 22(1): 1–13. https://doi.org/10.1080/10439463.2011.597856.

UNLIREC (United Nations Regional Centre for Peace, Disarmament and Development in Latin America and the Caribbean) and DCAF (Geneva Centre for the Democratic Control of Armed Forces). (2016). Armed private security in Latin America and the Caribbean: Oversight and accountability in an evolving context. Regional Study. DCAF and United Nations.

UNODC (United Nations Office on Drugs and Crime). (n.d.) UNODC statistics online: Intentional homicide victims." Retrieved July 7, 2020, https://bit.ly/3jzk22w.

Uruguay-CPP (Comisionado Parlamentario Penitenciario). (2019). Informe Anual 2018. Parlamento del Uruguay.

Uruguay-INE (Instituto Nacional de Estadística). (2020). Estimación de La Pobreza Por El Método de Ingreso 2019. Montevideo: INE.

Uruguay-MI-JF (Ministerio del Interior - Jefatura de Montevideo). (n.d.) Historia. Retrieved June 6, 2020, https://bit.ly/3fztboT.

Uruguay-MI (Ministerio del Interior). (2016). 421 Policías Cada 100.000 Habitantes. https://bit.ly/3jAXgXJ.

Uruguay-MI (Ministerio del Interior). (2017a). El 222. https://bit.ly/3eYYWqC.

Uruguay-MI (Ministerio del Interior). (2017b). Encuesta Nacional de Victimización 2017. https://bit.ly/3jBXj5N.

Uruguay-MI (Ministerio del Interior). (2019a). *Femicidios En Uruguay: Análisis Para La Homogeneización de Criterios y Su Categorización*. Montevideo: Ministerio del Interior, MIDES, INMUJERES.

Uruguay-MI (Ministerio del Interior). (2019b). Remuneraciones 2019. https://bit.ly /2CxoEpe.

Uruguay-MI (Ministerio del Interior). (2020a). Denuncias de Rapiña y Hurto: 1º de Enero Al 31 de Diciembre (2018–2019). Observatorio Nacional sobre Violencia y Criminalidad. https://bit.ly/3f1Jhag.

Uruguay-MI (Ministerio del Interior). (2020b). Homicidios: 1º de Enero Al 31 de Diciembre (2018-2019). Observatorio Nacional sobre Violencia y Criminalidad. https://bit.ly/2WNflZa.

Uruguay-OPP-DGE (Dirección de Gestión y Evaluación). (2014). Evaluación de Diseño, Implementación y Desempeño (DID): Seguridad Pública, 2011–2013. Oficina de Planeamiento y Presupuesto.

Uruguay-PN-DIGEFE (Policía Nacional - Dirección General de Fiscalización de Empresas). (2019). Informe Estadístico 2019. DIGEFE.

Vila, Alejandro. (2012). La Matriz Policial Uruguaya: 40 Años de Gestación. In *Uruguay: Inseguridad, Delito y Estado*, edited by Rafael Paternain and Álvaro Rico, 203–29. CSIC - Universidad de la República.

Vila, Alejandro. (2016). La Política de Seguridad Ciudadana Del Mujiquismo: Entre Acuerdos y Disensos. In *El Decenio Progresista: Las Políticas Públicas de Vázquez a Mujica*, edited by Nicolás Bentancur and José Miguel Busquets, 255–77. Fin de Siglo.

Vilalta, Carlos and Gustavo Fondevila. (2019). Prison populism in Latin America. Reviewing the dynamics of prison population growth. Strategic Note 32. Igarapé Institute.

Vigna, Ana, and Santiago Sosa. (2019). Muertes en las cárceles uruguayas. Magnitud del fenómeno y problemas para estudiarlo. *Revista de Ciencias Sociales* 32(45): 39–66.

Wakefield, Alison, and Mark Button. (2014). Private policing in public spaces. In *The Oxford Handbook of Police and Policing*, edited by Michael D. Reinig and Robert J. Kane, 571–588. Oxford University Press.

Weisburd, David, and John E. Eck. (2004). What can police do to reduce crime, disorder, and fear?" *Annals of the American Academy of Political and Social Science* 593 (May): 42–65. https://doi.org/10.1177/0002716203262548.

World Bank. (n.d.) World Bank Database. Retrieved July 7, 2020. https://bit.ly /30Ffzm5.

World Justice Project. (2020). *WJP Rule of Law Index 2020*. World Justice Project. https://bit.ly/3fVUAC0.

World Prison Brief. (n.d.) Highest to lowest: Prison population total. Institute for Criminal Policy Research. Retrieved June 6, 2020. https://bit.ly/2ZTUQMh.

Index

About the Contributors

Joseph Appiahene-Gyamfi (PhD) is professor of criminology and criminal justice at the University of Texas Rio Grande Valley, Edinburg, Texas. Dr. Appiahene-Gyamfi obtained his PhD and MA degrees in Criminology from Simon Fraser University in Burnaby, British Columbia, Canada in 1995 and 1999, respectively. Prior to his graduate studies in Canada, Dr. Appiahene-Gyamfi had received his BA (Honors) degree in Sociology with Psychology (1989) and a Certificate in Prison Administration (1985) from the University of Ghana, Legon. He also holds a diploma in Journalism & Public Relations (1979) from the Ghana Institute of Journalism, Accra, Ghana and worked for over two decades with the Ghana Prisons Service. Dr. Appiahene-Gyamfi publishes on crime in Ghana.

Monika Baylis is a teaching fellow in criminology at the University of Leicester. She is also based at the University of Huddersfield, UK, where she is finishing doctoral research after graduating with first class honors in criminology from the same institution. Her comparative study focuses on police decision making while addressing anti-social behavior (ASB) among young people in Poland and England. She is passionate about comparative research in policing. In 2020, she became a winner of the Huddersfield Association of Women Graduates' Annual PhD Prize. Monika's interest in this subject began when she was regularly invited as a Polish/English interpreter by police, courts, probation services, and local authorities in the UK. She has contributed to various national and local conferences and police officers' training within The European Union Agency for Law Enforcement Training (CEPOL). She has regular input on policing issues such as ASB and youth crime and Polish language and culture in West Yorkshire Police in England,

and at the Police Academy in Poland. She writes on the subject for Police magazines in both countries.

Mark F. Briskey (PhD) is senior lecturer in criminology and coordinator of the Criminology Internships program at Murdoch University, Australia. Prior to his academic career, Mark was both a State and Federal Police Officer where he served in both Australia and some long-term overseas postings. The Australian and Indonesian governments decorated him for his role in counter-terrorism investigations and for work in Pakistan, Afghanistan, and Sri Lanka. He is a former head of the Australian Graduate School of Policing and was involved in initial efforts to establish the Jakarta Centre for Law Enforcement Cooperation and Transnational Crime Centre in Indonesia. Mark obtained his PhD at the Australian Defence Force Academy at the University of New South Wales.

Mikkel Jarle Christensen (PhD) is professor WSR at the Faculty of Law, University of Copenhagen. He is principal investigator for the research project "The Global Sites of International Criminal Justice (JustSites)" funded by the European Research Council. JustSites is part of the Danish National Research Foundation's Centre of Excellence for International Courts (iCourts). MJC also serves as Chair for the COST Action on Global Atrocity Justice Constellations (JUSTICE360).

Mengliang Dai (PhD) is an assistant professor at Macau University of Science and Technology. He earned his PhD at City University of Hong Kong. His current research focuses on Strike Hard, wrongful convictions, and police discretion. Recent articles have appeared in British Journal of Criminology, Journal of Contemporary China, and Security Journal.

Sharyn Graham Davies (PhD) is associate professor of Indonesian Studies at Monash University in Melbourne. Sharyn has published extensively on policing in Indonesia as well as on gender and sexuality in the region. Her publications appear in Policing and Society, Australian and New Zealand Journal of Criminology, and Asian Studies Review. Sharyn .davies@aut.ac.nz

Federico del Castillo is an anthropologist researching the relations between police and adolescents in deprived neighborhoods. He is a PhD candidate in Social Anthropology at the Institute for High Social Studies, National University of San Martin (Argentina). He holds a Master's degree in Criminal Justice from John Jay College of Criminal Justice, CUNY (USA), and a Bachelor's degree in Anthropology from Universidad de la República

(Uruguay). He has published book chapters and articles on crime prevention, police reform, and restorative justice.

Giulia Fabini (PhD) is a research fellow in criminology at the Department of Legal Studies DSG, University of Bologna (Italy). She holds a PhD in "Law and Society" from the University of Milan and was a student researcher at the center for the study of law and society at UC Berkeley. Her research focuses on border control and the interaction between migrants and the police. She is also interested in migrants' struggles and immigration courts and the prison system from a gender perspective.

Lorna E. Grant (PhD) is an associate professor and director of the MSc program in the Department of Criminal Justice Department, North Carolina Central University. She earned her Doctorate in Juvenile Justice from Prairie View A & M University, Texas, BSc in social work and MSW in social work administration from the University of the West Indies, Jamaica. Prior to joining the faculty at North Carolina Central University, she taught at the University of the West Indies, Jamaica, and Clark Atlanta University, Atlanta. She is a member of the American Society of Criminology (ASC) and the Academy of Criminal Justice Sciences (ACJS). Her research interest includes but is not limited to youth gangs, juvenile justice issues, school violence, juvenile sex offenders, policing in Jamaica, community building, and project development & implementation. Dr. Grant has been conducting research in Jamaica for several years and has recently edited a book with two of her colleagues entitled "Crime and Violence in the Caribbean." Her second edited book is now with the publishers. She has published numerous research articles.

Ross Hendy (PhD) is a lecturer/assistant professor in criminology in the School of Social Sciences, Monash University. His research focuses on the development of theoretical and applied perspectives of police and policing, such as practitioner behavior and the effectiveness of police intervention. As a former sergeant with New Zealand Police, he has worked with researchers to enhance their understanding of the police environment, the limitations of police administrative data, and provided advice about real-world issues that criminal justice practitioners and policy-makers face in the criminological and criminal justice environments. His portfolio of applied research work at New Zealand Police's Evidence-Based Policing Centre focused on developing insight into operational policing issues such as the police use of lethal force and understanding of the increasing demand for mental health-related calls for service. His other research has involved the study of police officers from Australia, England, New Zealand, Norway and Sweden.

Dalibor Kekić (PhD) is associate professor at the University of Criminal Investigation and Police Studies, Department of Police Sciences, Belgrade, Republic of Serbia. He earned PhD title in Security Management Studies, specified in Police Management and Emergency Management. He is interested in HR, Emergency Management, Police Organization, and Security Management. Alone or co-authored, published about 130 papers, of which one is a textbook. Participated in more than thirty scientific national and international conferences. Organizing or participating in many seminars, workshops, and projects organized for different entitles and subjects.

Filip Kukić (PhD) is a physical fitness assessment and research expert in a Testing Section of Police Sports Education Center, Abu Dhabi Police, United Arab Emirates. He earned PhD in developing the screening model of physical fitness of police officers through the assessment of body composition. He is interested in integrating physical activity into occupational health of police offices by developing policies aligned with those of the agency. He published about sixty papers, of which one is a textbook. He participated in numerous scientific national and international conferences, and also organized or participated in many seminars and workshops and reviewed papers for journals of international and national importance.

Yik Koon Teh (PhD) received her BA in Law and Sociology, MA in Sociology from University of Kent, Canterbury, and PhD in Sociology (Criminology) from London School of Economics and Political Science. She was a Fulbright Scholar at University of California Los Angeles (2002); participant for the three-week Symposium of East Asia Security organized by US Pacific Command and US State Department (2012); individual expert in Criminology at the 13th UN Congress on Crime Prevention and Criminal Justice in Doha, Qatar; and Visiting Fellow at Rajaratnam School of International Studies, Nanyang Technological University, Singapore (2015). She is currently a professor at the National Defense University of Malaysia. Her latest book is *From BMF to 1MDB: A Criminological and Sociological Discussion.*

Samuel M. Makinda (PhD) is professor of security and counter-terrorism, and the Founding Chair of Security, Terrorism and Counterterrorism Studies at Murdoch University, Australia. He was awarded the Order of Elder of the Burning Spear by Kenyan President Mwai Kibaki in 2011. He was on the Australian Foreign Minister's National Consultative Committee for International Security Issues 2001–2008. In 1985–1986, he was a foreign affairs analyst in the Parliamentary Research Service of the Australian Parliament. He has been a researcher at the Brookings Institution; the

International Institute for Strategic Studies; St. Antony's College, Oxford University; and Global Security Programme, Cambridge University. A former editor of the Daily Nation in Kenya, Professor Makinda has published five books and numerous chapters and journal articles.

Skarlleth Martínez Prado, Nicaraguan independent researcher and political analyst with experience in the management and coordination of projects associated with the security and justice sector, defense, good governance, human rights and violence prevention in Latin America. She has participated in several joint research ventures with the Institute for Strategic Studies and Public Policies (IEEPP by acronyms in Spanish), Expediente Abierto and carried out research with the Norwegian University of Life Sciences (NMBU) about Community-Based Policing in Latin America. Her work and experience have been awarded by the United Nations Office for Disarmament Affairs with her inclusion in the Forces of Change III book, and the German Academic Exchange Service (DAAD). She is a MA graduate in Development and Governance from the University Duisburg-Essen in Germany, and a graduate from the William J. Perry Center for Hemispheric Defense Studies in Washington D.C.

Jephias Matunhu holds a PhD in Development Studies from University of Fort Harare in South Africa and is working towards a degree in Laws with University of South Africa. He is the Director of Tugwi Mukosi Multidisciplinary Research Institute of the Midlands State University and is the founding chairperson of the Development Studies department at the same university. In 2018 he was the overall winner of the Thailand International Cooperation Agency essay competition. Matunhu is an external examiner for eight universities scattered all over the world.

Viola Matunhu (PhD) is the current Deputy Dean in the Faculty of Arts at Midlands State University in Zimbabwe. She is also a lecturer in the Department of Development Studies at the same University as well as a Part Time Lecturer at Zimbabwe Open University in Zimbabwe. She is a public health specialist and holds a PhD in Public Management, Master's Degree in Human Resources Management, and several other public health related qualifications. She has published extensively on articles related to community health.

Jospeter M. Mbuba (PhD) is Professor of Criminal Justice and Public Administration at Purdue University Fort Wayne, USA. He has published widely and delivered numerous professional and invited presentations on the topics of crime prevention and public safety. He is also a curriculum development consultant, a three-time Fellow with the Carnegie African Diaspora Fellowship Program and a one-time Visiting Scholar with the Council for the Development of Social Science Research in Africa (CODESRIA). He is a member of the Academy of Criminal Justice Sciences, American Society of Criminology, and Kenya Scholars and Studies Association. He has chaired presentation panels at the annual conferences of these organizations. He is a 2014 alumnus of the FBI Citizen's Academy, Indianapolis Division and serves as manuscript reviewer for several journals, among his many professional engagements.

Miloš Milenković is team leader at the Emergency management sector, Ministry of interior, Belgrade, Republic of Serbia. He earned MSc title in Organizational Studies, specified in HR. He is interested in HR, Emergency Management, Police Organization and Security Management. He is the sole or co-author of about thirty papers and has participated in more than ten scientific national and international conferences. He has also organized/ participated in many exercises and workshops for different entitles and on various subjects.

Siddhartha Misra is an Assistant Professor in the Faculty of Law, University of Delhi. He obtained his Master of Laws (LL.M.) from Delhi University and the Doctor of Laws (LL.D.) from Meerut University. He has vast experience in teaching and research in law and related areas. His areas of interest include public international law, international organizations law, human rights, and civil and criminal liability law. He has written extensively and made numerous conference presentations. He has been a part of various sociolegal issues in India and is currently working on police reforms in India. He regularly writes for leading newspapers and magazines in India and serves on editorial boards of various law journals. He supervises master's and doctoral theses and dissertations and is a life member of the Institute of Constitutional and Parliamentary Studies, a member of African Initiative of Democracy and Human Rights and International Council of Jurists, London and an academic friend of the Advisory Committee of the UN Human Rights Council.

Joselyne Chenane Nkogo (PhD) is an assistant professor in the School of Criminology and Justice Studies at the University of Massachusetts Lowell. Her work has appeared in journals such as *Policing and Society: An International Journal of Research and Policy*; *Race & Justice*; *Youth Violence & Juvenile Justice*; and *The Prison Journal*. Her research interests include policing, race and justice, neighborhoods, immigration, and comparative criminal justice. She is currently conducting a study to examine social capital and perceptions toward the police among African immigrant women in the United States.

Timi Osidipe (PhD) is a senior lecturer in criminology at the University of Bedfordshire, UK. His research focuses on ethnicity and the criminal justice, victimization and the intersection between social justice and criminal justice, public policy and criminology. He is the joint course coordinator, BA criminology and sociology, University of Bedfordshire.

Leandro Piquet Carneiro (PhD) is a professor at the Institute of International Relations, University of São Paulo. Visiting fellow at the Taubman Center for State and Local Government from the Kennedy School of Government, Harvard University, from 2007 to 2008. He graduated in economics at the Federal University of Rio de Janeiro and received his Doctorate in Political Science. His major research field is crime and violence in Latin America. He is leading the Inter American Network for Police Development and Professionalization, a partnership program from the Organization of American States and the University of São Paulo and other police and academic institutions at the Americas Region. He was member of the Academic Council of the National Minister of Public Security (2018) and of the Rio de Janeiro City Hall Advisory Council (2010–2014).

Diego Sanjurjo holds a PhD in political science from the Autonomous University of Madrid and a Master's degrees in public policy and international development. He specializes in security and gun control policies and is currently a Postdoctoral Fellow at the Institute of Political Science, School of Social Sciences, Universidad de la República (Montevideo, Uruguay). His main areas of research include public policy theories, Latin American policies and security, and gun and drug policies.

Alvise Sbraccia (PhD), sociologist, is professor of criminology at the Department of Legal Studies DSG, University of Bologna (Italy). Through ethnography and biographical methods, his empirical research focuses on the process of migrants' criminalization in Italy, urban segregation and control, drug markets and police strategies. His main theoretical contributions are related to prison studies, post-colonial criminology and recidivism.

Jonathan South is a retired Police Officer who worked in various roles and Police departments. He has worked in education since 2010 either in teaching or training roles. He is the course coordinator for the new Degree in Professional Policing offered by the University of Bedfordshire, which is part of the Police Educational Qualification Framework designed by the

College of Policing, a degree he took the lead in designing. His research interests involve the investigation and management of Police Misconduct and Corruption and Community Policing.

Nicolás Trajtenberg holds a PhD in criminology from the University of Cambridge. He is a lecturer at the School of Social Sciences, Cardiff University, and associate professor at the Department of Sociology, School of Social Sciences, Universidad de la República. His research aims to understand what risk factors cause, mediate, or moderate the violence in low and middle-income countries (LMICs), as well as to investigate the transference and implementation of prevention and rehabilitation programs in the LMICs.

Mark Ungar (PhD) is professor of political science and criminal justice, Brooklyn College and Graduate Center, City University of New York. His publications include five books and about forty articles on police reform, citizen security, human rights, and violence. He works as a police reform advisor with the United Nations, Inter-American Development Bank, governments, police and NGOs in Latin America. His current initiatives include serving on the Citizen Security commission in Honduras, where he is helping draft arms control regulations; helping build environmental police forces in the Amazon Basin; and chairing the academic branch of the International Network for Environmental Compliance and Enforcement (INECE). He has received grants and fellowships from the Woodrow Wilson Center and the Ford, Tinker, and Tow Foundations.

Yunyun Yang (PhD) is a lecturer at Guangxi Normal University. She earned her PhD from City University of Hong Kong. Her work has appeared in Rural China and Social Science Research. Her research interests include social control, grassroots governance, county-level governance, and policing.

Lightning Source UK Ltd.
Milton Keynes UK
UKHW011838210521
384156UK00001B/14